DANNY KAYE
KING OF JESTERS

by David Koenig

Danny Kaye: King of Jesters by David Koenig

Published by
BONAVENTURE PRESS
Post Office Box 51961
Irvine, CA 92619-1961
USA
www.BonaventurePress.com

Cover art by Sebastian Cast (www.castdibujos.blogspot.com.ar)
Reprinted lyrics © Sylvia Fine Kaye (see page 4)

Publisher's Cataloging in Publication Data
Koenig, David G.
   Danny Kaye: king of jesters / by David Koenig.
      p. cm.
   Includes annotated references and index.
   ISBN 978-1-937878-01-6
   1. Kaye, Danny, 1911-1987. 2. Comedians—United States—Biography. 3.
      Entertainers—United States—Biography. 4. Comedy films—United States—History
      and Criticism. I. Title.

Library of Congress classification number
792.43´092—dc20
Library of Congress Control Number: 2012911799

Hardcover
ISBN-10: 1937878015
ISBN 978-1-937878-01-6

Printed in the USA
10   9   8   7   6   5   4   3   2   1

For my Old Time Movie buddies—
Brent, Charlie, Randy, Willem, Billy, Joe, and the gang—
for their friendship and for confirming that I wasn't the only crazy teenager
who enjoyed watching long-dead comedians in 50-year-old films.

CREDITS

Lyrics

All lyrics quoted © Sylvia Fine Kaye. Excerpts from previously published songs—including "Anatole of Paris," "The Lobby Number," and "Stanislavsky"—have been limited to individual lines and are reproduced in conjunction with the Fair Use Doctrine. Portions of the unpublished songs "Spies," "Shubert Alley," and "Cherry Blossom Time" are reprinted without objection by the Estate of Sylvia Fine Kaye. The estate makes no warranty or representation as to the creation of the lyrics, current ownership or rights in the lyrics, or other aspects of ownership in the lyrics. Its agreement not to object to use of the lyrics does not constitute an authorization, endorsement, or other expression of approval of this work.

Photos

Page 20 – White Roe Program, provided by John Weiner

P. 22, 23 – Images from Holly Fine Collection, provided by and reproduced by permission of Special Collections Library, University of Michigan

P. 29 – *Birth of a Star* lobby card

P. 31 – © BBC, from promotional still

P. 28, 46 – Provided by and reproduced by permission of Tamiment Playhouse Photographs Collection, Tamiment Library, New York University

P. 37 – Provided by Sam Locke

P. 50 – *Forecast* promotional brochure, © CBS

P. 59 – Provided by Benny Baker

P. 73, 75, 81, 99, 111, 119, 148, 150 – © Samuel Goldwyn, from original promotional stills

P. 87, 220, 236, 249, 274 – © CBS, from original promotional stills

P. 133, 257 – © Warner Bros., from original promotional stills

P. 140 – © 20th Century Fox, from original promotional still

P. 164, 169, 177, 193, 201 – © Paramount Pictures, from original promotional stills

P. 184 – © MGM, from original promotional still

P. 187, 205 – © Columbia Pictures, from original promotional stills

P. 265 – © ABC, from original promotional still

P. 272 – © Walt Disney Co., from original promotional still

P. 278 – © PBS, from original promotional still

CONTENTS

ACKNOWLEDGMENTS

My FIRST THOUGHT of writing a book about Danny Kaye came in 1982. Several buddies—fellow old-time movie buffs—had recently taken up writing histories on the likes of Laurel & Hardy, the Three Stooges, the Bowery Boys, Steve Martin, and animation. They all found publishers. I was a sophomore in college, not yet 20, contemplating a journalism career, and I wanted in on this grand adventure. Indoctrinated by local TV station KTLA's constant reruns of *The Secret Life of Walter Mitty*, I'd always been fascinated by Danny Kaye and, unbelievably, no book had ever examined his professional life. I began rummaging through any collection of old news clippings, scripts, and private collections that I could find and interviewing any old-timer who would speak to me. I had high hopes—but no expectations—that the project would one day be published. No matter, the exercise would be terrific practice in researching, interviewing, and writing, not to mention a priceless opportunity to meet once-famous Hollywood directors, writers and actors, and to learn more about the making of some of my favorite movies.

I spent several years compiling a rough manuscript. Oddly enough, no six-figure advances came my way from New York publishers. The consensus, according to my mountain of rejection slips, was that Danny Kaye was no longer popular enough and my book just wasn't juicy enough. So, in the mid-1980s, I packed all my scribblings into a big cardboard box and filed it away in the garage, considering it a nice memento and valuable training. I figured I needed a more marketable topic.

Growing up well south of Hollywood, in Orange County, California, I was equally entranced by Disneyland and realized there had never been an unauthorized, behind-the-scenes look at the Happiest Place on Earth. I changed all that. My first book, *Mouse Tales: A Behind-the-Ears Look at*

Disneyland, became a runaway best-seller (it's now in its nineteenth printing, and counting) and led to follow-ups on Disneyland, Walt Disney World, and Disney animation.

Still, my thoughts returned to that dusty old box in the garage. In 2008, looking for a brief respite from Disney, I figured I could dust off my old Danny Kaye notes, update the last chapter to include his passing, and—voila—six months later I'd have a new book. What I didn't count on was all the archival material that had become available during the intervening 25 years. Numerous colleagues of Kaye and several movie studios had donated personal papers, scripts, production logs, and other holdings to research libraries across the country. Best of all, Sylvia Fine Kaye had donated much of her and her late husband's papers to the Library of Congress. My six-month rewrite turned into several years of new research, interviews, and writing. The book is an infinite measure better for it.

Unfortunately, a handful of items slipped through the cracks during their 25-year hibernation in that cardboard box. Several yellowing news clippings lacked citations. Exhaustive lists of TV and radio credits provided by CBS and NBC vanished. And the names of several people who provided assistance were not preserved, so I apologize to anyone I omit from the following list.

My greatest research aide has been my close friend and kindred soul, Daniel Walshaw, who tends to the Library of Congress's Danny Kaye and Sylvia Fine Collection. A kinder, more good-hearted soul I have never known. I am also indebted to Walter Zvonchenko, Karen Lund, Denise Gallo, Jan Lancaster, and the rest of the staff at the Library of Congress; Barbara Hall, Linda Mehr, and Jenny Romero, Academy of Motion Picture Arts & Sciences' Margaret Herrick Library; Ned Comstock and Sandra Garcia-Myers, USC Cinematic Arts Library; Erika Gottfried and Peter Filardo, New York University's Tamiment Library; Lauren Buisson, UCLA's Special Collections Department; Kate Hutchens and Kathleen Dow, University of Michigan's Special Collections Library; Jonathon Auxier, Warner Bros. Archive; and Steve Massa, New York Public Library's Library of the Performing Arts.

I thank these interview subjects for generously providing their time and hospitality: Arthur Alsberg, Ray Anthony, Benny Baker, Norman Barasch, Earl Barton, Billy Barnes, Gary Belkin, Steve Binder, Frank Bracht, Sammy Cahn, Tony Charmoli, Horst Cerni, Ernest Chambers, Francisco "Chico" Day, Daniel Fapp, Rudi Fehr, Everett Freeman, Ron Friedman, Larry

Gelbart, Tommy Grasso, John Green, H. Bruce Humberstone, George Jenkins, Hal Kanter, Sheldon Keller, Perry Lafferty, Nolan Leary, Norman Lloyd, Sam Locke, Virginia Mayo, Jess Oppenheimer, Gil Perkins, Robert Pirosh, John Qualen, Donald Randolph, Bernard Rothman, Robert Scheerer, Melville Shavelson, Gary Smith, Leonard Spigelgass, Herman Stein, Peter Stone, John Weiner, Cara Williams, and Guy Wong.

I received kind, informative letters from Leon Askin, Herbert Baker, IAL Diamond, Henry Ephron, George Kennedy, Harvey Korman, Butterfly McQueen, James Newcom, Vin Scully, William Snyder, Mel Tolkin, Harry Tugend, and Joyce Van Patten.

Facilitating connections, granting permissions, and other assistance were provided by Edward Weidenfeld, Robert Bader, Jeff Abraham, Sam Goldwyn Jr., Richard Jordan, Marti Lomonaco, Roz (Prager) Memel, Lee Gary, Jack Marshall, Rusty Frank, and Jim Hill.

The terrific cover art was penned by Sebastian "Cast" Castiñeiras.

For their support, I thank my family—particularly ever-patient Laura, Zachary, and Rebecca; Koenigs Anne, Joe, Paul, and Maryanne; Hamlins Larry, Sheryl and Garth; and my movie-analyzing accomplices, Willem Bax, Charlie Christ, David P. Hayes, Bill Jagielski, Jeff Lenburg, Randy Skretvedt, and Brent Walker.

And, most of all, I owe everything to my Lord and my Savior Jesus Christ, whose goodness to me is unfathomable.

INTRODUCTION

IT WASN'T JUST the title of one of his movies. On stage, Danny Kaye *was* "Wonder Man," one of the most talented performers in the history of show business. He could sing straight or scat, dance, act, pantomime, tell stories, speak in dialects, handle broad physical comedy, and intimately connect with a live audience.

Kaye forged major conquests on Broadway, in the movies, on records and television, and in a patented stage revue in which he mesmerized seemingly everyone in the theater, from the big spenders in the front row and the royalty in the private boxes to the small children in the far, back shadows of the balcony.

Ironically, Kaye's greatest obstacle to mass popularity was that he could do too much, too well. He was impossible to classify. Without a brand, he found it difficult initially to make a name for himself and ultimately to keep that name remembered. For his most celebrated triumphs were live on stage, creating an in-person experience that could not be preserved to its full effect except in the memories of the individuals in the audience. Film, as it turned out, was possibly the worst medium at capturing a Danny Kaye experience—trapping him in a particular character and story, awkwardly trying to show off as many of his divergent talents as possible. A far better remembered film comedy contemporary, Bob Hope, was an equally capable dancer and singer, but realized he had to subjugate his other talents and focus on one-liners to catch—and keep—the public's attention.

Nonetheless, the motion picture is entertainment's most faithful time capsule and, consequently, offered Kaye his best-remembered roles: the storyteller Hans Christian Andersen, the daydreamer Walter Mitty, and the tongue-tied Court Jester with the vessel with the pestle. Or was it the flagon with the dragon?

This latter role best showcased Danny's unique talents. Still, as great as Kaye's physical gifts were, he was not the world's greatest singer, nor the most graceful dancer, nor the funniest comedian. He possessed two more important assets: first, an in-house content provider—his wife, who figured out how to best utilize his unique talents and to steamroll over anyone in the way, and, second, his own mental faculties. Danny's mind was razor sharp, able to quickly memorize complicated specialty songs and dance moves and entire scripts—including the parts of his co-stars. Yet he created his own material rarely, ad-libbed infrequently, and gladly ceded management of his career to others. His greater gift was an unbreakable concentration. Like the world's most skilled golfer attempting a difficult, high-pressure shot, he could block out every thought unrelated to the task at hand.

The technique helped Kaye master numerous show business disciplines, as well as countless hobbies. When Danny moved to Hollywood, he picked up golf and, within months, was playing at a near-professional level. Just as quickly, he perfected playing ping-pong, cooking Chinese cuisine, and flying his own plane. For fun, he spent so much time in operating rooms that world-famous surgeons were convinced he could have performed any of the procedures himself.

There was a personal cost. To devote himself fully to one subject, to submerge himself completely into that thought, Danny had to block out not only everything else, but everyone else. Years ago, his close friend Leonard Spigelgass explained: "When he's thinking about something, he can pass me on the street and he doesn't even know I'm there, because he's deeply involved with what he's thinking. He's thinking about (his daughter) Dena, or his airplane, or his television show, or the theater, or what he's going to do next, and all the world is blotted out."

To others, Kaye might come across as remote. "Sometimes he's indifferent," Spigelgass agreed, "and I get hurt. I worry, and then I realize that he's living in his own head, and don't we all? The difference is that he's a celebrity and so it matters. It doesn't matter when I live in my head—nobody knows it."

Stories are legion of Kaye, particularly in his twilight years of failing health, behaving poorly—snubbing autograph seekers, ignoring visitors, berating underlings. But there are just as many incidents of great kindness by the man, whether toward the children of the world through his 30 years of tireless efforts on behalf of UNICEF or toward friends and acquaintances who were able, even momentarily, to themselves become that one thing that

Danny was concentrating on.

"He was capable of great, great acts of friendship," composer Johnny Green recalled, with tears in his eyes. "When I first came out to California in 1942, I was having several deeply personal, soul-destroying problems. I took an awful nosedive and ended up in the hospital, discouraged and kind of a beaten guy. I didn't care about anything. Today I've a little sense of humor about the elegance of my attire and joke about myself: 'I wear white tie and tails for water polo.' (But) at that time I had actually become a slob. I was lying in the Good Samaritan Hospital downtown, suffering from what's known as hysterical paralysis. No brain damage or neurological injury, I was just in such a state of utter and total panic that I couldn't use my hands or arms. Danny Kaye came down to that hospital. He sat on the edge of my bed, and he shaved me. He turned me around and made me remember who I was, and what I was, and that this disheveled, mumbling, fumbling guy with ten days of beard on his face, lying on a hospital bed, was no picture of me. It was Danny Kaye who brought me out of that."

Danny, said Spigelgass, "is a dear, dear friend, but it is hard to make him your friend. He's a remarkable creature, and I can understand people hating him, because he has no patience with people who don't understand him, or know his life, or know his world, or know what he loves. But when he is your friend, there is nobody like him on earth. Let me tell you that when you've been ill, as I have been many times, when you're coming home from the hospital, and you look around the front door, there he is. When your mother dies, sitting sniveling suddenly becomes very strange because Danny is with you all the time. When my mother died, he was at my side constantly. Constantly."

Kaye's life and legacy have never been served by an accurate, balanced biography. His first serious biography (Kurt Singer's 1957 *Danny Kaye Saga*) was a rehash of press agent puffery, the last (Martin Gottfried's 1994 *Nobody's Fool*) a mean-spirited collection of tawdry tales. Truth did not seem to be a great concern for either author. As for me, I'll decline the roles of unthinking cheerleader, peeping tom, and armchair psychologist. Rather than examining Kaye's private life, I offer instead an appreciation of his many public lives — the performances for which he hoped to become known. As you will see, others usually created his material and coached his performances, but Danny always had a way of making them distinctly his own.

I.

ONCE UPON A TIME IN NEW YORK

DANNY KAYE WASN'T much different from most of the other young-sters growing up in slums of Brooklyn during the early years of the Twentieth Century. They all shared the same dream: to one day get the heck out.

Yet even beleaguered Brooklyn was considered the height of prosperity compared to where Kaye's father, mother and two brothers had migrated from—a small Jewish enclave in the Ukrainian town of Ekaterinoslav. In 1906, faced with Russia's rising persecution of the Jews, Jacob Kaminsky left behind Kiev—and his wife Clara and young sons Louis and Max—to sail for America. He traveled in steerage by steamship, arriving two weeks later in Philadelphia. A horse dealer in the old country, Jacob turned to sewing first saddlebags and, as his skills as a tailor progressed, dresses. For three years, he saved his pennies until he could pay for his family to join him. For a year, they shared a tiny apartment with fellow immigrants. But after Clara became pregnant, the family relocated from Philadelphia to New York. The Kaminskys settled into a two-family house at 350 Bradford Street, where on January 28, 1911, they welcomed their third son, curly red-haired David Daniel. Despite the hardships, Jacob retained his sense of humor and strong love of life, appreciative of his newfound freedoms in America. "Pop" enthusiastically led the family's joyous, musical religious festivities.

But little David relied more heavily on his mother. A gangly, carrot-topped kid needed plenty of support—and a sense of humor—to survive on the rough streets of East New York, where David's playmates grew up to join the notorious gang Murder Inc. A stark physical contrast to the typical dark-haired, dark-featured Russian Jews, David preferred to fit in with the crowd—no small feat considering the ethnic diversity of his neighborhood. Consequently, the boy who could speak only English, with snippets of Yiddish, eventually learned to mimic the accents and phrases of other cultures.

Mother Clara was the musical talent in the family. She taught David Russian and Jewish folk songs and recognized his natural gift for singing.

She took great pride in showing off her young singer at family gatherings. As an attention-craving youngest child, he was always ready to perform for anyone willing to listen.

His first public appearance came unexpectedly at the age of five. While drifting through a crowded Brooklyn shoe store, David suddenly broke into a silly, incoherent song called "Fifty, Fifty." But when customers started gathering around him to laugh and applaud, a clerk quickly patted the boy on the head and shooed him out the door.

David's first professional dramatic role came in a program staged by his class at New York City Public School 149. "It was a minstrel show," he recalled. "The backdrop was painted like a slice of watermelon. We seeds stuck our heads through the cutouts. We were told to cover our faces with burnt cork. I forgot to cover my ears. That, plus my red hair, stopped the show."

Clara also taught David to dance, but the lad preferred to devote his natural athleticism and agility to sports. In his neighborhood, a kid who could hit "two sewers" in punchball was the hero of the town. David could belt one and a half. He remained focused on athletics at Thomas Jefferson High School, spending most of his time pole-vaulting, playing handball, and swimming.

Away from school, he was shy and quiet and only slightly mischievous, though he hung out with the "rowdies," as he called them. "As a kid," he remembered, "I was scarcely the model for a well-behaved child, but I wasn't really bad either. For instance, as a teenager I was the kind of guy who stood behind the guy who whistled at the girls."

As a student, David, with his flypaper mind, was among the higher achievers—but he was bored. At 13, he ran away from home with another teen, Max Tirsch, intending to hitchhike to Florida. "He had a ukulele," Kaye said. "We started out with about $6 or something, hitchhiked all the way to Asheville, North Carolina, and we'd be picked up by people in cars. He'd play the ukulele and I'd sing songs, and we'd entertain them for a little while, so they'd give us a buck, or a couple of bucks, to get something to eat, and by the time we got back, we had more money than we started with."

David reluctantly returned to high school. But, a year later, at age 14, he lost his mother to tuberculosis. Life became even more difficult, emotionally and financially. Months before he was to graduate, the restless teen dropped out. He and dark-haired schoolmate Lou Eisen formed a harmony act, "Red and Blackie," to sing at parties. Most of their harmonizing, however, would be in front of the neighborhood candy store.

It was there, during the spring of 1929, that they caught the ear—and eye—of Nat Lichtman. An artist and Romanian immigrant, Lichtman had been hired the year before to bring a sense of professionalism to the entertainment offered at the White Roe Lake Resort of Livingston Manor, New York. White Roe was one of the hundreds of farms in the Catskill Mountains that had been converted to summer resorts for vacationing Jews. But owner Meyer Weiner wanted his establishment to be special. Lichtman created a stylish logo for the resort, picturing a leaping stag, and drew fancy covers for White Roe's weekly programs. He had professional sets built for the resort's threadbare stage. He helped create original stage productions and recreate current Broadway hits—albeit cut down to an hour in length and pieced together from notes he hurriedly scribbled in the dark while watching the plays himself. And he sought to hire experienced singers, dancers and comics.

Nonetheless, Lichtman noticed something special in those candy store singers. He needed a few more performers for the coming season, energetic kids willing to work without rest for $200 for the summer, including room and board.

The 18-year-olds were duly impressed by the dapper gentleman with the pencil-thin moustache. David and Lou, anxious for their first taste of professional show business, readily agreed. The boys, however, quickly discovered that at White Roe, new recruits spent less time as professional entertainers than as "tummlers" ("creators of tumult," in Yiddish). Their primary task would be doing anything necessary to keep the guests constantly entertained—or at least distracted—so they wouldn't think of checking out. David and Lou would chase each other through the halls with meat cleavers, jump fully clothed into fish ponds, and even perform conventional chores, such as waiting on tables. If the guests appeared to be growing bored, the tummlers would corral them for "porch sessions" or "lawn parties," dragging everyone outside to witness well-worn burlesque routines and song parodies. In particular, the boys were expected to dote on the young single women, who typically outnumbered the male guests three-to-one.

The lakeside resort stressed outdoor activities—swimming, horseback riding, golf, tennis, baseball—so on gloomy mornings, Mr. Weiner would rouse the tummlers extra early. "Pep up!" he'd charge. "Pep up the place!"

After completing the day's foolishness, the tummlers would start rehearsing the week's scripted performances, practicing into the early hours of the morning. Each evening had its own theme. Sundays featured a concert by the resident seven-piece orchestra. Another night was Game Night. Fridays showcased a pirated play. The first stage production David ever saw was at White Roe—and he was in it. In time, he'd take on roles in *Once in a Lifetime*, *Death Takes a Holiday*, *The Play's the Thing*, *Springtime for Henry*, *Reunion in Vienna*, *Awake and Sing*, and countless original dramas. The week's high point was Saturday, night of the musical comedy revue, featuring sketches, monologues, songs and dances.

David quickly took to acting, dancing and comedy. "Within five minutes of him being on stage, you knew he was going places," said Meyer Weiner's son, John. "He had it."

Because the boys would be needed in so many different stage roles, at White Roe they would no longer be the team Red and Blackie. Lou Eisen had already settled on a non-ethnic stage name, Lou Reed. David followed suit, opting to use his middle name and last initial—Danny Kaye (the same surname already adopted by his brother, Larry). At White Roe, at least, he was expected to maintain this warm, fun-loving "Danny Kaye" persona at all times.

After the summer ended, Red and Blackie resumed their act, singing at parties and occasionally on the radio, as Lou's school schedule allowed. Danny also tried his hand at an assortment of "real jobs"—soda jerk, office clerk, assistant to his brother Max's fledgling electrical business—but all ended disastrously. His failures confirmed to him that he was not meant for traditional employment.

He ended up spending a lot of time sleeping, irking his brothers. But their father realized that his youngest son's problem was more bad luck and confusion than laziness. "Leave Duvidl alone. He will find himself one day," Jacob would explain. Pop, meanwhile, slipped $5 bills under his youngest son's pillow, pretending to himself that he was sending him through college.

If Danny were ever going to make it in show business, he would require professional guidance. He returned to White Roe for the summer of 1930, as he would for the next three summers after that. Eisen would return as well, but as he progressed toward becoming a podiatrist, he gradually shifted to become White Roe's athletic director and spent less and less time on stage.

Danny quickly latched on to the resort's social director, Phil "Fishel" Goldfarb. This master of tummlery owned a novelty business and first came to White Roe several years earlier as a guest. But Fishel's antics, story-telling and jokes, often Yiddish, so entertained the other guests that Mr. Weiner begged him to stay longer, for free. Weiner then paid him to stay the next summer, and Goldfarb kept coming back, assuming the title social director.

Like Nat Lichtman, Goldfarb was only in his mid-20s, but Danny looked up to him as a wise, albeit clownish, father figure. Fishel helped cultivate Kaye's comic delivery, timing, vocal inflections, and facial contortions. As Danny became more comfortable on stage, he graduated to Goldfarb's stooge, and the two worked up comedy routines for the Saturday night revues. The revues featured about fourteen acts, often starting with a mono-logue—or "Fishelogue"—by Goldfarb, followed by songs, dances, and skits—usually one pairing Goldfarb and Kaye, with the duo appearing as, perhaps, hillbillies, wrestlers, sailors, or playboys.

While Fishel concentrated on making Danny funnier, Nat was more interested in making him more professional. Lichtman, according to Borscht Belt comic Herman Stein, "was extremely serious, and he would not allow anything that was tawdry or cheap of any kind to appear. Nat fre-quently would object to members of the cast who wanted to do something flashier, if it bordered on something that he would consider not in good taste. He was opposed to anything that dealt with normal kinds of burlesque or sex situations. He handled them in a way that was very dramatic and the-atrical, but not vulgar. He had a tremendous sensitivity to vulgarity.

"In many ways, Nat was Danny's mentor, particularly in those early years. He helped to discipline Danny, in the sense of advising and coaching and often demanding he stay within certain bounds to bring out Danny's best talents, rather than have him occasionally run amok, which he had a tendency to do and go all over the place in the interpretation of a character, because there were a lot of legitimate shows we did. In these plays, Danny really was a dramatic actor, sometimes comic and sometimes not. We did a lot of serious stuff.

"Also, I think Nat really tried to test diverse aspects of Danny's potential talent, ranging from the most wildly comic to the most deeply dramatic, whether it was musical or not musical. He had a tremendous range of opportunities for him. Nat was very mindful of wanting to help Danny com-mand a sense of theatrical discipline. He could give himself completely on the stage, but within bounds that made it authentic and plausible rather than a series of shtick."

Lichtman loved, in particular, the elegance of Danny's hands and worked with him to refine and highlight their graceful movement. Nat also helped Danny develop solo routines. The director had Kaye occasionally conduct the house orchestra, to comic effect—tripping as he stepped onto the bandstand, raising his baton and sending it flying over the audience, becoming overly emotional with the changing moods of the music.

With his quick and nimble tongue, Danny demonstrated exceptional skill at dialects and scat singing. So Lichtman suggested he incorporate his gibberish into Cab Calloway's jazz hit "Minnie the Moocher." Danny would sing a few lyrics of nonsense ("Git-gat-gittle-with-a-geet-gazay") and then prompt the audience to repeat them, back and forth, until the passages became ridiculously long and convoluted. Lichtman also suggested Kaye sing an old Yiddish song about teaching children Hebrew, "Oyfn Pripetshik," and created an entire sequence out of it, "Malamud in Cheder."

Recalled John Weiner: "Nat made a wonderful set of a little Hebrew school. Danny would wear a long beard and be the teacher to a group of small children. He'd sing these beautiful songs. And then he'd step in front of the blue curtain, rip off his beard, and sing 'Minnie the Moocher.'"

During the summer of 1932, White Roe hired a full-time dance director, Dave Harvey, who brought along his dance partner, Cathleene Young. "We had two professional dancers come up," Kaye recalled, "and we struck up quite a friendship. I knew I had to get into show business some way. I didn't know my left foot from my right foot as a dancer, but we made up an act and tried it out at camp."

Having a third member of the troupe broadened the possibilities of what they could do, so Harvey and Young invited Kaye to join them in the fall when they took their act to vaudeville. Billed as "The Three Terpsichoreans," the trio opened in Utica, New York. At one point during their act, Kaye was supposed to gracefully glide up to Miss Young and kiss her fingers. But when Danny reached out for the girl's hand, he fell flat on his face and split his pants. The audience roared. Danny, sprawled out on the stage, tried to get up as if nothing had happened, but Young whispered, "Wait for the laugh! Wait for the laugh!" From then on, the bit became a regular part of the routine. The Three Terpsichoreans were so well received that by the time they returned to White Roe for the summer of 1933, they

WHITE ROE PLAYERS
PRESENT
"SHADOWS IN BLUE"
Sunday Night, September 3, 1933

DAVE HARVEY, CUTHLEENE YOUNG
AND DANNY KAYE

PROGRAM NOTES: The new dance team of Dave Harvey, Cathleene Young, and Kaye was featured on the program cover for White Roe's big Labor Day weekend revue, just before they set off on their first vaudeville tour.

already had vaudeville bookings lined up for the next fall.

Their second vaudeville tour began in the Northeast and traveled westward. In Detroit, they were greeted by A.B. Marcus, the famed producer of an annual revue that toured "wherever no one else did." Marcus went backstage after one performance and announced, "How would you like to go to China?"

But by *you*, Marcus didn't mean everyone. Pointing to the dancers, Marcus decreed, "You I want. You I want." Then he pointed to Danny. "You I don't want." Harvey and Young, however, were too loyal to turn their backs on Kaye and convinced the producer to book the three of them for the price of two.

The trio joined the La Vie Paree troupe of 75 comics, singers, dancers, jugglers, acrobats, and fractionally-clad women. The caravan spent the following months traveling westward, doing 41 single-night engagements along the way. Upon reaching San Francisco on February 8, 1934, the company set sail for Asia. By this time, Kaye had finagled his way into eighteen of the 21 numbers and boosted his salary to $60 a week.

As soon as La Vie Paree hit Tokyo, Kaye had to begin adjusting to the strange new ways of the Orient. On opening day, the police objected to the casting of the half-naked women and confiscated all pictures of them. The women were allowed to perform, but their pictures spent a lonely night in jail.

"Our show couldn't help but be a hit—we had 40 girls in it," Danny recalled. "That was the first time in Japan that men and women had been allowed on the stage together. We got away with it, but the censors wouldn't permit anybody to kiss in the skit."

On another occasion, during a performance delivered to a Tokyo audience comprised predominantly of military men, Danny's routines met with stony silence, despite his increasingly desperate attempts at laughs. Finally, changing his strategy, he presented a sad ballad. Still no response. The depressed entertainer retreated to the wings where the theater manager, recognizing his despair, explained that the audience was too polite to disturb his lovely performance with noisy laughter and applause.

The tour of the Orient afforded Danny with a valuable opportunity to learn new techniques and perfect others. With the non-English-speaking crowds, he soon discovered the importance of making broad facial expressions, changing costumes quickly, adapting performances to particular audiences, and especially pantomime. "It was easy to make them laugh out

READY OR NOT: To publicize their upcoming vaudeville trips, The Three Terpsichoreans (Harvey, Young, and Kaye) posed for publicity photos, some serious, some silly, first in the fall of 1933 in New York (*above*) and then the following year in Chicago (*opposite*). [Special Collections Library, University of Michigan]

there," Kaye remembered, "broad stuff, like eating crackers and then trying to sing, with the crackers flying out of your mouth. That got 'em."

It was in Asia that Kaye fine-tuned his scat singing. "Most of the time we used pantomime," Danny recalled, "but after a couple of weeks I'd throw in a Japanese word here and there as a clue, just in case they weren't getting it. In one language or another, I've been doing it ever since."

"La Vie Paree" spent eight weeks in Tokyo, staging a pair of two-and-a-half-hour shows each day. The rigorous schedule continued in Shanghai, Hong Kong, and then Canton, where a terrified Kaye shared a dressing room with scorpions and flying cockroaches. Next, the troupe traveled to Singapore, Bangkok, and finally Osaka, where a typhoon struck and

blacked out all the lights in the theater, right in the middle of one of Danny's routines. The comic kept the crowd from panicking by sitting down on the edge of the stage, his legs dangling into the orchestra pit, shining a pair of flashlights on his face, and singing every song he knew.

Despite such perilous adventures, Kaye loved the Orient. There, he got his first taste of Chinese food, which in later years would become a passion, and—after years as a gigolo at White Roe—he fell head over heels in love with a fellow performer—tall, blonde dancer Holly Fine. He would remain smitten for several years, even after show business separated them.

The experience and skills, especially in comedic timing, Kaye acquired during the tour would prove invaluable. But when La Vie Paree ended its eight-month run and headed back for Seattle, Danny had had enough. Marcus planned to tour the eastern seaboard through the summer, before heading for Canada and ultimately back across the Pacific to Australia. Danny opted to leave, figuring, "I had no standing. I wasn't getting anywhere, so I left the show for a starvation routine. I came back to knock my brains out at the New York offices."

Harvey, Young and Fine stayed with the show. Danny began looking for work. He reluctantly returned to White Roe, when Meyer Weiner offered him $1,000 for the 1935 summer season—the most the resort had ever paid anyone. By this time, Weiner viewed Danny as an international celebrity and prominently advertised his discovery's return. He often featured Kaye's glamour photo on the cover of White Roe's revue program and marketed a new drink, the 30-cent "Danny Kaye Special."

To celebrate Kaye's return, Lichtman and writer Dick Diamond created an elaborate sequence, "The Song of the Miners," for the season's first big revue, on the Fourth of July. Extolling the virtues of the imperiled, unappreciated miner, the number earned Danny seven curtain calls.

Kaye continued performing sketches with Goldfarb. But whereas in the early years Fishel wrote himself most of the laugh lines, now Danny had graduated to playing the rube comic and Fishel played the straight man. A typical skit, "Rusty and the Doctor," opened:

Doctor (Goldfarb): Are you Rusty Kraus?
Rusty (Kaye): Guilty, your honor.
Doctor: Take your clothes off.
Rusty: Maybe I'm in the wrong place. I want to be an aviator, not a dancer.

Doctor: Come here.

Rusty: No.

Doctor: Come here.

Rusty: No.

Doctor: Come here.

Rusty: (walking over) I don't wanna.

Doctor: Born?

Rusty: What do you think?

Doctor: Where were you born?

Rusty: In the hospital.

Doctor: Why?

Rusty: I wanted to be near my mother.

Doctor: How many children in your family?

Rusty: Nine.

Doctor: All together?

Rusty: No. One at a time.

Doctor: How many boys?

Rusty: Four.

Doctor: How many girls?

Rusty: Four.

Doctor: What's the other one?

Rusty: Who knows, it's still a baby.

Doctor: What's your nationality?

Rusty: Russian.

Doctor: Were your parents Russian, too?

Rusty: No, they took their time. They were on the five-year plan.

Doctor: Your folks still living?

Rusty: No, father fell off a polo pony when he was 91 and my mother died at 108.

Doctor: What from?

Rusty: Childbirth.

Doctor: Quite a hearty couple, weren't they?

Rusty: Yes, Grandma and I hated to see them go.

Doctor: Ever dizzy?

Rusty: What do you mean—like seeing spots, blacking out, getting hazy?

Doctor: Yes.

Rusty: No.

Doctor: How much do you weigh?
Rusty: 150.
Doctor: Stripped?
Rusty: No, the drugstore was crowded.
Doctor: Have you traveled? Were you ever abroad?
Rusty: No, I was always a man.

The silly exchange continued for several more minutes, climaxing with a knockabout medical examination.

Kaye was now a Borscht Belt headliner at the age of 25, yet he was frustrated to still be slaving away in the same place where he started when he was 18. Fortunately, the season ended on a high note over the Labor Day holiday. Kaye's father stayed the weekend and saw his son go over big in his final Friday night play, *Accent on Youth*, and in the Saturday night revue, which showcased the best acts of the summer, including Danny's opening song "Black Coffee," "Cheder," and his star turn finale, "Song of the Miners." Better yet, in the audience were agents and one drama coach who requested that Kaye look him up when he returned to the city.

Yet solid offers never materialized. Having coffee one night in a Manhattan cafeteria, Danny ran into Nick Long Jr., an acrobatic dancer who had appeared in several films and was looking for a stooge to join his nightclub act at Billy Rose's Casa Mañana. They'd call the act Nick Long Jr. & Company. Danny would be the Company. Between Long's flips and leaps over long lines of showgirls, Kaye would run frantically around the stage and repeat his White Roe routines, like "Minnie the Moocher."

Early on in the Casa Mañana engagement, Danny unexpectedly received an encore call. He had no idea what to do, so he told the band to play the standard "Dinah." Kaye did it as a Russian: "Deenah, is there anyone feenah, in the state of Caroleenah...." The number went over terrifically, and it became a permanent feature of the act. Kaye soon devised a whole "Mad Russian" skit, using the song as a climax.

He followed up the Long booking with two variety tours: an eight-week campaign with Abe Lyman and his orchestra and a second in which he strategically positioned fans in front of stripper Sally Rand.

Between gigs, Kaye ended up sleeping back at his father's house and bumming meals at the tables of friends, like Nat Lichtman. "Nat adored Danny," said writer Sam Locke, "like a mother adores a baby who says, 'Look! Watch what I do!' And then the mother will 'Look! Isn't that...'

That was the quality in (Nat), and it was so warm. And I thought Danny was a warm guy then (because) Danny was always a reflection of the person who's closest to him. A mirror image. And because Nat was a very warm, good human being, Danny reflected that."

For the summer of 1937, Lichtman left White Roe for the President Hotel in Swan Lake, New York, and invited Danny to join him. Loathe as he was to return to the Catskills, particularly a resort that stressed Jewish entertainment even more than White Roe, Kaye had no other options. His role would be master of ceremonies. He refused to do any tummling. He was the acknowledged star of the troupe, around whom all the younger performers would gather to hear his tales and jokes, acted out in dialects. Danny was also a snappy dresser and more knowledgeable of women than were his naive sketch partners. Yet he didn't forget for a minute that he was still stuck in the theatrical minor leagues.

Danny and fellow President comic Herman Stein frequently went together to audition for radio programs. Stein said, "He and I would go to recital halls, and there were usually these three guys with hats and overcoats and cigars in the back of the hall while Danny did this extremely funny piece, which usually had people falling out of their seats when he had a mass audience. And here you had these three guys sitting there for the audition with their hands in their pockets. The 'Don't call us, we'll call you' kind of thing. But it was a very, very funny sketch, winding up with his 'Deenah' song. He was enormously frustrated."

By fall, Danny got his first big break—signing with a top-flight talent agent, Harry Bestry. Quirky yet connected, Bestry arranged to have Kaye audition his Mad Russian sketch for a vice president at Educational Pictures, an independent producer of two-reel comedies.

As Danny wrote to his long-distance girlfriend, Holly Fine: "I didn't feel any too confident about auditioning a sketch, but I did it anyway, and they thought I was terrific. They said they would let my manager know, and I surely thought it was going to be one of those things. You know the story, 'I'll let you know.' Well, in two days they called up and said they were sending their lawyer over with a contract—just on the strength of seeing me in one sketch!"

Educational initially proposed a four-year deal: a guaranteed $200 a week for 30 weeks the first year, increasing $100 a week each year until he would be making $500 a week in year four, for 40 weeks guaranteed. Kaye calculated he could make $64,000 in four years—far more money than he'd ever dreamed of. He realized he couldn't make 40 weeks worth of shorts in a year, but would instead be loaned out to other studios, earning his contracted amount while Educational pocketed the difference. Neither Kaye nor Bestry liked Educational's preference that Kaye be exclusively their property. So, instead Danny agreed to a non-exclusive deal of four shorts per year for two years.

Bestry then took Kaye to visit George White, producer of *George White's Scandals*, a series of Broadway revues and films modeled after the *Ziegfeld Follies*. White thought Kaye's act would fit perfectly in his next picture, contingent on Danny making a screen test. Bestry balked. "Let him see you in your picture (for Educational)," Bestry advised. "He'll be more anxious for you." Bestry would be mistaken.

DIME A DANCE

(Filmed mid-Nov. 1937; released Dec. 23, 1937)
Producer: Al Christie, for Educational Pictures
Screenplay: Arthur Jarrett, Marcy Klauber
Cast: Imogene Coca (Esmeralda), Danny Kaye (Eddie), June Allyson (Harriet), Hank Henry (Homer), Barry Sullivan (sailor)

Although Educational had been around for decades and its shorts were distributed by Twentieth Century Fox, the small studio was teetering on the edge of bankruptcy. Movie theaters were moving to double features, drying up the market for short subjects. Educational was known as the home of up-and-coming unknowns—making the first films of Bob Hope and the Ritz Brothers—and falling-fast has-beens, like Harry Langdon and Buster Keaton. Its credo was to produce a finished film as quickly and inexpensively as possible, usually filming a 20-minute short in about two days at and around the Astoria Studios on Long Island.

Kaye was to play in supporting roles at first and, if successful, move on to his own series based on his characterization of a brash, double-talking Russian, Nikolai Nikolaevich. His first, *Dime a Dance*, starred elfin comedienne Imogene Coca and ingénue June Allyson. Danny played a hapless sailor whose buddy convinces him to pretend to be a Russian prince to fool a girl at the dance hall.

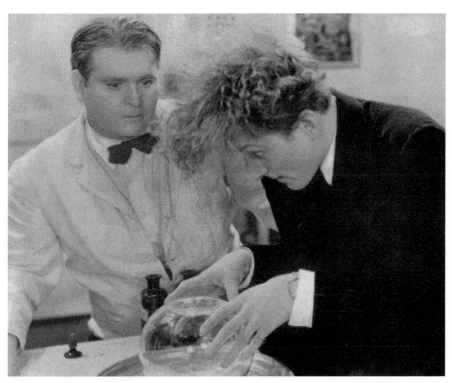

MAD RUSSIAN: Kaye played his manic Nikolai Nikolaevich character in most of his Educational short subjects, including *Getting an Eyeful* with star Charles Kemper.

GETTING AN EYEFUL

(Filmed Nov. 30 to early Dec. 1937; released Jan. 21, 1938)
Producer: Al Christie, for Educational Pictures
Director: William Watson
Screenplay: Billy K. Wells
Cast: Charles Kemper (Henry Groper), Danny Kaye (Nikolai Nikolaevich), Sally Starr (Eleanor), Clyde Fillmore, Jack Squires, Jack Hartley

Two weeks later, Kaye returned to the studio for *Getting an Eyeful*, starring comedian Charles Kemper as a sadistic eye doctor and Kaye as his ill-fated first patient, the excitable Nicolaevich. The two-reeler rivaled even the most violent Three Stooges short for sheer gruesomeness.

CUPID TAKES A HOLIDAY

(Filmed c. Dec. 1937; released Feb. 4, 1938)
Producer: Al Christie, for Educational Pictures
Director: William Watson
Screenplay: Billy K. Wells
Cast: Danny Kaye (Nikolai Nikolaevich), Douglas Leavitt (A. Swain), Estelle Jayne, Ruth Lockwood, Marion Martin, Pauline Myers

After the holidays, Kaye earned his first starring role, in *Cupid Takes a Holiday*. This time around, Nicolaevich must get married before his twenty-first birthday or, because of a Russian family tradition, he will go insane. He visits a series of prospective brides, but each has glaring drawbacks. In the end, Kaye's character in the film (like the film itself) would not be successful.

MONEY ON YOUR LIFE

(Filmed c. Jan. 1938; released May 13, 1938)
Producer: Al Christie, for Educational Pictures
Director: William Watson
Screenplay: M. Lewis, T. McKnight
Cast: Charles Kemper (Charlie Kemp), Danny Kaye (Nikolai Nikolaevich), Harry Gribbon (window cleaner), Sally Starr (Alice), Al Ochs, Jack Shutta, Eddie Hall

Danny reverted to a secondary role in his fourth film, *Money on Your Life*. This time around, Charles Kemper sells life insurance to Nicolaevich, only to discover that the crazy Russian fellow is being chased by hit men.

Audiences would have to wait patiently for such hilarity. In early 1938, Fox officially abandoned comedy shorts. Without distribution, Educational filed for bankruptcy. The studio, which typically released its shorts about three weeks after filming was completed, held on to Kaye's fourth picture for three months.

Although Danny could not be blamed for the weak material Educational forced him to deliver, his loud, abrasive, unfunny Russian characterizations did little to ease the pain. Kaye had distinct memories of his first movie-making experiences: "I'd rather forget all about them." To his dismay, years later scenes from his Educational shorts resurfaced in two compilation features—1944's *The Birth of a Star* and 1963's *The Sound of Laughter*.

Danny returned to Nick Long Jr. and the Casa Mañana. One performance was attended by Henry Sherek, who directed the cabaret shows at London's

EARLY TV: During his stint at London's Dorchester Hotel, Kaye was among Henry Sherek's caberet acts to be featured on the experimental BBC TV program *Autumn Laughter.* [BBC]

celebrated Dorchester Hotel. He was in America scouting for new talent. He had read Long's reviews and watched the dancer perform in Philadelphia, but wasn't overly impressed. Instead, Sherek was mesmerized by the lanky, red-haired buffoon. "He kept me laughing from the minute he leapt on the stage to the second he fell into the wings," Sherek said.

After the show, the director went backstage to book Kaye for $50 a week at the Dorchester. Danny, though, was under contract to Long. Sherek would have to hire both or none. He agreed, provided Kaye sing two solos, "Minnie the Moocher" and "Deenah."

Sadly, Europe had given the Black Death a healthier reception than the continent offered Kaye. He opened the eight-week stint in the spring of 1938, at the outset of the Munich Crisis, to a completely unresponsive audience. Kaye recalled one man in the audience sat with his back to the entire performance. The man never turned around, but at one point was heard to say, "I say, what's going on back there?"

As Kaye remembered, "I was the first atomic bomb in the history of the world. We were so desperately unsuccessful. It was awful."

Unlike his tour of the Far East, where he traveled with a close-knit troupe, Danny was basically alone in Europe. "I didn't know a soul in London," he continued. "I hated it. I hated England. I hated London. I hated everything connected with it, because it's terribly difficult to be happy in a place where you are completely unsuccessful."

Danny and the Dorchester would have liked to end the relationship right then, but Long had contracts with both of them. There were two high points. One show at the Dorchester was televised by the BBC under the title *Autumn Laughter*, although few people noticed because of the dearth of televisions in 1938. And one afternoon, Kaye made a well-received guest appearance at a band concert in Guildford (orchestra leader Jack Jackson noted "he was colossal"). Yet, the comedian was otherwise chilled by the cold British hospitality and left the country as soon as his contract with Long expired, in mid-November.

Back in the states, work wasn't exactly waiting for him. Danny could fill almost every job out there. And that was the problem. He was slowly perfecting every aspect of performing—mimicry, pantomime, singing, dancing, storytelling, improvisation, dialects, acting. Combined, the overload of talents translated into obscurity. He simply did too much. No one, not even his own agent, could categorize him. "Are you a singer?" casting directors would ask.

No, he wasn't really a singer.

"A dancer?"

Well, no, he couldn't call himself a dancer.

"A comedian?"

Not exactly.

"Well, what are you best at?"

"Nothing in particular," he'd answer.

And the agents would respond, "That's too bad…"

Dejected, Danny disappeared into hallway after hallway, accompanied by the echo of the word "Next!" He could just do too much, too soon.

II.

SYLVIA

DANNY CERTAINLY DIDN'T know it, but his ticket to stardom had also grown up in Brooklyn—right across the street. Her name was Sylvia Fine, no relation to Holly, and she knew well of Danny. But—two years his younger—she had yet to make an impression on him. When the lad was out in the streets playing punchball, she was inside, studying. Her father, Samuel Fine, was the neighborhood dentist, whose office 12-year-old Kaye would watch over during lunch hours—until he was caught drilling holes in the woodwork with the dental tools. At his earliest opportunity, Sam moved wife Bessie and the three Fine children to the more refined confines of Flatbush.

Like father, Sylvia was grimly serious, painfully shy, and not preoccupied with her looks. Her mother was more extroverted. Bessie loved to sing and had Sylvia begin taking piano lessons at age 6, as would her younger sister, Rhoda, and baby brother, Robert.

Smart as a whip and intensely ambitious, Sylvia began attending Brooklyn College at age 15. Exposed to the works of Gilbert and Sullivan and Mark Twain, Sylvia soon became interested in writing for laughs. She became editor of the college paper and penned a regular humor column, but eventually discovered her words were more effective in verse rather than prose. Her favorite composition of her college years was:

"The Great American Tragedy is
To have no date on Sagedy."

As a music major, Sylvia began writing songs for college competitions and class productions, employing her humor in ditties like "Can't Beat an Egg Like You" for the senior varsity show (for which she co-authored the book). Miss Fine bypassed a scholarship to Julliard Institute to continue her college training and graduated three months before her twentieth birthday.

Hoping for a career as a lyricist, she visited music publishers to pitch her songs, but they bristled at their complexity. "Why don't you find a nice young man and get married, little girl?" publishers responded. "These songs use too big words."

Instead, Sylvia began teaching piano lessons to the neighborhood kids.

For a while, she took a job selling kosher soap and later demonstrated soup mixes at a grocery store. In 1937, she was hired as a counselor at Camp Geneva, a girls' summer camp in the Pocono Mountains of Pennsylvania. There, she wrote songs and sketches and helped stage revues under the purview of composer Irvin Graham, who had several of his songs reach Broadway the previous year in Leonard Sillman's *New Faces of 1936*.

The following spring, Sylvia was contacted by Max Liebman, social director at Camp Tamiment, an adult-oriented summer resort in the Poconos. Liebman had hired several *New Faces* performers—Imogene Coca, her husband Robert Burton, and James Shelton—and tried to hire Graham. The songwriter, though, wanted to return to the children's camp, so he suggested Fine instead.

Like the Catskills resorts that Danny had been schooled in, Camp Tamiment offered a secluded spot of nature, with sports, games and entertainment for young singles. But, as the summer campus of the Rand School of Social Science, Tamiment aspired to something greater intellectually and culturally, offering daily lectures and classes. It also strove to present more sophisticated entertainment, particularly after Liebman was hired in 1933. Max insisted on original material, initially writing every song and sketch himself—and often appearing in them, as well. He also strove to hire professional comedians, actors, dancers and singers, who were committed to intense rehearsals through the week and could help to create new material. There would be no tummling.

Liebman was a master at "routining," or the art of ordering his numbers in a revue to maximize their effectiveness. His Saturday-night revues ran twelve to sixteen acts, kicked off by an opening number named after the show's theme (always something vague like "Shooting Stars," so it could encompass almost any act). He then rotated between sketches, songs, dances, and an epic production number finale. Liebman had no lowbrow specialty acts—like vaudevillian jugglers or animal routines. Even his comedy was serious. One week the dance numbers might be ballet, the next tap, modern jazz, or ballroom. Sketches, often musical, were his forte, along with satires of popular plays and movies.

In time, Liebman's Saturday night revues at the Tamiment Playhouse would become known as "Broadway in the Poconos." In hiring Sylvia, for the first time, he had someone else who could create the bulk of the musical numbers, leaving him time to concentrate on producing and directing.

Sylvia found the demands of crafting three or four new numbers every

CALLING ALL AGENTS: Sylvia Fine rehearsed the Camp Tamiment troupe, front-ed by comic Jules Munshin (*center stage*), for 1938's end-of-the-summer revue, designed to attract New York agents and casting directors. [Tamiment Playhouse Photographs Collection, Tamiment Library, New York University]

week, for ten weeks, along with acting as one of the camp's three rehearsal pianists, invigorating yet exhausting. She got three numbers into her first revue—the Benny Goodman-inspired "Rhythm Swing;" "The Man with the Axe," a comic piece for the imposing lead comic, Jules Munshin; and the show-stopping chorus number "ILGWU School of the Theatre." A parody of *Pins and Needles*, a Broadway revue produced by and starring members of the International Ladies' Garment Workers' Union, "ILGWU" was built around the notion that the best way to land a starring role on Broadway was to join a labor union. Tamiment's cast and crew loved the number because, as members of theatrical unions, they resented the success of a show by amateurs. It didn't hurt that ILGWU operated its own summer camp for labor union members, Unity House, right next door. The number went over so well it was repeated several times during the summer.

Under Liebman, Fine became a sponge, soaking in advice on what worked, what didn't, how to craft numbers, how to create characters in a song, and—to establish mood and save time—how to fold snippets of familiar melodies into her pieces for comic effect. Sylvia also discovered that, for a slow-working perfectionist like herself, working with a partner helped stimulate her creative energies and get projects moving.

Ironically, although Tamiment was ostensibly a camp based on a political philosophy and although Fine would have liked to work more of her left-wing politics into her work, Liebman discouraged it. He was convinced that being too political, or too Jewish, or too *anything*, prohibited mainstream success.

Her safe treatment of the war, for instance, can be seen in "Spies," which she wrote in July 1938 to be performed by Munshin, Coca, Burton, and Herman Shapiro:

> "Spying is our business and business is O.K.
> For we're the best intriguers in the diplomatic pay.
> We copy maps of every road, we never talk except in code.
> And no one dares hello us, we're offended if you know us.
> So call on Schpritsenwasser, Belchicoff, Scaramouche, and Madame Stinky.
> If you want inside information please,
> Schpritsenwasser, Belchicoff, Scaramouche, and Madame Stinky.
> Guys who even double cross their t's.
> We're so crooked that we often spy on one another.
> We'd even take the silver threads among the gold from our own mother.
> But who evolved the brilliant scheme
> for Lizzie Arden's vanishing cream—
> Schpritsenwasser, Belchicoff, Scaramouche, and Madame Stinky.
> We get answers before Professor Quiz,
> Schpritsenwasser, Belchicoff, Scaramouche, and Madame Stinky.
> G-men – G-women – G-whiz.
> We never slip, we never shirk,
> We turn out nice, clean, dirty work.
> We rob from cops and robbers, we even trim our barbers.
> Whenever we are sent to spy we always do our share
> For who can smell a plot out even when no plot is there—
> Schpritsenwasser, Belchicoff, Scaramouche, and Madame Stinky.
> We find out things and then we snitch.
> Schpritsenwasser, Belchicoff, Scaramouche, and Madame Stinky.
> You'd call each one a son of a—"

Over Labor Day weekend, agents and producers swarmed Tamiment to view the summer's final show—a restaging of the season's best acts. No offers came Sylvia's way. But she was hooked and, returning to New York, immediately began searching for similar opportunities. The previous spring, a group of politically minded artists called the Theatre Arts Committee had begun staging revues to raise money for war-torn Spain and China. They held the shows, called Cabaret TAC, in an old nightclub and were considered the "first group to take social satire out of the theater and endow it with the immediacy and informality of a cabaret setting." Some of the material was borrowed from shows like *Pins and Needles*, but most was original, some spoofs, but much of it political satire. The biggest hit to come out of Cabaret TAC was the pro-union production number "Picket Line Priscilla," sung by Beatrice Kaye and danced by Dorothy Bird.

Cabaret TAC was gearing up for a second season, starting November 27, 1938, and Sylvia offered her services. Her unpaid contributions were pointedly political, including "Curse of the Silk Chemise" (advising against buying silk from Japan) and "Down on Downing Street" (a wry castigation of British prime minister Neville Chamberlain's appeasement of Germany). The revues, however, lasted just four Sundays.

SUNDAY NIGHT VARIETIES

Keynote Theatre, N.Y. (March 5 to 19, 1939); Barbizon-Plaza, N.Y. (April 9, 1939)
Director/Set Designer: Nat Lichtman
Songs: Sylvia Fine ("Cock Robin," "Down on Downing Street," "ILGWU," "The Stage–What's Left of It"), Bernace Kazounoff, David Greggory ("Vultures of Culture"), John Latouche ("Blasé," "Physical Culture")
Sketches: Sam Locke, Richard Diamond
Cast: Danny Kaye, Irwin Corey, Claire Vermonte, Adele Jerome, Peggy Craven, Mervyn Nelson, Sherle Hartt, Betty Garrett, Bill Matons, Ailes Gilmour, Dolores Irwin, Alexis Rotov

In late January 1939, Sylvia learned that a fellow Cabaret TAC composer was writing songs for a similar revue, bankrolled by the radical leftist magazine *The New Masses*. Actually, the magazine had given all of $400 to a journeyman Borscht Belt director, one Nat Lichtman.

First, Nat found a mothballed loft nightclub on 52nd Street, the Club Miramar. He then had to round up people who could write a "show of social significance" for his star, Danny Kaye, and a group of other aspiring youngsters. Lichtman called in several talented yet still-unknown songwriters and two sketch writers—Dick Diamond from White Roe and 20-year-old Sam Locke, who had written for Nat at his last stop, Camp Copake. Locke set up his typewriter in the club's ladies' room, which he used as his office and where he was one day greeted by an overly excited Lichtman.

"Sam," Nat bubbled, "this girl came in with the most wonderful music and lyrics. She's so talented!"

"Is she pretty?" asked the young sketch writer.

"Well," Lichtman hesitated, "she's... handsome."

Originally, Miss Fine had been asked to merely send some of her satires to the club. She said she didn't have them. Instead, she brought herself down to personally audition the material. Lichtman flipped over her work and wanted to use a few of her numbers in the revue.

Danny was more flippant. In later years, Sylvia would recount how Kaye greeted her by asking why she wore hats with veils, since the only things he found more distasteful than hats were veils. In truth, Sylvia was the one who had always hated hats. What's undeniable is that from the start Kaye, too, was bowled over by her material.

Co-star Betty Garrett recalled, "I was with Danny in the little Manhattan club when Sylvia was brought in to write some special material. I observed the magic moment when they discovered each other. It was truly love at first sight. I think they fell in love with one another's talent as much as with one another."

As she had in Cabaret TAC, Fine received no pay for serving as both songwriter and rehearsal pianist on *Sunday Night Varieties*, nicknamed *Left of Broadway*. She did it for the exposure and, she hoped, to make a difference in the world.

"Everything we did in those days was political," said actor Norman Lloyd, who appeared in Cabaret TAC while his wife, Peggy Craven, appeared in *Sunday Night Varieties*. The casts and crews, he said, "were very talented, very hungry, and they had something to say."

Because everyone was looking for paid work on the side, the program had to be tweaked from week to week based not only on what worked in the previous show, but also on which performers showed up. The only time Lichtman could be sure all of the unpaid cast and crew would be present was at 3:00 in the afternoon, the hour he served the *New Masses*-supplied tea and cake. But the troupe, which fluctuated between 20-some and 30-some members, rehearsed vigorously for their once-a-week presentation, which was set to premiere March 5, 1939.

In addition to appearing as part of the ensemble in the opening and closing numbers, Danny was featured in about eight of the 20-plus numbers
performed each Sunday by the "Keynote Players." In various sketches and
musical numbers, he alternately played a fitness nut, culture snob, circus-
struck yokel, blasé nightclub visitor, and the "Wolf of Wall Street," who's
so busy he has his right-hand man and his left-hand man fill in for him at
his own wedding. Kaye also played Neville Chamberlain in both a sketch
by Sam Locke and in Sylvia's "Down on Downing Street," a shipping boy
in Sylvia's "ILGWU," and a hot jazz singer in the first number she would
write expressly for him, "Cock Robin."

The troupe tinkered with the content for each of their next three shows,
with Lichtman placing new numbers into rehearsal as quickly as the writers
could finish them. That way, he could advertise the show as being as current
as the day's newspaper headlines.

Danny dazzled Sylvia with what he could do with her numbers—his ability to quickly memorize and clearly enunciate, even at top-speed, her most
complicated lyrics, his dialects, his expressions, his wonderful body movement, his ability to fully become her quirky characters. He seemed the perfect vessel to deliver anything she could come up with. Sylvia just needed
to get their work more exposure. She found it difficult for the papers to take
notice of a once-a-week show in a rundown nightclub. *The New York Daily
Worker* did review opening night, noting, "There is more intelligence,
humor, pulchritude, and entertainment in the *Sunday Night Varieties* than
there is in any show I've seen this season on or off Broadway." Danny was
singled out for turning in an "outstanding performance" while "changing
costumes with confusing speed."

Ever aggressive, Fine contacted Gladys Andes, publicity director at the
Barbizon-Plaza Hotel, a plush 38-story tower across from Central Park that
had been set up as a creative and performing artists' residence, replete with
its own art galleries, studios, exhibit halls, library, concert auditorium, and
cozy little theater. Andes agreed to let *Sunday Night Varieties* play, at least
for one Sunday—Easter Sunday—so long as she, as director of the theater,
received top billing.

The move came just in time. Right before the curtain went up for what
was supposed to be the fourth and final night at the Keynote, the police
arrived, shut down the show, and evacuated the 300 persons inside. The
New Masses had never secured a theater license for the facility.

Appearing on a real stage would at least bring in reviewers from the likes

LEFT OF BROADWAY: During *Sunday Night Varieties*, Kaye played Neville Chamberlain in "Down on Downing Street," one of the first Sylvia Fine numbers he would ever perform. *(Betty Garrett at far right)*

of *Variety* and the *New York Post*. The critics uniformly agreed that Kaye and company tried hard and that "things will be a lot better off when they get out the old flit gun and do a bit of cleaning up." But there had to be money to go on, and the show closed soon after.

The revue's short run did not deter Sylvia. Through it, she had met Danny. Before the revue ended, Sylvia had called Max Liebman to tell him about this sensation she had run into. Tamiment needed a new lead comic, since Jules Munshin would not be returning that summer. Fine convinced Liebman to come down to the club to give Danny a look, but Max was unimpressed. He noted the kid had no style and didn't specialize. "But that *is* his style," Sylvia pleaded. Liebman finally consented, but the fact that Kaye's tag was that he had no tag would have to change.

Nat Lichtman wished Danny well, little knowing the two had worked together for the last time.

CAMP TAMIMENT REVUES

Tamiment Playhouse, Bushkill, Pa. (July 3 to Sept. 11, 1939)
Producer/Director: Max Liebman
Songs: Sylvia Fine, James Shelton
Sketches: Max Liebman
Cast: Imogene Coca, Danny Kaye, Robert Burton, Herman Shapiro, James Shelton, Jerome Robbins, Dorothy Bird, Bill Bales, Dick Reed, Albia Kavan, Hildegarde Halliday, Fred Danueli, Beatrice Joyce, Larry Burke, Mona Montes, Grant Muradoff, Leonard Frank, Lina D'Acosta, Ruthanna Boris, Anita Alvarez, Otto Ullbrecht, Meta Krahn

Danny was determined never to return to the Borscht Belt. Yet he recognized immediately that Tamiment was different. It was still a rustic summer camp. He shared a small room and slept in a cot, but there was fresh linen, only one roommate, and a bathroom in the same building. Even the vibe was different. Unlike the boisterous yet intimate atmosphere of White Roe, Tamiment was quiet, serious, impersonal. He was expected to spend most of his week rehearsing. There was no tummling, and romancing of the guests was no longer a mandatory job requirement.

Kaye marveled at the operation's professionalism and sophistication. Most of the material was original, crafted at the camp to showcase the gifts of each troupe member. Liebman, in fact, was skilled at quickly recognizing each performer's strengths and casting accordingly.

Never before had Danny been part of such a talented cast. Most of the performers were returning from Tamiment's breakthrough 1938 season. So, Kaye soon discovered that, for a change, he would not be the primary focus. On his opening night, July 3, most of the acts were borrowed from previous shows, both from Tamiment and elsewhere. Kaye appeared in four of the revue's fourteen acts, including his starring turn as "The Wolf of Wall Street" and singing as Dorothy Bird danced to "Picket Line Priscilla."

Sylvia, meanwhile, would write several songs each week, starting off with an opening number for the entire cast. But her first Tamiment number expressly for Danny, tailored to his specific talents and inspired by her own hatred of hats, would take longer. If Liebman insisted Danny needed something distinctive for audiences to remember him by, Sylvia was determined to make it her songs. She labored over every syllable of that first number and had finished the entire song except for two lines in the middle. They were fairly simple lines, but she had a particular rhyme in mind and it needed to be perfect. The single couplet took her weeks.

"People think I'm a very clever girl," said a young Miss Fine, "and maybe I am on paper after weeks of hard work. But when I go out, people expect me to make like Dorothy Parker."

By week four, the specialty number was ready. Danny was revved up. In addition to Sylvia's solo, he had a featured role in the night's finale, the elaborate, tongue-in-cheek musical "Here He Comes Now." Packed with six songs by Sylvia, the musical spoofed grand romantic operettas, making fun of dull song cues, bromides of direction, disguises, surprise endings, and other clichés, such as intoning, "Ah, here he comes now," every time someone new entered a scene. Kaye played the Masked Gondolier, the most notorious heartbreaker in Venice, who steals the heart of Mary Sue Ann (Coca), despite her engagement to wealthy rancher Bruce Benson (Shelton) and the objections of her father, Vanderveer (Burton), an important-looking executive who carries a mysterious black briefcase wherever he goes. After the inevitable love songs, chase sequences, and round of mistaken identities, we learn Benson is really a German spy, Vanderveer a diplomat carrying top-secret government papers, and the gondolier Secret Service agent Danny Davenport, who rescues Vanderveer, gets the girl, and saves the day.

The finale earned tremendous applause, but Sylvia's specialty number for Danny, slotted ninth on the program, went over even bigger. "Anatole of Paris" would become Kaye's most famous solo and the template for countless others—in which he'd adopt an eccentric character and spend the next five minutes giving the audience a witty dose of his history and personality, along the way detouring into other musical styles and dialects. In the case of Anatole, the effeminate Frenchman is "the result of the twisted eugenics of a family of inbred schizophrenics" whose bizarre hats stem from a curious preoccupation: he hates women. As Danny wove through Sylvia's clever, complicated lyrics, he'd suddenly forsake the French accent to jump into an unexpected quip about Brooklyn, Venice or "Old Man River." Nonetheless, Sylvia would refer to "Anatole of Paris" as about the simplest number she ever wrote for Kaye, saying anybody could sing it.

As Kaye wrapped up the song, the band launched into Irving Berlin's "A Pretty Girl Is Like a Melody" and Danny commented on a parade of women modeling ridiculous headwear. One girl wore a champagne bucket on her head, another a hat rigged with a miniature ping-pong net and paddles, one with a fire hydrant and a stuffed dog, one sporting a telephone ("for a lonesome afternoon conversation piece"), and one with a sharply angled dinner service.

Amazingly, two weeks later, Danny got an even bigger reaction. The latest rage on Broadway was updating Gilbert and Sullivan's operetta *The Mikado*. First came an all-black *Swing Mikado*, which inspired a similarly-jazzed-up *Hot Mikado*, which inspired a political sketch in *Pins and Needles*, "The Red Mikado." Liebman proposed a Yiddish Mikado. Set in a Hasidic village in Japan, "That There Mikado" was performed almost entirely in Yiddish, with a smattering of English words for comic effect. Despite Kaye's aversion to Yiddish humor, the spoof was the unqualified hit of the summer, one that cast members and guests alike would reminisce about for years after.

The Yiddish Mikado was also selected as the finale for the best-of-the-best revue over Labor Day weekend. That tenth show was so successful, it was repeated the following Saturday to pack the audience with even more agents and producers—among them Harry Kaufman, a longtime associate of Broadway's Shubert brothers. During the intermission, Kaufman went backstage to offer Liebman a contract to bring the revue to the New York stage. Two days later, he had the show in rehearsals. Two weeks later, it was to open on Broadway.

THE STRAW HAT REVUE

Ambassador Theatre, N.Y. (Sept. 28 to Dec. 2, 1939)

Producers: Lee & J.J. Shubert, Harry Kaufman
Director: Max Liebman
Songs: Sylvia Fine ("Crashing Thru," "Child Star," "Great Chandelier" score, "Anatole of Paris," "The Swingaroo Trio," "Soused American Way"), James Shelton ("Four Young People," "Our Town"), Glenn Bacon & Max Liebman ("Tramping on Life")
Sketches: Max Liebman, Sam Locke
Cast: Imogene Coca, Danny Kaye, Robert Burton, Alfred Drake, Jerome Robbins, James Shelton, Lee Brody, Jerome Andrews, Bill Bales, Leon Barte, Dorothy Bird, Ruthanna Boris, Maude Davis, Bronson Dudley, Gertrude Goldsmith, Dolores Granafei, Henriete Henning, Albia Kavan, Mata & Hari, Nana Matiss, Marjorie Moffet, Nan Rae, Richard Reed, Lilli Sandan, Pancho Scordi, Herbert Shepard, Vera Volkenau

Never before had a summer camp show been transported to the Broadway stage. So Kaufman suggested making that impossible dream—starving artists from the sticks reaching the Great White Way—the show's theme. The production, like the Labor Day weekend revue, would be billed as "the best of Tamiment's summer season," but there would be notable differences. First, it would use only the best of the season's "safe" material, avoiding anything too downbeat, political (like "Picket Line Priscilla"), or ethnic (such as the Yiddish Mikado).

Producer Kaufman preferred to distance the show from Camp Tamiment and its socialist politics. Liebman went along willingly, promoting the show as "an impudent musical" that "does not rely on newspaper headlines for material" and "has no social significance whatsoever." He even agreed to trim from the "Wolf of Wall Street" sketch a reference to President Roosevelt, when stockbroker Kaye picks up a ticker tape and exclaims, "Dammit, even when he's fishing I'm in trouble."

Second, only fourteen of the 24 acts on the bill were from Tamiment. As insurance, the Shuberts insisted on adding several established vaudeville acts—three specialty dancers, a monologist, and a comedy sister act—along with up-and-coming actor Alfred Drake.

Kaufman named the show *The Straw Hat Revue* and had Sylvia write an opening number "Crashing Thru," in which the entire cast, outfitted in the straw hats that were the stock in trade of summer theater, punched their fists through their hats to symbolize their arrival on the Great White Way.

Liebman was asked to write a new sketch about a playwright to show-case Drake, who broke onto the scene with his Orson Welles impersonation in *One for the Money*.

Kaufman also enlisted Sylvia to create an epic finale, a spoof of Carmen Miranda's "South American Way" number from the Shuberts' concurrent hit, *Streets of Paris*. Fine devised "Soused American Way" for Imogene Coca, who wore a shimmering costume similar to Miranda's, only tackier, and a turban topped not with tropical fruit, but with vegetables, complete with cobs of corn hanging from her waist.

Although *The Straw Hat Revue* was designed to feature Coca as the top star, Kaye appeared in ten numbers, one more than Coca. He was featured in four sketches and six musical numbers, including "Anatole," as well as ending the first act with the mini-musical spoof of operettas, which Sylvia had renamed "The Great Chandelier," to poke fun at the massive lighting fixture that, by tradition, appeared in at least one Shubert production each season. The Shuberts' hulking chandelier looked particularly ridiculous against the painted backdrops of Venetian streets.

The Straw Hat Revue was slated to open September 26, but had to be postponed three days when it was discovered that the Tamiment-supplied scenery didn't carry a union label. All the sets had to be reproduced by union workers.

BROADWAY DEBUT: Kaye, as the just-un-Masked Gondolier, won over Imogene Coca's Mary Sue Ann to conclude the operetta spoof "The Great Chandelier" and close out of the first act of the *Straw Hat Revue*. [Tamiment Playhouse Photographs Collection, Tamiment Library, New York University]

When the show finally opened, most critics were apologetically positive, as if embarrassed that they enjoyed it. They roundly praised the performers, but couldn't seem to shake the notion that it was still a summer camp revue not quite up to Broadway standards. Richard Watts Jr., of the *New York Herald-Tribune*, found it "a modestly pleasant show, with several numbers of genuine excellence, a lot of good tries, and a general air of unostentatious good humor."

Billboard noted Kaye "appears all over the place often, doing a seemingly endless variety of chores, and is uniformly successful in all of them. He's a major performer, of versatility and tremendous effect."

Attendance was modest. To drum up more ticket sales, a publicist mailed 10,000 former Camp Tamiment guests a postcard reading: "Max Liebman invites you to the freshest, funniest musical show in New York." Many of the recipients took the invitation literally and were outraged when the theater refused to give them free tickets.

Business was strong enough to keep the doors open, but not enough to make the Shuberts real money. So the producers immediately ordered changes. They rewrote or dropped several numbers, substituted new ones, and tinkered with the order. They added more vaudeville acts, like comic Cully Richards and the acrobatic Wiere Brothers. The changes were so constant and last-minute that rarely did the acts match the program. According to one critic, "Trying to follow the rapidly paced skits with current editions of the playbill is like trying to follow today's game at Yale Bowl with a Rodeo guide book."

Piece by piece, Liebman's finely tuned revue degenerated into a typical vaudeville show. He may have received billing for conceiving and staging the revue, but he understood it was no longer his show. Kaufman and the Shuberts were calling the shots.

The Straw Hat Revue closed after 75 performances, as soon as the Shuberts had recouped their $8,000 investment. The producers figured it would play better on a coast-to-coast tour of vaudeville houses, under a legitimate headliner, comic Phil Baker. Kaye, Coca and the rest of the cast were willing to go along, and expected to open in Boston on Christmas night. At the last minute, the project was shelved. Coca instead joined the Shuberts' nationwide tour of *Folies Bergere Revue*. The rest of the company was out of work.

Kaye, meantime, had saved up enough money from the show to afford him a couple of weeks' break from pounding on agents' doors. A week after *The Straw Hat Revue* closed, he caught a train to Florida with Max Liebman, for a chance to relax and mull over his future. Danny was realizing that Sylvia was able to cultivate and showcase his strengths better than he thought imaginable. He'd spent ten years struggling to achieve small-time success. She got him to Broadway in eight months.

But their partnership was no longer all business. Sam Locke recalled writing with Sylvia at her parents' home: "Danny would come over, and he'd bring frankfurters, which was typical of Jewish courtship. He called them mom and pop, and Danny was so typical of the young man, although he's not that way as a person. There's nothing particularly Jewish about him. He was playing the role." Locke also began to notice that Kaye, who earlier had reflected the gentleness of Nat Lichtman, now began taking on the toughness of Sylvia.

Locke remembered Sylvia confiding in him how upset she was over Danny romancing an older buxom blonde at Tamiment. "Sylvia told me how humiliating it was," Locke said. "Danny wanted to marry (Sylvia), but she didn't know (if she wanted to). It would be sort of a comedown for this girl to marry a kid from East New York. It may have been a real feeling. Actually, it was typical of the kind of girl who's building up her own image."

After a few days in Florida, Kaye decided to make their partnership permanent. He called Sylvia and asked her to elope. She packed her bags and cobbled together her last $40. Danny and Sylvia were married in Fort Lauderdale on January 4, 1940. Liebman stepped in as best man. To avoid upsetting Sylvia's parents, they returned to their respective families' homes and kept the wedding a secret for several weeks, until they could be remarried in a formal Jewish ceremony at a synagogue.

Of greater concern once they were back in town was how to promote their professional partnership. They didn't have to wait long. Agent Harry Bestry contacted Norman Corwin's radio variety show *Pursuit of Happiness*, which earlier had Danny perform his annoying waiter shtick from the *Straw Hat Revue*. Corwin agreed to another guest spot, this time with Kaye playing a Russian. The second appearance went over even better—so much so that Danny would be asked back three more times, to play a bookstore clerk, an accountant, and a play producer.

Bestry also discovered that Dario Borzanni was having trouble finding appropriate entertainment for his chic Manhattan nightclub, La Martinique. Festooned in Latin décor, the nightspot was located in the basement of the Medical Arts Building on West 57th Street and catered to a sophisticated clientele. Borzanni agreed to give Kaye a two-week tryout, for a guaranteed $250 a week plus an option to continue if successful.

The challenge was figuring out what Kaye would do once he took the stage. Most of Fine's previous writing for Danny were group pieces. At La Martinique, he'd take the stage alone. He could sing "Anatole" and then,

instead of having showgirls model the silly headgear, he could use members
of the house orchestra. Sylvia had been working on another number,
"Stanislavsky," that allowed Danny to use his Russian accent playing a student of the lengendary master of the Moscow Art Theatre, whose secret to
method acting is suffering. But the number wasn't coming off quite right.
She contacted Sam Locke, who had earned $100 for the use of his skit "The
Wolf of Wall Street" in *The Straw Hat Revue*. Fine suggested that if Locke
would like to join her writing for Danny, they would split all the money that
the trio was sure to make.

Locke helped Fine trim out all the excess and penned several new lines,
including a concluding stanza ("Finally I play in the greatest role of my life.
I play part of antique mahogany bureau, so convincing that in the second act
my drawers fall out."). Sylvia was thrilled with his suggestions.

Kaye took the stage at La Martinique for the first time at a dinner-hour
performance in early February 1940. Ill at ease in a new suit and alone on
stage, he gamely introduced each number and then burst into character. The
audience all but ignored him. Danny was far more comfortable performing
in a theater, where an audience is there expressly to see the show, rather
than a nightclub, which an audience may visit primarily to eat, drink,
smoke, relax or chat. "I was the biggest disaster," Kaye recalled. "They
wanted to pay me off right then."

Though crushed, Kaye was convinced by the club's press agent, Eddie
Dukoff, to at least go through with the midnight performance. Danny reluctantly delivered the same string of tunes, but this time each number elicited
howls of laughter and thunderous applause. Evidently, the hipper clientele
attended the late-night show, and they refused to let this innovative satirist
go. After an hour, Danny had exhausted his repertoire of routines, from
"Minnie the Moocher" to "Deenah." In desperation, with the crowd still
screaming, he instructed the bandleader to "play something, anything."
When the orchestra began beating out a sultry rhythm, Kaye improvised a
conga dance, accompanied by his own ad-libbed lyrics of Latino gibberish.
As the band played faster and faster, he pleaded for them to stop and ultimately ended the number by pretending to knock himself unconscious. Two
waiters carried him off the floor. The ad-libbed "Conga Song" became a
permanent addition to the act—as well as a handy escape tactic.

Danny returned the second evening, this time a bit more confident.
Unfortunately, his timing was thrown off by an obnoxious guest who,
throughout the entire show, kept pounding his table and laughing uncontrol-

ZANY FOR HIRE: After several appearances on *Pursuit of Happiness*, CBS Radio ordered a publicity shot of Kaye. [© 1940 CBS]

lably—in all the wrong places. Kaye finally identified the convulsive culprit. It was Jack Benny, who had praised Danny the year before after a benefit at Madison Square Garden. For the rest of the week, Benny returned each night with a different group of celebrities to cheer on the young comic.

The buzz surrounding Danny's new act and his encore on *Pursuit of Happiness* convinced *Variety* to send to the club a reviewer who had earlier seen Danny with Nick Long Jr. The critic now found Kaye "a self-assured worker on the floor" whose "style embraces a lot of things... On his own now, Kaye is a big, breezy and refreshing personality with a unique style of general kidding that should carry him along in good style, depending on his material."

At first, Danny's act at La Martinique was very rigid, but eventually his inventiveness began to overpower his insecurities. "I used to come out and make a formal announcement of a song," he recalled. "Then I'd be crazy and wacky in the song. Then I'd get behind the facade of dignity for another announcement. Well, one night I was doing just a plain pop tune, and suddenly I felt comfortable. I felt like me. I began to have confidence in myself as a person. Therefore I could be me on stage; I didn't have to hide behind the formal facade any more."

Danny and Sylvia continued working one-on-one to develop more specialty numbers. From here on out, she would concentrate exclusively on solo character pieces, such as combining a sneezing routine with the oft-parodied Ukranian folksong "Otchi Tchorniya." Danny would play a stodgy Russian opera singer whose allergy gets the best of him as he tries to make it through the song. Sylvia credited Danny with helping to compose it. "Danny and I work together," Fine said. "We sit at the piano, and I'll start or he'll start, and we'll work up a number from nothing. That's how the sneezing opera number started. We worked up a lot of opera numbers that day. A stuttering opera singer, one with a tic, a perspiring opera singer, and a few others. The sneezer is the one that caught on, though."

As Kaye added new elements to his performance, everything seemed to work. It helped, of course, that Sylvia sat six feet away, at the piano. She realized that an impromptu atmosphere benefited Danny's performance, but if he ever seemed to be going overboard, she'd pound her keyboard.

"I used to control him from my piano bench," Fine said. "If I thought he was hitting a number too hard, I'd change the octave so that I played it higher and lighter, and without his knowing it—he has a very sensitive ear—he'd ease up and become lighter, too."

She was also developing into his coach. She evaluated Kaye's every action and criticized every facet of his performance, for constructive purposes. Sylvia wanted Danny to learn from his mistakes and didn't mince words, often commenting, "That stinks."

She, like Nat, tried to take advantage of Kaye's undulating hands, despite Shubert scout Harry Kaufman's earlier insistence that Danny would "never get anywhere until he learns to keep those cockeyed hands under control." The nightclub critics and columnists, however, regularly fawned over his hands' constant, graceful movement. Kaye remembered, "I heard so much praise of my hands that suddenly they seemed to me to be two large chunks of meat dangling from my wrists. I was conscious of them for the first time and thought I'd never get over it."

Borzanni doubled, then tripled Kaye's salary and extended his engagement indefinitely. After fourteen weeks, La Martinique was set to close for the summer, so Bestry began lining up A-list gigs on the road, beginning with a three-week run in June as master of ceremonies at the swank Ben Marden's Riviera nightclub in New Jersey, followed by Chicago's Chez Paree, a vaudeville engagement, and a booking in Florida. Kaye's notoriety grew with every stop.

He garnered particularly strong notices in Chicago, where he appeared with singer Kitty Carlisle. Noted one critic: "Kaye's act is particularly impressive... Kaye has no jokes or gags. He is a personality comedian with a fresh twist of extremely clever satire and burlesque... It's smart stuff throughout in the writing and made more impressive by Kaye's distinctive style in selling it."

By now, Max Liebman wanted back in the picture. He convinced Sylvia to spend the bulk of the summer, between the Riviera and Chez Paree engagements, writing at his side in Tamiment.

Most of Tamiment's regulars also returned, minus the headliners. Imogene Coca came back to guest star one week, and Kaye returned for at least two of the shows, to reprise "Anatole of Paris," the Yiddish Mikado, and other old favorites, as well as to try out an ambitious new number, "Partner of Pavlova," before taking it on the road. Fine and Liebman had written the satire of the Russian ballet in the "Stanislavsky" mold, but with a nice flourish near the end. To take advantage of Kaye's quick tongue, they included a rapid-fire recitation of the names of more than a dozen Russian ballet masters, real and imagined, from Toumanova to Schagrevsky.

But, for Danny, there was a far more prestigious opportunity waiting.

LADY IN THE DARK

Alvin Theatre, N.Y. (Jan. 23 to June 15, 1941;
without Kaye Sept. 2, 1941 to May 30, 1942)
Producer: Sam H. Harris • **Director**: Moss Hart
Book: Moss Hart
Songs: Ira Gershwin & Kurt Weill ("Tschaikowsky")
Cast: Gertrude Lawrence (Liza Elliott), Victor Mature (Randy Curtis), Macdonald Carey (Charley Johnson), Bert Lytell (Kendall Nesbitt), Margaret Dale (Maggie Grant), Natalie Schafer (Alison Du Bois), Danny Kaye (Russell Paxton), Donald Randolph (Dr. Brooks)

Orson Welles, Greta Garbo, everyone who was anyone had to fight—and heavily tip—to get in to see the newest nightclub sensation. At La

Martinique, stage producer Max Gordon was so impressed by Kaye that a few nights later he returned, dragging along playwright Moss Hart. Hart, having been burrowed away writing the much-anticipated *Lady in the Dark*, was a reluctant guest, yet he found himself equally captivated. After the show, Hart went backstage to tell Danny that if he ever wrote a revue-style show, it would be for Kaye.

But even after the playwright arrived home, he couldn't shake his amazement over the young performer. He especially enjoyed "Anatole of Paris," and, based on the character of Anatole, Hart wrote a part for Danny as an effeminate photographer into *Lady in the Dark*. Hart then phoned the Kayes, simultaneously offering the role and apologizing for it: "It's a very small part, and I can only pay $250 a week..."

"Mr. Hart," Sylvia answered, "for this chance *we* will pay *you*."

"Don't you want to see the script?" Hart asked.

"If you say it's good for Danny, I'm sure it is," she replied. Danny signed in July 1940, four months before rehearsals were to begin.

Big, bold and experimental, *Lady in the Dark* was destined to be something special. Hart was pouring his soul into the book, determined to establish himself on his own, apart from frequent collaborator George S. Kaufman. For lyricist Ira Gershwin, it would be his first musical since the death of his brother, George, in 1937. And for German composer Kurt Weill (*The Threepenny Opera*), it was a chance for his first big-time success in America.

The producers originally envisioned actress Katharine Cornell in the lead, but as the music became the driving force of the play, they instead opted for stage legend Gertrude Lawrence. Kaye's character was incidental to the story and spent the majority of the play off stage. Still, he was given several of the juiciest lines and two comic solos, the bouncy "It's Never Too Late to Mendelssohn" and the brief "Tschaikowsky."

Gershwin penned the latter after hearing Kaye, at breakneck speed, perfectly enunciate the tongue-twisting list of ballet dancers in "Pavlova." It reminded Gershwin of "The Music Hour," a poem he had published in *Life* magazine in 1924. In it, he compiled the names of 47 Russian composers, drawn from the back covers of brother George's piano and orchestral scores. Ira rearranged "The Music Hour" list, removing five names and adding eight others. Several additions weren't technically Russian composers, but rather Polish composers, a Yiddish playwright (Rumshinsky), and the birth name of Vernon Duke (Dukelsky).

Kaye arrived for the first day of rehearsals, visibly nervous. Sitting down for the first read-through, he glanced around the room at the show's first-class talent—Hart, Gershwin, Weill, producer Sam Harris, and co-stars Lawrence, Bert Lytell, Macdonald Carey, Victor Mature. Danny began trembling. When they broke for lunch, Kaye sidled over to Donald Randolph, who was playing the psychiatrist, and asked, "Mr. Randolph, how come you're so cool? I'm nervous as hell." Randolph tried to put the young actor at ease, explaining that he was equally nervous but, like the others, had trained himself to keep it within.

Yet even after the rehearsals did get rolling, Danny didn't. Without an audience to play off, Kaye appeared listless. His co-stars took note. Producer Harris, star Lawrence, and others suggested Hart find a replacement. After ten days of languid rehearsals, Hart finally took Sylvia aside. Privately, he confessed, "Sylvia, I don't know what to do. George Kaufman, Sam Harris, and everybody want me to replace Danny. They say that you can't make a nightclub performer into a theatrical performer, and I don't know what to do. He just doesn't seem to be rehearsing."

Fine explained that Danny always walked through rehearsals because he really couldn't perform to empty seats. If he wanted to see the real Kaye in action, he would have to bring in some kind of an audience—even just two or three people.

For the run-through that evening, Hart positioned Harris and a few secretaries in the audience. Electrified, Kaye sang "It's Never Too Late to Mendelssohn" as he never had before. The number had been planned as a simple bridge, rather than a high point of the show. It went over so well, the producers reluctantly decided to pull it from the show, to prevent it from ballooning one of the dream sequences out of proportion. Kaye was devastated, moaning, "There is nothing left of my part." Musical director Maurice Abravanel tried to comfort him: "There is still 'Tschaikowsky.'" Danny laughed, derisively, "Thirty seconds—'Tschaikowsky.'"

Yet from then on, no one questioned Kaye's ability. Before *Lady in the Dark* opened in New York, there would be a two-week tryout period in Boston, where the final changes and cuts would be made. The second act opened with a circus dream sequence, in which Kaye as the ringmaster got to sing his sole number. On opening night in Boston, Danny followed his cue and leapt down from a wooden horse to sing "Tschaikowsky."

In a miraculous 38 seconds, Kaye rattled off all 50 Russian composers, from Malichevsky and Gretchaninoff to Nowakofski and Rachmaninoff, with precise clarity. Kaye finished with a wide upward swerve of his hand and leapt back on top of the horse. The moment he landed, thunderous applause erupted, said co-star Donald Randolph, "like a thousand machine guns went off. I had been in about 30 Broadway opening nights, and I'd never seen anything like that."

The hysteria stopped the show cold. Gershwin lit a cigarette, walked out of the lobby, and down the street. When he returned to the theater, the applause was still going strong.

At first, as Danny stood proudly atop the wooden steed, he felt exhilarated. But then came a terrible thought. Sitting in a swing on the other side of the stage was the show's temperamental star, Gertrude Lawrence, waiting to sing her own number. If she wanted, she could demand that "Tschaikowsky" be yanked. Danny's shoulders fell, as he sank lower into his boots, muttering to the cheering crowd, "Stop... stop!"

When the applause finally died down, Lawrence rose from her swing and slowly walked to center stage. She stopped and smiled at Danny as the orchestra ripped into "The Saga of Jenny." Everyone expected her to belt out her big number with even more enthusiasm than she had in rehearsals. Instead, she sang "Jenny" very softly, accentuating the words with the uninhibited bumps and grinds of a backstreet stripper.

"This time," Randolph said, "2,000 machine guns went off. They told me later that this had never happened in the history of the Broadway theater—a real showstopper followed immediately by one bigger than the previous, all in one show. We would never have an empty seat, the entire run."

Kaye and Lawrence's rivalry would not last long, at least on stage. One evening, Kaye was running through "Tschaikowsky" when he detected that the audience wasn't really with him. He glanced back to see Lawrence nonchalantly waving a red handkerchief. The next night, as she launched into "Jenny," the audience began to titter. She turned to see Danny playfully mugging in the background. The two called a truce.

Kaye was the talk of the town before the show ever got to New York. *Lady in the Dark* catapulted him to stardom, and he knew it. "You can't have the kind of success he did at La Martinique," his friend Johnny Green said, "and then move into a class double-A Broadway show and be the smash that Danny Kaye was and not know you were going someplace. I mean, when you have a line in the show that becomes part of the language—and Danny had in that show. In one scene he had a line: 'I'm so mad I could spit!' That became New Yorkese. (For) every smart-ass person in New York, that became part of the language. Danny Kaye was already a trademark."

Buoyed by his Broadway success, Kaye inked his first recording contract, a one-year deal with Columbia that began with his singing six songs from *Lady in the Dark*. He also re-upped at La Martinique, where each night after *Lady in the Dark's* final curtain, he'd rush six blocks to put in two late-night performances of his nightclub routines. He added "Tschaikowsky" to his stage act, with a twist—each night he'd try to set a new record in how fast he could finish it. La Martinique had multiplied his salary so many times, that the club was forced to give Danny a percentage of the gross. The producers of *Lady in the Dark* were not quite as generous. They bumped his pay from $250 a week all the way up to $300.

Kaye suddenly found himself the object of an endless string of reporters. By this time, Danny had begun shaving two years off his age, to emphasize that he was in his youthful 20s, instead of the grizzled, old age of 30. And, in every interview, he was emphatic on two points: his "overnight success" and his wife's "assistance." Quizzed about his instant stardom, Danny would retort with a trace of irritation: "The thing no one realizes is for twelve years you've been playing every tank town in America and beating your brains out all over the world."

Herman Stein, who used to audition with Danny unsuccessfully for radio work, remembered, "When he was a smash hit in *Lady in the Dark*, the head of CBS was in the nightclub one night and said to Danny, 'Why didn't you ever try radio?' And Danny almost, but not quite, spilled a pitcher of ice water on his head."

Interviewers also liked to ask if his wife had been much help to him. "That is a pale and watered-down way of putting it," Kaye would reply. In every interview, Danny would publicly thank his wife for her invaluable efforts, at one point admitting, "I'd say Sylvia is 80 percent of my career." After all the false starts, he knew he sure couldn't have created all this excitement on his own.

LET'S FACE IT

Colonial Theatre, Boston (Oct. 6 to 25, 1941); Imperial Theatre, N.Y. (Oct. 29, 1941 to Feb. 27, 1943; without Kaye to March 20, 1943)
Producer: Vinton Freedley • **Director**: Edgar MacGregor
Book: Herbert & Dorothy Fields, based on 1925 play *The Cradle Snatchers* by Russell Medcraft & Norma Mitchell

Songs: Cole Porter ("Farming," "Ev'rything I Love," "Baby Games," "Let's Not Talk About Love," "I Hate You, Darling"), Sylvia Fine & Max Liebman ("A Fairy Tale," "Melody in 4F")

Cast: Danny Kaye (Jerry Walker), Eve Arden (Maggie Watson), Benny Baker (Frankie Burns), Mary Jane Walsh (Winnie Potter), Edith Meiser (Cornelia Pigeon), Vivian Vance (Nancy Collister), James Todd (George Collister), Sunnie O'Dea (Muriel McGillicuddy), Nanette Fabray (Jean Blanchard), Jack Williams (Eddie Hilliard)

Because *Lady in the Dark* would go dark for eleven weeks for the summer, the actors were signed only to six-month contracts. The producers figured that if the show were successful, everyone would be anxious to re-sign in the fall. Instead, the stars all became targets for the Hollywood scouts and their deep pockets. For Danny, motion pictures certainly appeared to be the next logical step in his career. His first serious opportunity came in early 1941. MGM offered him $3,000 a week, but Sylvia said no. Kaye explained, "I would work for much less, believe me, almost for nothing, if they would give me character roles and let me learn how to act. But I know they would just put me into a specialty spot here and there, and one bum picture would put me back two or three years. I'm very young. I've got lots of time. My wife doesn't want me to go into pictures for at least a year, and then as an actor and not as a specialty performer."

Sylvia preferred to have Danny first develop as a lead in the theater. Fortuitously, in stepped famed Broadway impresario Vinton Freedley. The producer was planning a new musical comedy, inspired by a news snippet he had noticed in *Variety*. It concerned several patriotic housewives who wanted to do their part to boost Army morale by inviting servicemen to their homes for weekends. Freedley turned to Cole Porter for the music and, for the book, Herbert Fields, who previously had written *Hit the Deck, DuBarry Was a Lady,* and *Panama Hattie* for him. But Fields and his partner/sister Dorothy Fields thought the military setting was overused—until they recalled an old play, *The Cradle Snatchers*. In it, three faithful housewives hire three bachelors to make their three husbands jealous. The Fieldses turned the three bachelors into soldiers stationed at nearby Camp Roosevelt on Long Island.

Freedley just needed a cast. He considered Milton Berle, Jack Haley, and Benny Baker as the three soldiers, playing opposite Martha Raye or Binnie Barnes. But he had a better idea, once he learned that Broadway's newest sensation was looking for a meatier role for the fall. Freedley offered Kaye $1,000 a week plus fifteen percent of the gross over $20,000. If every show sold out, he'd earn about $2,900 a week. As soon as *Lady in the Dark* broke for the summer, Freedley announced he had signed Kaye as head gigolo in *Let's Face It.*

Moss Hart was furious, the news coming just after he learned that Victor Mature, Macdonald Carey, and Bert Lytell were also leaving the cast. But Hart took Danny's defection personally. He saw himself as the one who had given the young unknown his first big break. Kaye feigned surprise at Hart's reaction. He didn't view Hart's earlier $50-a-week raise as a bonus, but rather as justification for leaving. Since Hart's wife, Kitty Carlisle, was fast becoming one of Sylvia's closest friends, the playwright would soon get over his anger, in time to escort Fine to the premiere of *Let's Face It.*

Danny had never before starred in anything major, so naturally he was tense. The score was not one of Cole Porter's best, but he did write one song to showcase Danny's quick, nimble tongue, "Let's Not Talk About Love," filled with a litany of complicated rhymes—timidity, stupidity, solidity, frigidity, avidity, turbidity, viscidity. But, to put Danny at greater ease, Porter permitted two specialty numbers by Sylvia and Max Liebman to be integrated into the show. Unfortunately, the ploy seemed to backfire. Danny was particularly uneasy over the first routine, a "cutesy monologue" called "A Modern Fairy Tale" that grew out of his penchant for kidding Sylvia at home in baby talk. He was embarrassed at the thought of goo-goo-ga-ga'ing on Broadway. Kaye insisted that if the number wasn't an immediate hit, it be pulled from the show.

He was more comfortable with Fine and Liebman's second contribution, the scat "Melody in 4F." In 90 seconds, Kaye git-gat-gittled the military life of an inductee, from draft notice to medical inspection, drill instruction, combat and, ultimately, medal of honor—using fewer than two actual words per each eight bars of music. The only discernible lyrics were sporadic punctuations of phrases like "Shaddup" or "Flat feet!"

Sylvia and Max attributed a large share of the song's creation to Danny. In fact, the number was actually just a stylized version of a routine Kaye had ad-libbed one night after watching surgeon friend/neighbor Al Weller perform an operation. "When we came home," Danny said, "we attended a gathering of jazz musicians. Al loved to play guitar and to hold jam sessions in his home. Somebody said, 'What did you do today, Al?' and he said, 'I did an operation,' and he began to describe it. I stopped him and said, 'I'll tell you what it was like.' I told them how he made the incision, and about the operation, and about the sponges and everything, and how he sewed it up. I did it all in double-talk plus pantomime."

LET'S FACE OFF. Brooklynite Kaye *(left to right)* and Brooklyn Dodgers manager Leo Durocher squared off against St. Louis Cardinals manager Billy Southworth and Missouri native Benny Baker, during the heat of the 1942 pennant race.

Although Fine and Liebman's experience on Broadway was limited, their expertise in staging was not. They did what they could to make sure the production showed off Danny in his best light, according to co-star Benny Baker. "Max and Sylvia would be sitting out in the audience," Baker recalled. "All of a sudden, I'd see Max lean over and whisper to Sylvia, and then a couple of minutes later Sylvia would stand up and walk down to Mr. Freedley and say, 'Just a minute. I think we ought to do so-and-so.' And the whole thing would be changed around, because they had a director, Edgar MacGregor, who knew nothing — an old-fashioned stage director who said, 'Put your hand here, move two steps to the right.' A traffic cop, not a director."

Predictably, Danny discouraged everyone when he sleepwalked through rehearsals in September 1941. Sylvia assured the uneasy Freedley and Porter that there was nothing to worry about. She promised that on opening night, with an audience, they would see an entirely different performer.

Sure enough, the audiences and the critics liked the show during the tryouts in Boston and loved it when it opened at New York's Imperial Theatre. "Fairy Tale" went over nicely, but the scat song, "Melody in 4F," stopped the show cold — even though Kaye's timing was a split-second off. Immediately after the final curtain, Sylvia slipped backstage and pushed through the excited admirers clamoring to congratulate the show's star. As the throng continued to sing his praises, Danny turned to Sylvia and, still smiling, said, "Syl, I loused up your song, didn't I?"

"You sure did," she nodded, dampening an otherwise triumphant evening.

Drama critics thought otherwise. "The oncoming Danny Kaye is brilliantly funny and has one exceptional comic number," wrote Richard Watts Jr., of the *New York Herald Tribune*. "One strange thing about the score is that the most striking number has not been contributed by Mr. Porter at all. It is something called 'Melody in 4F,' and it is the work of Sylvia Fine and Max Liebman. The narrative of the career of selectee, it is done in what I can only describe as triple-talk. At least, it seems to go a step beyond mere double-talk, in that it doesn't even pretend to be using words."

Because the show referred to current events, the script had to occasionally be tweaked, to adjust to the shifting military headlines. As well, Benny Baker stopped using one line—in which to escape the ladies' clutches he joked that he'd act like "the Japanese high command"—because he was afraid the audience would boo him off the stage. And Cole Porter had to rewrite several lines in his song "Farming," concerning how chic celebrities were buying their own farms, after actress Carole Lombard was killed in a plane crash.

The smash opening of *Let's Face It* convinced the Kayes that they'd finally secured a dependable, long-lasting source of income. Right away, they ran off to find the most luxurious homestead New York could offer—a twelve-room apartment filled with flowers and fancy furniture that overlooked Central Park. Danny put his attorney, Louis Mandel, in charge of the family finances, but held back $50 a week each for he and Sylvia to cover day-to-day expenses. He also hired Eddie Dukoff, La Martinique's hyper-aggressive press agent, to act as his personal publicist. Dukoff would remain with Kaye for fifteen years.

Danny could also afford to go back to his old stomping grounds, the Catskills, now as honored guest instead of laborer—although one visit was memorable to Kaye for another reason. Co-star Benny Baker recalled, "I went with him to buy his first car: a Cadillac convertible. (Soon after,) we drove up to Grossinger's, and at that time I was very fond of creamed pickled herring. I had it for breakfast, I had it for lunch, and I had it for dinner. The next day I had it. Monday morning I had it. We were there two and a half days, and as we started to leave to go to the theater, all of a sudden, I said, 'Danny, you better stop quick!' I had the worst case of diarrhea in the history of the world. He stopped about every 20 minutes all the way back. At 8:00 that night I walked to the theater and I was hanging on everything. I was afraid that I was going to let go at any moment, especially on stage.

"We had one scene where we were all sitting on the bench, and I'm supposed to see Lieutenant Wiggins, and I say, 'Ut-oh, Lieutenant Wiggins!' He's coming along with Danny's girl, so we jumped up on top of this set to be the three statues, which is a thing that Herbert Fields put in because this was a scene that his father of Weber and Fields had done many years ago. It was a tremendously funny scene because every time Wiggins would turn, we would go into these various poses. Well, this night I said, 'Ut-oh, ohhhhhh… Lieutenant Wiggins…' and (excrement) started to go right down the sides of my pants. Now we jump up on it. We're sliding all over it, and Danny got so hysterical laughing that he couldn't continue, and he closed the scene."

For hobbies, Kaye enjoyed watching surgical procedures — La Martinique, after all, was located in a Medical Arts Building — and baseball. The comic became fast friends with Leo Durocher, after the Brooklyn Dodgers manager began frequenting the Imperial Theatre because he had a crush on star Nanette Fabray. Durocher supplied Danny and Benny Baker with Dodgers tickets, baseballs and gloves, so the actors could play catch backstage. Unfortunately, after co-star Louis Calhern was injured by a Kaye fastball, the producers banned baseball equipment for the duration of the show's run.

Meanwhile, Sylvia kept Max Liebman on the family payroll, to continue writing special material for Danny's stage appearances and helping to achieve her dream of one day writing the score for a "book musical." By now, the team had it down to a science. "About material," Sylvia explained, Danny "doesn't know a thing. We never show Danny a number 'til it's finished and then if he laughs, we throw it away. If he doesn't like it, we're pretty sure we've got something. You see, he hardly knows what he's going to do with a phrase 'til he begins to work on it, but we can guess how he'll make a face here and how he'll do a phrase somewhere else. But sometimes all of us get surprised."

Sylvia and Max obsessed over Danny's every mannerism and inflection, and his dependence on them professionally began to seep into their personal lives. One tale has it that the writers were so controlling that late one night Fine and Liebman arrived home to find Kaye waiting up for them, seething. "Well!" Danny exploded. "I was waiting for you to tell me I could go to the bathroom!"

Fine and Liebman also used their pens to do their bit for the war effort.

One of their contributions was dreaming up a soldier revue. Dubbed "Local Board Makes Good," it was a collection of songs and sketches that could be performed by the servicemen themselves. Soon after, Sylvia vowed to permanently abandon writing political satire, explaining that she couldn't work fast enough to keep up with the headlines. (In the mid-1960s, she would write several songs to promote Lyndon B. Johnson's re-election campaign.)

Danny matched their efforts by insisting on keeping up a hectic schedule of bond rallies. In March of 1942, Kaye suffered an attack of nervous exhaustion. He was hospitalized at Mount Sinai Medical Center and for several weeks was forced to spend all his free time and nights at the hospital to ensure a full recovery.

By submerging himself into scores of rallies and radio appearances for the troops, Kaye hoped to avoid armed service himself. But the Army would wait no longer. He received notice to report to the draft board February 3, 1943 — just weeks before he was supposed to head to Hollywood. Danny received a 90-day deferment, the first of three postponements he'd finagle before ultimately being classified 4F due to a bad back, thanks to a note from his neighbor, Dr. Weller.

Meanwhile, fifteen months into its run, *Let's Face It* was still selling out weeks in advance. In January 1943, Kaye met with Vinton Freedley to discuss the fate of the show. Danny said he would have to leave at the end of the month, for the Army or the movies. Without Danny, the show would have to go on at least through February and hopefully longer, depending upon the success of Kaye's replacement. Days later, the producer corralled Benny Baker to announce his new lead: Jose Ferrer.

"Jose Ferrer for Danny?" Baker asked, dumbfounded.

"Oh, yes," Freedley smiled. "He's very funny. He did *Charley's Aunt*."

"But what's he gonna do at five minutes to eleven when Danny comes out and stops the show?"

"Oh, he's going to come out in that lady's dress that he wore and a big cigar."

"That's fine," Baker nodded, "but what's he gonna do when he gets to the middle of the stage?"

"Oh, he'll be very good in it."

In place of "Melody in 4F," Cole Porter added a song he'd previously written for Ferrer, "Taint Etiquette," to be performed as a duet with Baker. With no "Danny Kaye" on the marquee, *Let's Face It* closed on schedule, three weeks later.

III.

HELLO, HOLLYWOOD

SINCE THAT FIRST INVITATION by MGM to come to Hollywood in the spring of 1941, the Kayes had regularly been fielding additional inquiries. Danny caught early interest from William Goetz, head of Twentieth Century Fox, and independent producer Samuel Goldwyn.

In May of 1941, Goldwyn enlisted advisor Leo Spitz to check out Danny's stage act and report back on the comic's prospects for pictures. Spitz telegrammed back: "Kaye's performance superb. He is a comedian of unique and unusual talent, however seriously doubt advisability of starring him in an expensive picture at this time. Bob Hope meant nothing in his first two or three pictures, despite the fact that he was much better known than Kaye. Would not hesitate, however, to give him important feature role in any picture."

Goldwyn, though, wasn't looking for a second banana. A decade earlier, he had turned Broadway comic Eddie Cantor into a movie star. Goldwyn wanted the next Eddie Cantor. After watching Danny in *Lady in the Dark* and at La Martinique for himself, Goldwyn was convinced he'd found him. While in New York, the producer arranged several meetings with Danny, Sylvia and their new agents from William Morris, and was impressed by them all. Goldwyn laid out his case: he wasn't interested in a specialty performer; he was interested in grooming stars. He didn't juggle dozens of projects simultaneously; he produced them one at a time. Every production received his full attention. He made no B pictures. He spared no expense. He hired only top talent and big-name directors. He continually ripped up scripts and demanded rewrites until he got gold. Goldwyn suggested a five-to-ten year deal; Danny would make no more than one picture a year, filmed during the summer, so he could spend the rest of the year performing on Broadway or in clubs.

Goetz, on the other hand, proposed a one-picture deal, to test the young comic's drawing power and give him a break to do Broadway. Goetz also insisted on an option, that if the picture were a hit, Danny would quickly return to Hollywood and do three to four pictures within a year "so that his audience would build quicker."

Danny and Sylvia were both sold on Goldwyn, preferring—per an internal memo from William Morris agent John Hyde—"to lay Danny's career in the hands of such an able individual and producer, rather than go with a major studio where Danny's career would be in the hands of multiple producers and directors of varied talents. We here would very likely favor Goldwyn, because as an individual he would be Danny's employer, producer and sponsor. Furthermore, Goldwyn is ripe and eager to make stars from comparative unknowns and, of course, we believe, with Goldwyn's help, Danny must reach the top in movies."

Sylvia, though, had preached patience. She made Goldwyn wait a full year, with Danny seven months into his *Let's Face It* run, before they were ready to sign. By that time, Warner Bros. had joined the bidding, but Goldwyn remained the prohibitive favorite. As further incentive, Goldwyn had hired Kaye's friend and fellow Tamiment alumnus Don Hartman to oversee his studio's return to broad comedy. At Paramount, Hartman had helped map out the first three *Road* pictures for Bob Hope and Bing Crosby. Goldwyn traded Paramount one use of his contract player, Gary Cooper, for two uses of Hope, and put Hartman in charge.

In May of 1942, Danny signed an exclusive deal with Goldwyn to make five pictures over five years, $100,000 each for the first two pictures, $125,000 for the third, and $150,000 each for the fourth and fifth. The contract, however, was a joint deal with Sylvia. According to the contract, two years prior, on August 7, 1940, the couple had "entered into a partnership and under which the services of the artist may be contracted for only with the consent of both second parties; that the term of said agreement is for ten years, and that under the terms thereof each is entitled to half of the earnings of the artist." Sylvia, according to the deal, had to grant her permission for Danny to accept any performance deals and would split the proceeds 50-50, receiving separate checks.

Production on the first film would begin the following spring, after Kaye had fulfilled his *Let's Face It* commitment. Between pictures, Kaye would be allowed to do radio and stage work, as long as it didn't interfere with Goldwyn's shooting schedule. In addition, Fine and Liebman would contribute to the writing of the first picture, with options for each successive film.

Both parties also had the option to make up to one additional picture together each year, but considering how much time and money Goldwyn would lavish on each film, there likely wouldn't be time. Sylvia felt confident that Goldwyn would not treat Danny as just another performer.

"Goldwyn was an original," recalled contract writer Mel Shavelson. "He was the original pirate, and everybody else was a copy. I've worked for all of them—Goldwyn, Harry Cohn, and Jack Warner—and Goldwyn was the toughest of all, but his standards were the highest. He was always disappointed when he made a picture and it wasn't a glove. Because that was his business (when he emigrated to America), he was a glove-maker. And to make a glove, you bought the best materials, you hired the best workmen, you made the best glove. Well, he bought some of the best material, hired some of the best people, and managed to make some of the worst pictures. And he also managed to make some of the best. When Willie Wyler was making *Best Years of Our Lives*, the way he made it was he barred Goldwyn from the set. But Goldwyn's intent was always good. He was an immigrant, he still spoke with an accent, but he had, I suppose, the people's taste."

Goldwyn attracted the limelight not only for his classy pictures and outspoken nature, but also for his often-awkward way of phrasing things. His garbled pronouncements— like "A verbal contract isn't worth the paper it's written on" or "I read part of it all the way through"—became so legendary that reporters, disgruntled employees, and Goldwyn's own press agents began fabricating counterfeit "Goldwynisms." Danny had even sung Goldwyn's line "Include me out" in Cole Porter's song "Farming" in *Let's Face It*.

As Kaye was finishing up his commitment to Broadway, Fine and Liebman flew to the West Coast to begin preparations on Danny's first picture. Typically, they started by tinkering with different pop music styles, usually to spoof them. One afternoon Don Hartman, who was both writing and associate producing Kaye's first film, overheard one of Sylvia's compositions and complimented her, saying it sounded almost as good as Gilbert and Sullivan.

"Who are Gilbert and Sullivan?" asked an eavesdropping Goldwyn.

"They are the greatest lyricists and composers in history," Hartman explained, patiently.

"Well, then," the producer demanded, "why don't we hire *them*?"

UP IN ARMS

(Filmed June 21 to Sept. 18, Dec. 23, 1943;
released N.Y. Feb. 17, 1944, wide March 27, 1944)

Producer: Sam Goldwyn, for Avalon Productions, Samuel Goldwyn Productions, RKO Radio Pictures
Director: Elliott Nugent
Screenplay: Don Hartman, Allen Boretz, Robert Pirosh (uncredited Phil Rapp)
Original Story: Character from 1923 play *The Nervous Wreck* by Owen Davis
Songs: Music by Sylvia Fine & Max Liebman ("Melody in 4F," "Lobby Number," "Jive Number" based on "Tess's Torch Song"), Harold Arlen & Ted Koehler
Cast: Danny Kaye (Danny Weems), Dinah Shore (Virginia Merrill), Dana Andrews (Joe Nelson), Constance Dowling (Mary Morgan), Louis Calhern (Col. Phil Ashley)

Most Broadway stars who jumped straight to leading roles on the screen, such as Eddie Cantor or the Marx Brothers, brought along their hit stage play as their first film, to ensure a profitable start. But when Goldwyn signed Danny, Paramount purchased *Let's Face It* for Bob Hope, although Fine and Liebman retained the rights to their contributions. For Kaye's first picture, Goldwyn insisted on a wartime setting, so he could at least use "Melody in 4F." Hartman and Allen Boretz (*Room Service*) were put to work on a first treatment and screenplay—but certainly not the last.

According to scenarist Shavelson, "When you turned in a script to (Goldwyn), he said, 'I don't like it.' You said, 'What don't you like about it, Mr. Goldwyn?' And he said, 'I don't know, but when it's right I'll know.' Which is the most frustrating kind of work to do. But as I said, his standards were very high, he always wanted to do the best, and he never stinted on money. And also he was a one-man operation. He not only ran his studio, he financed his own movies, and he released his own movies. So you know he was a pirate and a pioneer. I learned a hell of a lot working for him. I also developed an ulcer."

Goldwyn had a few musts. The writers had to work in appearances by his handpicked bevy of models, the Goldwyn Girls—no small feat, considering most of the action was to take place aboard a troop transport. They also were to give Danny's character a gimmick, like Eddie Cantor had as a sneezing, wheezing hypochondriac in his first picture, *Whoopee*. "You know Eddie was a hypochondriac," he'd remind his writers, "now maybe we can get something like that." But Goldwyn was so insistent on the point that Hartman quickly realized the producer didn't want something *like* that character. He wanted exactly that character.

Goldwyn was intent on remaking Kaye as Cantor. In fact, Danny used to joke that for their first three years together, Goldwyn used to call him "Eddie." The writers' challenge was that a timid, Eddie Cantor-type character was the direct opposite of the extroverted personas Danny assumed for Sylvia's routines. The trick was to figure out ways to logically work in the numbers so it didn't look like Danny's character had a split personality.

But why would *anyone* ever break out into a high-speed scat song like "Melody in 4F"? In their initial screenplay, Hartman and Boretz had newly drafted Danny visit a Staten Island beer garden before he shoves off. When someone spikes his milk, he insists on singing with the house band, despite his impaired condition. In the writers' second draft, Danny volunteers to sing during a dance on the ship, to distract the soldiers' attention from a girl he's smuggled on board. He's so nervous, most of the words are gibberish and he finally ends the song with a frantic "Conga!" In a later version, Danny begins to sing at normal speed, but a prankish GI instructs the band to play five times too fast, forcing Danny to sing his high-speed specialty. Ultimately, the writers had Danny deliver the song as if he's making it up on the spot. He's been composing a song on the life of a solider, he explains, "but I haven't thought of all the words yet."

An easier method for including specialty material was to fold it into a dream sequence. So, the writers had Danny daydream that he's a great lover, the "Purple Flash," and Fine and Liebman composed a colorful jive take-off on "Tess's Torch Song," for Kaye to show off his scat singing and dance moves.

Since Hartman was familiar with Kaye's stage act, he could try to incorporate established routines into the script. In one early draft, Danny's best pal, Joe, was to be an orchestra violinist, as an excuse for Kaye to visit Radio City Music Hall and watch "Barber of Seville," so he could perform the bit in which he overly reacts to the mood of the music—crying when it's sad, delirious when it's happy, increasingly frantic as it becomes more upbeat. Danny gets so excited, he begins pulling on another guest's tie, practically choking him and setting off a riot that stops the opera and gets Joe fired. The routine didn't make it past the one draft, but that didn't stop Hartman from trying, again unsuccessfully, to work it into Kaye's second picture.

Besides having to run everything past the rewrite-happy Goldwyn, the writers also had to please Sylvia. She disliked their first drafts, which were filled with drawn-out subplots and sequences highlighting the ingénues and other soldiers, but having nothing to do with Danny. (In the end, Danny would be needed on all but one of the film's shooting days.) After two rough scripts, Goldwyn reassigned Boretz to his Bob Hope pirate picture. Also working on the Hope film was Robert Pirosh, a former Marx Brothers writer who had worked with Hartman on *The Road to Zanzibar*. Hartman asked Pirosh what he thought of the Kaye screenplay and songs, and so loved his suggestions he asked Goldwyn to reassign Pirosh to *Up in Arms*.

At the time, Fine and Liebman were trying to come up with a third number for the picture, but couldn't logically fit any more into the plot. For Pirosh, they described some of their more crowd-pleasing numbers, like *The Straw Hat Revue's* "Great Chandelier" and a similar song Sylvia wrote at Tamiment the year before, "Shubert Alley," in which a clichéd Broadway show is quickly reenacted in song, from overture, to opening curtain, opening chorus, and through a series of stereotypical characters—the comic, the prima donna, the juvenile whose mother objects, the count, the jazz stepper, and the villain, who is unmasked. As the song opened, "People go to a musical show, but what they've seen they can't recall. I maintain it's very plain. If you've seen one, you've seen them all."

Pirosh thought that one of the numbers might work if, instead of spoofing musical plays, they changed it to spoofing motion pictures, cued by Danny waiting in line at a movie theater lobby. Since movie satires were a regular standby at Tamiment, Fine and Liebman had a treasure trove of snappy lyrics to draw upon—the main narrative of Mary Sue Ellen and Cowboy Dan and the many disguises from "The Great Chandelier," spoofing tropical pictures in "Soused American Way," Manic Depressive Studios from the sketch "Yes, Mr. Manic," the notion of starting a show in the middle because the audience arrives in the middle from "Opening Opening," and the Busby Berkeley production number "Cherry Blossom Time." ("When it's Cherry Blossom time in Orange, New Jersey, we'll make a peach of a pear. Oh, honeydew be mine, because we cantaloupe. I'll take you to the chapel, as the apple of my I declare, the month of May is merry, for girls n' boysenberry...")

Titled "The Lobby Number," Fine and Liebman's first draft aimed to make fun of tropical pictures and centered on the faux film *Hips, Hips Hooray* ("The opening scene is a private yacht, but 85 chorus girls are right on the spot."). Incorporating the character of Cowboy Dan convinced the writers to switch their setting to a ranch in Fresno, California—but not before first running through an endless string of credits. In rapidly increasing tempo, Danny would relay, "Manic Depressive Pictures presents (lion roar) *Hello, Fresno, Goodbye.* Produced by R. U. Manic, and directed by Depressive. Now you know the name of the picture and you'd like to see it—but no!" He'd then rattle off the countless writers, art directors, photographer, and other crew, before going on to describe the movie itself—another of those typical musical-comedy-western-gangster-dramas, which are just riddled with clichés (such as from "The Great Chandelier": "You must let me marry Cowboy Dan! He owns the biggest ranch in Texas, Bar None!"). The song climaxes with Carmelita Pepita, the Bolivian bombshell, crying out, "Conga!" and a spastic Danny leading the waiting audience in a line out the lobby door—at which point he spies new arrivals and starts the number all over again.

With the script going through countless permutations, Goldwyn was also concerned how much work Danny would require to be ready for the big time. Goldwyn mandated that Kaye report to the studio in August 1942, during *Let's Face It's* summer hiatus, to make a series of screen tests. The producer's greatest concern was Danny's unique nose, and he encouraged the comic to undergo plastic surgery. According to his contract, Kaye would not be forced to undergo an operation, but if he agreed to, the cost and risk would be his own.

Danny found the screen tests extremely uncomfortable. His movement restricted by the stationary camera, he came off stilted. Bob Hope, at the time filming *They Got Me Covered* on the lot, suggested Kaye borrow his director, David Butler, an accomplished comedy foreman. Butler placed the camera on a dolly in order to follow its roaming subject. Now Kaye, accompanied by Sylvia on the piano, was able to perform naturally.

A different aspect of the screen test worried Goldwyn. On the Technicolor test film, Danny's reddish-brown locks made him look scraggly, almost sinister. Subsequent tests, shot from every imaginable angle, showed no improvement. Goldwyn would allow Danny to keep his nose, but he insisted Kaye's hair be bleached an innocent blond. After all, it worked fifteen years earlier with Harpo Marx, who switched from a red to a blond wig to achieve a more angelic, impish look.

Danny was more concerned that the general public would even like him. Fearing his stay in Hollywood would be short, Kaye didn't buy a home when he moved west, opting instead to rent a big, eleven-room house in Beverly Hills. Danny felt ill at ease and, Pirosh said, "that's understandable because he had been a big sensation on the New York stage and now in his first picture, Goldwyn brought him out at a huge price and starred him in his first picture as 'Danny Kaye in *Up in Arms.*' That doesn't happen too often. Very, very few in motion picture history came out and starred in their own pictures, (but slowly) he got over that as the development of the script went on."

Goldwyn had equally ambitious plans for Kaye's leading lady, Virginia Mayo, whom he had discovered on the New York stage, in a musical comedy act featuring Pansy—two guys in a horse suit. "I was brought from New York to play the lead in *Up in Arms*," Mayo recalled. "I was seen by Mr. Goldwyn in New York, and he brought me out to California on a five-year contract. He tested me for it, and they didn't think I was ready for the lead, so they made me a Goldwyn Girl, for experience sake. But actually I think it was Mrs. Kaye who didn't think I was ready. They were worried about it being Danny's first picture, and they didn't want somebody who was also inexperienced with him."

In truth, Sylvia didn't want Danny making his film debut alongside the girl who used to work with Pansy the horse. Mayo's lead role was given to the equally unknown Constance Dowling and, for one picture, Mayo was demoted to play a featured Goldwyn Girl. She received more lines than the other models, she was typically positioned front and center, and the camera lingered on her a little longer.

Sylvia may have been new to Hollywood, but it didn't take long for her to make her presence felt as Danny's de facto agent, coach and personal director. Wherever she went, conflict arose. Her motive was justifiable—looking out for her husband's best interests—but her manner was harsh, quickly leading to a sour reputation and plenty of fodder for gossip columnists. Walter Winchell once ran the story:

Miss Fine called the Goldwyn Studio, where a film cutter happened to answer the telephone. "Hello," she said in a firm voice. "This is Sylvia Fine."

No response. "Hello," repeated Miss Fine. "Why don't you answer? What's wrong?"

"Nothing," the editor replied at last. "I was merely bowing."

Actually, the incident never took place. The story was entirely fictitious, although the feelings portrayed of studio workers were accurate. Sylvia was fully aware of her reputation. One day, her sister, Rhoda, was visiting the Kayes' home when she noticed a newly painted portrait of Sylvia. "Isn't there a lot of green in that face?" Rhoda observed.

"Well," Sylvia replied, "that's how a lot of people see me."

On the set of *Up in Arms*, mild-mannered director Elliott Nugent proved no match for hurricane Sylvia. Throughout the filming, whenever Nugent shouted, "Cut!," Danny would look right past him to see if his wife agreed with the director's commands.

When the disagreements concerned Sylvia's own numbers, Goldwyn usually took her side. He trusted that Sylvia knew what she was doing, even if he didn't. During the filming of "The Lobby Number," Sylvia stopped the orchestra and insisted on different tempos. She had structured the song to allow for where the laughs were. The musical conductor was furious. Rehearsal halted and busloads of extras stood around doing nothing but making money, until Goldwyn stormed on to the set. Sylvia and the conductor each voiced their opinions. "You will do it Miss Fine's way," the boss decreed. "Except for one question I'd like to ask Miss Fine: What is the reason for the whole number?"

Even after "The Lobby Number" was filmed, Sylvia still wasn't happy with it. In particular, she thought that one passage lifted from "Pavlova," in which Danny suddenly becomes a Russian ballet dancer, looked out of place. She convinced Goldwyn to shoot extensive retakes. But since a month had passed, all the stars and extras could not be costumed and lined up to fill the lobby in exactly the same way as before. So, Danny filmed the new sequences in extreme close up and on a staircase in the lobby background, where in the original footage the extras were less conspicuous. The punchline of the now-deleted "Pavlova" sequence, though, had been the lead-in to the number's finale: "*Too impulsive*—why that's the password of the FBI!" On the soundtrack over "Too impulsive," Kaye dubbed the punchline of an earlier joke ("Bar none!") as the new FBI password.

For Danny, shooting the elaborate number, especially the frenzied conga finale, was exhausting. He needed a ten-minute break between every take to recuperate. Kaye also discovered that performing and capturing his trademark specialty songs on film presented a unique problem. Motion pictures' standard practice—of first recording the sound and later photographing the singer mouthing in synchronization—was not designed for scat. "Melody in 4F" required take after take to ensure sight matched perfectly with sound. But in time Danny mastered the process so well that it became almost impossible for audiences to detect.

Goldwyn's insistence that everything be perfect typically resulted in costly, last minute changes. In all, shooting lasted 76 days—eight days over schedule. The production, originally budgeted at $1.5 million, cost nearly $2 million. Goldwyn's biggest budget buster was his late decision to add— and then delete—an expensive cartoon finale.

Hartman got a kick out of slipping animated sight gags into live action pictures, such as animating the mouth of a talking camel in *The Road to*

LOBBY CARD: In *Up in Arms,* Kaye sang the mapcap "Lobby Number," a movie spoof based on snippets of earlier numbers Sylvia and Max Liebman had written at Camp Tamiment. [© 1944 Samuel Goldwyn]

Morocco. So, he thought he had the perfect climax for *Up in Arms*. The movie was originally supposed to begin with "actual footage" of a triumphant Danny leading in a pack of captured Japanese soldiers at gunpoint, when the image suddenly dissolves. The narrator blames the disintegrating film on tropical mildew or those pesky "weavie-weavies." Then, during the movie's climax, dozens of Japanese soldiers—bayonets drawn—corner

Danny in a cave and are about to attack, when, according to the script, "animated caterpillar worms, with almost human faces, appear from everywhere and start chewing holes in the film. As they eat chunks out of the film, we hear a sound like rabbits noisily chewing carrots."

The narrator panics: "O-o-o-oh! I'm sorry, folks, it's those weavie-weavies again! Can't seem to keep them off the film! Get off of there, you worms! Folks—look! You can still see some of the fight going on!" The narrator then describes Danny heroically facing off against a battalion of Japanese soldiers, but every time the enemy is about to strike, an animated weavie-weavie chews the image right off the screen. Finally, one of the creatures gulps down the remaining fragment of the film in one huge swallow. The weavie-weavie then turns to the audience and, in a high, effeminate voice, announces, "Now you'll never know what happened! I'm the only one who knows and I'll never tell! Never, never, NEVER!" He belches loudly and slithers off the screen.

Goldwyn hired Walt Disney Studios to animate about 90 seconds of munching weavie-weavies. The footage was drawn by Mickey Mouse artist Ub Iwerks and laid over live action footage of Kaye doing hand-to-hand combat on the side of a mountain.

Although it was a novel gag, the producer didn't think a suddenly fearless Kaye vanquishing the enemy off-screen provided a logical, or satisfying, conclusion. After great expense, Goldwyn demanded the sequence edited out. A brief new scene was shot in which a stand-in for Kaye, disguised as a Japanese general, leads the enemy soldiers into a pit.

Once the movie was completed, Goldwyn put just as much energy into promoting it, intent on making Danny Kaye a household name. Yet the boss's passion for publicity was so intense, he drove *Up in Arms'* frustrated press agent to the verge of quitting. While vacationing in Palm Springs, Goldwyn called his publicist to find out what happened to all of the exposure he was promised.

"Well, what newspapers have you been reading, Mr. Goldwyn?" the press agent asked.

"What do you mean 'What newspapers have I been reading?' Don't you know I'm in Palm Springs for a rest?"

Up in Arms opened at the Pantages in New York on March 3, 1944. The critics generally enjoyed the movie despite its far-fetched storyline about smuggling female GIs on to a troop transport headed for the Pacific. The writers were so intent on giving the public a thorough introduction to

JIVE FANTASY: The popularity of Sylvia's jive take-off on "Tess' Torch Song" (performed by Danny in the "Purple Flash" dream sequence, shown with Louis Calhern and Constance Dowling) convinced the couple—and Goldwyn—to make room for another jive number in his next picture. [© 1944 Samuel Goldwyn]

Kaye's many facets that the story became little more than an excuse to tie one routine to the next. Consequently, the film can be hilarious one moment and pedestrian the next. Bosley Crowther, in the *New York Times*, called "the whole picture is little more than a blunt enlargement upon 'Melody in 4F.'" Fortunately, no one in this booming box office year seemed to mind, and the film made Goldwyn a huge profit.

As for Danny, his debut earned him a nationwide following. Overnight, *Up in Arms* had the industry speculating that Danny Kaye would be the Forties' gift to the comedy world. Danny and Sylvia would come to regard the reception afforded *Up in Arms*—with filmgoers boasting they had seen the picture six or seven times—as the gold standard to aim for on all future films.

WONDER MAN

(Filmed July 13 to 17, Aug. 7 to Nov. 16, 1944; Jan. 18, Jan. 23, 1945;
released June 8, 1945)
Producer: Sam Goldwyn, for Samuel Goldwyn Productions, RKO Radio Pictures
Director: H. Bruce Humberstone
Screenplay: Don Hartman, Melville Shavelson, Philip Rapp, Jack Jevne & Eddie Moran
(uncredited Ray Golden, Edmund Beloin, Jo Swerling, Sylvia Fine)
Original Story: Arthur Sheekman
Songs: Sylvia Fine ("Bali Boogie," "Otchi Tchorniya," Opera number, patter for "So in
Love"), David Rose & Leo Robin
Cast: Danny Kaye (Edwin Dingle/Buzzy Bellew), Virginia Mayo (Ellen Shanley), Vera-
Ellen (Midge Mallon), Donald Woods (Monte Rossen), Steve Cochran (Ten Grand
Jackson)

Soon after filming wrapped on *Up in Arms*, Goldwyn began looking for
another project that could highlight Kaye as a mild-mannered milquetoast
who saves the day by somehow transforming into a frantic extrovert.
Goldwyn selected *The Wonder Man*, a 45-page treatment by former Marx
Brothers and Eddie Cantor writer Arthur Sheekman. Danny was to play
Edwin Tilson, a timid super-genius who can write with both hands at the
same time and spends his days researching at the library. Virginia Mayo
would be Ellen, the junior librarian who invites Edwin to her apartment for
dinner. There, she encourages him to apply for a job opening she saw post-
ed at the library. Edwin gets the job—as a G-man—and goes undercover as
a chorus boy at a vaudeville theater linked to a recent murder. Edwin gradually works his way up to featured performer, while he and Ellen solve the
crime.

Goldwyn turned the short story over to Don Hartman, who had just finished polishing Bob Hope's *The Princess and the Pirate* with Mel
Shavelson, a writer for Hope's radio show. But Hartman and Shavelson
envisioned something more ambitious than a conventional comic mystery,
something that allowed Danny to play his extroverted stage persona
throughout the picture. Goldwyn, however, insisted on retaining the timid
Eddie Cantor character. The writers struggled with a solution for keeping
the two polar opposite Dannys on screen at the same time. Then it hit them:
why not film two Dannys? Why not set Kaye in a dual role, as super-identical twin brothers? And what if the murder victim was one of the brothers,
who—in the vein of recent fantasies like *Here Comes Mr. Jordan, I Married
a Witch*, and *Topper*—returns to earth to help his brother solve the crime?
Having a second, flamboyant Danny also provided room for a second lead-

ing lady, Vera-Ellen, a pert tap expert whom Goldwyn recently discovered in Broadway's *A Connecticut Yankee*.

Hartman and Shavelson's first treatment opened at a dinner club with Midge Miller (Vera-Ellen) tap dancing, followed by comic Buzzy Bellew (Kaye) performing "Deenah." Not only has Buzzy stolen Midge from Hundred Grand Jackson, he's also blackmailing the hood. So, while Midge performs a Balinese boogie dance, two hired guns from Kansas City trail Buzzy to his dressing room, shoot him, and dump his body in the East River. Buzzy's spirit rides a golden elevator to the Pearly Gates, where an angelic doctor must first remove the slugs from his body—only to discover that Buzzy has only half a soul, due to a life of gambling, drinking and other vices brought on by hatred of his super-identical twin, Edwin. In flashback, we see their parents beaming with pride at kind, brilliant Edwin, but dismayed at his brainless, troublemaking brother. The only way for Buzzy to get into heaven is if, within the week, Edwin also dies, because his kindness would make up the difference. Buzzy's ghost returns to earth, but he's not allowed to bump off his brother. Instead, Buzzy convinces Edwin to assume his identity, purportedly to help figure out who killed him—but actually to set him up to be killed by Jackson's men. Buzzy must teach Edwin his speech, mannerisms and routines, thereby leading to a duet with Kaye singing both parts. Edwin, though, hasn't been warned about Midge, and ends up at a classy restaurant racing between Midge upstairs and Ellen downstairs. When Jackson arrives, he runs out on both dates.

Buzzy's ghost later leads Edwin to a pool hall that Jackson frequents. Jackson mistakes Edwin for Buzzy, and challenges him to a game for the money he's owed. Edwin calculates the trajectory of his shots with chalk and a yardstick, but Jackson still wins the first game. With Buzzy's help, Edwin wins the second. But Buzzy leaves his brother to lose the final, double-or-nothing match. Jackson gives him until midnight to come up with the cash or else—confirming to Edwin that it was Jackson who killed his brother.

Meanwhile, the hit men from Kansas City return to town, upset that they've been accused of not killing Buzzy. When Edwin can't come up with the money, Jackson hires two new goons. They chase Edwin to the opera house, where he disguises himself as a tenor and performs one of Danny's club routines in which a female singer "sings long passages with great gusto, while he joins in here and there with a single note, almost swallowing his beard each time." The hoods finally drag Edwin to Jackson's hideout where, as Jackson levels his pistol at Edwin, the lights go out. Bang! When the lights return, we see the two hit men from Kansas City have shot Jackson. Buzzy then arrives to knock out Edwin, place the gun in his brother's hand, and call the cops.

In court, Edwin is about to be convicted for the murder of Jackson, when Buzzy has a change of heart. He supernaturally demonstrates for the jury that the ghost story Edwin has been telling is true. For this selfless act, Buzzy is permitted into heaven, where a bevy of angelic Goldwyn Girls await.

The primary problem with Hartman and Shavelson's scenario was that Buzzy's a despicable cad who spends the entire movie trying to get his brother murdered. But before the screenwriters could start on a second draft, Hartman filed suit against Goldwyn for payment of back earnings, and Goldwyn forbid Hartman from setting foot on the lot.

The producer turned *The Wonder Man* over to *Topper* writers Jack Jevne and Eddie Moran. Although their Buzzy became more sympathetic (he returns to earth to help Edwin), the overall story became darker. Most of Buzzy's scenes take place in a cemetery, where he trades one-liners with two ghosts playing checkers on a tombstone. However, they made two key additions: giving Buzzy the ability to possess Edwin's body and having Edwin make several comical sidetrips to Schmidt's Delicatessen, where every time he arrives to buy potato salad, he hears harp music and blurts out a location that Buzzy wants to lead him to. On a dinner date with Ellen, when Edwin starts hearing the harp music, he tries to block out the sound by loudly singing "The Star Spangled Banner"—causing the other café patrons, as well as Buzzy and the other two ghosts at the cemetery, to stand at attention. The writers also had nightclub owner Monte be the one who's pining for Midge, so that Edwin can bring Ellen to the chapel at the same time that Buzzy was supposed to marry Midge. Both women would walk down the aisle side by side, before they realize they're being two-timed. Ellen would run off in tears, and Monte would step in to marry Midge.

Jevne and Moran were nervous that Goldwyn might find their scenario too dark, since Buzzy spent so much time in a cemetery, talking with ghosts. Goldwyn, however, objected not to the setting, but rather that the scenes forced Buzzy's ghost to "operate at a distance, instead of being close at hand," removing the zany Kaye from the action and missing out on possible interactions between the brothers.

After Jevne and Moran were given a second crack, Goldwyn reassigned Shavelson to the next draft with a new partner, Jo Swerling. A frequent

Frank Capra collaborator, Swerling insisted that his participation be kept confidential. Shavelson and Swerling added a Christmas-time backdrop, a proper English valet for Buzzy, and a big chase finale through a department store. Edwin would try to dodge the hoods up and down elevators and through a frenzied nylon sale, a fashion show featuring the Goldwyn Girls, and a puppet show. Reaching the toy department, Edwin takes the place of the store Santa. When one boy informs him that he has scientifically disproved the existence of Santa Claus, Edwin advises him to stop being a "quiz kid. Stay away from books or you'll grow up to be a dope!" Edwin finally escapes down a package chute. But when the hoods make it to the street, they notice there's a Santa on every corner. Edwin finds the DA— and a room full of gangsters—enjoying Midge's performance at the nightclub, so Edwin takes the stage and lyrically spills the beans on Jackson's criminal past, providing all the characters and sound effects. We close as newlyweds Edwin and Ellen head to bed, wondering if they'll ever hear from Buzzy again—as an invisible hand magically draws the shades.

In the end, the writers decided to combine the finale of Edwin musically filling in the DA with the earlier idea of him, in disguise, performing a double-talk opera. They then handed off the entire scene to Sylvia. Her lyrics and comedy business, set to music from Verdi's *Il Trovatore* and *Rigoletto*, were not only hilarious, it also was the only number she would ever write for Goldwyn that advanced the plot. Typically, her specialties were tangential to the storyline. "My work for Danny's movies is a kind of a mixed-up thing," Sylvia said. "I know the story down to the last detail, and I figure out where it needs a number. Then I write it—separately from the regular script—and work it in."

Goldwyn, meanwhile, wasn't crazy about the movie's title, so he had his staff dream up some new ones. They suggested *Heavenly Brother, Heaven Only Knows, Two for the Show, Heavenly Spirit*, and *The Christmas Spirit*, because of the script's holiday tie-ins and the film's planned December release date. Goldwyn didn't care for any of the submissions and thought there were already too many Christmas-themed movies of late. He reluctantly decided just to shorten *The Wonder Man* to, simply, *Wonder Man*.

His director, H. Bruce "Lucky" Humberstone, was more concerned with the script itself, finding it protracted and overly plotty. But, to keep from falling behind, he started filming on schedule, on July 13, 1944.

Although Danny had played a fidgety milquetoast in *Up in Arms*, the Edwin role required restraint to contrast with Buzzy's flamboyance. Danny wasn't accustomed to playing restrained. So during the first several rehearsals, he played both characters zany.

Director Humberstone pulled him aside and said, "Look, Danny, we can't be Danny Kaye on both sides of the screen. You've got to play Danny Kaye on one side of the screen, you're supposed to be a Broadway hoofer, but on the other side of the screen, you've got to be entirely different. What you have to visualize is that the other side of the screen, you should play it as though, let's say, I had Edward Everett Horton playing the part."

Kaye thought toning down his personality too much would wash out the character, but the director insisted, "I promise you, if you play the intellect as Edward Everett Horton would play it, and you're on the other side of the screen playing it as Danny Kaye, you as Edward Everett Horton will steal every scene from yourself as Danny Kaye."

Kaye was mortified. "Well, then I'm not a good comic, am I?"

Humberstone encouraged him: "Yeah, you're a hell of a comic, but you're playing a deadpan over here, and the audience is going to be attracted to the deadpan. You're still Danny Kaye, and you're gonna steal every scene that you play with your brother." Kaye agreed to try it, even though he couldn't envision himself as Edward Everett Horton.

The crew planned to begin filming with the most strenuous production number, "Bali Boogie," Sylvia's dance duet for Danny and Vera-Ellen combining jive with Balinese music.

On the fourth day of production, just as filming of the number was coming to a close, disaster struck. Humberstone recalled, "How that accident ever occurred I don't know, because that's the first accident I'd ever had on a picture. This silly (number) was all rehearsed. We had a big drum in the middle of the set—a drum that was at least six feet across—and I had mattresses in it because the drum was probably four feet tall. Danny was on the level of the stage and had to run and jump into the drum, which he did. He jumped in and his leg just cracked. He might have gone through a mattress and hit one of the cross-sections that kept it together."

In actuality, Kaye had severely wrenched his knee and, with a single scene in the can, the entire production had to be shut down for three weeks. "On the other hand," the director added, "it was probably the best thing that happened to the picture. I wasn't particularly happy with the story when we started, and I got a new writer in, Phil Rapp, and the result was that we improved the script by at least 50 percent. It clicked together. We practically rewrote the whole script. It made a big difference to me, because I was

OPERA MAN: In the Sylvia-crafted climax of *Wonder Man*, Kaye disguised himself as the lead in an opera to attract the attention of the district attorney, seated in the audience. [© 1945 Samuel Goldwyn]

happy all the way through the picture."

The biggest change was scrapping the entire department store scene, which would have required elaborate sets and two weeks to film. The switch wasn't a problem for the marketing department, either, since the production delay required postponing the movie's release past Christmas. Script-wise, Buzzy still needed a location on the way to the opera house where he could tell the fleeing Edwin that he was on his own. So, Rapp had Edwin once again drop in on Schmidt, the beleaguered deli owner.

The delay also gave Sylvia more time to decide on a solo routine for Edwin/Buzzy to perform in the nightclub. In the end, she opted for "Otchi Tchorniya," the sneezing Russian opera singer routine she had written for Danny's first appearance at La Martinique and which had become a staple of his stage act. Sylvia was intentionally drawing from the pieces she had created before re-teaming with Max Liebman. Their partnership had been growing strained as the ambitious student attained more power than the teacher. Fine convinced Goldwyn to allow her to work solo on *Wonder Man*. Liebman agreed to dissolve the team and remained on the East Coast, where he would soon begin grooming Sid Caesar for his start in *Tars and Spars* and, later, *Your Show of Shows*.

Everyone on the lot clearly understood Fine's role as the wall around Kaye. Screenwriter Mel Shavelson recalled, "Sylvia was the basic part of the operation with Danny. Sylvia was the creative brains, and she had her own ideas about what was best for Danny. She was a tough, very difficult woman to get along with, but I never had any trouble. She was inventive and creative, because what Danny was doing when he broke in was Sylvia Fine's material and that helped create Danny Kaye, and he never forgot it— she never let him. In those days, we didn't do a picture without Sylvia first. We pitched the stories to her and the scripts to her. Danny would be there, but Sylvia was the one who would say yes, or no, or what should be done."

Others didn't fare as well. Virginia Mayo said, "I'm sure that people did have trouble going through her, because she was a tough cookie. She knew what she was developing. She knew Danny's potential. She knew his qualities, and she wanted to protect him, naturally. It goes with the domain. She was his mentor. She guided him. She fought for good scripts, because she knew what was good for him, and it's doubtful he could have made the great success without her help."

Director Humberstone, whom Goldwyn had borrowed from Fox especially to direct *Wonder Man*, had heard of Sylvia running roughshod on *Up in Arms*. Humberstone said, "When a man is in a loan-out that automatically makes him pretty important or he wouldn't be asked to be borrowed from another studio. So when you're riding high, you can make demands that you normally can't make. So when I had my first interview with Goldwyn, the first thing I said was, 'I just want one thing understood. If I'm to do this picture, I don't want Sylvia Fine on the set at all when I'm shooting, unless

I send for her.' And he said, 'Well, that's going to be a tough thing to do, but I understand why you're saying that because she did cause us a lot of trouble with the director on the last picture.' So he okayed it. The result was Sylvia Fine was never on the set at any time when I made the picture, with one exception. I sent for her because one of the numbers in the picture was a number called 'Otchi Tchorniya,' which consists of a run of Russian dialect comedy you just can't put on paper, and no one else would have been able to play the piano to do the accompaniment during the number except his wife.'"

The script, in fact, describes the number as "the wording of which is known only to Danny Kaye and Sylvia Fine."

Humberstone continued: "I knew nothing about it, and it wasn't the type of musical number that I could have any control over, because Danny couldn't have any control over it himself. By that I mean Danny has to have an audience in order to do the number. Usually with musicals, we make a soundtrack and then synchronize, but we couldn't do that with 'Otchi Tchorniya.' It had to be made live. So, I had to have an audience. I think I had about 70 or 80 extras behind the camera to react to what Danny was doing while I photographed him in front of the camera, which meant you got an open mic. I had to have Danny come through over and above the laughter of the extras, so we had problems getting our mics under control. And we actually did a hell of a number. I had three cameras on him, and I just let him go. There's no direction to it. He just goes, and he never knows how long he can go or how short it's going to be. He's got to be wound up to do it, and as long as they're laughing, he rolled. So naturally this off-stage group of extras that I had was laughing their heads off, because they'd never heard it before."

Another late addition to the script, by Rapp, provoked a battle with the censors. Rapp suggested Buzzy give Midge an engagement ring inside a jack-in-the-box, out of which popped a miniature Buzzy head. Then, as the picture was about to close, the camera would move from Edwin and Ellen's bridal suite to Monte and Midge's room, where the ghost of Buzzy would magically freeze Monte so he can't join Midge in bed. On the dresser, the little Buzzy-in-the-box would pop up and crack, "I'm a little devil, ain't I?" At the censor's request, Rapp toned down Ellen's suggestive dialogue, but left the principals wearing pajamas and in their bedrooms. The censor reiterated that everyone was to be fully dressed and standing on balconies outside their hotel rooms. The filmmakers again ignored the request and shot

the scene their way. But, seeing it on film, they realized that the final gag
should center on Edwin not Monte, a minor character who'd gotten less
than six minutes of screen time. So they re-filmed the scene with Buzzy
freezing Edwin—even if it defied logic. Buzzy had ample motive to want
Monte away from his fiancée, but none to keep Edwin away from Ellen.
Even more curious, how did Midge's engagement ring box end up in
Edwin's hotel room?

Filming went sixteen days over schedule, but only three percent over its
$1.9-million budget. And *Wonder Man* provided Kaye with his second solid
hit, earning $3.1 million at the box office.

Critics roundly praised Danny's performance. The film showed, according to the *New York Times'* Bosley Crowther, "a wholesale, complete and
exhaustive demonstration of Mr. Kaye... The tremendously talented young
man manages to give an exhibition of most everything he can do. And all of
it is amusing."

RADIO

In the 1940s, nearly all the great movie clowns starred on their own
weekly radio shows. Yet the medium was not an ideal match for Kaye, since
it was blind to his facial expressions, body movement, and other physical
gifts. Yet in his formative years, Danny was desperate to break into anything, and radio seemed the most achievable medium. Red and Blackie got
several gigs on local radio in the early 1930s. In the late 1930s, Kaye got to
perform a few of his nightclub routines on the shows of Benay Venuta and
Walter O'Keefe.

Then, in 1940, after his recurring appearances on *Pursuit of Happiness*,
Danny was asked by CBS to create a pilot for a possible series of his own.
Titled *When You Were 21*, each week Kaye would appear in sketches based
on the "fads, fashions and foibles" of a different year, from 1900 to 1940,
suggested by listeners. Sylvia was invited to join the writing staff, but not to
contribute musical numbers. The show aired as part of the summer series
Forecast, which "auditioned" prospective series and promised to turn those
that generated the most fan mail into regular series. The *Forecast* episode
that aired immediately after Danny's, *Suspense*, and the episode that ran the
next week, *Duffy's Tavern*, were picked up as regular series. Danny's was
not. Sylvia recognized that radio didn't highlight what Danny did best.

Thereafter, she was content to limit his broadcast exposure primarily to guest appearances, often tied to war relief efforts.

By the time Kaye began work on *Wonder Man,* the offers from networks and sponsors were continuing to pour in. The most insistent suitor was brewer Pabst Blue Ribbon, which was quietly looking to replace Groucho Marx as host of CBS's underperforming *Pabst Blue Ribbon Town.* (When Groucho discovered his lame-duck status, he asked for—and was granted—an early release.) Danny finally agreed to a three-season pact, provided he and Sylvia were given total creative control. Kaye would receive more than $16,000 a week, out of which he'd first have to pay his own staff—including writers, actors and orchestra—then pocket any remainder.

"I'd spend it all to make good on the air," Kaye promised. Sylvia, with the title "supervisor," was put in charge of assembling the creative staff. She initially wanted Phil Rapp, creator of *The Baby Snooks Show* and *The Bickersons,* to ride herd as producer, director and head writer. But Rapp wanted $3,500 per episode—nearly a quarter of the program's entire budget—and the writer insisted the sum be guaranteed for the run of the series, even if he left after getting it started. Instead, Sylvia retained Groucho's producer, Dick Mack.

Mack concurrently produced Abbott and Costello's radio show, and had their announcer, Ken Niles, work double duty on Danny's show. The sponsor loved Niles because, as he showed with Abbott and Costello, he could be built up into one of the featured performers, making it easier to integrate his extended pitches for Pabst Blue Ribbon beer. To join him, they recruited Danny's deadpan *Let's Face It* co-star Eve Arden, gravel-voiced character actor Lionel Stander, Droopy-sound-alike Bob Jellison, and trumpeter Harry James and his Music Makers.

Mack oversaw a staff of about six writers. The best known scribes were Milt Gross, whose Yiddish comic strips had heavily influenced Fishel Goldfarb, and Howard Snyder and Hugh Wedlock Jr., former gag writers for Jack Benny who had spent the last few years writing screenplays for Universal. Sylvia handled Danny's musical arrangements and special material, and during broadcasts accompanied him on the piano.

Retitled *The Danny Kaye Show,* the radio program broadcast from Los Angeles at 5:00 Saturday evenings, so it was heard live at 8:00 p.m. on the East Coast.

As a practice run, and to promote the upcoming show on any of the 150 stations willing to carry it, the team wrote a teaser show to perform at 7:00

p.m. PST on the Saturday prior—December 28, 1944. The script consisted primarily of banter between Kaye and Niles, but also a few minutes of Kaye introducing Arden, James, Stander and Sylvia. Since Sylvia detested public speaking, her brief exchange consisted of one- and two-word responses, culminating in Danny's remark "Talkative wench, isn't she?" In the preview, Kaye sang "Shoqtatsonvitch's Fifth" and a number Mack and Fine wrote especially for the episode, "Pabst Blues" ("I've got those how-can-it-be-splendid, if it isn't blended blues…").

THE DANNY KAYE SHOW
SEASON ONE
(21 shows)

Producer/Director: Dick Mack
Writers: Dick Mack, Sylvia Fine, Milt Gross, Howard Snyder, Hugh Wedlock Jr., Jack Harvey, Robert Fine (shows 6-21), Jay Sommers (8-21), Stanley Davis (11-21), Elon Packard (11-21)
Cast: Danny Kaye, Harry James & His Music Makers, Ken Niles (announcer), Eve Arden, Lionel Stander, Bob Jellison, Buddy Devito, Kitty Kallen

Episode 1 (aired Jan. 6, 1945) • **Guests**: Eddie Cantor, Frank Nelson
[Danny performs all the parts in a play, *Ingrid Nuttlemyer, Girl Grandfather*. Danny sings "Tschaikowvsky," "Minnie the Moocher."]

For the regular show, the format would be a loose one—start with the introductory fanfare from James' theme song, "Ciribiribin," and Kaye git-gat-gittling. Niles introduces Kaye as "33 fine talents, blended into one great comedian." Interplay between the main characters. A musical number by James. A Pabst pitch by Niles, then a longer, often unrelated sketch culminating in a Kaye specialty number. A main objective was to use as many of Danny's vocal talents as possible: the dialects, jokes, singing, scatting, funny noises. The first show was a sign of what was to follow, with Danny playing a half-dozen nationalities, both sexes, and assorted ages, along with a large percentage of the animal kingdom.

Episode 2 (aired Jan. 13, 1945) • **Guest**: Doris Singleton
[Fictional recounting of Danny's life story, "A Kaye Grows in Brooklyn." He sings "Alphabet Song," "Lobby Number"]

Episode 3 (aired Jan. 20, 1945)
[Danny accidentally buys a milking machine at auction. Inspector H.I.J. Kaye tackles the Case of the Missing Toothpick. "Pabst Blue Ribbon Blues," "Deenah"]

RADIO FREQUENTLY: For his weekly series, Kaye brought along *(left to right)* Lionel Stander, Harry James, himself, Eve Arden, announcer Ken Niles, and composer/pianist Sylvia. [© 1945 CBS]

Episode 4 (aired Jan. 27, 1945) • **Guests**: Leo Cleary, Grif Barnett, Martha Wentworth
[Danny flies to Washington, D.C., for a March of Dimes benefit. "Scat Song," "Molly Malone"]

Episode 5 (aired Feb. 3, 1945)
[Danny returns from Washington with a baby. King Danny of Brooklyn attempts to save the mortgage on Ebbets Field from Queen Eve of Manhattan. "Airy Fairy Pipers," "King of Brooklyn," "Countess of Coney Island"]

Episode 6 (aired Feb. 10, 1945) • **Guests**: Leo Cleary, Verna Felton
[Danny plays Cupid in a Valentines Day play. "It's Never too Late to Mendelssohn," "Stanislavsky"]

Episode 7 (aired Feb. 17, 1945) • **Guests**: Ed Emerson, Pinto Colvig
[Danny's new dog gets him evicted from his hotel. The cast performs *Uncle Daniel's Cabin*. "I've Got a Song," "Accentuate the Positive"]

Episode 8 (aired Feb. 24, 1945) • **Guest**: Shirley Mitchell
[Danny tangles with an amorous building inspector as he puts the finishing touches on his Little Playhouse. In its first production, Inspector H.I.J. Kaye solves the Case of the Murdered Meatball. "Let's Not Talk about Love"]

Although the show's ratings were acceptable, critics panned the writing. The jokes missed more than they hit, episodes rarely carried a cohesive storyline from start to finish, and the program had no recurring characters of its own—since the stars were basically playing themselves. New writers were added to the staff, including Sylvia's brother, Robert Fine, who was trying to break into the business. To provide a more predictable framework, they introduced a handful of repeating characters—Shirley Mitchell as a seductress, Benny Rubin as an Italian music professor—and devised a running storyline that the cast, instead of randomly staging spoofs, would perform them as productions in Danny's Little Playhouse.

Episode 9 (aired March 3, 1945)
[Danny has jitters on opening night at the Playhouse, before playing Donavitch Kayeoff. "Russian Love Song," "Pavlova"]

Episode 10 (aired March 10, 1945) • **Guest**: Shirley Mitchell
[Little Theatre Guild performs *Romeo and Juliet* in the styles of a radio soap opera, the Lone Ranger, and the Whiz Kids. "Accentuate the Positive," "ABCD Song"]

Episode 11 (aired March 17, 1945) • **Guests**: Shirley Mitchell, Benny Rubin
[Danny goes shopping for a new suit, then visits a tongue coach. The guild performs *One Irishman's Family*. "Concerto for Tongue & Orchestra," "Eileen"]

Episode 12 (aired March 24, 1945) • **Guests**: Ken Roberts, Lee Brody, Arthur Elmer, Leo Durocher, Harry Sosnick & his Orchestra
[Danny applies for a job with the Brooklyn Dodgers. Kaye broadcast this and the following episode from New York, at 8 p.m. EST. "Jenny"]

Episode 13 (aired March 31, 1945) • **Guests**: Frank Sinatra, Arthur Elmer, Sosnick & his Orchestra
["Nightmare Song," "Opera"]

Episode 14 (aired April 7, 1945) • **Guests**: Benny Rubin, Harry Lang
[Danny's diary recounts his return train trip from New York. "Cannonball Express," "Minnie the Moocher"]

Episode 15 (aired April 21, 1945) • **Guests**: Shirley Mitchell
[The guild performs *Dublin or Nothing*, featuring New York cop Daniel O'Kaye. The episode was written for the week earlier, but all regularly scheduled radio programs were cancelled April 14 to allow for news, memorial services, eulogies and other tributes to FDR, who had died two days earlier. "Farming," "Molly Malone."]

Episode 16 (aired April 27, 1945) • **Guests**: Jimmy Durante, Garry Moore, Benny Rubin
[Inspector H.I.J. Kaye carries over from Durante & Moore's show to help crack the Case of the Missing Umbriago. Danny plays all the parts in a courtroom drama. "Airy Fairy Pipers"]

Many of the top-rated radio stars performed their programs twice each evening, three hours apart, so they could get the same prime-time spot on both coasts. Danny performed his show only once, and his early start time hurt ratings on the West Coast. So, CBS moved the show from Saturdays to Fridays, airing at 7:30 p.m. in Los Angeles and, therefore, 10:30 p.m. in the East. As a stunt to promote the schedule change, Danny guest-starred on the lead-in *Jimmy Durante and Garry Moore Show,* beginning a comic mystery storyline that was then carried over to his own show, on which Durante and Moore appeared. The switch to Fridays did have one fatality—Stander would not make the move.

Episode 17 (aired May 4, 1945) • **Guests**: Benny Rubin, Doris Singleton, Frank Nelson
[Danny buys an engagement ring. "Blue Skies," "Deenah"]

Episode 18 (aired May 11, 1945) • **Guests**: Benny Rubin, Shirley Mitchell
[Danny sells war bonds door to door. "Bond Song"—Fine lyrics to Arthur Sullivan's "Lord Chancellor Song"]

Episode 19 (aired May 18, 1945) • **Guests**: Benny Rubin, Shirley Mitchell
[Danny learns his blarney in Killarney. Live remote from Birmingham General Hospital for veterans in Van Nuys, California. "It Ain't Necessarily So," "Danny Boy"]

Episode 20 (aired May 25, 1945) • **Guests**: Charley Lung, Maxine Marx
[Live remote broadcast from the stage of the Pantages Theater, combining a War Loan Rally with a showing of the upcoming *Wonder Man.* "When You're Lying Awake," "Lobby Number"]

Episode 21 (aired June 1, 1945)
[In his season finale, Danny dreams of his recurring characters—the Irish Daniel O'Kaye, British Inspector H.I.J. Kaye, adolescent Danny Kewpie Kaye, and Russian Donavitch Kayeoff. "Bali Boogie," "Modern Major General"]

Within days of performing in the season finale, Danny began work on his next film, *The Kid from Brooklyn.* His contract with Pabst's advertising agency, Warwick & Legler, allowed him to appoint a replacement show for the summer, so he let Harry James take over. During the break, *The Danny Kaye Show* would be completely retooled. The Kayes wanted someone new in charge.

SEASON TWO
(29 shows)

Producer/Director: Goodman Ace (22-38), Willie Shore (39-50)
Writers: Goodman Ace (22-38), Sylvia Fine, Abe Burrows (22), Eddie Pola (22), Bud Gagnon (23-38), Henry Howard (23-38), Byron Wingate (23-33), Lee Brody, Herbert

Baker, Jess Goldstein, Arthur Alsberg, Hal Kanter, Al Lewis (39-50)
Cast: Danny Kaye, Dave Terry & His Orchestra, Dick Joy (announcer), Butterfly
McQueen, Jim Backus, Goodman Ace, Everett Sloane, Kenny Delmar

Episode 22 (aired Sept. 28, 1945) • **Guest**: Ward Wilson
[The second-season opener was the only episode to credit Abe Burrows, although he
may have provided uncredited doctoring to earlier episodes. "Girl with the Blue
Eyes." The premiere was a remote broadcast from Chicago before 10,000 War
Fund workers, before Kaye set off on a USO tour. Until he returned, CBS each
week substituted a different program in his place—Frank Sinatra and Judy Garland
(Oct. 5, 1945), *Easy Aces* (Oct. 12, 1945), *Burns & Allen* (Oct. 19, 1945), *Jack
Benny Show* (Oct. 26, 1945), *Duffy's Tavern* (Nov. 2, 1945), and Eddie Cantor
(Nov. 9, 1945).

Back in January, four days after Danny aired the first episode of his
radio show, Goodman Ace broadcast the final installment of his long-run-
ning situation comedy *Easy Aces*. Ace was renowned for his razor-sharp
wit—the quality purported by critics to be most lacking in Kaye's show.
So, after entertaining several competing offers, Ace agreed to replace Mack
as producer, director and head writer for the second season of *The Danny
Kaye Show*. Ace would be paid $3,500 a week and have the show relocate
to New York. He would also replace the entire cast and crew, except for
Danny and Sylvia.

Impressed by Ace's wit, reputation and intelligence, Kaye gave his new
producer full rein. According to incoming scribe Arthur Alsberg, "Goodman
Ace had a nice library in New York, and we worked in his apartment. Kaye
came up one day and was looking over Ace's beautiful books. And Ace
said, 'What are you doing, Danny?' He said, 'I was just looking at the kind
of books you have so that I know what to put in my library.' (Danny) was a
very bright guy, enormously talented, but not an intellectual."

In addition to upgrading the quality of the humor, Ace was also concerned about story and character. Sylvia's contributions, in particular, usually appeared to be haphazardly tacked on. Ace wanted to better integrate
her work into the show rather than just cut away to one of her specialty
numbers—the supply of which had already been exhausted. So Sylvia took
on two assistants to craft longer, more frequent musical pieces—former
Camp Tamiment castmate Lee Brody and the young Herbert Baker.
Herbie's style meshed perfectly with Sylvia's, and he became fast, dear
friends with the Kayes. Baker would continue to write for Danny, with and
without Sylvia, for the next 30 years.

Ace insisted on creating an ensemble cast of *characters*, rather than just personalities. Danny couldn't take on a fictional personage; he had to play Danny Kaye, the performer who could do anything. So Ace developed characters whom Kaye would constantly run into while putting together his weekly radio show—Jim Backus as Pabst executive Mr. Singleton, Butterfly McQueen as the overeager president of the Danny Kaye Fan Club, Kenny Delmar as Mr. Average Radio Listener (who heckles Kaye outside the studio), and Ace himself with Everett Sloane as subversive gag writers Al and Joe.

Regular characters also provided a better opportunity to develop catch phrases and running gags. Mack's ideas—such as Danny drawing out, "Ken Niles! Am... I... glad... to... see... you!"—never caught on. Ace had a better suggestion: each week having writers Al and Joe try to sneak in corny old jokes. In their first show, while trying to come up with material for Kaye, Joe suggests, "This is easy for him, Al... no hard words or anything... remember the one where the guy says to another, 'My sister married an Irishman,' and the other says, 'Oh, really?' and the first guy says, 'No, O'Riley'?"

Kaye protests: "'Oh, really?' 'Oh, Riley!' My grandfather told me that joke!" Then, each week thereafter, Al and Joe would try to slip different variations of the joke past Danny ("I am from Russia." "Oh, really?" "No, Odessa." Or "I like Russian songs." "Oh, really?" "No, 'Otchi Tchorniya.'" Or "That's quite a mop of blond hair you have. Is it unruly?" "No, un-Riley."). Al and Joe even convince scatterbrained Butterfly McQueen to tell an O'Riley joke, but she inadvertently substitutes the punchline "No, Flanagan." The "Oh, really?"/"Oh, Riley" writers became the most talked-about feature of the program.

Episode 23 (aired Nov. 16, 1945)
[Danny returns from Tokyo and meets his new boss, fictional Pabst executive Mr. Singleton. "Bali Boogie"]

Episode 24 (aired Nov. 23, 1945) • **Guest**: Lily Pons
[Danny disguises himself as a Russian delivery boy to bring a case of beer to Pons. "Blue Skies," opera medley]

Episode 25 (aired Nov. 30, 1945) • **Guest**: Leo Durocher
[Danny and the Brooklyn Dodgers manager rehearse a vaudeville bit. "How-How-How," "Sally," "Good Evening Friends," "Korean Folk Song"]

Episode 26 (aired Dec. 7, 1945) • **Guest**: Sophie Tucker
[Mr. Singleton wants to share a private dinner with Tucker. "Stanislavsky," "Steam on the Beam," "Some of These Days"]

Episode 27 (aired Dec. 14, 1945) • **Guests**: Shirley Booth, Georgia Gibbs
[Booth plays her ditzy Brooklyn character, Dottie Mahoney. The cast holds a musical business conference. "It Might as Well Be Spring," "Barrel-House Boogie"]

Episode 28 (aired Dec. 21, 1945) • **Guest**: Martha Raye
[Christmas pageant. The show was Backus' last as Mr. Singleton, as he headed to Hollywood to become a regular on *The Alan Young Show*. "My Ship Has Sails"]

Episode 29 (aired Dec. 28, 1945) • **Guest**: Georgia Gibbs
[Short of time, Danny searches for a thirteen-month calendar. "Accentuate the Positive," "Auld Lang Syne"]

Episode 30 (aired Jan. 4, 1946) • **Guest**: Betty Hutton
[Kaye and Hutton seek a bank loan to start their own film production company. "Stanislavsky," signature songs medley, "Trolley Song"]

Episode 31 (aired Jan. 11, 1946) • **Guest**: Shirley Booth
[Waitress Dottie Mahoney pleads to sing on Danny's show to get back her boyfriend. "Delicatessen Song," "Railroad Song"]

Episode 32 (aired Jan. 18, 1946) • **Guest**: Shirley Booth
[Dottie Mahoney returns to co-star in a Brooklynese opera. "Frim Fram Sauce," "Countess of Coney Island"]

Episode 33 (aired Jan. 25, 1946)
[Danny guests on his own show, plus a spoof of *Court of Human Relations*. "Babbit & the Bromide," "Anatole of Paris"]

Episode 34 (aired Feb. 1, 1946) • **Guest**: Helen Jepson
[Remote broadcast from Milwaukee—Pabst's hometown—in honor of the city's 100th anniversary features Jack and Jill opera. "Frim Fram Sauce," "Jenny," "Minnie the Moocher," "Jack & Jill"]

Episode 35 (aired Feb. 8, 1946) • **Guest**: Ann Sothern
[Sothern plays her CBS radio character Maisie, who wants Kaye to co-star with her in a Broadway musical. "Molly Malone," "I Love a Rhyme," "Triplet Song," "Triple Tongue," "Concerto for Tongue & Orchestra"]

Episode 36 (aired Feb. 15, 1946) • **Guest**: Carmen Miranda
[Danny tries to hire an interpreter for Miranda. "Tropical Song," "South American Way"]

Episode 37 (aired Feb. 22, 1946) • **Guests**: Jack Pearl, Georgia Gibbs
[Pearl plays wild storyteller Baron Munchausen. "It's a Sin to Tell a Lie," "Wishing"]

Episode 38 (aired March 1, 1946) • **Guests**: Orson Welles, Georgia Gibbs
[After Welles turns Kaye's running gag into a play, *The Wife of O'Riley*, Danny turns Welles' *Julius Caesar* into a musical comedy. "Cannonball," "McNamara's Band"]

Despite the changes, the show's ratings remained modest. Worse, Ace bristled at dealing with the authoritative, overprotective Sylvia. For one show, Ace had written exceptionally witty dialogue for guest star Betty Hutton. "If you give her lines like that," Fine objected, "Danny ought to do something special. Maybe the 'Tschaikowsky' number."

Ace responded that while he admired the piece, he thought it had already been overused. "Well, you'll have to do something!" Miss Fine protested.

"Tell you what," Ace conceded. "We'll have the orchestra louse up Hutton's numbers."

Another week, Sylvia wanted to re-use one of Danny's signature numbers, because she wasn't able to come up with anything new. Ace said that would be fine—so long as the rest of the joke-writers be allowed to repeat *their* old material.

Hal Kanter, who joined the series' writing staff a few shows into season two, remembered Danny had recently hired a pianist, Sammy Prager, to accompany him on stage and during USO tours. "Sam traveled with him quite often when Sylvia didn't," Kanter said. "Sylvia used to accompany him on his numbers on the radio show, and Sylvia, for some reason, always wore operatic gloves when she played the piano. One week she was ill and could not make the broadcast, and Sammy Prager filled in for her. The next day, Sylvia was talking to Goody Ace and said, 'How did Sammy do?' And Goody said, 'Remarkably well, considering the fact that he plays without wearing gloves.'"

The changes didn't make Danny much happier with the show, either. The addition of all the colorful new characters increasingly took the spotlight off of him. After one morning read-through, all the cast and crew smiled with satisfaction—except Kaye. He folded his script and grumbled, "Well, I'm the highest-paid straight man in show business." Without looking up, Ace retorted, "Jack Benny makes three times the money you do."

Danny and Sylvia reluctantly had to admit that radio was not the best place for his talents. In addition, being tied to New York was costing him lucrative stage bookings and would conflict with his need to be in Los Angeles in the spring to begin work on his next movie. Ace, Kaye knew, was dead set against relocating to the West Coast. So, in January 1946, Danny asked for an early release from his contract. Warwick & Legler suspected the comic was interested in launching another show, with a new sponsor, and refused.

So, in early March, Kaye headed for Hollywood—and took the show with him. About half the writers made the trip. Ace was not among them. "Goodman Ace didn't particularly want to live in California. He was quite a wealthy man, and he preferred New York," recalled Alsberg.

To replace Ace, Willie Shore was hired as producer/director and Al Lewis (who later created *Our Miss Brooks* for Eve Arden) became head writer. Lewis, according to Alsberg, "had been in radio quite a while. Although the three of us (dialogue writers) who came out here knew the show pretty well, they figured we needed a head writer to guide us who had more experience than we did at the time."

Although the writers retained the show's format and characters, the move back to Hollywood did allow them to feature a celebrity guest every week.

Episode 39 (aired March 8, 1946) • **Guests**: Peter Lorre, Georgia Gibbs, Lee Brody, John Brown
[Lorre invites Danny to his spooky house. "You Made Me Love You," "Lobby Number"]

Episode 40 (aired March 15, 1946) • **Guests**: Edward Everett Horton, Georgia Gibbs
[Danny teaches Horton to speak Brooklynese. "Frim Fram Sauce," "Oh, Mr. Horton"]

Episode 41 (aired March 22, 1946) • **Guests**: Dick Powell, Benay Venuta, Dickie Monohan, Dick Ryan
[Kaye, Powell and Venuta play dysfunctional private eyes. "Johnny One Note," "Trio Detective Number"]

Episode 42 (aired March 29, 1946) • **Guests**: Jean Hersholt, Georgia Gibbs
[Danny recalls his childhood after being hypnotized by Dr. Christian. "Blue Skies," "Triplets," "Nightmare Song"]

Episode 43 (aired April 5, 1946) • **Guests**: George Jessel, Georgia Gibbs
[Kaye and Jessel play starving songwriters the Dolly Brothers, a spoof on Jessel's first picture as a producer, *The Dolly Sisters*. "Songwriters," "Airy Fairy Pipers"]

Episode 44 (aired April 12, 1946) • **Guests**: Georgia Gibbs, Jim Backus, Jerry Hausner
[Danny trains for a prize fight. "Babbit & the Bromide," "I Got a Song"]

Episode 45 (aired April 19, 1946) • **Guests**: Joan Blondell, Dick Ryan
[Spoof of radio's *Quiz Kids*. "Shoo Fly Pie," "Information Please"]

Episode 46 (aired April 26, 1946) • **Guests**: Billie Burke, Georgia Gibbs, Walter Craig, Hal Kanter
[Burke throws a house party. "Bali Boogie," "3 B's, Barrel-House Blues"]

Episode 47 (aired May 3, 1946) • **Guests**: Andrews Sisters, Jim Backus
[Danny is named Sheriff Kaye. "Farming," "Jack and Jill"]

Episode 48 (aired May 10, 1946) • **Guest**: Basil Rathbone
[Rewrite of Orson Welles show. "Deenah," "Julius Caesar"]

Episode 49 (aired May 24, 1946) • **Guest**: Arthur Treacher
[Rewrite of *Countess of Coney Island* episode was intended to feature David Niven on

May 17. But when the show was postponed, Niven was unable to appear and fellow Brit Treacher stepped in. "Don't Marry That Gal," "Countess of Coney Island"]

Episode 50 (aired May 31, 1946) • **Guests**: Carmen Miranda, Hal Kanter, George Sorel, Jay Novello
[Rewrite of Miranda's earlier interpreter show. "Babooshka," "South American Way"]

Without Goodman Ace, Kaye thought the show suffered. He renewed efforts to be released from his contract. At the beginning of May, Warwick & Legler finally consented, with the stipulations that over the next year Kaye would be limited to ten guest broadcasts and was prevented from taking on a new sponsor. Pabst would have first dibs on the option of sponsoring four of the appearances, at $5,000 each.

With the news out that the show was ending, the writers merely rewrote earlier scripts for the final three broadcasts. In the last show, they wrapped up all the running gags. Instead of sniping at Kaye, Mr. Average Radio Listener approached him sobbing: "Friday nights are gonna be a lot different... I'm gonna start listening to the radio again."

And Danny voluntarily agreed to one last O'Riley joke. "Last month my sister *did* marry an Irishman," Kaye told announcer Dick Joy. "Oh, really?" "Just happens to be the fella's name—Thomas J. O'Really."

Wonder Man director Lucky Humberstone was not surprised at the series' premature ending. He had tried to dissuade Kaye from doing the show in the first place, pleading, "Danny, don't do it. Don't go on radio because you aren't made for radio. You're a 'sight comic.' And if you're on radio, nobody sees you; they only hear you. You're extremely funny when you're working with a live audience, but they're laughing at your facial expressions and what you do with your hands, because you've got the most graceful hands of any man I've ever known. You won't have either your hands or your face on radio, so in my personal opinion I think you'll be a flop on radio, and I would advise you not to do it."

"Well," Humberstone shared years later, "he was conceited enough not to agree with me, and he did radio and he died quick. And that's the reason he died. You'd hear the audience laughing like hell on the radio, but people sitting home listening would say, 'What the hell's everybody laughing at?' because he hadn't said anything funny. It's what he was doing that was funny."

Other sponsors tried to get Danny to return to radio. CBS even offered him another crack at his own show just a year later. But Kaye decided to stick to guest appearances on others' programs and GI series like *Command*

ON THE RADIO

Pursuit of Happiness (CBS, c. late 1939) •
(Jan. 28, 1940) • (Feb. 11, 1940) •
(March 10, 1940) • (April 21, 1940)

Forecast (CBS, July 22, 1940)

President Roosevelt's Diamond Jubilee
(CBS, Jan. 31, 1942)

Command Performance (AFRS, March 1,
1942) "Pavlova" • (Aug. 19, 1944) opera
parody • (Dec. 23, 1944) "Lobby
Number" • (July 19, 1945) "Bali Boogie"
• (Aug. 15, 1945) "Lobby Number" •
(May 12, 1946) • (June 30, 1946) • (May
29, 1947) • (Feb. 10, 1948) • (Feb. 8,
1949) • (Feb. 22, 1949) • (Dec. 20,
1949) • (March 14, 1950)

Mail Call (AFRS, March 29, 1944)
"Deenah," "Tschaikowsky" • (Oct. 25,
1944) "Minnie the Moocher" • (Feb. 1,
1945) • (Sept. 24, 1947) • (Oct. 13,
1948) • (Feb. 1949)

Jack Benny Program (NBC, May 28, 1944)
"Stanislavsky" • (April 28, 1946)
"Concerto for Tongue & Orchestra" •
(CBS, March 1, 1952) "Jack's Song" •
(March 6, 1955)

Hollywood Democratic Committee (Oct.
8, 1944)

Democratic National Committee Program
(CBS, Nov. 6, 1944)

Esquire Jazz Concert (NBC, Jan. 17, 1945

Jimmy Durante Show (CBS, April 27,
1945)

Jubilee (AFRS, April 28, 1945)

GI Journal (AFRS, May 8, 1945) • (March
16, 1946)

Lux Radio Theater (CBS, 1945) "Up in
Arms" • (March 25, 1946) "Wonder Man"

Stars in the Afternoon (CBS, Sept. 22,
1946)

Philco Radio Time (ABC, March 19, 1947)
"Dena's Lullaby"

Hollywood Fights Back (ABC, Oct. 26,
1947) • (Nov. 2, 1947)

Camel Screen Guild Theatre (CBS, Nov.
3, 1947) "Secret Life of Walter Mitty"

Leo Forbstein Memorial (April 25, 1948)

Red Cross Flood Relief Show (CBS, June
13, 1948)

**Hollywood Bowl Symphonies Under the
Stars** (AFRS, Aug. 5, 1948)

Red Feather Round-Up (CBS, Sept. 3,
1948)

Wrigley Christmas Special (CBS, Dec. 25,
1948) "Tubby the Tuba"

A Salute from the USO (Feb. 1, 1949)

On with the Show USO (1949)

Suspense (CBS, Jan. 13, 1949) "The Too
Perfect Alibi" • (Jan. 5, 1950) "I Never
Met the Dead Man"

Saturday at the Shamrock (ABC, Feb. 18,
1950)

The Big Show (NBC, Jan. 28, 1951)

Hedda Hopper Show (NBC, April 1, 1951)
"Lobby Number," "On the Riviera"

Academy Awards (March 20, 1952) Host

Of Thee We Sing (Syndicated, 1952)
"Thumbelina"

Bud's Bandwagon (AFRS, 1954)

Guest Star (March 21, 1954) "Not Since
Ninevah"

Stagestruck (CBS, April 4, 1954) • (May 2,
1954)

A Tribute to Gertrude Lawrence
(Syndicated, 1955)

**Photoplay Eleventh Annual Gold Medal
Awards** (ABC, Feb. 10, 1955)

Close to Your Heart (Syndicated, Feb.
1956) "Knock on Wood"

Biographies in Sound (NBC, Sept. 10,
1957)

Here's Hollywood (NBC, Nov. 19, 1962)

Bob Crane Show (AFRS, Nov. 1967)

Michael Jackson Show (KABC, Jan. 1970)

Bob Hope Story (BBC, May 17 to June 7,
1978)

Performance, often with *Danny Kaye Show* writer Hal Kanter doubling as scribe and straight man.

Danny had discovered that he could entertain audiences with just his voice; he just couldn't sustain it on a weekly basis.

THE KID FROM BROOKLYN

(Filmed June 4 to Oct. 9, Oct. 15, 1945; released March 21, 1946)
Producer: Sam Goldwyn, for Samuel Goldwyn Productions, Trinity Productions, RKO Radio Pictures
Director: Norman Z. McLeod
Screenplay: Don Hartman & Melville Shavelson (uncredited Everett Freeman & Ken Englund, Edwin Moran, Czenzi Ormonde, Philip Rapp)
Original Story: *The Milky Way* screenplay by Frank Butler, Richard Connell, & Grover Jones, from 1934 play by Harry Clork & Lynn Root
Songs: Sylvia Fine & Max Liebman ("Pavlova"), Jule Styne & Sammy Cahn
Cast: Danny Kaye (Burleigh Sullivan), Virginia Mayo (Polly Pringle), Vera-Ellen (Susie Sullivan), Steve Cochran (Speed McFarlane), Eve Arden (Ann Westley), Walter Abel (Gabby Sloan), Lionel Stander (Spider Schultz)

Back in Hollywood, Goldwyn was ruminating over what to put Danny in next. The producer wanted to expand James Thurber's short story "The Secret Life of Walter Mitty" as Kaye's third picture, but was unhappy with how the writing was progressing. So Goldwyn turned to regulars Don Hartman and Mel Shavelson.

"Because we had to meet a date, we had to get something going fast and we didn't have any material," Shavelson recalled. "In our sessions, Don would be talking about different pictures, and he mentioned *The Milky Way* with Harold Lloyd was one of his favorites. So I said, 'Why don't we try it with Danny?' And that's how that started. That was the easiest picture of all to write because we started out with a very funny premise, and it was a Broadway play originally."

Lloyd played welterweight milkman-turned-boxer Burleigh Sullivan, who is unaware that his astounding victories were fixed, to set him up for a big fight against the champ. Because *The Milky Way* was only ten years old, there was concern that it was too soon for a remake. But Goldwyn was determined that the prior version be forgotten quickly and permanently. When he paid $125,000 for the story rights, he also acquired the original negative and all of Paramount's theater distribution prints—then promptly had them all destroyed. (*The Milky Way* survives to this day in pristine form only because Harold Lloyd preserved his own original nitrate print.)

Casting became a quick and easy job, as well, since Goldwyn turned to his contract performers (*Wonder Man* players Mayo as leading lady, Vera-Ellen as the second lead, and Steve Cochran as Danny's rival) and Danny's radio co-stars Eve Arden and Lionel Stander, who repeated his role from *The Milky Way*. As director, Goldwyn assigned broad comedy specialist Norman Z. McLeod, whose experience included overseeing the Marx Brothers, W.C. Fields, and even several scenes of *The Milky Way* when Leo McCarey fell ill. The mild-mannered McLeod, according to Shavelson, "was a very nice guy—too nice to be a director."

In their first draft, Hartman and Shavelson stuck close to the original's script, but tried to work in routines specially suited to Danny's skills. In one omitted scene, boxing promoter Gabby Sloan and his entourage arrive at Burleigh's apartment door. Burleigh asks, "Who is it?" Learning it's the hoods, he hides behind the furniture and pretends his voice is coming from the radio: "*Who Is It?* That brand new radio quiz program! Here is our first contestant. What is your name, sir? (switching to a Swedish accent) Ayban Svenson Svenson Swanson." The ruffians enter Burleigh's apartment, and Gabby switches off the radio. Nonetheless, Burleigh, as the Swede, continues: "Ay just arrived yesterday, by yumpin' yimminy, from Yacksonville. Got a yob as a yanitor in a yoke box yoint in New Yersey—but I guess I'm ay'm a yerk—ay like it better in New *Jork*."

Their first script also exhibited Hartman's penchant for extra-natural, anthropomorphic sight gags. He suggested having the film end with victorious fighter Burleigh, dazed after having just been accidentally walloped by a dowager, mooing like a cow. Earlier, in Burleigh's second fixed fight, he was to face Kangaroo Kelly, the Australian assassin. Burleigh is so frightened, he visualizes Kelly as a kangaroo (played by a man in a kangaroo suit). Burleigh gets slapped kicked, banged, punched and headlocked by the marsupial, before a little kangaroo wearing boxing gloves pops out of its pouch and starts belting Burleigh. When Burleigh finally connects with a punch, the imaginary kangaroo flips backwards, whacks Burleigh in the face with his long feet, and knocks him out. Burleigh's awakened by Gabby with smelling salts, only to discover he's sitting in his corner and the fight hasn't started yet.

Despite the tightness of the original script, five more writers were called in to add polish, straight through filming. Among them, Everett Freeman remembered the constant rewriting was Goldwyn's idea, not the director's. "McLeod loved the script and didn't ask for many changes. As a matter of

MILKING LAUGHS: In *The Kid from Brooklyn*, milkman Danny pleaded with boxing promoter Walter Abel, as Steve Cochran, Lionel Stander, and Eve Arden looked on. [© 1946 Samuel Goldwyn]

fact, Sam Goldwyn used to get the best out of people—or what he thought was the best—by challenging. We once had a scene in which he was hollering at McLeod for not demanding any changes. He said, 'What are you doing not asking for any changes? All the great directors, Frank Capra and all the rest of them, ask for changes, but you sit there and tell me you like the script!' And McLeod said, 'Well, I like it.' 'What the hell kind of director are you…?' and so forth. It was pretty wild, and I felt sorry for poor Norman, that he was taking such a beating simply because he liked the script as it was."

Freeman and partner Ken Englund focused primarily on working musical numbers into the script. Vera-Ellen would be Burleigh's kid sister, a nightclub dancer, and love interest Virginia Mayo would have aspirations of becoming a singer. More difficult was working in a specialty routine for a timid milkman. There seemed to be two places they might be able to work in numbers: at a garden party celebrating now-cocky Burleigh's successful boxing tour and, earlier, at his sister's nightclub, when he's begged on to the stage by his adoring public. The writers suggested that Burleigh, as a child, loved to sing. The other kids hated it and would throw bricks at him, so he learned how to duck. This backstory would explain why the otherwise-shy

Burleigh agrees to sing at the nightclub and could be used for the lyrics to his song.

Sylvia, however, thought the idea contrived. More so, she was beginning to feel that Goldwyn and others around the lot were trying not only to work around her, but also to turn Danny against her. Flustered, Goldwyn gave her husband a long speech about how he shouldn't rest his entire career on one woman. The producer suggested that there were many people available who could write the type of songs Kaye and the picture required.

When Danny relayed the conversation to Sylvia, she exploded, "By all means! It wouldn't be bad to have Ira Gershwin or Frank Loesser writing for you. It's all right with me!"

Goldwyn, coincidentally, pursued Loesser for the film, but Loesser declined. Instead, Goldwyn retained Sammy Cahn and Jule Styne for the bulk of the numbers, but none for Danny. Cahn said that he and the Kayes "were friends a good many years, but I always kept my distance. I knew that Sylvia wrote for him, so I didn't want to trespass."

Meanwhile, the cameras started to roll. Danny's greatest concern was that, even though he portrayed an inept fighter in the film, he wanted to make his pugilism look believable. So Goldwyn hired well-known trainer John Indrisano to teach Kaye how to box. Within weeks, Danny was able to appear as if he actually knew what he was doing, occasionally subjecting himself to mild abuse to make the scenes look credible. He enjoyed the bouts in spite of being forced to spar with only fighters who towered above his six-foot height, so he would look more heroic.

A month after production began, Jerry Seelen and Lester Lee agreed to write a routine for Burleigh to perform at the club about how he loved to sing as a child. Seelen's lyrics for the "Cavalcade Number" exhibit a marked absence of Sylvia-sharp wit and puns, instead relying on Danny's vocal talents: his widdle boy voice as young Burleigh and his Austrian dialect as Professor Beesmyer, the music instructor who taught him to love happy songs (so he sings everything, even tragic lyrics, in a happy voice).

The number was orchestrated and recorded. Danny filmed the lead-in on the nightclub stage, along with audience reaction shots to be intercut with the number. Filming of the number itself, however, was scheduled for the end of production, in hopes that by then Sylvia—who had returned to New York—would have cooled off and supplied a number that could be used in the garden party scene.

With filming more than halfway completed, Goldwyn's wife, Frances, called Sylvia in New York. Mrs. Goldwyn explained that her husband, while he would never admit it himself, was quite sorry and hoped Sylvia would return to California and work up something for the picture. Sylvia finally offered her and Liebman's five-year-old ballet spoof "Pavlova" to use in the garden party scene. But Fine's friend Irving Berlin advised her, "You charge him $25,000 for that number. That's what he paid me for one use of 'Always' in *Pride of the Yankees*." Goldwyn, thankful to have anything on such short notice, paid her price without blinking an eye. Cahn and Styne, in comparison, split $20,000 for the eight songs they submitted. And, as a final peace offering, Goldwyn cut the "Cavalcade Number."

Mechanically, the insertion of "Pavlova" was easy enough. Burleigh originally was to arrive at the garden party amid a contingent of Scotsmen wearing kilts and playing the bagpipes, as in *The Milky Way*. As a bridge to the Russian ballet specialty, he instead arrives with a contingent of Russian dancers, musicians and tumblers. Logically, though, "Pavlova" was a horrible fit. There's no explanation (aside from Burleigh's newfound confidence) how he could perform such a complicated character number, which prevents audiences from believing Danny as the Russian dancer. It's simply jarring, and the number's subtle humor is lost.

Although Kaye was not in any of the other numbers, Goldwyn insisted they be as fabulous as possible. He borrowed famed dancer/choreographer Kay Thompson from MGM, for $1,050 a week. The loan ended up costing Goldwyn plenty more when Thompson requested that Vera-Ellen's two big dance numbers be reworked after they had already been filmed, pushing production an extra two weeks over schedule.

Thompson also appeared in the opening scene as the matron who oversees the Sunflower Dairy milkmaids. But when previews found the film too long, Thompson's part ended up on the cutting room floor.

The lavish musical sequences slowed down the picture and pushed its cost near $2.5 million. *The New York Times'* Bosley Crowther called the movie uneven, finding Danny at his funniest, but noting the film dragged "when Mr. Kaye isn't anywhere to be seen." Audiences didn't seem to mind, making *The Kid from Brooklyn* Danny's most successful outing to date, collecting close to $3.5 million in its first run.

Forces inside the studio must have pointed out to Danny that the film Sylvia was least involved with became his most profitable. Virginia Mayo maintained that having Sylvia around benefited Danny. "It's good," she said, "to have somebody you can go to and say, 'Is this right or is this not right?' Because when you're in the spot where you're new in the business, you have nobody who's going to tell you what's good and bad. Sylvia was Danny's sounding board, and it was wonderful to have that."

The only problem was that Danny was no longer new in the business, and he began resenting being led everywhere by her hand. As he cracked at the time, "Sylvia has a fine head on my shoulders."

THE SECRET LIFE OF WALTER MITTY

(Filmed April 8 to Aug. 21, Sept. 3 to 4, 1946; Feb. 17, May 21, May 28, 1947; released N.Y. Aug. 4, 1947, wide Sept. 1, 1947)

Producer: Sam Goldwyn, for Samuel Goldwyn Productions, RKO Radio Pictures
Director: Norman Z. McLeod
Screenplay: Ken Englund & Everett Freeman (uncredited Czenzi Ormonde, Mel Shavelson, James Thurber, Philip Rapp)
Original Story: "Secret Life of Walter Mitty" by James Thurber
Songs: Sylvia Fine ("Anatole of Paris," "Symphony for Unstrung Tongue")
Cast: Danny Kaye (Walter Mitty), Virginia Mayo (Rosalind van Hoorn), Boris Karloff (Dr. Hugo Hollingshead), Fay Bainter (Mrs. Mitty), Ann Rutherford (Gertrude Griswold), Thurston Hall (Mr. Pierce), Gordon Jones (Tubby Wadsworth)

In 1939, humorist James Thurber wrote the short story "The Secret Life of Walter Mitty" for the sophisticated *New Yorker*. Four years later, the short story would be reprinted by *Reader's Digest*, instantly transforming the tormented daydreamer into Thurber's most famous character. Four years later, Mitty would also become one of Danny Kaye's most famous characters—but not without a fight.

At the end of 1944, Goldwyn was fishing around for a follow-up to *Wonder Man*. Screenwriter Everett Freeman thought Danny would make a perfect Mitty. Goldwyn wasn't impressed. "Who wants to do a picture about a guy who daydreams?"

Story editor Pat Duggan, however, liked the idea. A few Broadway producers had already made offers for the rights to Mitty, and several movie studios were also showing interest. Twentieth Century Fox envisioned George Jessel in the role. International Pictures' Nunnally Johnson wanted it for Jack Benny. MGM saw the story as a musical comedy revue, with a series of Technicolor dreams starring Judy Garland and friends.

Thurber's agent asked for $15,000. Goldwyn was stunned. The story was only a few pages long! Thurber, though, considered it his most important single story, and thought length had no bearing on its value. Goldwyn asked *Up in Arms* director Elliott Nugent, co-creator with Thurber of *The Male*

Animal, to talk some sense into his friend. But Nugent agreed with Thurber. Goldwyn reluctantly paid the $15,000.

On January 2, 1945, Freeman began work turning the 2,000-word story into a 180-page screenplay. With Danny in the lead, certain changes in the character were inevitable. Instead of Thurber's middle-aged, henpecked husband, Mitty would be younger and single, bullied by an overbearing mother, fiancée, mother-in-law-to-be, and boss. In place of the story's uneventful shopping trip, Mitty of the movies would have to encounter adventures exciting enough to sustain a two-hour movie.

Freeman's initial scenario opened with Mitty daydreaming as he rides the train to work as a proofreader at a pulp magazine publishing house. As he begins to nod off, the girl of his dreams sits down next to him. Another passenger grabs her wrist. Mitty, thinking it's all a fantasy, punches the man and promises the woman that she won't be bothered again. But the man belts Walter. "Strange!" Mitty says, rubbing his chin. "This never happened before."

At Penn Station, the woman offers to have her limousine driver give Walter a ride to his office. But after he's dropped off, Mitty realizes he's left his briefcase in the limo. He rushes to the woman's hotel room, where he discovers the driver has been murdered. Though frightened, Walter agrees to have lunch the following day with the woman. On his way, he daydreams himself as Inspector Mitty of Scotland Yard, solving the mystery of the slain limo driver. Walter's also being followed by two hoods, who've noticed that his little black book looks a lot like the one they're after.

In the end, Mitty loses his fiancée, but wins the girl of his dreams, asserts himself over his mother, and gets his own office with his name on the door. As Freeman closed his brief treatment: "Nor must we overlook the fact that we have told a little tale that is completely faithful to the character created by James Thurber, gives Danny Kaye scope for his talents as a comedian and entertainer, and if handled properly, might very well win an Academy Award. Who knows?"

It didn't take long for news to spread of Goldwyn's insistence on a thriller plot. The New York literary community was up in arms over the idea of Walter Mitty going Hollywood. "Watch your step, Goldwyn old boy," warned *New Yorker* columnist Frank Sullivan. "You are playing with dynamite." Soon, letters of protest started appearing in newspapers across the country.

To expand the idea to a full-length treatment, Goldwyn assigned Freeman a writing partner who was a fellow Thurber admirer, Ken Englund. The writers agreed to temper the thriller storyline, to give Mitty a more "Thurberish" life.

But while the pro-Thurber group had been cursing on the outside, an opposing group had been forming inside the studio gates. The studio executives and advisors reminded Goldwyn that he was supposed to be making a Danny Kaye movie. The short story should serve as an inspiration, without dictating the tone of the entire film.

Goldwyn weighed both sides and called the writers into his office. Giving Mitty a dull life, the boss claimed, would make a dull picture. Therefore he insisted on an exciting life. Englund argued that subtle wasn't dull. "Ken," Goldwyn explained, "I can't keep listening to you on this point. Frankly, let me tell you something for your own good as a writer in Hollywood. Outside of a few thousand people in Manhattan, you are the only one in the rest of America that ever reads that *New Yorker* magazine!"

But, Englund responded, "Mitty" had since been published in *Reader's Digest*. Millions had come to know and love the character. But, Goldwyn decreed, to break even on a big A picture, he had to sell more tickets than the combined readership of the *New Yorker* and *Reader's Digest*. Argument ended. Boys, go forth and write me a Danny Kaye comedy. Retain the excitement. Play up the damsel in distress. And add three musical numbers. Oh, and the Goldwyn Girls.

Freeman and Englund fleshed out the thriller plot—mystery woman Rosalind seeks Walter's help delivering a valuable black book to a man she thinks is her uncle, but who is actually the murderous Boot. When the Boot thinks Walter has the book, he sends his henchmen, including the villainous Dr. Hugo Hollingshead, after him.

The writers tweaked Thurber's five dreams—Walter as a submarine pilot, surgeon, prosecuting attorney, RAF fighter pilot, and closing with, instead of Walter stoically facing a firing squad, cowboy "Slim" Mitty besting an ambush by outlaws. They also retained Thurber's "ta-pocketa, ta-pocketa," the ingenious, all-purpose sound effect of the short story's daydreams.

Working in musical numbers while retaining a Thurberesque mood was a little more difficult. The writers thought a ballad might be least intrusive. In Thurber's RAF dream, Captain Mitty downs one last brandy and hums a popular French tune as he heads out for an impossible mission. The screenwriters placed Captain Mitty in a desert café, agreeing to sing "a little Cockney song"—before being attacked by a burly Arab, who's actually a

Nazi agent in disguise.

To set up a second number, the writers had a salon manager discover Walter and Rosalind in a dressing room, searching through corsets for the black book. Rosalind explains that Walter is the famous hat-maker Anatole, allowing Mitty to sing "Anatole of Paris" to the Goldwyn Girls as he continues searching through hat boxes. He then must emcee a fashion show, cluelessly describing Anatole's creations—until the real Anatole arrives.

Goldwyn could tell the boys were still a ways off. He pushed *Mitty* to the backburner and reassigned Freeman and Englund to polish *Kid from Brooklyn*. When they returned to *Mitty*, charged with writing the first full screenplay, the writers realized that the dreams had been the best-received component of their earlier work. So, they expanded the dreams from five to eight. Real-life Walter suddenly bursting into song seemed out of character, so he'd instead play Anatole Mitty in a dream. He'd also be sea captain, surgeon, RAF pilot, riverboat gambler, action serial star, knight and gunslinger. In the action dream, triggered when Mitty is drugged by the Boot, adventurer Walter defeats aliens in a forest and gorillas in a dungeon to rescue Rosalind just as a black-cowled figure is about to administer a hypodermic. In the knight dream, triggered when Mitty is about to wed fiancée Gertrude, Sir Walter Mitty arrives in a medieval courtyard to claim his princess and defeat Hollingshead in a sword fight, only to learn the Lord (played by Uncle Peter) has no niece.

The new dreams were fun, but brought the climax to a standstill and overpowered the few musical elements. Freeman had had enough. He had been against making the film a musical from the beginning and especially resented being forced to write in spots for the Goldwyn Girls. He courageously went to Goldwyn's office and told his employer exactly what he thought of his sense of humor. Freeman was canned.

"In fact," Freeman remembered, "I think I was responsible for that now-famous line which Goldwyn told Pat Duggan about me: 'That man will never work for me again… unless I need him.' As it turned out, he subsequently needed me, to come back on *Walter Mitty* and see it through and (for) a follow-up picture."

Still, the confrontation did cause Goldwyn to think. Was there a way to please—or at least quiet—the Thurber-backers? He decided to see what Thurber himself had to say. Late in November 1945, Goldwyn brought the 160-page screenplay to Thurber in New York. Goldwyn explained that while he was sure they were on the right track, he considered the last half of

the script to be "too blood and thirsty." Upon reading it for himself, Thurber
announced that he was "horror and struck." He thought the story was outra-
geously melodramatic.

Goldwyn returned to California in need of a release. So, the first thing he
did was release Ken Englund. A week later, Goldwyn called Englund back
to his office and handed him a plane ticket to New York. Englund was to
work with Thurber smoothing out the rough spots. Englund asked for
specifics. "I'll be specific!" Goldwyn thundered. "I hate the last 60 pages!"

Englund spent ten days with Thurber, beginning December 3, reading the
script section by section, six hours a day. With only ten days, Thurber was
convinced that it was too late to delete the thriller plot, so instead sought to
cover it up. He and Englund devoted some time to expanding Mitty's humdrum real life—building up conversations among the supporting players
during a card game and at a celebratory dinner at a Chinese restaurant and
giving Walter an early monologue at his office window feeding cookies to a
pigeon, Elmer, dreamily imagining where his feathered-friend has traveled.

Yet the outlet for most of the Thurber-style humor had to be the dreams.
And the bigger, the better, the more *time-consuming* Mitty's dream life, the
less time there would be to spend in reality. Thurber inserted dialogue from
his short story straight into the sea captain, surgeon and fighter pilot
dreams. He also suggested using more characters from Walter's real life in
his dreams. Mitty's rival in the gambler and cowboy dreams could be fellow
suitor Tubby. During "Anatole of Paris," Walter's acquaintances could be
modeling the hats—his fiancée Gertrude in a fur hat that's actually her dog
and barks into the camera, her mother in a hat made from the curtain rods
and muslin she wants from the department store, his mother wearing a
crown of flowers surrounding a sprinkling can that waters when she bends,
his boss Mr. Pierce sporting a birdcage derby with Elmer the pigeon inside,
and Rosalind in "a startling creation" with letters that spell WALTER.

Thurber wanted to add his short story's firing squad dream, inserted as a
resigned Walter stands in the rain outside a drugstore, where his mother is
buying him a sedative following a restaurant celebration dinner-gone-horri-
bly-wrong. Mitty, an international spy, declines a handkerchief and heroically faces a German firing squad. Major von Pierce lowers his sword. The
guns fire ta-pocketa, pocketa. Walter falls. Nurse Rosalind, crying, runs to
his side, kneels beside him, cradles his head in her lap, and strokes his face.
He looks happy and triumphant, even in death.

In the most recent script, Thurber detested a scene in which Walter was forced to visit the menacing Dr. Hollingshead, posing as a psychiatrist, who insists that Mitty merely imagined that the girl of his dreams was real. Thurber was concerned that the audience, too, would think Mitty crazy and lose sympathy for him. Instead, Thurber wanted Mr. Pierce to refer his own doctor, Ravenscroft, who advises plenty of rest and settling down with Gertrude.

In the chapel, in place of the knight dream, Thurber and Englund devised a Dutch dream. As Gertrude walks down the aisle, the electric fans in the background would dissolve into the windmills of Holland. The villagers would sing, dance and shower newlyweds Walter and Rosalind with tulips. The gaiety would be interrupted as Walt Van Mitty notices a trickle of water by his wooden shoes. The dyke has sprung a leak. Walter runs to plug the hole with his finger and sends Rosalind off to save the town. He gives her his wooden shoes to place by her heart, just before an avalanche of water crashes over him.

Englund incorporated Thurber's suggestions into his next draft. Goldwyn was unsure. He asked others on the lot, including Sammy Cahn, to read the script. Cahn loved it. "This is one of the most incredible scripts I have ever, ever read," Cahn said. "I've never read anything quite as good as this."

"Just wait 'til I get through with it," Goldwyn replied.

Indeed, the latest version made the entire studio brass nervous, fearing the Thurber stamp might cover the broad comedy that past Kaye writers emphasized. The solution: call in a past Kaye writer, Phil Rapp. Thurber was not pleased with the newest addition to the staff—and for good reason. One by one, Rapp began peeling away Thurber's changes. The first to go was the Dutch dream. Next was Thurber's beloved, yet equally fatalistic, firing squad dream. Instead would be a scene of equal emotion that allowed Kaye to sing a ballad from his stage act. After returning home from the psychiatrist, Walter looks down from his bedroom window and sees a policeman, stationed to keep an eye on him. The scene blurs to a Dublin alleyway, where Irish tough guy Walter O'Mitty is eluding the police in a final, mad desire to reach the side of his beloved Molly. But it's too late. Molly is dead, and Walter sadly sings "Molly Malone."

Thurber liked the Irish daydream, and was relieved to hear Rapp was integral in its creation. The humorist was devastated, though, to lose the firing squad sequence. In a last ditch effort to save it, he sketched out an entire courtroom dream, inserted during the psychiatrist examination, in which defendant Walter is sentenced to be executed, leading to a minimally revamped firing squad sequence.

By this time, with filming set to begin within days, Sylvia had become an even more active force on the project, albeit long distance. She had just learned she was pregnant, at risk, and her doctor advised against her flying back and forth between coasts. So she remained in New York, readying the musical numbers and sharing her wishes for the story by phone call and telegram.

Since, for the first time, romance was the primary motivation for Kaye's character (and Virginia Mayo would, for the first time, share top billing), Sylvia was determined that Danny look like a leading man. When she received photos of the costume tests, she immediately wired Goldwyn her displeasure: "Am certain it was not your wish that Walter Mitty be made into unattractive grotesque obvious comedy character. Since this is much stronger love story than other three pictures am almost sure you agree with me that it is necessary for Danny to look very personable although hen-pecked by his mother and boss in order make believable Rosalind going for him. Think he should be dressed at least as well and unobtrusively as Dingle in *Wonder Man*."

Sylvia's songs were also in flux. She had finished arranging "Anatole" and "Molly Malone." But adding the latter meant they couldn't use a ballad in the RAF scene. Hearing she was one number short, Sylvia's radio show protégé, Herbie Baker, suggested a new psychiatrist dream. Using trick photography, Walter could fantasize that he was lying on a therapist's couch, consulting with Shtickfortz Zolzein Von Mitty-Glick, the "Great Owstrian psychiatrist." Although the suggestion didn't address the film's need, Sylvia liked the idea and would later work with Baker to turn it into a specialty for Danny's stage act, "Stickfitz" ("Under the spreading psychiatry, the village psychoanalyst stands...").

Fine hatched her own idea for an RAF dream number, after hearing Prokofiev's "Peter and the Wolf," in which each character has its own musical theme and instrument. In Sylvia's composition, Danny would simulate the sounds of each instrument by "triple-tonguing," a skill she'd employed the year prior for a radio show number, "Concerto for Tongue and Orchestra." In the dream, Commander Mitty's fellow pilots would call on him to do his impersonation of their old music teacher, Professor Grünwald, and he'd perform "The Symphony for Unstrung Tongue" (later recorded as "The Little Fiddle"), introducing the heroine fiddle who resides with her wicked guardian, the French horn. They live substantially droll lives until along comes the handsome, young trumpet who, upon seeing the enchanting fiddle, "gets so excited that he has a solo passage." The cruel French horn is recognized as a German officer in disguise and is chased into a kettledrum, which is boiling. For Kaye, the number was a git-gat-gittle tour de force— exactly the type of number despised by Thurber.

As filming proceeded, Rapp continued making changes sure to irk Thurber. The straight psychiatrist, Ravenscroft, seemed superfluous, so Hollingshead conducted the examination—which included a shot of a Goldwyn Girl in a bikini.

Rapp also preferred that the movie end in real life instead of with a dream. In the script, newly promoted Mitty kicks back with an issue of his cowboy magazine and we close on his dreaming of overpowering Toledo Tubby. Rapp suggested closing the picture instead with a big gag, capitalizing on the casting of Boris Karloff as Dr. Hollingshead. At his new office, Walter would take Rosalind into the next room to show how the doctor's parole was working out—Karloff would be posing for the cover of *Terror Stories*, made up as the Frankenstein monster.

Even Thurber's title wasn't safe. Goldwyn engaged Audience Research Inc., the motion picture arm of the Gallup Poll, to survey random Americans on what they thought of the story and the title. The story tested off the charts, registering the highest audience acceptance rates they'd ever seen. But the title tested poorly, and few respondents had any idea it was a comedy. A substitute title, *The Beautiful Dreamer*, fared better, but still below average.

So Goldwyn had everyone involved in the production submit alternate titles. Among the suggestions: *The Great Mitty, Mitty the Great, Mighty Mitty*, and *The Schizophrenic Kid*. Staffers who were outraged that Goldwyn would even consider changing the title submitted a single suggestion, over and over again: *The Secret Life of Walter Mitty*.

Goldwyn then had Audience Research Inc. test the alternate titles. Some rated slightly worse (*Mitty, Walter Mitty's Secret*), some better (*Mitty's Private Affair, The Mighty Mr. Mitty, High Time),* and a handful significantly higher (*That's Life, That's My Affair*). Respondents, particularly women, most liked *I Wake Up Dreaming,* since the title suggested love, romance, dreaminess, music and mystery.

Twentieth Century Fox, however, had recently released a horror picture called *I Wake Up Screaming*. Goldwyn got permission from Daryl Zanuck to use his own variation, but eventually realized that publicity for the Fox picture may have skewed the testing. So, he decided to throw out all the test results and stick to *The Secret Life of Walter Mitty*.

Returning director Norman McLeod was among those who had hoped to stick as close to Thurber's tone as possible and put up mild resistance, unsuccessfully, to Goldwyn's changes. Art director George Jenkins recalled one of Goldwyn's correctional sessions: "Suddenly one day I had a call from Sam Goldwyn to come up to his office, and, also, the director had a call to come up to his office. I didn't know what it was all about. (Goldwyn) said, 'Sit down, please.' And he began to bawl out the director for not being captain of the ship. I was wondering what I was doing there. Actually, I was there to embarrass the director."

As expected, Danny found himself most in Thurber's world in the dreams. Aesthetically, the stark settings were heavily influenced by Jenkins' background on the New York stage. The art director recalled, "The dreams are sort of a milestone in the designing of motion pictures. I think that the skeletonized set of a western street is the first time skeletonized sets were used in films. And it started a trend, especially when television came along and everything was skeletonized, sort of in the same manner. But skeletonizing had been used in the theater, and I used it in the theater, so it was not any big deal."

Whereas Kaye's previous movies had him alternate between terrified milquetoast and hyperactive extrovert, the daydreams provided his first opportunity to play calm and collected. Despite tremendous dangers, he's "cool as a cucumber," whether portraying the seafaring Captain Mitty ("It's nothing. Just a broken arm."), the respected Dr. Mitty ("Your brother will play the violin again. I just grafted new fingers on him."), or "Slim" Mitty, the Perth Amboy Kid, throwing Tubby around the paper-thin props and porches.

The Mississippi gambler dream presented a special challenge. The script called for a sleight-of-hand artist whose fingers would be photographed performing fancy shuffles. But each time the camera closed in on his hands, the stand-in gambler would suffer an attack of stage fright and fumble the cards. Danny never enjoyed retakes, even if they were not of him. Impatiently watching from off screen, he volunteered, "Here, let me see if I can do that," taking the cards and his place at the head of the table. On the first try he had the deck ruffled and stacked so expertly that Kaye's hands, not stunt doubles, are the ones used in the final film.

Soon after primary filming was completed, Danny and Sylvia appeared

DREAMBOAT: Mitty's fantasy life, particularly the Riverboat Gambler and Irish day-dreams, afforded Kaye his first opportunity in movies to show his calm, confident side. [© 1947 Samuel Goldwyn]

on the radio show *We, The People* and talked about their upcoming movie. "It is based on a story by James Thurber," Sylvia said, adding in a low voice, "*was.*"

The constant changes pushed the production 21 days over schedule and well past its $1.85 million budget. But even by early 1947, with the entire film edited, Goldwyn still wasn't happy. The picture's running time far exceeded two hours, an eternity for a musical comedy. The Frankenstein gag at the end always seemed awkward, so it was an easy cut. The leads did have to be called back to re-shoot the office scene, though, to have Rosalind and Pierce appear together before Mitty drifts off to the cowboy dream. William Seiter, who was on the lot preparing for *The Bishop's Wife*, stepped in to direct the revised sequence.

There was also the problem of the cowboy dream itself. It seemed anti-climactic, since all the movie's conflicts had been resolved and Walter had already bested Tubby in real life. It was finally decided to move up the cow-boy dream, to when Walter is racing from the wedding chapel to the Boot's mansion. Howard Hawks, who was directing Danny in his next picture, oversaw shots of him eyeing a parade cowboy on the streets of Pasadena.

Into the summer of 1947, the picture was screened for preview audiences, and Goldwyn could tell problems remained. "It's too long," complained one viewer. "There's too much talk of always sending Danny to bed. The thought made me sleepy."

During previews, audiences loved the action scenes, but were bored by all the small talk involving Mrs. Mitty and Gertrude. Much of the gabbing set up the engagement dinner at the Chinese restaurant. Deleting the restaurant scene permitted removal of discussion of the celebration during the card game, Walter inviting Pierce to the dinner, and the henchmen driving away from the restaurant, realizing that they'd taken the wrong book from Mitty. The cuts quickened the film's pace considerably, despite creating an error in logic when, back home, Walter is shocked to see he still has the black book.

Preview audiences most enjoyed the dream sequences, with one exception—the touching yet depressing Irish dream. Danny Mandell, who had taken over as editor after shooting wrapped, always thought the dream detracted from the flow of the storyline. "I thought the whole thing was out of character," Mandell said. "The picture was much too long anyway. I didn't think it belonged in the picture. So I suggested dropping it out. (Goldwyn) didn't like the idea because he thought it was well done. About a week later, I suggested it again. He said, 'Let me think about it.' So about a week after that I was in his office and somebody came in. Mr. Goldwyn said, 'Listen, I've got an idea. I was thinking. Now just try to visualize this: The last thing we see is so-and-so and then instead of going to this, we leave out the 'Molly Malone' number. What do you think of it?' The visitor's comment was 'Not a bad idea, not a bad idea. Mmm, hmm.' So I said nothing and about a week later, Mr. Goldwyn asked me what I thought. I had already had the picture mounted in such a way so that all we'd have to do was to leave the reel out of the picture, as the sequence was mounted on a separate reel. That's how sure I was that he'd come around."

Sylvia was so distraught to hear the Irish dream might be cut, she suggested dropping "Anatole" instead, arguing that it was the sequence that "holds up story movement unnecessarily... I think cutting 'Molly' or for that matter any of the Irish dream would take away an important quality it gives the picture, since it differs radically from the other dreams in photography, mood and treatment."

At first, Goldwyn denied everything. "I have no intention of cutting 'Molly Malone,'" he replied. "Whoever told you that is not acquainted with the facts." A month later, he conceded, "I certainly have tried to keep the

'Molly Malone' dream in, but I find that it stops the comedy dead, and it is hard to pick it up afterwards."

Thurber's defeat was complete. Following a preview, the humorist remarked, "Anybody catch the name of this picture?" His disappointment was inevitable. Too mundane a Mitty would have made a boring movie, and too many dreams would have become repetitive. Even within the dreams, Thurber and the filmmakers were at odds. In the original short story and in the movie dreams Thurber championed (firing squad, courtroom, Irish, Dutch), Mitty stood heroic despite certain failure. Every daydream that survived the cutter's blade presented Mitty the Undefeated, victorious. Even as Anatole, he is a character in control.

The public loved the picture, ponying up more than $3 million—just short of *The Kid from Brooklyn's* take. Critics generally seemed to enjoy *Mitty*, but felt compelled to show some remorse over the exaggeration of the original. *The New York Times'* Bosley Crowther, in an all-too-typical review, pointed out that: "Much of the flavor of the Thurber character is lost because of the lack of contrast between Walter Mitty's dream world and actual experiences."

The lack of contrast, of course, was intentional. The short story's humdrum real life would have been torture to sustain for twelve Technicolor reels, so *Mitty: The Motion Picture* purposely sacrificed it in giving Walter two secret lives: his dream life and his perilous adventures in reality that go unacknowledged by everyone else. The picture is a success when judged not as a watered-down Thurber piece, but as a witty Danny Kaye romp.

A SONG IS BORN

(Filmed June 16 to Sept. 26, 1947; released N.Y. Oct. 19, 1948; wide Nov. 6, 1948)
Producer: Sam Goldwyn, for Samuel Goldwyn Productions, RKO Radio Pictures
Director: Howard Hawks
Screenplay: (uncredited Harry Tugend, Philip Rapp, Daniel Fuchs, Mel Shavelson, Ken Englund, Robert Pirosh, Everett Freeman, Roland Kibbee)
Original Story: *Ball of Fire* screenplay by Charles Brackett & Billy Wilder, from story "From A to Z" by Billy Wilder & Thomas Monroe
Songs: Don Raye & Gene de Paul
Cast: Danny Kaye (Hobart Frisbee), Virginia Mayo (Honey Swanson), Benny Goodman (Magenbruch), Hugh Herbert (Twingle), Steve Cochran (Tony Crow), O.Z. Whitehead (Oddly), Mary Field (Miss Totten), and as themselves Tommy Dorsey, Louis Armstrong, Lionel Hampton, Charlie Barnet, Mel Powell, Buck & Bubbles

Despite the wild success of their four films with Goldwyn, Danny and

Sylvia were miserable, professionally and personally. Since the days of *Let's Face It,* Kaye had been having a none-too-secret affair with co-star Eve Arden. Equally difficult, Danny had grown increasingly resentful of Sylvia's micromanagement of his career—simultaneously realizing that no one was better able to utilize his greatest talents.

Sylvia thought Goldwyn was the one smothering Danny. She wanted more control over his pictures and better integration of her music. She also was unhappy with the increasing attention being paid to Danny's leading lady. According to Virginia Mayo, Sylvia "didn't like my constantly being played opposite Danny. They wanted somebody different once in a while, and I could see how he would. After all, four pictures opposite him is a lot. But it didn't seem to bother Goldwyn, and he was the boss. Goldwyn was the one who cast, and he was not going to take any backtalk from Sylvia or whomever."

Even more, Fine was convinced that Goldwyn and his Hollywood henchmen were driving a wedge between her and her husband. Her pregnancy forced her to spend more time away from the studio, increasing her paranoia. Fine was contracted to pen a biography of Danny, hired a ghostwriter to do the actual writing, and—after seven months of research and writing—demanded the woman drop the project. The birth of daughter Dena, on December 17, 1946, consumed even greater amounts of time and energy.

After the holidays, Goldwyn had to decide on their fifth and final film together. Kaye's regular writers had been working on a period picture, *Hip! Hip! Hipplefinger!*, with Danny as a professor at a men's college that welcomed its first female student.

Goldwyn wasn't crazy about the story, but it did remind him of a superior romantic comedy he had produced six years earlier—*Ball of Fire*. In it, Gary Cooper played a shy professor who falls for stripper Barbara Stanwyck while researching the word "slang" for an encyclopedia. As he did with *The Milky Way* and *The Kid from Brooklyn*, Goldwyn figured he could take the earlier script, tweak the lead for Kaye, and add a bunch of musical numbers. Although he would be saving some pennies by remaking a property he already owned the rights to, Goldwyn vowed to make the next film the most elaborate musical he had ever done.

Goldwyn hired Harry Tugend, formerly an executive producer at Paramount, to develop the story, under the title *That's Life*—a title that had tested well as a possibility for *Mitty*. Tugend's primary task was transforming the old professors into classical musicologists researching jazz.

His first draft featured Kaye as Elmer Frisbee, an expert on pitch, who is constantly identifying the tones of car horns and other background noises. (When he overhears the crack of the housekeeper being socked on the chin, he comments, "D flat.") He and his five grizzled housemates are researching a history of music, but are fearful that they'll lose their funding with the passing of their benefactor, musical instrument manufacturer Daniel Totten. Yet when Totten's daughter pays a visit, she overhears the servant's son (Sugar Child Robinson) playing a raucous swing tune on the piano and consents to give the professors more time to incorporate modern music into their encyclopedia. For research, Frisbee visits a nightclub and ends up on stage performing a staple of Kaye's stage act—an overeager, off-key "Begin the Beguine." He later leads the professors in "When You and I Were Young, Maggie" at his bachelor's dinner, "The Battle of Jericho" during the rousing finale, and serenades singer Bubbles Brown with an undetermined "sentimental ballad." After Bubbles moves into their home to hide from the cops, the now-perky professors awaken the next morning and, one by one on their instruments, join a cheerful mockingbird in song. Frisbee joins in last, gently singing the tune toward Bubbles' window. As their song nears its finish, Bubbles groggily approaches the window, slams it closed, and returns to bed, pulling the covers over her head.

Naturally, Tugend's basic plot remained the same as *Ball of Fire's*—much to his boss's surprise. Upon reading the first draft, Goldwyn exploded: "This is lousy! Here I'm paying you big money, and all you did was change the words!"

Tugend's second stab incorporated more slapstick, particularly during the early scene in which the professors meet Miss Totten. An organ grinder is performing outside, and his monkey sneaks in an open window. The animal hides underneath the table where Frisbee and Totten are sitting, and starts slapping their knees—to Totten's gigglish pleasure and to Frisbee's nervous compliance. As Totten gets up to leave, the monkey slips a banana peel in her hand. Frisbee is inspired for his quest when the monkey starts playing jazz piano (using a piano-playing chimp that was currently performing at the Hollywood nightclub Slapsy Maxie's).

For a musical, the story still didn't feature much music. So an early idea was to hire Benny Goodman and other famous jazz artists to play the parts of the professors. The filmmakers, however, quickly realized that casting young hepcats as the professors worked against the premise of the movie—since they all were supposed to be out-of-touch codgers. So, after casting

Goodman as one of the old-timers, the rest of the parts went to grizzled character actors. The change in direction puzzled Goodman, who wondered why he was cast as one of the "longhairs."

Goldwyn then hired Don Raye and Gene de Paul ("Cow-Cow Boogie," "Mr. Five by Five,") to write two hip tunes—an establishing number for the leading lady ("Daddy-O") and a group number on the history of music, in which Frisbee would conduct the guest artists ("A Song Was Born").

In late February, Sylvia arrived on the lot, exactly as she had at the end of the four previous winters, to begin writing special numbers for Danny. She hated not just Tugend's script, but the whole idea for the picture. She thought jive was dated. That the gangster story was overused and too similar to *Wonder Man*. That the professor character, "as written and conceived for Gary Cooper, didn't begin to be rich enough in comedy values for Danny." And, most of all, she considered it ridiculous to remake a well-known picture after only six years, unless it was changed so completely "that the audience thought it was seeing something fresh." Goldwyn asked what if they turned it into a period picture? Sylvia loved the idea, saying that that single switch should satisfy all her objections. She got to work writing specialties for Danny and, after four weeks in California, returned to New York.

Days later, she learned that Goldwyn had not only changed his mind about the period setting—making most of her work unusable—but also claimed that Sylvia's involvement so far, in fact her entire visit to California, was unsolicited. He insisted that he had never requested her to leave New York. Fine was stunned.

Tugend was able to incorporate some of Sylvia's ideas into his third screenplay, which resurrected a theme alluded to in *Ball of Fire*—comparing the nightclub singer and the professors to Snow White and the seven dwarfs. The picture would open outside the institute, where Frisbee would be telling the neighborhood kids, in song, the story of Snow White, accompanied by his fellow professors on their instruments. Each character in the tale would have his own musical theme. Frisbee's increasingly uncomfortable and sensual descriptions of Snow White would betray his own repressed desires. Thereafter in the script, characters would make frequent references to plot points in Snow White. Sylvia also wanted to use one of Danny's standbys, the high-pitched "Airy Fairy Pipers," for the window-side serenade.

When the time came for a fourth draft, the first of seven rewriters—Phil

Rapp—was brought in to punch up the comedy. When the nightclub singer (renamed "Honey" since they could no longer use "Bubbles" once they signed musical duo Buck and Bubbles) leads the professors in a jam session, Rapp suggested she sing the text from a racing form to the melody of *Rigoletto*. And, at the climax, as the professors race to New Jersey to break up Honey's shotgun wedding to a gangster, Rapp suggested one professor be shown riding on a motorcycle with a second sitting on the handlebars, another professor on a fire truck, one in a police car, one in an ambulance, one in a tank leading a line of tanks, and the seventh crazily driving Miss Totten's car.

To direct, Goldwyn wanted Howard Hawks, who helmed *Ball of Fire* and was just finishing up *Red River* with John Wayne. Hawks hated the idea of remaking his earlier hit and had no desire to ever work again for Goldwyn. He preferred to produce his own pictures, and had little patience for Goldwyn's endless suggestions and revisions. Finally, Goldwyn offered Hawks the astronomical sum of $25,000 a week. Hawks reluctantly agreed, solely for the money. Both were miserable during the production, Hawks knowing that he had sold out and Goldwyn knowing that he'd overpaid for his services.

Hawks, feeling that he'd done the story perfectly the first time, did everything he could to change the remake back to the original. He reinstated original dialogue that the revisionists had dropped, had the names of several of the professors revert back to their former names, hired the same actress to play Miss Totten, and, whenever possible, directly copied staging and camera angles from *Ball of Fire*.

Most of all, Hawks wanted nothing to do with any of Sylvia's numbers. As a goodwill gesture, Goldwyn told her he would pay for up to two numbers at $35,000 each, with the stipulation that Danny not be allowed to perform the numbers on stage or radio for five years—a clause sure to be rejected by the Kayes. Sylvia opted instead to devote her time to developing ideas for Danny's next film—apart from Goldwyn. Kaye would be left without a single song in the entire picture.

Once filming began, Kaye acted nothing like an unflappable Gary Cooper. His mind was preoccupied with Eve Arden, who had separated from her husband months before and whose divorce would become final in late July. Coupled with his growing resentment toward Sylvia and pending split with Goldwyn, Danny was uncharacteristically somber on the set. He began seeing a psychiatrist.

Virginia Mayo remembered Kaye, during filming, as "a little depressed, but I thought perhaps it was just because he didn't have any numbers in the picture." Hawks, on the other hand, found Danny a "basket case."

A tipping point came midway through filming, on August 22, 1947, when the Kayes signed a long-term deal with Warner Brothers. The contract signified not only a break with Goldwyn, but also a new commitment to Sylvia. For the first time, she would also serve as associate producer, ensuring even greater micromanagement for the next five years.

Less than two weeks later, on September 4, Danny moved out of the Kaye home. The parting was not amicable. "They were bloody well estranged," said family friend Johnny Green. "It was a terribly, terribly unhappy time for both of them and a very difficult time for people like my wife and I, who wanted to be friends. We didn't want to take sides. We wanted to be open and there for both of them, and it was not easy. We did all we could do to juggle the balls."

To the papers, Sylvia blamed her husband's moodiness: "Danny and I talked things over for a week," she provided, "so I cannot say he walked out on me. The trouble just seemed to snowball into something definite... I love Danny. He's nervous and unhappy, and it's been difficult for him with the baby in the house."

Her husband gave his view of the split: "No outside influence caused the separation. In the process of becoming successful professionally, our personal relationships got a little bit lost. So we decided on a temporary situation so we could stand back, look at our marriage objectively, and try to figure out a way to make a go of it.

"Don't think I fail to appreciate Sylvia. She was perfectly content to work through me, let me be the big guy. But I didn't want things that way. I believe in people standing on their own feet and retaining their own identity. I think that to belong to somebody truly, you must first belong to yourself. To make other people happy, you must first be capable of making yourself happy. So I'm chiefly interested in Sylvia's finding a personal happiness and keeping her own individuality. If we, as two distinct individuals, can work toward the same goal, I think our marriage is saved."

As much could not be said for the latest picture, which was going through its own identity crisis. Halfway through production, Goldwyn had again turned to Audience Research Inc. The title of the featured tune, "A Song Was Born," tested slightly higher than *That's Life*. But the present tense, *A Song Is Born*, rated even one point higher. So Goldwyn adopted the

DISCHORD: The less-than-harmonious musical *A Song Is Born* reteamed a sullen Kaye with Virginia Mayo. [© 1948 Samuel Goldwyn]

latter, forcing disk jockeys who played the song to introduce it as "from the motion picture of *almost* the same name."

That picture turned out to be a forgettable one. Kaye's character not only doesn't sing, he rarely smiles. Somehow, all the charm of *Ball of Fire* was lost in the translation. The jazz overlay made the remake loud and disjointed, and left no screen time to differentiate between, let alone develop the supporting cast. The professors of the original movie were like seven lovable dwarfs, each with his own special area of interest. Those of the remake, in studying the same subject, became a pack of indistinguishable white beards. In fact, they're so interchangeable, that in early drafts of the screenplay, most of their dialogue was attributed to "A Professor" or "Another Professor."

Ball of Fire scenarists Charles Brackett and Billy Wilder were so mortified at *A Song Is Born* that they refused screenwriting credit. Harry Tugend, too, wanted his name left off the film and, to his deathbed, was miffed whenever someone uncovered his participation. "I don't know how you got my name," Tugend would say. "There were other writers on it, but the director did what he pleased. I know of no other picture with no writing credits."

The only writer who wanted credit was Thomas Monroe, who helped Billy Wilder with the short story that inspired *Ball of Fire*, thereby forcing Wilder to receive some billing, as well.

Through one of the most extravagant advertising campaigns in the studio's history, Goldwyn attempted to persuade the public that Kaye left him on a high note. It didn't work. The film's cost had ballooned to $2.85 million—nearly a half-million dollars over budget and far beyond what it could ever hope to recoup at the box office. Danny, suddenly alone, had his first flop in Hollywood.

IV.
INTERNATIONAL ICON

A MAJOR FACTOR in leaving his wife and his boss, the two people most responsible for Kaye's previous successes, was a constant striving to be famous as himself. The public associated him with Sylvia's lyrical characters and Goldwyn's movie milquetoast; neither was the persona he wished to be known as.

The closest he'd come to developing his own version of "Danny Kaye" was on stage. Even after he'd made his mark in Hollywood, Danny continued to perform on stage while between pictures. Live audiences gave Kaye a feeling that no movie could.

Danny had moved beyond nightclubs. He had graduated to playing "presentation houses"—large movie theaters that featured live acts between the picture showings. A dance team would open, followed by singer Georgia Gibbs, and then Kaye would perform a half-dozen or so routines. In between each number, as his comfort increased, he began fine-tuning this character of Danny Kaye, part silly, part sophisticated, completely endearing.

To become more accessible and demonstrate that he wasn't strictly a zany, he'd typically include a ballad. Initially, Sylvia and Max Liebman wrote him an Irish folk-type song, "Eileen." He later substituted "Molly Malone." By the late 1940s, he'd instead perform a subdued version of the jazz standard "Ballin' the Jack," a simple, catchy song that his audience could leave the theater humming, and one that accentuated the graceful, fluid motions of his hands, arms and legs. His hands had, in fact, become such a noticeable feature of the show that he added a routine just for them. The house lights would go dark and a lone spotlight would shine on his two hands, as he flickered them about, as if they were playing a harp or performing a ballet.

Kaye aspired to break the anonymity that typically exists between performer and audience. "The first time I violated that anonymity was in Chicago," Danny confessed. "I had the audience snapping its fingers with me when suddenly I stopped and said, 'Somebody isn't snapping! Turn on the house lights. I want to spot the culprit!' They turned the house lights on and the stage lights off, and the audience was transformed into performers. I looked at all those people and said, 'So this is who I've been dealing with?' It drew one of the biggest laughs I've ever heard, although it was an embarrassed laugh, for suddenly I had contrived to put the audience on the stage."

In early 1948, he decided to give this "Danny Kaye" character the ultimate test: a six-week engagement at the London Palladium. Danny had heard all the rumors about staid, emotionless Englishmen. Fellow American performers, including the recently embarrassed Mickey Rooney and Rita Hayworth, related horror stories of their poor receptions in Europe. Kaye himself remembered his own disastrous stay at the Dorchester ten years previous.

When he arrived in London, Danny invited the press up to his hotel room. He was surrounded by a tribe of savage reporters anxious to pounce on another Hollywood personality. Kaye, though, acted like a curious kid from Brooklyn. To their surprise, he pretended to be uninformed and open-minded regarding international politics, but willing to listen and learn. The meeting became casual and comfortable, and the next day's coverage was kind.

Despite the head start, Danny remained apprehensive come opening night, February 2. The first half of the program—a parade of singers, dancers, comics and acrobats—went over well with the packed house. Now it was time for the second half, featuring just Kaye. The master of ceremonies, comedian Ted Ray, sped through a brief introduction, concluding with "… and here is Danny Kaye!" While a surge of applause followed, Danny didn't. He remained frozen backstage until a production manager, prompted by Ray's second "… and here is Danny Kaye!," shoved him on stage.

All Danny needed was the push-start, for it jolted him into an electrifying 55-minute performance. The entire audience appeared breathless, mesmerized by every imitation, story, song and dance. Every routine seemed fresh and spontaneous, as if he made it all up on the spot. For his finale, Kaye led the enthusiastic throng through each verse, pronounceable and otherwise, of "Minnie the Moocher."

After the show, Danny was mobbed by well-wishers, including one visitor in particular: a frail, stern old man with flowing white hair and a black opera cape. He stared grimly at Kaye. The performer looked up to face Hannen Swaffer, the most famous and most feared of all London critics. "My boy," the gentleman began resolutely, "I have been going to the music

halls for 50-odd years and I have never seen a greater personal triumph." He
paused for a moment, as if the compliment had left a bad taste in his mouth,
and then added gently, "Mind you, you didn't make *me* laugh."

Kaye went on to make headlines for the remainder of the run. He
received more than a thousand fan letters and gifts a day, inundating his
dressing room. Audiences were convinced that they'd just spent an hour not
with a stage character, but personally, intimately interacting with the real
Danny Kaye.

"Never have I encountered such warmth, such enthusiasm, such deep
emotion," Danny was quoted. "Here, when I give the audience some emotion, I can feel it coming up from them. It goes back and forth in waves."

It was during his stint at the Palladium that Kaye first worked out the
most sincere element of his act, the "sit down spot." As Danny recounted:
"I had been playing golf that morning. I was doing a dance routine. I felt a
little beat, so I sat on the apron of the stage—that's the space on the audience side of the footlights—and I said to the crowd, 'I think I'll sit here and
rest for a minute.' I bummed a cigarette from someone in the first row, and I
told them what had happened to me that day on the golf course. So after
sprawling there on the stage apron and having a little visit with the folks
until I felt refreshed and relaxed, I stood up and went on with the performance. Since then, I've always worked that interlude into my shows."

Breaking conventions themselves, King George VI and his queen attended a Kaye performance. It would be the first time not only that the royal
family attended a vaudeville show that was not a command performance,
but also the first time they bypassed the royal box for the cozier front row
seats. During the show, Danny casually ad-libbed that he could use a cup of
tea. A stagehand tiptoed behind him with a steaming cup in hand. "Danny,"
the King pointed, from his seat, "your tea."

In preparation for the special performance, accompanist Sammy Prager
went to great extremes to impress his kingship. He bought a new suit and
got a haircut. In the middle of the show, noticing his assistant's trim, Danny
politely pointed a finger and chanted, "Sammy got a haircut, Sammy got a
haircut, Sammy got a haircut!" The audience roared and joined in the chant.
Later, Prager admitted, "I could feel the blood rushing to my face until I
was sure I looked the color of a Maine lobster. I glanced out into the audience and could hardly believe my eyes. There was the King singing along
with the crowd, 'Sammy got a haircut!'"

After another evening's performance, Kaye was posing for photographers when they suddenly redirected their focus. Danny turned to find Winston Churchill laughing heartily and stealing the cameramen's attention. "Hey!" Kaye shrieked. "Come on back here now! I'm the star of this show and a guest in the country besides!"

In a private chat, Churchill conceded, "Young man, you have a fantastic ability. You lift your little finger and they respond. I'm very happy you're not in politics. You'd make a formidable adversary."

Meanwhile, Danny had achieved what he had set out to do: to be successful as himself. It wasn't the sneezing Russian tenor or the off-key ham warbling "Begin the Beguine" that the audience loved, but rather the entertainer behind the routines. Kaye realized that, mentally, he had conquered the primary barrier that separated him from Sylvia. So, the couple spent a lot of time together on the phone during the rest of Danny's stay in London, each having softened a little.

On closing night at the Palladium, the audience refused to let Kaye quit. When the show went past 11:00, the hour the last bus left and underground transportation called it a night, the crowd shouted, "We'll walk home!" As the mandatory closing hour of midnight approached, the evening had to end. As Kaye wrapped up his final goodbyes, someone started to sing "Auld Lang Syne." The crowd joined in. Danny began to cry.

Before returning home, Kaye sent his family all the gifts from the admiring British. He showed up on the doorstep soon after. "I'm sure it's going to work out this time," Sylvia promised. "We're going to try hard to make a success of our marriage." Seven months had been enough time to sort things out and come to an understanding. Kaye broke off his relationship with Eve Arden, permanently. He would have many more romances in the years to come, but henceforth it would always be understood that he would never divorce Sylvia. He owed her too much, he told inquiring friends. And, too, now that he had proven to himself that he could be loved and appreciated as "Danny Kaye," rather than Sylvia Fine's puppet, he could better appreciate—rather than resent—her direction.

When Danny returned from England, he came home for good. Convinced they were no longer temporary roommates, the Kayes bought their first home, a roomy white brick Georgian fronted by a large pool and patio in Beverly Hills. They would also maintain a luxurious apartment in New York, which allowed them both to be closer to entertainment's main hubs, even when Danny's temperament required they be separated.

Soon after, Kaye received a return invitation to the London Palladium, this time to appear in the Royal Command Variety Performance on November 1. Never before had the King requested a specific performer for the annual benefit. This time, Sylvia would be coming along.

Firsthand, she witnessed the hysteria. Ticket prices for the single show were doubled, up to $84 per seat. The theater accommodated 2,800. It received 100,000 applications for tickets. Egged on by Eddie Dukoff, shrieking mobs of bobby-soxers had to be restrained by police. Five girls fainted. A clanging fire engine stopped nearby to answer a false alarm, heightening the tension.

The three-hour extravaganza featured 300 performers in 30-some acts, including thirteen-year-old soprano Julie Andrews. But everyone was waiting for Kaye. He stayed on for 30 minutes, twice as long as anyone else. He did not disappoint. As the royal family left the theater, Sylvia was presented to them. "Tell your husband how much we enjoyed seeing him again," the Queen said.

Sylvia, though, was a much tougher critic. "This is what caused all the excitement six months ago?" she thought, as she headed for Danny's dressing room. She greeted him with a litany of complaints about his performance, until she noticed a British reporter scribbling in the corner. Reading her own critique in the morning paper, Fine vowed to become more sensitive to her husband's moods. "I've learned not to jump on him as soon as a number which didn't come off is over," she would say. "I've learned to wait a week before discussing it. Right after the show is definitely not the time to bring it up; however, Danny can tell by my face how I have reacted. I can't hide it from him."

Kaye's trips to London had firmly drawn the line between the former Borscht Belt clown and the new world-class entertainer. Ed Sullivan accurately summed up the phenomenon when he later wrote: "Danny Kaye has registered the greatest success any American or, for that matter, any British act ever scored at the Palladium."

Kaye's stage act—not to mention Kaye himself—would never be the same.

THE INSPECTOR GENERAL

(Filmed Aug. 16 to Nov. 10, Dec. 6 to 11, 1948; Jan. 8 to 13, July 13 to Aug. 1, 1949; released N.Y. Dec. 30, 1949; wide Dec. 31, 1949)

Producer: Jerry Wald, for Warner Bros.
Assistant Producer: Sylvia Fine

Director: Henry Koster (uncredited David Butler, Philip Rapp)
Screenplay: Philip Rapp, Harry Kurnitz (uncredited Ben Hecht & Charles Lederer, Jack Rose, Peter Viertel, Millard Lampell)
Original Story: *Inspector General* play by Nikolai Gogol
Songs: Sylvia Fine ("Medicine Show Number," "Brodny Brodny," "The Inspector General," "Soliloquy for Three Heads," "Happy Times," "Gypsy Drinking Song," "Lonely Hearts")
Cast: Danny Kaye (Georgi), Walter Slezak (Yakov), Barbara Bates (Leza), Elsa Lanchester (Maria), Gene Lockhart (Mayor), Alan Hale (Kovatch), Walter Catlett (Colonel Castine), Rhys Williams (Inspector General)

During negotiations with Warner Brothers, Danny's agent, Abe Lastfogel, sought $200,000 per picture for Danny and $100,000 for Sylvia, plus half the profits. Lastfogel contended that Goldwyn was willing to pay a similar salary, plus 25 to 30 percent of net receipts, but the deal fell through due to a disagreement over television rights. No matter how close the agent claimed he was on a deal, privately the Kayes were dead set against another long-term deal with Goldwyn.

Professionally, Sylvia had won the battle over Danny—convincing him that she, not Goldwyn, knew what was best for him in movies. Although Goldwyn was willing to put forth the cash and the class, at the end of the day, each picture would ultimately be a Goldwyn picture, with Danny's talents and Sylvia's music shoehorned in. Sylvia convinced Danny that they should be providing input from the start. She needed to be a primary force in creating the project and following it through from first concept through filming to final edit, the whole time tailoring it to Danny's unique talents.

Midway through filming *A Song Is Born*, Danny and Sylvia signed a five-year, five-picture deal with Warner Brothers. Danny would receive $150,000 per film to star, Sylvia $50,000 to act as composer and associate producer. Plus, they would share one-third of the profits—stipulating they were to be paid in separate checks. The couple would also get their own office on the lot. Danny would receive his own secretary, accompanist, "star dressing room," stand-in, and the right to approve choice of story, director and leading lady. Virginia Mayo, who was released by Goldwyn when he realized that with no Kaye he would have no use for her, was also headed for Warners, but she knew that the Kayes "would not stand for" her re-teaming with Danny.

Kaye was to make one picture a year—all musicals, all in Technicolor—with the freedom to make movies for others in between. And if the first deal worked out, he had an option for a follow-up ten-year deal.

Sylvia was charged with approving an appropriate story idea. She suggested remaking *Three Men on a Horse*, about a milquetoast who's held captive in a bar when the patrons discover he has a knack for picking the winning horses out of a racing form, or *The Man from Blankley's*, a turn-of-the-century play about a drunk who, wandering into a fancy dinner party, is mistaken for a special guest. Producer Jerry Wald bought the rights to *Father Goose*, envisioning Kaye in the role of a young comedian discovered by Keystone comedy director Mack Sennett.

Instead, they settled on *The Inspector General*, a 100-year-old Russian play that Sylvia first considered for Danny's return to Broadway. The period piece concerned a rascally visitor to a small town who, mistaken by the corrupt local officials as an investigator for the czar, begins demanding bribes and woos the mayor's wife and daughter. The impostor escapes, just as the town learns his true identity—and that the real government inspector is on his way to visit the mayor.

Although the play made for biting satire in the 1840s, Warners insisted on substituting an unidentifiable central European backdrop in place of the politically incorrect Russian setting. In addition, the play had no love interest and zero sympathetic characters. Sylvia suggested the story be rewritten as if for Charlie Chaplin, in the vein of his pathos-filled *City Lights*. Most importantly, the music was to progress—not interrupt—the story.

For the screenplay, Warners hired Ben Hecht and Charles Lederer, the team behind *His Girl Friday* and other top screwball comedies. Sylvia met with Wald and the screenwriters in late October 1947 to hash out a plan of attack. They decided to depict Danny as a soldier who has just finished fighting in some minor offshoot of the Napoleonic wars, arriving home weeks after everyone else. An opening sequence would establish his character as "Chaplinesque—pure in heart, ingenuous still ingenious. He is a little man concerned with little things." He bursts excitedly into town, but by now the locals are tired of closing up their shops to have parades to greet returning soldiers. Learning he's lost his girl and his job, he leaves in search of a new life. On the way, he falls in with a crafty, world-wise "Svengali." They reach a town run by crooked officials, who confuse Danny for the inspector general. His first impulse is to tell them they're mistaken, but he is quieted by his companion. Danny catches the eye of the mayor's amorous daughter, but he is attracted instead to a peasant whose family has been bankrupted by the authorities. Eventually, Danny is exposed and leaves the town—the citizenry enriched, but himself no better off than when he arrived.

The story conference was so productive, the group agreed there was no need for a detailed treatment. Work could begin immediately on a screenplay. Six weeks later, Hecht and Lederer handed in a 200-page snoozer, ironically titled *Happy Times*. Kaye was to play Fefi, a Hungarian army cook captured by the French, who is given his freedom after posing as a slain soldier in Napoleon's victory portrait. The starving simpleton wanders into a village and, unsuccessful begging for food, tries to fool a waitress into thinking he has money by rattling his money pouch, which is full of nails. He's nabbed attempting to swipe a goose from a diner's plate. Fiesty peasant Gita follows him to jail, where the corrupt councilmen assume he must be Napoleon's inspector. They release Fefi and throw him a party, where he's propositioned by the mayor's wife and daughter and nearly poisoned by an assassin. The officials then try to bribe Fefi, even as he's stalked by the French-hating peasants, led by Gita's father. In the end, Fefi locates the peasants' pilfered riches, and they jail the mayor and his cronies. As they begin to throw Fefi a party, the Hungarian army arrives—refusing to believe the war has ended—and tears their old cook away from Gita.

The problems with the script were glaring. It was too talky, with dull, pages-long conversations between extraneous characters. It lacked both warmth and comedy. Fefi and Gita spent little time together. There were no dance numbers. There was zero suspense, since at no time was Fefi in danger of being exposed. And the story didn't really get started, with Fefi being mistaken as the inspector general, until nearly an hour in. In fact, as story consultant Harry Kurnitz noticed, the hero walked around in a complete daze until page 107.

With Kurnitz's help, Hecht and Lederer were given six more weeks, imperiling the hoped-for spring start date, because Sylvia—determined to integrate her songs into the storyline—couldn't begin work on the music until she knew what the story was.

Their second screenplay placed greater focus on "Fefe" and gave him a comic sidekick—Minerva, a dancing circus bear he rescues from gypsies. Gita is even more fiery, anxious to raid the jail to free Fefe. And Fefe is more proactive—he unsuccessfully tries to get the bear to perform in a tavern, he introduces himself as the inspector general, and he buys a farmhouse for Gita's family, endearing him to the peasants who earlier wanted to kill him. The French army arrives and imprisons Fefe and the other officials. But, with the guillotine ready, Fefe is rescued by his friends in the Hungarian army and Gita encourages him to return with them to war.

The story improved, but now read like a patch job. It was time to take a step back. Other writers, including Jack Rose (who was busy readying *Three Men on a Horse* for Danny), were temporarily pulled off their projects to produce a treatment. Rather than a soldier, Danny became Georgi, a hapless gypsy who's ejected from camp by burly Yakov because he's too honest. Yakov promises Georgi the bear when he gains some experience in deception and "accomplishes something." The writers also wanted to make Georgi's love interest and the rest of the peasants more sympathetic and downtrodden, rather than a bloodthirsty mob. The villagers just want their church organ back. It's the town council that will plot to kill Georgi. At the finish, the real inspector general shows up, and Yakov pickpockets his credentials. But, unable to stand silent as the inspector is to be executed, Georgi confesses. For his honesty, the inspector general is about to anoint him the new mayor, but Georgi declines, preferring to rejoin the gypsies and his bear.

Kurnitz and Phil Rapp then expanded the treatment into a full screenplay. Rapp's primary focus was adding laughs. He was finally able to work in Danny's "Busy Eater Routine," which he'd earlier, unsuccessfully, tried to slip into *The Kid from Brooklyn* and *A Song Is Born*. The bit—in which Kaye maniacally without pause chewed, drank, seasoned, cut, buttered, etc.—was born one night years before when Danny went to dine at a Chinese restaurant. Sitting nearby was a man who was energetically filling his face without pause. Kaye was so intrigued by his eating style that he spontaneously began imitating the customer. From then on, Danny could send friends into convulsions whenever he sat down at a dinner table. The routine would not play quite so hilariously on film.

Finally, filming could be scheduled to start at the end of the summer and Sylvia could begin work on the music. In May 1948, she proposed five numbers—a "Medicine Show" number for Georgi to sell Yakov's worthless elixir, a "Road Song" as Georgi wanders in search for food, a long specialty piece "like the 'Lobby Number'" as Georgi at a reception describes the arts in Vienna, a hiccupping song, and a quartet Georgi sings with reflections of himself in giant mirrors, like Harpo Marx's triple harp number in *The Big Store*.

Sylvia incorporated the hiccupping idea into the medicine show number when she realized she also needed a town anthem and a love song. But by the time filming began on August 16, she had barely started work on the two elaborate specialty numbers. By then, another full script had been completed, but Kurnitz still wasn't happy with it, convinced that it ran too long and lacked laughs. So he and Rapp would spend their days on the set, trying to devise gags on the spot and slowing down production.

The cast wasn't even secure yet. Production was already underway when Warners struck a deal with Twentieth Century Fox for their stock actor, Lee J. Cobb, to play the mayor. Cobb refused. More than two weeks into filming, Warners finally signed Gene Lockhart instead. Cameras were rolling for over a month before the studio recruited Elsa Lanchester as the mayor's wife, after being unable to hire Joan Blondell, June Havoc, or Eve Arden. To Danny at least, Arden's "no" must not have come as a surprise.

Warners also hired Walter Catlett to play the inspector general's near-sighted war buddy—but they had to pay him daily and weren't allowed to announce that the venerable comic was in the picture until it was finished. Catlett, it seems, owed a fortune in back taxes. Co-star Benny Baker explained, "When actors owed money, the IRS would look at *Variety* and *Hollywood Reporter* every day to see who was working, and they would run right to the studios and garnish their salaries. (Catlett) wouldn't work by the week, he'd work by the day. He'd get paid every day. Although he worked twelve weeks, he was getting paid every day, so they couldn't get the money from him."

It didn't help that there were more producers than they knew what to do with—studio head Jack Warner, producer Steve Trilling, executive producer Jerry Wald, line producer J.W. Wright, and associate producer Sylvia.

Although Danny and Sylvia technically reconciled after his return from London in February 1948, working together remained touchy. Johnny Green, who composed the film's score and acted as musical director, said, "Sylvia and Danny were not exactly enthralled with one another during the making of that picture. It was a terrible atmosphere most of the time. Those things create like smog. It becomes very hard to breathe. The atmosphere was not charged with love and amity, (and) the word was that Sylvia, who was an important creative force on the picture, was hard to please."

Henry Koster was an accomplished director of musicals who had just finished *The Bishop's Wife* for Goldwyn, but was ill prepared for Hurricane Sylvia. Behind his back, she had been complaining about many of the director's changes to the script.

Then, come the first day of rehearsals—for the medicine show number to be shot at Corrigan Ranch—Sylvia had so many suggestions and directions, even calling music director Green out to the ranch to discuss finer points, that the crew couldn't even line up their lighting instructions. The Warners executives were incredulous. "You're not lighting Bette Davis!" one exploded. "This is a comedy!" But the brass knew they had to tread carefully with Sylvia, while simultaneously not driving off the director. Koster made clear that he had the authority on the set. He said he was happy to listen to Fine's suggestions, but in the end all decisions would be his. The studio just asked that he not "cross any bridges," and that they would step in if she caused further trouble.

Fortunately, Sylvia was primarily preoccupied with her musical numbers and, once she had made her preferences clear, returned home to resume actual writing of the numbers. But whenever she was on the set, Koster was miserable. After each shot, Koster would ask Danny to shake his head to indicate whether or not he was happy with the take. Kaye would first respond "yes," then "no," then back to "yes," unable to make up his mind— a notorious habit of his wife's. Then someone noticed Sylvia, off to the side, directing her husband which way to shake his head.

Fine didn't make life any easier for editor Rudi Fehr. "Johnny Green was very friendly with the Kayes," Fehr remembered, "and he came to my cutting room on the first day of shooting and said to me, 'Now, I want you to meet Mrs. Kaye, Sylvia Fine. She's going to work with you on the editing,' which didn't make me too happy because who wants the new associate producer to tell you how to cut the film? But I am somewhat of a diplomat, and I said, 'Wonderful. I'd love to work with you, Miss Fine.' And we got along fine. All of a sudden I realized she was making crazy cuts. She had one-frame cuts and things like that. When Danny Kaye said, 'Beep!,' she ordered a cut of just the 'Beep!' But we could hardly see it; it's not right. I also knew she had her mind set on what she wanted. So I did something naughty as far as Mrs. Kaye is concerned. I cut two versions and ordered two prints. I ordered a black-and-white and I ordered a color print. And during the day I worked with Mrs. Kaye and cut it all the way she wanted it, and then I came back at night and cut it the way I wanted it.

"And then came the day of reckoning, the sneak preview, and Mrs. Kaye did not know it was not going to be the version she had cut. After the preview, Sylvia said to me, 'Fine friend you are.' I felt terrible and I said, 'Sylvia, I didn't know what to do. I didn't want to argue with you. And yet my obligation is to cut the picture the best I know how. It's very unusual that an associate producer who has never worked as an associate before tells me how to cut a film after I have cut so many pictures myself. Jerry Wald

IN TUNE: Family friend Johnny Green wrote the score for *The Inspector General*, while helping to keep the peace around the set. [© 1949 Warner Bros.]

came to my rescue, but she still went up to the front office and complained about me. But Mr. Warner knew what I was doing."

At Sylvia's insistence, Green wrote a score to stress every movement Danny made on screen. "Johnny Green did a fantastic job," acknowledged Fehr. "He was so meticulous in the score. He actually what we call 'Mickey-Moused' the music. Danny worked with his entire body, so a twitch of the face, (Green) would catch it with the music. He'd cue a gesture of the arm. He timed it with his walk and all." The score would win Green a Golden Globe Award.

Because Danny had agreed to return to London November 1 for the Royal Command Performance, he hoped to finish the film by the end of October. Kaye worked overtime to complete as many of his scenes as possible, and Koster juggled the shooting order, saving the scenes Kaye wasn't in until after he had left. With Danny and Sylvia in Europe, Koster spent the first week of November directing the other actors' scenes. Then he was done. After 66 days of shooting, he'd met his contractual obligations and, with a new project looming, he was finished with the Kayes, even though Sylvia still hadn't completed her two main specialty numbers. Editor Fehr directed a day of "pick ups," then filming shut down for several weeks to give Sylvia and the gag writers an opportunity to catch up.

David Butler stepped in as the new director and began rehearsing a gypsy violin and sword dance sequence on November 29. It led to an audience participation number, in which Danny broke the audience into thirds and had each section sing a different nonsense phrase. "The Gypsy Drinking Song" became the highlight of the film and a permanent addition to Danny's stage act.

Butler oversaw six days of rehearsals, followed by six days of shooting new sequences and re-shooting a few that seemed to lay flat, particularly the medicine wagon show. Butler thought he'd finished the picture, even though Sylvia was still scrambling to finish her "Triple Mirror Number." A few weeks later, the director agreed to five more days of filming, adding little bits of business, retakes, pick-ups, and continued tinkering with the medicine show.

For all the fiddling, "The Medicine Show Number" never did click. All the additions and subtractions created a disjointed mess that kept stopping and restarting. The filmmakers even knowingly retained a continuity error (at one point, Danny leaps on to the wagon inexplicably wearing spectacles), to avoid drawing out the scene any further.

Unfortunately, a series of sneak previews confirmed that the film was still short on laughs. Sylvia insisted her musical numbers be re-cut and the mirror song be filmed. So Phil Rapp was called back to write and for eleven days direct four new scenes, namely a slapstick encounter involving wrestlers and tumblers, and Sylvia's "Triple Mirror Number." In the song, Georgi ruminates on how best to play the inspector general, whether arrogant (Russian), elegant (Englishman), or smart (Viennese). But fitting

Danny and three full-sized reflections into the movie frame at one time proved difficult. So the number became "Soliloquy for Three Heads," with the heads of Danny's three doubles floating above him.

The one hang-up was the censor board misunderstood Sylvia's climactic lyric as a profanity. The three visages urged Georgi to "Give 'em the fist. Give 'em the wrist. Give 'em the finger." Sylvia had to explain that "giving the finger," with an index finger alongside the nose, represented the Viennese Danny's thoughtful attitude.

At the same time, the author of a Canadian radio program, *The Happy Time*, threatened to sue if Warners used the title *Happy Times*. The studio reluctantly reverted to *The Inspector General*.

"Eighteen months I worked on this picture," Fehr noted. "It was the longest picture I've ever worked on. When we had it all together, it didn't work somehow. It laid there. There was no excitement. We added sequences, and still there wasn't enough entertainment. We took it out for previews, and we still felt the audience was somewhat bored. We monkeyed around with it different ways. And it just wasn't there. The (additions) made the picture somewhat come to life."

The Inspector General was finally released on the last day of 1949. Reviews were mixed. Despite two years in the making, with everyone striving to create something epic and unique, the film turned out to be yet another vehicle that Danny had to carry by himself. Sylvia's numbers, as it turned out, were the only things worth carrying. The story overworked tiny incidental gags at the expense of the best one—Kaye never takes advantage of his tramp suddenly gaining power. He's too busy being sympathetic.

Such flaws weren't detected by many in the audience, but only because there weren't many in the audience. Some had begun buying televisions and spending their evenings at home. Even costlier for the studios, the end of the war closed off countless foreign markets. Some of Kaye's films for Goldwyn had made almost as much money internationally as they did in the U.S. *The Inspector General*, on the other hand, grossed nearly $2 million in the states—and next to nothing overseas. Danny took the picture's losses particularly hard. He saw how Sylvia's fingerprints were all over the troubled production. Her role had to be tweaked.

Warners wasn't any happier with the experience. Still, the studio hoped for smoother sailing with the Damon Runyon gangster yarn *Stop, You're Killing Me*, to be directed by Rapp and produced by Kurnitz as payback for their standing by *The Inspector General* for so long.

Danny didn't want to go through a fiasco like that again. He was supposed to begin rehearsals for the new picture on January 2, 1950, but asked for a one-week extension. During the break, he approved the casting of Lauren Bacall as his leading lady, but then asked to postpone the start of production for another two weeks so he could accept a stage engagement in Florida. When he returned, he could stall no longer. Less than six weeks after the release of their first film together, Kaye persuaded Warners to release him from the five-year contract. Sylvia was paid for the fourteen weeks she'd put in so far as producer on *Stop, You're Killing Me*.

All parties maintained that the contract was torn up "on a friendly and amicable basis." Few at Warners were looking forward to working again with Sylvia. And, Danny was through being a studio's long-term contract player. He consented that, if an acceptable story could be found, he'd be happy to work again for the studio, under a single-picture deal. It would take 20 years before he'd make another Warners-distributed film, as a supporting player in an independent production.

As Kaye would later say: "Even a picture like *The Inspector General* taught me something. It taught me never to make another movie like that one!"

MOVIE CAMEOS

I Am an American (Warners, 1944)

Screen Snapshots: Out of This World Series (Columbia, Nov. 27, 1947)

Screen Snapshots: Hawaii in Hollywood (Columbia, Jan. 22, 1948)

Screen Snapshots: Hollywood Friars Honor George Jessel (Columbia, July 8, 1948)

It's a Great Feeling (Warners, filmed Aug. 20 to Oct. 16, 1948; released Aug. 12, 1949) During production on *The Inspector General*, Warners required Danny to put in one day's worth of work on the cameo-fest *It's a Great Feeling*. Kaye and the other guest stars were not originally slated to appear, but right before filming began star Dennis Morgan uncharacteristically rejected the script. Yet, an expensive score had been written. Production was to start in a few weeks. There was no time to build new sets. So writers Mel Shavelson and Jack Rose were called in, and decided to have the story take place in a movie studio. All the studio contract players were rounded up to contribute one quick scene apiece. Danny performed a short comedy routine at a railway station.

Paramount News No. 75 (Paramount, May 1954) In Johannesburg, South Africa.

Paramount News No. 83 (Paramount, June 1954) In Johannesburg, South Africa.

Screen Snapshots: Hollywood Beauty (Columbia, May 5, 1955)

Screen Snapshots: Playtime in Hollywood (Columbia, Jan. 19, 1956)

ON THE RIVIERA

(Filmed Sept. 18 to mid-Dec. 1950, late Feb. 1951;
released N.Y. May 23, 1951; wide May 25, 1951)
Producer: Sol C. Siegel, for Twentieth Century Fox
Director: Walter Lang
Screenplay: Valentine Davis, Henry & Phoebe Ephron
Original Story: 1934 play *The Red Cat* by Hans Adler, Rudolph Lothar, adapted by Jessie Ernst
Songs: Sylvia Fine ("On the Riviera," "Scotch Number," "Popo the Puppet," "Rhythm of a New Romance," "Happy Ending"), Chris Smith, Jim Burris, & Andre Touffel ("Ballin' the Jack")
Cast: Danny Kaye (Jack Martin/Henri Duran), Gene Tierney (Lilli Duran), Corinne Calvet (Colette), Marcel Dalio (Philippe Lebrix), Jean Murat (Felix Periton), Henri Letondal (Louis Foral), Clinton Sundberg (Antoine), Sig Ruman (Gapeaux)

Although Warners had promised that they would cast Danny in a wide range of films and allow him to approve major facets of each production, at the end of the day, they would all be "Warner Brothers-type" films, drawing from the studio's limited stock company. Warners was not equipped to produce, for instance, musicals of the distinction and originality of MGM or the opulence of Twentieth Century Fox.

So, once unfettered from his Warners contract, Danny became a free agent, able to pick and choose from any type of role, from any studio. Immediately, the Kayes jumped at two offers—both true, big-budget musicals, one from Fox, one from MGM.

Under production chief Daryl F. Zanuck, Fox was known for provocative dramas with the likes of Gregory Peck and Tyrone Power and over-the-top show biz spectacles with Betty Grable and Alice Faye. All-out comedies were not its forte. Danny would receive his most adult role to date, one quintessentially Fox rather than Kaye—since Fox had created the role years before, for other actors.

But Danny seemed a natural choice, since it was another "double" role that required singing and dancing. The sexual farce (about a nightclub entertainer hired to impersonate a playboy financier, confusing the performer's jealous partner and the businessman's wife and colleagues) had been used by Fox twice before—as *Folies Bergere de Paris* (1935) with Maurice Chevalier and as *That Night in Rio* (1941) with Don Ameche and Carmen Miranda. Zanuck went to the well a third time looking for a tax deduction. The previous summer, while vacationing on the French Riviera, he shot loads of footage of the beach, cliffs and town. Zanuck would then produce a film called *On the Riviera* in which his actors would play their scenes in front of a rear-projection screen showing his home movies.

Zanuck enlisted Valentine Davies (*Miracle on 34th Street*) to revise the screenplay. Davies' primary contribution was turning the amorous financier into a world-famous aviator, Henri Duran. But his script was short on humor and heavy on dialogue. Henry and Phoebe Ephron were brought in for a polish and to trim Duran's interminable speeches. They focused on playing up Kaye's nightclub alter ego character, Jack Martin, as both a singer and a celebrity impersonator, even suggesting a comical scene in which Martin, impersonating Duran, boards a private plane and begins inventing aeronautic terms. The Ephrons also, inspired by Davies' inclusion of a Chevalier impression as a tribute to *Folies*, had Kaye do a brief impersonation of Carmen Miranda, with a wastebasket on his head, as a nod to *That Night in Rio*.

The Ephrons' scripts were rife with sexual innuendo that slipped past the censor board. In Duran's first scene, as he disembarks from a two-day, non-stop, round-the-world trip and is passionately greeted by a bevy of women, he announces that he is so tired all he'd like is a bottle of champagne. "After that, I would like to go to bed for a week. Who will join me..." he briefly pauses, "...in cheering my brave comrades?"

What did catch the censor's eye was Davies' climax, in which the aviator heads to the bedroom with his wife, while pretending to be the entertainer. "The last part of the story," warned the board, "seems to be based in large measure on the suspicion of illicit relationships between the various characters." The censor suggested changing the sexual escapade to merely romantic advances and eliminating the shot of Duran heading to the bedroom door. The Ephrons eliminated the shot, but retained the possibility that Duran spent the night with Lilli. Again, the censor reiterated: "It should be *affirmatively* clear that he does *not* go into her bedroom." The final film cuts past the entire incident, but it becomes abundantly clear after the fact that he and his wife slept together.

Fox engaged Sylvia to write the musical numbers, but to do no more. The news of her behavior at Warners had gone viral and, as a condition of employment, she was barred from the set of *On the Riviera*.

Davies' original script provided her with suggestions for four musical numbers for Kaye's entertainer character: an opening song (Chevalier's standard "Valentine"), a closing song ("Goodbye, Girls, I'm Through"), an extravagant, showgirl-packed production number in which the entertainer impersonates Duran, vowing to end his days as a Lothario, and "Bebe

Needs Nouvelles Chaussures," a comical song for the entertainer to perform on television, based on the introduction of crap tables at Monte Carlo, describing a Frenchman's bewilderment at such terms as "petite Joe" and "les yeaux de serpent."

The Ephrons tweaked the list: opening with a Chevalier-like rendition of "On the Riviera," impersonating Jimmy Durante singing "Some Enchanted Evening," and intimately crooning Kaye's latest recording, "C'est Si Bon," in the nightclub lounge.

As her first bona fide musical, Sylvia would compose or arrange ten numbers before she was through—although only about half would make it to the final film, including "On the Riviera," the big production number "Rhythm of a New Romance," the "Happy Ending" finale, and a snippet of a "Scotch Number."

Since Danny was playing a comical nightclub performer, he was filmed performing three of his regular nightclub routines, the nonsensical "German Concert Song," the off-key "Begin the Beguine," and "Ballin' the Jack." For each, he was accompanied by Sammy Prager, outfitted in a fake mustache to make him look French. Prager shared the stage with Kaye for the first two numbers and played as part of a lounge trio during "Ballin' the Jack."

As filming drew to a close, however, Zanuck wasn't happy with the preponderance of solo pieces. He loved gaudy, over-the-top production numbers. In addition, the "German Concert Song," coming seconds after "On the Riviera," slowed down the start of the picture. It was cut.

In place of "Begin the Beguine," Zanuck preferred something more elaborate—but filming was drawing to a close and Sylvia was a notoriously slow writer. That's when director Walter Lang overheard Danny humming "Popo the Puppet," a tune his wife had written to entertain their three-year-old daughter. Upon hearing the lyrics, Lang suggested costuming Danny as a marionette and suspending him by ropes like Howdy Doody. Kaye and the other dancers would be controlled by eight puppeteers who employed a system of counterbalance weights to operate the ropes and the performers.

The child's song became the most memorable feature of an otherwise adult film. The tune, though, showed that Sylvia's proclivity for borrowing was not without risk. She, Danny and the studio were sued over "Popo the Puppet" by one Count Popo DeBathe, a well-known San Francisco Bay Area clown who often included puppetry in his act. The clown claimed they stole his name. After three years of litigation, Popo settled out of court.

STRINGS ATTACHED: Danny frolicked as a life-sized marionette in "Popo the Puppet," Sylvia's eleventh-hour addition to *On the Riviera*. [© 1951 20th Century Fox]

Viewing a rough cut of the picture, the Ephrons were torn. "It didn't seem to have many laughs, which bothered us," Henry Ephron recalled. "But it was definitely a picture with class, well made, quite beautiful, and Danny's performance, as usual, was marvelous. It wasn't and never could be *An American in Paris*, but it wasn't a clinker either. In any event, the picture cost $2.7 million, and no matter what ideas we might have about new scenes or new shooting, there wasn't a chance that Zanuck or (Fox president Spyros) Skouras would put up another penny."

For his parts, Danny seemed comfortable in both roles—as both fast-talking entertainer Martin and as Duran, suave, well-dressed, monocled, with a touch of gray at his temples to add distinction. Since Martin's a nightclub performer, Kaye could play the character crazier when he was performing and straighter once he stepped off the stage. (Although, once the "German Concert Song" got cut, there wasn't much frantic Danny remaining even on stage.) Playing calmer, more realistic characters didn't necessarily do the film any favors. As *New York Times'* Bosley Crowther pointed out, Kaye's "stern impersonations of the two look-alike men are so close in pattern and texture that the contrast lacks humorous novelty."

So, too, Danny's best roles were those tailored specifically to his talents. This was warmed-over Don Ameche—acceptable if you were Ameche or any other of Fox's interchangeable leads of the period, whose songs were presented as on-stage acts, rather than integrated into the storyline.

On the Riviera didn't quite break even at the box office. Undeterred, five years later, Fox asked Kaye to star in *Can Can*. Danny declined, and Frank Sinatra got the part.

Meanwhile, the other picture Kaye had agreed to in early 1950—a musical *Huckleberry Finn*—had been in the works at MGM since 1944. But it wasn't until late summer 1951 that the studio settled on a final script and score. Arthur Freed would produce, Vincente Minnelli direct, and Gene Kelly choreograph and star as con artist The Duke, with Kaye as his comic sidekick, the Dauphin. Although Dean Stockwell as Huck and William Warfield as runaway slave Jim would be the central figures, the story would be shaped to give extended screen time to the Duke and Dauphin.

Rehearsals began in the fall of 1951, but just before the start of filming, both Kaye and Kelly pulled out. Kelly, wrangling at the time with MGM over a contract, opted to go to Europe to create the experimental *Invitation to the Dance*. Kaye—according to Kelly—was dissatisfied with playing a supporting role in the picture. Danny took the time, instead, to prepare for a larger role, one that would leave little doubt as to who was the star.

HANS CHRISTIAN ANDERSEN

(Filmed Jan. 21 to May 26, 1952; released N.Y. Nov. 25, 1952; wide Dec. 19, 1952)
Producer: Sam Goldwyn, for Samuel Goldwyn Productions, RKO Radio Pictures
Director: Charles Vidor
Screenplay: Moss Hart (uncredited Konrad Bercovici, Gilbert Gabriel, Myles Connolly, Robert Ardrey, Harold Lamb, Allen Scott, Jo Swerling, Henry Bellous, Ted Sears at Disney, Don Hartman & Mel Shavelson, Noel Langley, Samuel Taylor, Frank Partos, Ken Englund)
Original Story: Myles Connolly

Songs: Frank Loesser ("Anywhere I Wander," "I'm Hans Christian Andersen," "Inch Worm," "The King's New Clothes," "No Two People," "Thumbelina," "The Ugly Duckling," "Wonderful Copenhagen")
Cast: Danny Kaye (Hans Christian Andersen), Farley Granger (Niels), Renée Jeanmarie (Doro), Joseph Walsh (Peter), Philip Tonge (Otto), Erik Bruhn (Hussar), Roland Petit (Prince), John Brown (Schoolmaster), John Qualen (Burgomaster)

In the three years since Kaye and Goldwyn parted ways, the actor had become an international phenomenon, despite starring in two under-performing movies. The producer, meanwhile, had begun cutting back on production. Goldwyn was searching for a crown jewel to cap his career, something big and colorful, an epic musical to surpass even his Oscar-winning *The Best Years of Our Lives*. So in 1950, he committed to finally producing a film on the life of Hans Christian Andersen.

As Goldwyn told Kaye, "I am out to make this picture the greatest thing I have ever made. I honestly believe that if it is handled properly, it can be even greater than *Best Years*—and believe me, I have never said or even dared to think that much about any other picture. This picture can open a new era in motion picture making because it has such a combination of universal appeal, human tenderness, believable comedy, magnificent spectacle, and opportunity for unparalleled artistry. If its elements are handled with the touch they deserve and put together with the loving care they should have, we will have a triumph the like of which has never been seen in the history of this industry."

Certainly, Goldwyn had nursed the project along slowly. He first got the idea to depict the beloved Danish writer of fairy tales back in 1934. The real-life Andersen was, by all accounts, a lovable figure, though his life was hardly the stuff of fairy tales. His father was a small-town cobbler, his mother a washerwoman, and his grandfather an asylum inmate. His difficult childhood, scarred by his father's death, was eased only by the tales he heard from his grandmother. At his earliest opportunity, Hans moved to Copenhagen, where he became an actor, singer and dancer. Benefactors encouraged him to write a play, put him through school, and—after he relocated to Paris—produced his dramas and novels. The highest praise, though, was reserved for his fairy tales.

Goldwyn envisioned the story as a drama for Gary Cooper or Walter Huston. His first treatment, penned in 1937 by biography specialist Konrad Bercovici, employed names, places and events from Andersen's life, but dramatized them with creative license. Bercovici titled the story *A Stranger at Home*, because Andersen would find fame first in foreign countries. The writer invented a gypsy woman who predicts that newborn Hans will one day achieve greatness, rather than grow up to be a cobbler like his father. Yet 25 years later, Hans finds himself running his father's workshop, despite his talent for writing. He's content to stay home and marry Selma, the miller's daughter, but his mother convinces him to go to Copenhagen to fulfill the gypsy's prophecy. Hans leaves a trail of broken hearts as he pursues his writing career in Copenhagen, Germany and Paris. But after one of his plays flops, he returns to Denmark. This time it is Selma who sends him back to the world capitals to continue his career and ultimately prove the gypsy correct.

Goldwyn turned the treatment over to drama critic and novelist Gilbert Gabriel, who pointed out its myriad flaws—the story rambled and lacked both conflict and a climax. Gabriel suggested cutting the number of women in Hans' life down to two—since "the romantic tug belongs to the stay-at-home peasant girl and the world-famous (singer) Jenny Lind." Writing should be Andersen's "habitual escape from sophisticated grown-ups into the world of elves and witches, where he could be again a happy kid." Aware that Goldwyn had noted choreographer George Balanchine on the payroll, Gabriel suggested including snippets from operas and ballets, and ending with a grand ballet finale featuring favorite characters from his fairy tales. "After all," Gabriel told Goldwyn, "Andersen was no holy historical character, and nobody outside of the city fathers of Copenhagen can object if we give the facts of his life more color and vigor."

Goldwyn had several other writers pen treatments before passing the project to Myles Connolly, who had written novels featuring a youthful, good-hearted iconoclast, Mr. Blue. Connolly noted the earlier scripts failed because their star was "a drab and petty figure." Andersen had to be more like Mr. Blue, and his life story needed to be more like a fairy tale. Connolly renamed the story *Once Upon a Time* and envisioned Hans identifying more with the children than the adults. In fact, whenever the kids of the village can't be found, the parents and teachers deduce they are in the cobbler's shop, listening to stories. A famous ballerina also takes a liking to Hans when, after repairing her slippers, he shares the story of the "Loyal Tin Soldier" (illustrated on the screen in ballet). After the town gossips see Hans with the ballerina, his sweetheart realizes he doesn't belong in a small town ("You're a swan in a pond of ducks") and encourages him to strike off for Copenhagen. Arriving first in France, Andersen gets a job at the king's castle, where he befriends the gardener (who's really the king in disguise).

Convicted by the lessons of Hans' tales like "The Naked King," the king takes pity on the peasants and institutes major reforms.

Goldwyn continued passing the project from writer to writer, who expanded the ballet connections and stressed the idea of a cobbler with revolutionary ideas, adding increasingly political overtones as World War II approached. In 1941, Goldwyn considered teaming up with Walt Disney, who was developing his own Andersen picture, *Stagecoach to Odense*. Goldwyn would produce the live action segments—told in flashback, as a triumphant Andersen returns by coach to Odense—and Disney would create six animated fairy tales.

The project then lay fallow, until it was dusted off in early 1945 with Kaye in mind. Don Hartman and Mel Shavelson, however, recognized that the Andersen under consideration did not fit into the mold that Goldwyn had earlier mandated for Danny.

As the writers instructed Goldwyn: "If we look at Danny Kaye in terms of Eddie Cantor, this is not a vehicle for him. It can, however, we believe, be made into a most original, imaginative, important and successful picture, combining all the elements desired for a Danny Kaye picture, and no one we know could play the part of Andersen more superbly than Danny.

"It must be done as a fairy tale and not the conventional love story. It, therefore, must not be thought of in terms of a conventional boy-meets-girl Hollywood story. The love story is mainly between Hans and the children of the world, who would be represented in our picture by one outstanding child of the caliber of Margaret O'Brien. She would be the sister of Anna, the girl in Odense, with whom Hans is in love.

"It is a necessary part of the story, and we have no interest in this property, unless Hans leaves the little town of Odense for the city of Copenhagen for the sole purpose of going to see the King, and unless it maintains the theme of greed and cruelty versus kindness, gentleness, and happiness (this does not have to be political).

"Wherever we could we would accent the story for comedy possibilities to brighten it up for Kaye, and we already have several ways of inserting music even in typical Danny Kaye style. We also believe we could eliminate the ballet dancer and the Dumas scene and the publishing of the books, which have no relation to the fairy story."

Instead, Hartman and Shavelson's narrative, entitled *The Cobbler and the King*, revolved around a little girl following Hans to Copenhagen, where they meet the king disguised as a gardener. The boss promptly shelved the project, for the next five years.

By 1950, Goldwyn had seen Kaye's public persona mature, to the point where he could finally accept him playing more than warmed-over Eddie Cantor. Danny coveted the role of Andersen, as did Jimmy Stewart. Since Goldwyn wanted to make a whimsical musical, Kaye was the natural choice. Casting Stewart would necessitate a straighter, more down-to-earth drama, with the music reserved for the ballet sequences. Stewart did share Goldwyn's preference for Henry Koster as director—and Stewart's interest would help in negotiating with Kaye.

Kaye's agents demanded $200,000 for a maximum of sixteen weeks of work—the same conditions Danny had gotten from Fox for *On the Riviera* and from MGM for *Huckleberry Finn*. Goldwyn tried to haggle, offering less money and asking for more time and an option on a second picture, *The Adventures of Walter Mitty*. Danny held firm, arguing that it wouldn't be fair to make different deals at different studios. Kaye also refused to sign for more than one picture, since he didn't know when—if ever—Goldwyn planned to make the *Mitty* sequel and didn't want a commitment hanging over his head. And, finally, after the nightmare of *The Inspector General*, he would not, under any circumstances, work with Koster ever again. Danny didn't require director approval; *anyone* else was fine.

Goldwyn still needed a script. He told the newest flood of writers that one element was non-negotiable: like the recent hit *The Red Shoes*, his movie also had to revolve around a ballet version of Andersen's tales. In fact, he'd already signed *The Red Shoes'* star, dancer Moira Shearer, to play Hans' love interest. Through the first five months of 1951, four different writers, alone and in pairs, cranked out eleven more scripts. Most retained Andersen's revolutionary publishing of "The King's New Clothes," although Goldwyn was cooling on the idea. The mood of the country had changed considerably since the pre-war days that originally inspired the plot point. Other scripts started from scratch. One had Andersen drift off into a dream world of his fairy tales, in the vein of *The Secret Life of Walter Mitty*. Others wove in more details from Andersen's real life, heeding the requests of outside forces calling for a more accurate portrayal of their beloved storyteller.

With time running out, Goldwyn—according to Mel Shavelson—"decided he wanted a real heavyweight on it." The producer took the two screenplays he liked best, Connolly's fifth draft and Jo Swerling's second, and began offering the job to some of the biggest writers in the business—

Robert Sherwood (*Best Years of Our Lives*), Ruth Gordon and Garson Kanin, Paul Osborn. He finally signed *Lady in the Dark's* Moss Hart, for $75,000 plus five percent of the profits.

Hart insisted on scrapping all 27 outlines, treatments and screenplays that came before him. Goldwyn did force him to retain several plot points from *Once Upon a Time*, including the ballet finale and the idea of making Andersen's life a fairy tale. Consequently, Connolly would be credited for the original story—a sore point for Hart, who maintained that he never read any of Connolly's (or anyone else's) previous drafts.

Hart's approach, he told Goldwyn, was "that the same innocence of the fairy stories should be preserved in the character of Andersen himself, and in the story you finally choose to tell. There must have been in Andersen a strong vein of child-like purity and naiveté that both impelled him and allowed him to create the stories themselves, and I suggest that the story of your picture be an innocent and disarming one, so that the fairy tales seem a complimentary part of it and further the telling. Once embarked on his journey, his adventures in Copenhagen should have the same fairy-tale unreality of the man himself. His is the kind of child-like faith that moves mountains, for people no matter how cynical or sophisticated are somehow touched by innocence. In short, Andersen applies to the ordinary rules of human behavior the unswerving belief of a child that all things are possible, and in his contacts with the ballet dancer and the kind, it is this quality which proves the open sesame and enables him finally to complete his journey back to Odense with the same fairy-tale reality of one of his own stories."

Hart boiled every element down to its simplest form. Hans the cobbler loves sharing stories with the children, to the dismay of the schoolmaster. So apprentice Peter encourages Andersen to head to Copenhagen, where he falls in love with a ballerina. He writes her a fairy-tale ballet, but returns home when he realizes she loves another, her husband, the harsh director.

For the music, Goldwyn unsuccessfully tried to get Richard Rodgers and Oscar Hammerstein. He momentarily considered Sylvia, but Hart wanted Frank Loesser, whose *Guys and Dolls* was the talk of Broadway. Loesser demanded a substantially higher paycheck—ten percent of the profits. Goldwyn agreed, realizing he had to get the project moving.

Loesser worked closely with Hart to make the music part of the storyline. He wrote nine songs for the picture, although one—"The Shoe Song," in which Hans advertises his services as he arrives in the Copenhagen marketplace—was replaced by a reprise of "I'm Hans Christian Andersen." Other tunes were the exuberant "Wonderful Copenhagen," the love song "No Two People," the ballad "Anywhere I Wander," and four fairy tale songs ("The King's New Clothes," "Inchworm," "Thumbelina," and "The Ugly Duckling").

Although it took Hart four drafts to please Goldwyn, his basic story remained unchanged from his first version to his last. The revisions were primarily cuts, since adding in all of Loesser's songs plus three ballets— including a marathon seventeen-minute finale—could have pushed Hart's early drafts to three hours.

As well, director Charles Vidor had changes of his own. One alteration, however, Hart successfully resisted. Vidor wanted to play up Hans' anguish and motivation for returning to Odense by having the ballerina kiss the ballet master in front of Hans. Hart pointed out that by that point in the scene, the ballerina was already aware of Hans' feelings for her. "Thereafter," Hart argued, "she tries as best she can to shield him from further hurt and would not ever even impulsively kiss Niels in Hans' presence or make any overt gesture of love towards Niels."

Another suggestion Hart gave in on. On the first pages of the script, Hart used as his symbol for Andersen a kite that yearns to soar. So, he planned to end the movie as Hans and Peter are walking back to Odense. Hans vows that he's finished with storytelling, just as they come across a little girl, crying because her kite is caught in a tree. As Andersen starts untangling her string, he tells the story of the kite that refused to rest, leading Peter to observe that Hans would never stop telling stories. Vidor, though, wanted to end the picture musically and in a less complicated, drawn-out fashion, with a reprise of the song that described Hans' transformation, "The Ugly Duckling." Hart suggested a compromise—that they instead reprise "Thumbelina" after Peter rescues the kite. Finally, Hart relented and wrote a new, substitute ending, with Hans back in the village, singing a brief medley to the children and the now-appreciative adults.

Days before rehearsals were to begin, Moira Shearer discovered she was pregnant and had to drop out of the cast. With such short notice, choreographer Roland Petit volunteered the star of his Paris Opera Ballet company, his wife-to-be, Renée Jeanmarie. Although an exquisite dancer, "Zizi" threw tantrums over her costumes and haircut and, once the cameras started rolling, suffered an acute spell of stage fright. Worse, she spoke very little English and labored to learn how to pronounce her lines, one word at a time, through her thick French accent. One scene in particular, in which she

SPINNING TALES: In *Hans Christian Andersen*, Danny first showed his special connection with children. [© 1952 Samuel Goldwyn]

was supposed to call her husband an oaf, required take after take as she kept calling him a "great oof" and a "great off." Danny showed little patience for the dancer's poor English speaking skills. After a preview, Sylvia even complained to Goldwyn, "There were occasional lines of Jeanmarie's that I found impossible to understand."

On film, Kaye came across as positively charming. Admittedly, Hart's story and dialogue were simplistic, the ballets ran too long, and the songs—while glorious—told all the fairy tales, so there was never an opportunity to represent the tales visually. Yet Danny, lighting up the screen whenever he broke into song, carried the show.

Over the last two years, Kaye had begun recording songs and stories for children, but *Hans Christian Andersen* caught his special rapport with kids for the first time on film. "He was so pleasant and wonderful with children," confirmed John Qualen, who played the burgomaster. "He loved the kids, and he had them all in love with him."

In the public's eyes, the film would forever link Danny with the sweet, wide-eyed storyteller—to the point that moviegoers believed the character replicated Kaye's off-screen personality. Moviegoers didn't believe Danny Kaye was Hans Christian Andersen so much as they went away thinking Andersen was like Danny Kaye.

That, of course, was sacrilege for Andersen's legions of admirers. As soon as word got out that Goldwyn had settled on a completely fictitious storyline, the Andersen worshippers came out in full force. Just as *The Secret Life of Walter Mitty* was attacked for giving Mitty a daily life comparable in thrills to one of his fantasies, *Hans Christian Andersen* was criticized for turning the storyteller's life into an Andersen-like fairy tale. Danes were against any deviation from the facts of Andersen's real life. Most vociferously, they criticized the casting of Kaye as their beloved folk hero, fearing he would "clown up" the role.

The Danish foreign office asked Goldwyn if it could produce a historically accurate short film that could be shown in tandem with his Hollywood version. Goldwyn refused, explaining that he wasn't pretending to make a factual biography. Instead, he started the picture with a quasi-disclaimer: "Once upon a time there lived in Denmark a great storyteller named Hans Christian Andersen. This is not the story of his life, but a fairy tale about the great spinner of fairy tales." The Danes were left to issue a pamphlet on Andersen's life, featuring an introduction by Danish American actor Jean Hersholt, that they hoped would be handed out at theaters showing Goldwyn's film.

After filming was completed, Kaye headed to Europe. After four straight years appearing at the Palladium, he instead agreed to a three-week tour of British music halls. Danny ended the trip with a conciliatory stop in Copenhagen. "I came here to see if you would murder me," he told the Danes. Kaye went from the airport directly to a mammoth statue of Hans Christian Andersen in one of Copenhagen's central parks. There, he laid flowers and scaled the monument to embrace Andersen's likeness. By the time he climbed down, the thousands of onlookers were cheering. Danny had to be carried on the shoulders of policemen to get through the mob. Later that afternoon, Kaye visited the Danish Premier at the Parliament and handed him a copy of Moss Hart's script. The next day, Kaye visited Andersen's birthplace-turned-museum in Odense, where he was asked to

ALL SMILES, AT LAST: Kaye, Zizi Jeanmarie, and producer Sam Goldwyn were back on friendly terms at the premiere of *Hans Christian Andersen*.

pose for photos in Andersen's bed—infuriating the Hans Christian Andersen Society.

Still, Danny returned to the country's good graces the following evening by appearing in a charity BBC radio broadcast. During the one-hour benefit, he even sang a popular Danish folk song.

Copenhagen grew even more thankful when the release of Goldwyn's film and, in particular, the song "Wonderful Copenhagen" boosted tourism by 50 percent—even though the song incorrectly pronounced the city as Copen-haw-gen instead of Copen-hay-gen. In addition, experts soon discovered that the bed Kaye reclined on at the Andersen Museum was a replica. The genuine four-poster was found safely stashed in the museum's attic.

By the time Danny returned home, Sylvia had hatched a plan to promote the movie, as well as her husband's image and pocketbook. In the film, Danny sang every song in the score. Each one had hit written all over it. Kaye immediately added several of the tunes to his stage repertoire. So Sylvia proposed Danny record them all for an album to be sold in movie theater lobbies. As she explained to Goldwyn, "When people come out of a musical, that's when they want to buy the record." Loesser was furious. "Listen! I'm not in the Danny Kaye business! I'm in the Frank Loesser business! I'm not interested in Danny's record being *the* record. I want everybody who sings to record these songs." Nonetheless, Sylvia figured everyone benefited—and it helped promote the movie, so Goldwyn was on board.

Both the film and the soundtrack album became unqualified hits. Although production records show the movie cost just a few thousand dollars more than its $3-million budget, Goldwyn touted its price tag as closer to $4 million. Reviewers, on the whole, praised Loesser's songs, but found the story syrupy. "For the most part," *New York Times'* Bosley Crowther wrote of Kaye, "he is bound and restricted by Mr. Hart's sentimental script to pretend to the moody behavior of a sort of amiable village dunce. Although he is supposed to be a fellow with a fantastic gift of gab and a hypnotic way with children, he has little to say of interest—except in song."

Some were disappointed by the ending, since Hans ended up not winning the ballerina, but walking home with his apprentice. One Hollywood wag described the story as "Boy meets girl. Boy loses girl. Boy gets boy."

Nonetheless, the film raked in $6 million—and immortalized Danny as the gentle charmer of children.

AUDIO RECORDINGS

As was customary at the time, Kaye's first audio recordings were released as singles on 78-inch vinyl. In later years, they would be grouped together, in various combinations, on albums. (* written or co-written by Sylvia Fine; ** added or updated lyrics by Fine)

Columbia
"Jenny" (recorded Feb. 28, 1941) From *Lady in the Dark*
"My Ship" (Feb. 28, 1941) *Lady in the Dark*
"Princess of Pure Delight" (Feb. 28, 1941) *Lady in the Dark*
"Tschaikowsky" (Feb. 28, 1941) *Lady in the Dark*
"It's Never Too Late to Mendelssohn" (March 24, 1941) *Lady in the Dark*
"One Life to Live" (March 24, 1941) *Lady in the Dark*
"Deenah" (May 5, 1941)
"Minnie the Moocher" (May 5, 1941)

"Molly Malone"** (May 5, 1941)
"Fairy Pipers" (Jan. 9, 1942)
"Farming" (Jan. 9, 1942) *Let's Face It*
"Let's Not Talk about Love" (Jan. 9, 1942) *Let's Face It*
"Anatole of Paris"* (Jan. 23, 1942)
"Babbitt & the Bromide" (Jan. 23, 1942) *Funny Face*
"Eileen"* (Jan. 23, 1942)

Decca
"Bloop Bleep" (May 7, 1947)
"I Got a Song" (May 7, 1947) *Bloomer Girl*
"Tubby the Tuba" (May 13, 1947)

"I Wonder Who's Kissing Her Now" (May 14, 1947) *I Wonder Who's Kissing Her Now*
"What's the Use of Dreaming" (May 14, 1947) *I Wonder Who's Kissing Her Now*
"Bread & Butter Woman" (Sept. 27, 1947, with Andrews Sisters)
"Civilization" (Sept. 27, 1947, Andrews Sisters) From *Angels in the Wings*. Though several Kaye songs would crack the Top 5 in the U.K., "Civilization" was his only single to achieve that distinction in the U.S. It spent 11 weeks on the pop charts, peaking at #3. Others to reach the U.S. Top 30: "Bloop Bleep" (hitting #21 during 3 weeks on the chart), "Woody Woodpecker Song" (#18, 6 weeks), "I've Got a Lovely Bunch of Cocoanuts" (#26, 2 weeks), "C'est Si Bon" (#21, 1 week), "Blackstrap Molasses" (#29, 1 week), and "Thumbelina (#28, 1 week).
"The Little Fiddle"* (Nov. 28, 1947) *Secret Life of Walter Mitty*
"In Enterprise of Marital Kind"** (Dec. 2, 1947) *The Gondoliers*. Kaye's first eight Gilbert & Sullivan recordings were issued as singles, as well as packaged in an album of four 78s. His versatile voice and nimble tongue making him perfect for G&S, Danny had performed several of their songs on his radio show, but had never appeared on stage in a G&S pro- duction (he would later decline an invita- tion to tour with the prestigious D'Oyly Carte company). The recordings, howev- er, would not be carbon copies of G&S's originals. The music first had to go through Sylvia. She had learned, during her camp counselor days, that the kids better enjoyed G&S if she tweaked the tempo and updated topical lyrics. She would do the same for Danny's versions.
"Judge's Song"** (Dec. 2, 1947) *Trial by Jury*
"When First My Old, Old Love"** (Dec. 2, 1947) *Trial by Jury*
"If You're Anxious for to Shine"** (Dec. 4, 1947) *Patience*
"Nightmare Song"** (Dec. 4, 1947) *Iolanthe*
"Policeman's Song"** (Dec. 4, 1947) *Pirates of Penzance*
"Oh By Jingo" (Dec. 10, 1947) *Linger Longer Letty*
"St. Louis Blues" (Dec. 10, 1947)

"Amelia Cordelia McHugh" (Dec. 12, 1947, Andrews Sisters)
"Beatin', Bangin' & Scratchin'" (Dec. 12, 1947, Andrews Sisters)
"Mad Dogs & Englishmen" (Dec. 14, 1947) *The Third Little Show*
"Triplets" (Dec. 14, 1947) *Between the Devil*
"Lullaby for Dena" (Dec. 17, 1947) Sylvia's Camp Geneva mentor Irvin Graham wrote this song for her newborn. It was recorded on Dena's first birthday.
"Molly Malone"** (Dec. 17, 1947)
"Ballin' the Jack" (Dec. 18, 1947)
"The Moon & I"** (Dec. 19, 1947) *Mikado*
"The Moon Is Your Pillow" (Dec. 19, 1947)
"Big Brass Band from Brazil" (Dec. 20, 1947, Andrews Sisters) *Angels in the Wings*
"It's a Quiet Town" (Dec. 20, 1947, Andrews Sisters)
"Lobby Number"* (Dec. 20, 1947) *Up in Arms*
"Put 'em in a Box" (June 4, 1948, Andrews Sisters) *Romance on the High Seas*
"Woody Woodpecker Song" (June 4, 1948, Andrews Sisters)
"Candy Kisses" (March 29, 1949, Regalaires)
"Thank You" (March 29, 1949, Regalaires)
"Honey Bun" (April 18, 1949) *South Pacific*
"There's Nothing Like a Dame" (April 18, 1949) *South Pacific*
"All I Want for Christmas Is My Two Front Teeth" (Sept. 14, 1949, Andrews Sisters)
"Merry Christmas at Grandmother's House" (Sept. 14, 1949, Andrews Sisters)
"John Wellington Wells"** (Sept. 28, 1949) *Sorcerer*
"When I Was a Lad"** (Sept. 28, 1949) *HMS Pinafore*
"I've Got a Lovely Bunch of Coconuts" (Oct. 2, 1949)
"Peony Bush" (Oct. 2, 1949)
"Happy Times"* (Nov. 11, 1949) *Inspector General*
"Love Me Or Leave Me" (Nov. 11, 1949)
"Handout Song" (Dec. 14, 1949)
"Wreck of the Old '97" (Dec. 14, 1949)
"Coca Roca" (Dec. 24, 1949)
"C'est Si Bon" (Feb. 10, 1950, Lee Gordon Singers)
"Wilhelmina" (Feb. 10, 1950, Lee Gordon Singers) *Wabash Avenue*
"Confidentially" (Feb. 15, 1950)
"Paper Full of Fish & Chips" (Feb. 15, 1950)

"Pigalle" (May 18, 1950)
"Hula Lou" (May 19, 1950)
"Ladies, Ladies" (June 17, 1950)
"Popo the Puppet"* (June 27, 1950) *On the Riviera*
"Tubby the Tuba at the Circus" (Aug. 18, 1950)
"Ching-Ara-Sa-Sa" (Sept. 28, 1950, Andrews Sisters)
"Orange Colored Sky" (Sept. 28, 1950, Patty Andrews)
"Little White Duck" (Nov. 12, 1950)
"The Thing" (Nov. 12, 1950)
"I Left My Hat in Haiti" (Jan. 16, 1951, 4 Hits & a Miss) *Royal Wedding*
"I Taut I Taw a Puddy Tat" (Jan. 16, 1951)
"Liar Song" (Jan. 16, 1951, Carol Richard) *Royal Wedding*
"Happy Ending"* (March 8, 1951) *On the Riviera*
"On the Riviera"* (March 8, 1951) *On the Riviera*
"Rhythm of a New Romance"* (March 8, 1951) *On the Riviera*
"I'm Late" (March 9, 1951) *Alice in Wonderland*
"Walrus & the Carpenter" (March 9, 1951) *Alice in Wonderland*
"Black Strap Molasses" (Aug. 12, 1951, Jimmy Durante, Groucho Marx, Jane Wyman, 4 Hits & a Miss)
"How D'Ye Do & Shake Hands" (Aug. 12, 1951, Durante, Marx, Wyman, 4 Hits & a Miss) *Alice in Wonderland*
"Eat Eat Eat" (Sept. 26, 1951)
"Riley's Daughter" (Sept. 26, 1951)
"Santa Claus Looks Like My Daddy" (Sept. 26, 1951)
"Mademoiselle de Paree" (Sept. 27, 1951)
"Tongue Twisters" (Sept. 27, 1951)
"You're for Me Mimi"** (Sept. 27, 1951)
"There's a Hole in the Bottom of the Sea"* (Dec. 20, 1951)
"Uncle Pockets"* (Dec. 20, 1951) Macy's hired Sylvia to create a patter song about a character whose bottomless pockets are filled with products, vowing to display the records and sheet music in their department store windows.
Hans Christian Andersen soundtrack: "Anywhere I Wander" • "King's New Clothes" • "Wonderful Copenhagen" •

"Inchworm" • "Thumbelina" • "Ugly Duckling" • "I'm Hans Christian Andersen" • "No Two People" (Aug. 11 to 13, 1952, with Jane Wyman)
"In My Neck o' the Woods" (Oct. 29, 1952)
"What More Do You Want" (Oct. 29, 1952)
"Anatole of Paris"* (Dec. 20, 1952)
"I Belong to Glasgow"/"Good Old 149" (Dec. 20, 1952)
"Tschaikowsky" (Dec. 20, 1952)
"I Love You that's One Thing I Know" (Feb. 27, 1953)
"I'll Buy the Ring" (Feb. 27, 1953)
"Night of My Nights" (Oct. 27, 1953) *Kismet*
"Not Since Ninevah" (Oct. 27, 1953) *Kismet*
"All About You"* (Feb. 26, 1954) *Knock on Wood*
"Knock on Wood"* (Feb. 26, 1954) *Knock on Wood*
"Monahan O'Han"* (Feb. 26, 1954) *Knock on Wood*
"Stories of the Ballet's Magic Toyshop" (March 9, 1954)
White Christmas soundtrack: "The Old Man"/"Gee, I Wish I Was Back in the Army" • "Snow" • "White Christmas" • "The Best Things Happen While You're Dancing" • "Choreography" • "Manhattan Mambo" • "Blues Skies" • "I'd Rather See a Minstrel Show" • "Mandy" (April 10, Sept. 2, Sept. 9, Oct. 19, 1954, with Bing Crosby, Peggy Lee, Trudy Stevens)
"Yon-u-ary"* (Aug. 30, 1955)
"I Love You Fair Dinkum" (Aug. 30, 1955)
Court Jester soundtrack*: "Life Could Not Better Be" • "Where Walks My True Love" • "You'll Never Outfox the Fox" • "My Heart Knows a Lovely Song" • "Willow, Willow Waley" • "Pass the Basket" • "Maladjusted Jester" • "I Live to Love" • "I'll Take You Dreaming" (Sept. 7 to 12, 1955)
"Madam, I Love Your Crepe Suzettes" (Sept. 17, 1955) *Du Barry Was a Lady*
"My Darling Jenny Macoo" (Sept. 17, 1955)
"The Court Jester"* (Sept. 4, 21 to 22, 1955)
"Laugh It Off Upsy Daisy"* (Dec. 20, 1955, Dena Kaye)
"Little Child" (Dec. 20, 1955, Dena Kaye)
"Delilah Jones"** (March 22, 1956)
"Molly-O"** (March 22, 1956)

Capitol

"Ciu Ciu Bella"** (Nov. or Dec. 1956)

"Love Me Do" (Nov. or Dec. 1956)

Mommy, Gimme a Drinka Water album: "I'm Five" • "Bathtub Admiral" • "Playing on the Seesaw" • "Thank You Letter" • "New Baby" • "Crazy Barbara" • "Colored Kisses" • "I'm Hiding" • "Just Imagine" • "Don't Tickle Me" • "I Like Old People, Don't You?" • "The Puddle" (recorded late 1957; released Feb. 3, 1958) Kaye's most famous stand-alone recording project, in which he plays a precocious five-year-old, was the brainchild of Milton Schafer, an aspiring composer who was under contract to Frank Loesser's publishing firm. Loesser knew just the person to record the songs. As noted the *Saturday Review*, "Loesser could not have done a greater favor for Schafer (or himself) for the perceptive Kaye not only enters completely into the spirit of the songs, but, even more importantly, into the skin of the small boy they depict." Whereas Kaye's baby talk could sometimes come across as cloying, the album captured the shtick at its most charming.

Merry Andrew soundtrack: "Pipes of Pan" • "Chin Up, Stout Fellow" • "Everything Is Tickety Boo" • "You Can't Always Have What You Want" • "Square of the Hypotenuse" • "Salud" (vocals taken from film soundtrack, recorded summer 1957)

Reprise

"Dodgers Song"* (Aug. 18, 1962) Sylvia and Herbie Baker wrote this patter song for diehard Dodgers fan Danny, to celebrate the fierce pennant race with the rival San Francisco Giants. They even included a nod to their old radio show—"Oh, really? No, O'Malley." The Dodgers would lose the crown to the Giants in a season-ending, best-of-three playoff series.

"Myti Kaysi at the Bat"* (Aug. 18, 1962)

Dot

Five Pennies soundtrack*: "Five Pennies" • "Bill Bailey" • "Indiana" • "Lullaby in Ragtime" • "Five Pennies Saints" • "Follow the Leader" • "Good Night, Sleep Tight" • "Carnival of Venice" • "Music Goes 'Round & 'Round" • "Jingle Bells" (vocals taken from film soundtrack, recorded Oct. to Dec. 1958, with Louis Armstrong, Susan Gordon)

Dena

Danny Kaye Rambler album: "Great Come & Get It Day" • "C'est Si Bon" • "Oh, Baby Mine" • "Ciu Ciu Bella" • "Down by the Riverside" • "South Rampart Street Parade" • "Ballin' the Jack" • "I've Got a Lovely Bunch of Coconuts" • "Story of Alice" • "Turn Around" (recorded early Dec. 1963) Kaye, with TV series back-ups Paul Weston and his orchestra, the Clinger Sisters, and Earl Brown Singers, recorded this album as a premium for sponsor American Motors. Dena Records produced 200,000 albums, to be given away by Rambler automobile dealers.

Columbia

Two by Two sountrack: "Why Me" • "Put Him Away" • "Gitka's Song" • "Something, Somewhere" • "You Got to Have a Rudder on the Ark" • "Something Doesn't Happen" • "Old Man" • "Ninety Again" • "Two by Two" • "I Do Not Know a Day I Did Not Love You" • "When It Dries" • "You" • "Golden Ram" • "Poppa Knows Best" • "As Far as I'm Concerned" • "Hey, Girlie" • "Covenant" (Nov. 15, 1970)

Golden Records

Six Stories from Far Away Places: "Big Oven" • "Farmer of Babbia" • "Master of All Masters" • "Most Remarkable Cat" • "Nail Broth" • "Tale of the Name of the Tree" (recorded fall 1960; released Jan. 1961)

Fairy Tales from Hans Christian Andersen: "Princess & the Pea" • "Perfectly True" • "Tinder Box" • "Match Girl" • "Ugly Duckling" • "Steadfast Tin Soldier" (1962)

Grimms Fairy Tales: "Clever Gretel" • "Water Nixie" • "Bean" • "Straw & Coal" • "Snow White & Rose Red" • "Musicians of Bremen" • "Fox & the Geese" • "Rumpelstiltskin" • "Sweet Porridge" (1962)

V.
PEAKING AT PARAMOUNT

IN THE WAKE of his triumphs at the London Palladium, Kaye quickly lost interest in returning to Broadway, where he would be forced to play someone else's character. Instead, he placed renewed emphasis on his own stage act. His manager began booking him into larger venues, where he would no longer be side entertainment between movies. He would be the show. Taking his cue from the vaudeville acts of the Palladium, he lined up more and varied acts as his lead-in.

Sylvia hired her protégé from the radio series, Herbie Baker, to help develop more material for Kaye's stage act, though they were careful to incorporate new numbers slowly, knowing how comfortable Danny liked to be with his material.

Kaye, for his part, continued to grow ever more at ease portraying himself. Interacting with the audience expanded beyond sing-a-longs and the sit down spot, to become an ongoing feature of the act. He regularly conversed with individuals in the audience, such as one woman whom he caught rising from her seat to leave early to tend to dinner at home. "What are you having?" Danny asked. The woman said she was making a pot roast. So Kaye had a phone brought out on the stage, and he called her house to ask her family to put a little more water on the roast, because the show was running late and he wanted her to stay until the end.

Danny worked especially well with children. During one show in Boston, he asked onto the stage a little boy dressed up with holsters and two tiny six-shooters. "What's your name?" Kaye asked.

"Jimmy McDonough," the feisty lad answered.

"How old are you?"

"Nine!"

"Do you want to be a pilot?" Danny asked. The boy shook his head. "Do you want to be in the Air Force, or in the Army, or a baseball player?" Kaye continued, exhausting all possibilities. He finally gave up. "What do you want to be?"

"A crook!" the boy said, bringing down the house.

Once in Omaha, Danny had just finished his final number when a baby in the front row began to cry. The mother tried in vain to quiet her child. Kaye said he would sing one more song, a lullaby. So he started to sing, but the baby only cried louder. All the while singing, Danny walked off the stage, picked up the baby, and went back on stage. The child slowly grew quieter and finally silent. Kaye put a finger to his lips to stop any applause and quietly returned the baby to mother. Danny, still with a finger to his lips, walked back up on the stage and off into the wings.

Increasingly, Danny discovered that in sacrificing laughs and applause to do things like swap recipes with audiences, he moved into their hearts. Now even in the U.S., his "Palladium-type show" was receiving Palladium-type ovations. But there was one theater that Danny had never performed in, an American equivalent of the Palladium, a big city palace with a history of showcasing the ultimate in entertainment, the prestigious Palace Theatre in New York.

But by 1953, the Palace was known more for its history. Back in the Teens and Twenties, "playing the Palace" meant reaching the zenith for a vaudevillian. By the 1950s, vaudeville was, for all practical purposes, dead. Undeterred, the Palace was trying to rejuvenate the format by combining programs of vaudeville acts with one-man shows. Judy Garland's engagement broke all the house records. Then came Betty Hutton, and she outsold Garland. Now it was Danny's turn. When he opened on the evening advertised as his fortieth birthday (in publicity years, since he was actually turning 42), he felt at the top of his game. "I'll tell you a little secret," he whispered to the opening night crowd. "There is nobody in the world likes to hear me entertain better than me."

There was a time when Kaye would rather be anyone other than himself, but now he wouldn't want to be anyone else. "Back around '42 or '43," said Max Liebman, "if a mimic did an impersonation of Danny, he'd do it as a Russian character, or a scat singer, or a Frenchman, or whatever Danny happened to be doing at the time. Today, that would be obsolete. He's become less stylized, more difficult to impersonate. The instinctive realization that he could charm an audience by being himself must have come through slowly and gradually, obviously. When I first knew Danny, he was more or less an inarticulate man before an audience. Every word was rehearsed. He used to hide behind his characters. He doesn't have to anymore."

Thereafter, whenever the William Morris Agency booked a stage date for Kaye, they would send the theater owner a warning to ensure proper billing: "Attention! In all publicity and advertising, please refer to Danny Kaye as

an international entertainer. This is just about the best description of his performance. Avoid using words such as 'comedian,' 'comic,' etc., as these do
not properly or accurately describe his particular talents."

Originally scheduled to play the Palace for eight weeks, his record-
breaking run was extended to four months. The show was so popular, Decca
repackaged eight of his singles into an album called *Danny Kaye at the
Palace*.

During his run at the Palace, Danny's stage act took a monumental
detour, when Eugene Ormondy, conductor of the Philadelphia Symphony
Orchestra, asked him to perform his act at a charity benefit. Kaye declined.
"Danny, I understand perfectly," Ormondy said. "But you know the people
in the orchestra got to know you so well and they like you so much that
they'd even play if you conducted them."

"Well, you know... what? The Philadelphia Orchestra would play if I...?
Wait a minute," Kaye bubbled, thinking. Comically conducting the house
band had been part of his stage shtick since White Roe, but he'd never
before had the opportunity to lead a world-class orchestra. He quickly
learned two pieces, Strauss' "Tritsch-Tratsch-Polka" and Sousa's "Stars and
Stripes Forever," for the March 7, 1953 concert. Danny contributed eight
minutes of conducting and clowning, enough to earn a tidy sum for the
Musician's Pension Fund.

Word of the hit concert spread quickly. Soon, invitations arrived from the
Los Angeles Philharmonic, Stockholm Symphony, and Israeli Symphony.
Kaye gradually worked his conducting act up to 25 minutes. But after
agreeing to conduct the Boston Symphony, Kaye got hold of a flyer adver-
tising his upcoming appearance: "Special Pension Fund Concert. Danny
Kaye, Guest Conductor. 7-8:30."

"Seven to 8:30!" Kaye stammered. "What am I going to do for an hour-
and-a-half?" Immediately, it occurred to Danny that he could fill time by
getting his own guest conductor. He talked Charles Munch into leading
"The Sorcerer's Apprentice" as the opening number. It would run eleven
minutes. He still had 79 minutes to fill. So Danny compiled a stack of symphony recordings and memorized them all. His appearance went over
tremendously and became the template for dozens of appearances thereafter.

Audiences were warned from the outset to expect the unexpected. A typical playbill would introduce the symphony as "Under the Direction of
Danny Kaye," followed in small print by: "The Management assumes no
responsibility for this portion of the program." At the start of a typical per-

formance, he would wind up for his first downbeat—and send his baton flying into the audience. To get the musicians to play progressively softer, he'd progressively break little pieces off of his baton. He'd coach his orchestra on how to rise to acknowledge applause and how to be seated. He'd have them sing a chorus. He'd dance on the podium. He'd even lie on the podium and conduct with his feet. He'd lead "Flight of the Bumblebee" with a flyswatter. And he always found time to give his impressions of the classical types of conductors, including the coffee grinder, the meat chopper, the baby carriage pusher, the emotionally explosive leader, and the one with an allergy.

Although the material was entirely different from his regular stage act, he did retain one element—informality. One evening, he borrowed the chair of his solo violinist, set it up on the podium, and had a heart-to-heart talk with a woman whose opera glasses he had borrowed. During one performance with the St. Louis Symphony, Danny was in the middle of a number when he noticed that one violinist was pregnant. He stopped the playing immediately and brought her a glass of milk and a little stool for her to rest her feet.

Amid Kaye's antics, all the music was played straight. Danny had perfect pitch, incomparable grace, and the ability to maintain complete control over both orchestra and audience. "Everybody is a Walter Mitty," he remarked. "Everybody has wanted to lead an orchestra. It gives a wild feeling of power. It is your castle, your kingdom. You are the reigning monarch."

Despite the fact that he couldn't read a note of music, Danny effectively conducted, quite brilliantly at that. He'd continue leading orchestras for the next 33 years, along the way raising more than $6 million for musicians' pension funds.

Danny's four-month run at the Palace eventually had to end, so he could return to Hollywood. New York critics shook their heads, unable to comprehend why the ultimate stage performer felt compelled to annually demean himself by appearing in movies.

Theatre Arts critic Walter Kerr was one who recognized that Kaye stood tallest in person, on a stage. He considered Danny's affinity for Hollywood "perhaps the most conspicuous waste of talent in the contemporary theater." His greatest charm was his ability to directly bind himself with his audience; the sparks would fly and each would recharge the other. Kaye couldn't bind himself with a motion picture camera, and neither could the audience bind itself with a screen.

Kerr explained, "The trouble with Danny Kaye in pictures is that he has chosen a medium which is inhospitable to his most striking characteristics, a medium which draws no certain of his talents, especially the lesser ones, and tends to reject or to tone down the more fabulous ones. Kaye is a zany, a man of grimaces, an explosion of nervous energy. But the screen has never been a very congenial instrument for personal extravagance, for the broader and more stylized mannerisms of antic performers... It is in the nature of Danny Kaye's talents that he must hire a hall, that the modulations of the film frame cannot contain him."

KNOCK ON WOOD

(Filmed June 1 to July 10, July 20, Aug. 12 to 19, Aug. 24, Nov. 14, 1953;
released L.A. April 6, 1954; N.Y. April 14, 1954)

Producers/Directors: Norman Panama & Mel Frank, for Dena Productions, Paramount
Screenplay: Norman Panama & Mel Frank
Songs: Sylvia Fine ("All About You," "Chacun a Son Gout," "Knock on Wood," "Monahan O'Han")
Cast: Danny Kaye (Jerry), Mai Zetterling (Ilse), Torin Thatcher (Langston), David Burns (Marty), Leon Askin (Gromek), Abner Biberman (Papinek)

By the early 1950s, Hollywood's studio system had begun to fade. With fewer people going to the movies, the studios cut back on film production and no longer needed nor could afford to keep a huge stable of actors and craftsmen under contract. Simultaneously, many actors, directors and producers wanted more control over and a greater financial stake in their pictures. They formed their own production companies and convinced the studios to fund their projects for a share of the profits. Actors with their own production companies would then receive a percentage of their films' profits, rather than a huge salary, reducing their tax liability.

More power and money appealed to Danny—and especially to Sylvia. Kaye first considered forming his own production company in 1947, as he was preparing for life without Goldwyn. He almost became partners with Cary Grant and twice nearly joined forces with Don Hartman. Both times, just as they were finalizing plans, Hartman was offered a production chief job, first at MGM and a few years later at Paramount.

Kaye found kindred souls when he ran into Norman Panama and Melvin Frank at a party one evening. Danny asked the prestigious comedy writing-directing-producing team if they had done any work on any of the projects they'd proposed to him a while back. Panama and Frank sheepishly admitted that, no, they hadn't given much thought of late to a Danny Kaye movie. But within the next couple of days, they hatched a plotline they thought would be perfect for Kaye—about a ventriloquist who gets mixed up with a spy ring. They dropped the script they had been working on for two months and jumped right into writing *Knock on Wood*.

Danny and Sylvia were so impressed by their work that they formed their own production company with Panama and Frank as junior partners and *Knock on Wood* as their first release. In exchange for half the profits, Paramount agreed to provide funding, equipment, soundstages, crew and distribution for two films. The Kayes christened the firm after daughter Dena. But although Dena Productions was a legitimate company, with its own offices on the Paramount lot, its methods deviated from those of a typical business. The principals claimed that their most common business technique was hollering. The group would build their movies by gathering in a room and yelling their ideas at each other.

"There are no restrictions with us," Sylvia said. "If we have a sudden inspiration, we can call one another up in the middle of the night and tell about it. We did that frequently during the filming of our first picture. Imagine doing that with most prominent studio executives. They'd think you mad, but we could be just as mad as we pleased. Thus no idea was ever lost through growing old."

The creative team agreed that none of Danny's past movie roles had been able to capture the "real" Danny Kaye. So their primary focus became creating a character similar to the one he sold himself as on stage—warm and winsome, spontaneous and romantic, yet complicated. For a change, Danny would be a believable, relatable human. Instead of Edwin, Hobart, Walter or Burleigh, he'd get a normal, albeit bland, name—Jerry Morgan.

Cast as a ventriloquist, he'd still have an excuse to exhibit a split personality. Yet any outlandish gags and specialty material were to flow naturally from the plot. Panama and Frank even thought to incorporate Kaye's gift for tongue-twisting delivery—showcased to great effect in Sylvia's songs—in the film's dialogue. Danny's character, impersonating a British car salesman, must rattle off make-believe features (describing the hubcap as the "overhead, underslung, oscillating compression decravinator") and, later, recap the shenanigans of foreign spies ("Gromek got it from Brodnik, who brought it to Shoshnik, who in turn gave it to Brutchik").

The tricky lines were a snap for Kaye. According to assistant director Francisco Day, "There was no problem *ever* with dialogue. If there was something that they were rehearsing and it didn't work out the way they thought it would work out, why just like that Danny would rehearse it once and that's all. He had a real photographic mind. If the directors had something new for him, something that was better, Danny would take it always."

Although the production company may have been short on formalities, it refused to cut any corners in making the best possible movie. They spent a bundle just on Danny's wooden co-stars, Clarence and Terrence. The twin dummies were patterned after photos of Kaye as a child and were often required to smile widely, a la Joe E. Brown, to reveal a full set of teeth. But Kaye felt the usual wooden-painted or wooden-plated teeth would look too cheap. He ordered the dummies filled with a full set of plastic dentures, installed by a licensed dental technician. Each dummy also boasted glass eyes, a sponge rubber face, toupee by Max Factor, and wardrobe by Edith Head. Terrence alone cost $800.

Although Dena Productions was spending the studio's money, it was motivated to keep expenses under control. First, Paramount had to approve all budgets. More importantly, although Kaye, Fine, Panama and Frank were paid modest salaries during production, the real money was in their split of any profits.

Plans to make the film in 3-D were quickly abandoned. So, too, were a number of scenes. Panama and Frank calculated that their original script required building 66 sets and, once filmed, would run over two hours—too long for either a taut spy thriller or a rollicking comedy. They agreed to cut the sets to fewer than 40 and lop fifteen minutes off the running time, primarily by eliminating scenes of our hero fleeing in a stolen car through a police roadblock and becoming mixed up in an English foxhunt.

To keep costs down, Panama and Frank also had hoped to shoot the film overseas. Planned were twelve weeks at London's Pinewood Studios, four weeks on location in London, and two weeks of second unit work in France and Switzerland. Yet, as soon as they laid out a shooting schedule to start June 1, 1953, news came that Queen Elizabeth II's coronation, televised internationally, was to take place June 2. Suddenly, it seemed easier and less expensive to make the movie on a Paramount soundstage, with a Paramount crew.

For the exteriors, a second-unit crew spent the two weeks before principal photography began filming the London-based leading lady before she left for Hollywood, cavorting throughout England and Zurich alongside a double for Kaye. Unfortunately, Danny's regular double, Jon Pertwee, was unavailable for the final three days of filming, and another—noticeably taller and lankier—actor had to fill in for several shots scurrying about the streets and sidewalks of London.

Panama and Frank first envisioned Moira Shearer or Deborah Kerr in the lead role. Yet, Danny had other plans after seeing the Swedish film star Mai Zetterling on stage during his trip to London in 1953. Kaye was intrigued by the blonde, green-eyed beauty's firm personality, since instead of playing opposite a singer, dancer, librarian or nurse, this role called for a psychiatrist. Per Danny's wishes, Zetterling got the job and the character's name was changed from Dr. Leslie Symmons to Dr. Ilse Nordstrom.

Zetterling, however, did not enjoy making the film, mostly because she was uncomfortable with the strange ways of Hollywood. "We used to have a (nickname) 'Meyer,'" recalled assistant director Day. "We used to say, 'Hey, Meyer!' to everybody, and she used to think that we were saying 'Mai,' that we were calling to her. And she would answer. Pretty soon we just stopped using it, because it disturbed her." As soon as filming was complete, Zetterling returned to Europe. She would never again make another film in Hollywood.

Sylvia's contributions were held to four—a conventional love song ("All About You"), dance number ("Knock on Wood"), scat-singing duet for Danny and dummy ("Chacun a Son Gout"), and an Irish drinking song ("Monahan O'Han"), in which a disguised Kaye must spontaneously ad-lib a heroic tall tale of bluster and brogue.

Although Fine served an integral role as business partner and songwriter for *Knock on Wood*, she stayed out of Panama and Frank's way on the set. Still, she was called into service for Danny's duet with the dummy. During recording, Kaye initially sang his own part, while Sylvia sang Terrence's part. But her voice went unrecorded, audible only to Danny and the orchestra leader. Afterwards, Kaye's vocal was played back while he recorded the part of the dummy.

Production went smoothly, and on schedule, until seven weeks in, when the only things left to film were the two big dance routines—the "Knock on Wood" vaudeville flashback and an epic comic ballet. But while filming the flashback, dance partner Patricia Denise severely strained her calf muscle and had to be taken, by Danny, to the doctor. She would be out of commission for four weeks. In the meantime, the producers turned off their cameras and focused entirely on the ballet.

Choreographer Michael Kidd, fresh from Broadway's *Guys and Dolls*,

LIFT OFF: *Knock on Wood's* ballet spoof finale, featuring New York City Ballet star Diana Adams, took more than two months to train for, rehearse and film. [© 1954 Paramount Pictures]

had already been training dancers for a month. The intricate ballet finale would take another full month to rehearse and six days to shoot. Like the opera in the Marx Brothers' *A Night at the Opera*, the ballet in *Knock on Wood* was presented straight, with our hero hilariously trying to fit in. Though intentionally fumbling, Danny's natural grace still shines through.

Ironically, Kaye could be equally clumsy. "Danny has the facility for movement that equals any good dancer," said choreographer Tony Charmoli. "(But) between my assistant and I, we refer to Danny as the 'Porcelain Princess' because he was strong, but he was prone to bumping into things. If something was physical and you could possibly get hurt on it, he would get hurt. Going through a doorway, if the doorway wasn't wide enough, he'd bump an elbow. Such a gangly one."

As a result, Kaye was constantly using *Knock on Wood's* assistant director as his guinea pig, to ensure every stunt was safe. Francisco Day recalled, "Whenever he had to do something, he wanted me to do it first. Like he had to climb one of those backstage ladders in a theater, way up onto the roof, and he didn't want to do it until I did it. And when we were on the street and he had to run and then slide, he wanted me to go and do it for him.

Nonetheless, while rehearsing a scene in side-by-side showers, Danny bumped his knee on the edge of the shower door, cutting and bruising it— neither the first nor last of his many on-set injuries (*see chart below*).

After the final edit, Panama and Frank were pleased with the finished product, except for one element—the break-off with Jerry's fiancée, Audrey. As originally filmed, Clarence disparages Audrey on stage, as Jerry's agent and the French nightclub manager look on in displeasure. Audrey has been waiting in Jerry's dressing room, and when he arrives, she presses him to select a wedding date, because she's been offered a role in a ballet in London. The dummy insults her. Upset, she returns her engagement ring and storms out.

Three months after the production closed, Panama and Frank revised the scene. This time, Audrey would be the one looking on from the wings in

On-Set Injuries

Wonder Man (July 17, 1944) Kaye severely twists knee jumping through giant drum during "Bali Boogie."

(Aug. 16, 1944) Kaye bruised by wire harness while swinging from tree in Prospect Park scene.

Inspector General (Sept. 28, 1948) Kaye sprains ankle hopping about mayor's bedroom.

(July 11, 1949) Kaye sprains right wrist after falling from top of six-man pyramid.

(July 14, 1949) Kaye skins knee after falling from exercise ladder in gym scene. (The previous week, he was 400 miles into a flight home from England when the plane's engine caught fire, forcing the

pilot to turn back. After his second on-set injury in four days, Kaye joked, "Take me back to the plane already!")

Knock on Wood (June 1, 1953) Kaye cuts and bruises knee in shower scene.

White Christmas (Dec. 4, 1953) While rehearsing "The Best Things Happen While You're Dancing," Kaye swings on bar, lands on side of right foot, and twists ankle.

Court Jester (Feb. 18, 1955) Kaye picks up small girl visiting the set, and she accidentally scratches his eyeball.

Five Pennies (Fall 1958) Kaye simulates so much trumpet playing, that his lip blisters and eventually splits.

horror as Clarence badmouths her on stage, and—upset from the start—she would confront Jerry as he walks off the stage.

Despite the retakes, Panama and Frank were able to keep the production within range of its $1.2-million budget. The result, similar to Kaye's schizophrenic character, was two films in one. Casting Danny as a ventriloquist sounds inspired, wide open for comic exploration. Yet after the brief scat duet, the dummy turns evil, has his skull smashed in by the raging ventriloquist, and is thrown into a box, not to speak another word until the film's closing moments. Worse, Danny's angry outbursts come across as unsettling, a little too realistic and uncomfortable to witness in a whimsical clown. So, too, showing Danny's serious side made him a believable romantic lead, but muffled the comedy. The first half of the film is also bogged down by endless plot machinations between the supporting players. Never before had a Danny Kaye movie gone so long with Kaye off screen. Yet, at the midway point, once Danny realizes he's being chased, the movie and the merriment take off in hysterical high gear.

The film was a big hit with audiences, grossing $4 million. And, in later years, Danny would refer to *Knock on Wood* as his favorite film. Despite an aversion to looking back on his career, he would admit: "Things like the ballet, the bit under the table—I hate to use the word, but those were *classic* routines."

WHITE CHRISTMAS
(Filmed Sept. 21 to Dec. 10, 1953; released N.Y. Oct. 14, 1954)
Producer: Robert Emmett Dolan, for Paramount
Director: Michael Curtiz
Screenplay: Norman Krasna, Norman Panama & Mel Frank (uncredited Jack Rose, Mel Shavelson, Barney Dean)
Songs: Irving Berlin ("White Christmas," "The Old Man," "Mandy," "Heat Wave," "Blue Skies," "Sisters," "The Best Things Happen While You're Dancing," "Snow," "Minstrel Show Number," "Choreography," "Gee, I Wish I Was Back in the Army")
Cast: Bing Crosby (Bob Wallace), Danny Kaye (Phil Davis), Rosemary Clooney (Betty Haynes), Vera-Ellen (Judy Haynes), Dean Jagger (Major Waverly), Mary Wickes (Emma)

As pleased as Paramount was to partner on Kaye's first independent production, it had even higher hopes for another musical it was preparing, *White Christmas*. The studio had budgeted the holiday spectacular at over $3 million and was using it as the first vehicle to showcase its patented VistaVision process. Paramount had been the only major studio to pass on

CinemaScope, an even wider-screen process that forced directors to stretch their action too broadly and forced most theaters to drastically cut down on their projection's height, to fit the entire image on standard movie screens. At a width-to-height ratio of 1.85 to 1 (versus CinemaScope's 2.55 to 1), VistaVision offered a sharper, more practical widescreen image.

Paramount had been nursing *White Christmas* along for years. The idea had seemed simple enough—build a movie out of the recording industry's all-time best-selling tune, re-teaming Bing Crosby, who introduced the song in 1942's *Holiday Inn*, with his *Holiday Inn* co-star, Fred Astaire, and composer, Irving Berlin.

But Paramount didn't own the rights to *Holiday Inn*. So rather than a straight sequel, *White Christmas* was to be a hybrid "re-imagining." They would start with similar characters to *Holiday Inn's*—Crosby as reluctant romantic Chuck, who must play watchdog for his playboy stage partner Johnny, played by Astaire. Norman Krasna's storyline, about a song-and-dance team that comes to the aid of their retired commander from World War I, and Irving Berlin's songs ("We'll Follow the Old Man," the vaudeville duet "Monohan and Callahan," "What Can You Do with a General?") would be lifted from *Stars on My Shoulders,* a five-year-old stage musical that never made it to the stage.

In late 1952, Crosby's wife, Dixie, passed away, and he decided to pull out of *White Christmas*. He said that he didn't want to return to work until the fall and that he had promised his fourteen-year-old son that they would spend the spring together touring Europe. The news was just the excuse his co-star had been looking for. Astaire was already skeptical of the script and his role as a veteran of the first World War, and asked to be released as well. Paramount had originally announced a release date of Christmas 1952. Now, its heavily promoted revised date of Christmas 1953 was in jeopardy. The studio announced it would quickly recast the leads. Privately, however, the executives must have realized that producing a film called *White Christmas* without Crosby made about as much sense as producing a Lassie movie without a dog.

After three weeks of negotiation, Crosby agreed to return—starting in August, at a higher salary of $150,000 plus a full one-third of the profits. Berlin and Paramount would each collect a third. Astaire, however, could not be lured back. The studio went looking for a new dancer and settled on Donald O'Connor. Crosby had been concerned that his character not be too frivolous or "young in nature." So, he liked how the addition of O'Connor could help the story by allowing an older GI/younger GI relationship. O'Connor's character (with a new, less world-wise name of Phil) could be the excitable kid, who adores big-time performer Bob, and the action could be moved to World War II. That way, instead of starting the picture on a nightclub stage, the story could begin on the battlefield, before Bob and Phil team up. Best of all, producer Robert Emmett Dolan could work "White Christmas" into the scene, since he had received so much mail from ex-GI's begging him to recreate the common wartime sight of home-sick soldiers listening to the song.

The addition of O'Connor allowed for broader comedy, including a drag version of "Sisters." Berlin also changed the "Monohan and Callahan" number to "A Singer-A Dancer," and tailored two dance numbers for the young hoofer, "The Best Things Happen While You're Dancing" and "Choreography."

Yet not long after inking the deal, O'Connor fell gravely ill with Q fever, a tick-borne disease he had contracted from his previous co-star, Francis the talking mule. The actor struggled with the illness for months and by the time August rolled around, he was still too weak to return to work. Paramount could wait no longer. Executive producer Don Hartman was sent to see if he could persuade Kaye to step in. Danny had a full schedule of stage appearances lined up. But—for his pal Don—he agreed to step in for the ridiculous amount of $200,000 (more than twice what O'Connor had agreed to) plus ten percent of the profits, convinced that Paramount would pass. Out of options, the studio agreed to pony up the $200,000, if Crosby and Berlin each gave up five percent of their cuts for Kaye. Both happily agreed, figuring that the picture—and, in turn, they—would make more in the long run with Danny in the cast.

Kaye had one added stipulation: that Panama and Frank be given $25,000 and three weeks to rewrite the script. During an emergency story conference at Hartman's home, director Michael Curtiz spent an hour acting out the entire script for Panama and Frank. After pantomiming the grand finale, Curtiz asked, "How do you like it?"

"Is that it?" Frank replied. Hartman nodded. "Don, that's the lousiest story I've ever heard."

"That's the lousiest story you ever heard?" asked Curtiz. Panama and Frank nodded. Curtiz turned to Hartman: "If that's the lousiest story they ever heard, then why am I doing this picture?"

Nonetheless, Panama and Frank left the basic story intact and began

SNOW JOB: Kaye agreed to a supporting role alongside Bing Crosby in the holiday classic *White Christmas*—his most profitable picture. [© 1954 Paramount Pictures]

rewriting most of Danny's lines, even as the crew started rehearsals. They also left in O'Connor's two dance numbers, although during "Choreography" Kaye would step aside during the most complicated moves for a professional dancer.

Berlin was ecstatic that the addition of Danny allowed for great comedic opportunities in the vaudeville duet with Bing. The composer rewrote "A Singer-A Dancer" yet again, as "A Crooner-A Comic." But in the end, it was dropped in favor of a medley of Berlin standards. Also cut, to save money, was an elaborate "Winter Fantasy" number the four principals were to perform as they anticipated all the snow that awaited them in Vermont. Berlin replaced it with the simpler "Snow," borrowing a melody he had discarded from *Call Me Madam*. Producer Robert Emmett Dolan mandated another cut: a closing pull-back shot of snow falling on a miniature lodge. Dolan conceded that it would have made a better ending than having the actors point out the snowfall from the inn door, but said the studio "could not, in all honesty, spend $40,000 or $50,000 on a shot that we had no assurance the audience would still be in the theater to see."

Paramount's marketing department used the film's long, troubled production to its advantage. They spent nearly $1 million building the long-awaited release into an event. Audiences took the bait. *White Christmas* became the top-grossing film of the year, earning $12 million for Paramount, Berlin, Crosby and Kaye to divvy up. Despite its story problems, the movie remains a gorgeous holiday classic—even though the film process didn't last. According to *White Christmas* editor Frank Bracht: "The VistaVision system, although beautiful to see, proved impractical due to difficulty in handling and added cost to the exhibitors, as extra men were required in the projection room."

ASSIGNMENT: CHILDREN

(Filmed June 14 to July 2, 1954; released Feb. 9, 1955)
Producer: UNICEF, Paramount
Cast: Danny Kaye (Himself)

By the closing number of one of his stage performances, Kaye had convinced most of the audience that they knew the real Danny Kaye. That connection, though, was a relationship that could be established only with hundreds at a time, not millions. For a mass audience, Danny was more difficult to know, since he so wholly became the characters he played.

Perhaps emboldened by years of therapy, Kaye increasingly acted as if he were disinterested in what the outside world thought of him. He was far from image conscious. He wore comfortable, loose-fitting clothes—a floppy hat, half-buttoned sweater, and "space shoes" (odd-looking footwear custom molded around the shape of his feet). He never performed for reporters; in fact, he regularly lost patience with them. And he spent more and more time with royalty and celebrities of all fields—popular entertainment, classical music, sports, politics, medicine.

Publicist Eddie Dukoff detected a separation growing between Danny and the general public, particularly after his "coronation" in England. In publicity materials for *On the Riviera*, Fox had advertised that in his role as stage performer Jack Martin he was playing the "real" Danny Kaye. But, increasingly, Kaye in public resembled aviator Henri Duran, the cultured international celebrity. Playing Hans Christian Andersen provided a more likable, accessible role. But Dukoff advised Danny he needed "a rapport with the people."

That rapport began on a flight back from London to New York in 1953, during which Kaye got to talking with fellow passenger Maurice Pate, executive director of the United Nations International Children's Emergency Fund. The two hit it off. Danny expressed interest in UNICEF's mission of providing aid to the poor children of lesser-developed countries. A full year later, as he was preparing for his next trip abroad, Kaye received a note from Pate: "I understand you're going around the world again. Could we have lunch together? I have something interesting to talk to you about."

When the two met, Pate further explained his group's goals and wondered if Kaye could stop by some of UNICEF's outposts. The nonprofit organization needed all the publicity it could get. Perhaps Danny could mention on the radio or write a magazine article about the work UNICEF was doing in the field.

"I'll do better than that," Kaye volunteered. "I'll take my camera and shoot some film, and when I come back you can have it." Danny then visited Paramount to see about that camera. The studio had an even better idea. It would supply the camera equipment, 40,000 feet of color film, and a crew that included two professional photographers. The idea was to make a documentary film that explained UNICEF's efforts to bring medical help to millions of kids lacking adequate food, shelter and protection from disease. The film, *Assignment: Children*, could then be shown at movie theaters before the scheduled feature, to promote UNICEF and solicit donations.

Kaye would pay his personal expenses, while Paramount would cover all filming-related costs. Danny would receive the official title "Ambassador at Large" and full diplomatic status for the tour. He began in London, attending a charity premiere of *Knock on Wood*. Then he was off to South Africa to fulfill theater engagements in Capetown, Johannesburg, Durban and Rhodesia.

Next, he went to work for UNICEF. In India, he was welcomed by Prime Minister Nehru and Madame Pandit. Thereafter, few of those he was to meet had any idea who Danny Kaye was. These were the starving, stricken children of India, and then Burma, Thailand, Hong Kong, Japan and Korea.

The children spoke no English and lived in cultures totally unlike Kaye's. Yet language was no barrier to Danny; the kids understood perfectly his sounds, signs, singing and dancing. Smiles and hugs are universal.

"One thing I learned is that children are essentially the same all over the world," Kaye said. "They are exactly alike when acting instinctively. If they are hungry, they cry. If they are amused, they laugh. It is only when they assimilate culture, language and customs of their society that they become different from one another. Most adults are too inhibited to behave like children with children."

Danny was the exception. As he explained, "Did you ever find yourself leaning over a baby crib with a three- or four-month-old baby, making the oddest noises and sounds and faces? Well, if anybody had walked in and caught you doing that, you probably would be embarrassed. Most people would. Well, fortunately for me, I am uninhibited in the sense that I can do it comfortably with people watching."

Kaye didn't really play for the kids, he played *with* them. He also wasn't the one there to do the doctoring. "I don't come with any hypodermic needle and inject them against malaria or tuberculosis or whatever it might be," he said. "I may be present while it's being done, but I don't come as a medical man. I don't come as a spreader of gospel. I don't come as a teacher. I come as somebody who can maybe communicate with a child."

While Danny cavorted, UNICEF representatives fed the starving children and administered medical care to fight malaria, tuberculosis, yaws and other tropical diseases. Danny's favorite keepsake from the trip was a snapshot of a healthy young boy he called Sam, sitting on his lap and chewing the end of some toffee he had stretched from Kaye's mouth. Two weeks before, Sam—his body covered with large, open sores caused by yaws—had received his first shot of penicillin.

Assignment: Children was released in early 1955 to theaters "in every country which has a projection machine, whether behind the Iron Curtain or not." Kaye went on a second international UNICEF tour, this time to promote the film. Within a year of its release, the 20-minute color short would be translated into 23 languages, seen by 91 million people, and reportedly shown in more theaters than any other movie ever made. All monies collected during the showings went to UNICEF, and in the years forward 16mm prints were supplied to hundreds of libraries across the country to keep spreading the message.

Danny also profited from the venture, for as one journalist noted: "Kaye may get honors for *Assignment: Children*. In fact, he deserves them, but I'll wager nothing will touch him as much as the thanks (Far East fashion, with palms together and bowed head) of the children themselves."

The reviewer found just one shortcoming in the film: "It isn't long enough. Some of the tots laugh, some cry big tears... all are tremendously appealing. Here's hoping that some day someone will make a full-length feature on this fascinating subject."

THE COURT JESTER

(Filmed Nov. 22, 1954 to Feb. 16, Feb. 25 to March 12, March 18, 1955; released N.Y. Jan. 27, 1956)

Producers/Directors: Norman Panama & Mel Frank, for Dena Productions, Paramount
Screenplay: Norman Panama & Mel Frank
Songs: Sylvia Fine & Sammy Cahn ("Baby, Let Me Take You Dreaming," "Life Could Not Better Be," "My Heart Knows a Lovely Song," "Outfox the Fox," "Ritual of Knighthood;" Fine only "The Maladjusted Jester")
Cast: Danny Kaye (Hubert Hawkins), Glynis Johns (Maid Jean), Basil Rathbone (Sir Ravenhurst), Angela Lansbury (Princess Gwendolyn), Cecil Parker (King Roderick I), Mildred Natwick (Griselda), Robert Middleton (Sir Griswold)

The popularity of MGM's Best Picture-nominated *Ivanhoe* inspired a bounty of medieval epics — *The Sword and the Rose, Knights of the Roundtable, Prince Valiant, The Black Knight, King Richard and the Crusaders*. Panama and Frank thought the time ripe for a spoof. The challenge was that such period pieces, done right, didn't come cheap.

Paramount agreed to put up at least $1.5 million, so the writers began devising their own epic, loosely based on the legend of Robin Hood. They envisioned Kaye not as the swashbuckling Robin Hood character, but as circus performer Hubert Hawkins, who helps the show's midget acrobats escape from their indentured servitude. They vow to repay the favor and, in the last reel, help Hawkins and the Black Fox restore the infant king to his rightful throne.

Though a mere circus clown, Hawkins aspires to be strong and courageous. By having him impersonate a jester, the writers could work in Kaye's patter songs, dialects, and all-around silliness. Then, having him hypnotized, Kaye could play the bold, cocksure hero of Walter Mitty's dream world.

Sylvia approved of the basic plot, but noticed that the main story — the Black Fox's plot to overthrow the fake king — is firmly in motion before

Kaye ever arrives on screen. She thought, wherever possible, Danny's should be the character that drives the story. Sylvia wanted Hawkins to make multiple attempts to infiltrate the castle in different disguises, first as a monk, then as a hairdresser, a doctor, and finally as a jester. She thought Hubert should only pretend to be hypnotized, placing him in conscious control of the storyline. She suggested that Hawkins, after swinging by a vine to the princess' chamber, gets dizzy and thinks there are two people in her room instead of one. And, at some point, Sylvia wanted Hubert sent to a torture chamber, where he could fake suffering noises and simulate the sounds of the rack, iron maiden, and other devices. Panama and Frank agreed that the story's basic premise should be that Hawkins "tries to be a hero and keeps falling on his ass." Yet they ignored all her specific suggestions.

Ideally, Panama and Frank would shoot some footage in London, using the interiors and exteriors of real castles. No expense was to be spared, or so they hoped.

To ensure Sylvia's music was the highest quality, they assigned her a collaborator—Sammy Cahn. Panama and Frank initially asked for six songs, all for Kaye—a "Man of Many Faces" number for him and the midgets to perform at the circus; a lullaby to soothe the baby in a hut; a "Merry Minstrel" song to sing on the wagon in the rain in the courtyard outside the castle gates, and three songs for the main hall—a love song, a specialty jester routine, and a "Pass the Basket" number, with Hawkins urging the chorus to keep passing around a basket, to keep the king and his guards from discovering the baby inside.

Fine and Cahn began working together at the Kaye home in the summer of 1954 and, by the time cameras began rolling during Thanksgiving week, were still at it. Sylvia, explained Cahn, "was very, very, very, very, very, very, very—a whole page of verys and then there's—slow. And I am very, very, very, very, very, very, very fast. And this was very, very troublesome to me. (Writing the songs) seemed forever."

Still, Sylvia and Sammy's working relationship was pleasant. "I can't work in conflict," Cahn said. "A song written in conflict sounds like a song written in conflict. (But) I always had a feeling that she was writing behind me. I was only there because they wanted me to be there. It's like if I was the exclusive writer for Sinatra and he brought somebody else in to write for him. There would be a natural kind of feeling of trespassing. And I felt like I was trespassing, because I knew that nobody writes for Danny Kaye like Sylvia Fine. And who's this fellow? What's he doing here?"

In all, Fine and Cahn composed a dozen songs for the picture, including two love songs ("Love Me Again" and "I'm Young Again") they quickly discarded. Yet Fine alone took charge over the specialty number (alternately titled "I Make a Fool of Myself," "The Court Jester's Lament," and "Nobody's Fool" before being renamed at the last minute "The Maladjusted Jester"). Cahn said, "All the special material she did. I had nothing to do with it. I didn't even know about it. This was her domain. No one was going to get in there."

As the start of production neared, the estimated budget had ballooned to $1.9 million. There would have to be cuts. Two more songs were chopped—to save money and to tighten the narrative. Out was "I Live to Love," which the hypnotized jester was to sing as he wooed the princess. Instead, the screenwriters incorporated snippets of its lyrics into the scene's dialogue ("I live to love, I love to live, I leap from my sleep when danger cries"). As well, the ballad "Where Walks My True Love" was deleted, but its melody retained as background music for the scene in which Hawkins and his love interest, Jean, begin their journey in the wagon.

Panama and Frank also abandoned plans to film overseas in and around authentic castles. Most everything would be shot on a Paramount sound-stage, except for a few special effects (a stuntman on a swinging vine, a cat-apult) on the backlot and exterior shots requiring an ocean background, using the cliffs of the Palos Verdes Peninsula.

More significantly, Panama and Frank estimated they could lop off $250,000 in production costs by scaling back their plans for trick opening credits and elaborate opening scenes at the circus and in town. The opening did establish why the midgets were indebted to Hawkins and how they were so nimble and adept at being thrown about by catapults. But dropping it saved a week of filming that covered 22 pages of the script and eliminated the need to build several elaborate sets and pay a cast of hundreds (for the circus audience, acrobats and dozens of animals, including a trained bear).

The opening scene's replacement, "You'll Never Outfox the Fox," estab-lished Hawkins' desire to be a hero, while summing up his relationship with the midget acrobats in a few lines of dialogue. The elaborate number also began driving back up the project's cost. In fact, by the time filming was to begin and all predicted expenses had been itemized, the budget stood at near-ly $2.5 million. Panama and Frank refused additional cuts and, using Don Hartman as their middleman at Paramount, received the go-ahead to proceed.

As filming was about to begin, Panama and Frank replaced choreographer James Starbuck with Robert Alton. After one week of filming, they replaced cinematographer Ray Rennahan with Ray June, adding an extra $8,000 to the production costs.

Panama and Frank's five previous producing and directing experiences were much smaller in scale—in no way comparable to *The Court Jester's* huge cast, hulking sets, intricate props, and elaborate costumes. Everything ended up costing more than they had anticipated. Filling up huge backdrops, particularly the cavernous Main Hall, meant additional actors, outfitted in additional costumes, and lit by additional lamp operators. The frantic "midget battle" finale, in particular, was far more difficult than expected to stage and film, with countless actors engaged in constant action. The scene required three weeks to complete, its price tag nearly doubling to $424,000. The main titles had to be remade several times, increasing their cost from $2,500 to $37,500. The dueling scene on the parapets, budgeted for $72,000, would cost $184,000.

The production fell so far behind schedule that on many days sets would have to be disassembled and temporarily moved aside to accommodate the start of other films, further driving up costs.

Sylvia helped slow down the process, as well. Pre-recording the songs, Fine and Kaye style, was inherently expensive. As Roy Fjastad, head of Paramount's music department, noted in a memo to explain the cost overruns for music to his bosses: "On the days that pre-recording took place, additional hours of orchestra time were consumed, due to changes, new ideas, vocal inflections, etc. As a matter of fact, the final pre-recording of 'Nobody's Fool' took seven-and-three-quarters hours instead of three hours, which we would normally budget."

Sylvia's last-minute tinkering with the opening number, "They'll Never Outfox the Fox," meant the music wasn't ready when time came for filming. The scene's plentiful cast had to be paid to sit around for five days, waiting. Budgeted for $120,000, the scene cost $217,900.

On March 1, 1955, with the number finally completed, Hartman pulled Kaye aside. They were more than a month over schedule, approaching $1 million over budget, and there was still one more musical number left to be filmed, the extensive "Pass the Basket." Hartman said omitting the number would save at least $75,000. Danny consented to cut it, with Panama and Frank's permission. "Pass the Basket" was chopped and the song that led into it—"Willow Willow Waley"—reduced to a brief lead-in to "The

POINT TAKEN: Kaye's overmatched *Court Jester* miraculously defeated Robert Middleton's Sir Griswold. [© 1956 Paramount Pictures]

Maladjusted Jester."

Sylvia was disappointed, but had Danny voice-record the full version of "Willow Willow Waley" anyway, along with "Pass the Basket," "I Live to Love," and "Where Walks My True Love." She had just co-founded Dena Music Company, with herself as president, and planned *The Court Jester* soundtrack as her company's first release, hoping to replicate the success of the *Hans Christian Andersen* soundtrack. Yet since the finished film contained only five songs, the four deleted numbers were needed to fill up both sides of an album.

For his part, Danny had to be a little hesitant about doing his first period picture since *The Inspector General*. His first challenge was looking the part, since—clad in tights—his skinny legs showed little definition. Kaye also bristled at learning he'd have to wear a suit of armor. "A nice comfortable suit of armor?" he asked. Costume designer Edith Head looked dubious. She explained that making comfortable armor wasn't one of her tricks of the trade.

"Let's drop the picture," Danny said, sounding serious.

Miss Head knew what she had to do. She quickly devised a suit of flexible aluminum. Kaye reluctantly agreed to wear the armor, but hated it even so.

Danny felt more at ease behind the tip of a sword. Olympic fencing instructor Ralph Faulkner was brought in to coach him on the fine points of fencing. On film, Kaye would square off against Basil Rathbone, though age 62, a highly proficient swordsman. Kaye, Rathbone recalled, "had never fenced before, but after a couple of weeks of instruction, Danny could completely outfight me. Even granting the difference in our ages, his reflexes were incredibly fast and nothing had to be shown or explained to him a second time. His mind worked like a camera."

During the scene when Hawkins is hypnotized into believing he's a master swordsman, Kaye suddenly began whipping his blade so quickly that Rathbone couldn't keep up. To retain the ultra-perfect timing—and prevent Rathbone from being skewered—coach Faulkner dressed as Rathbone's character and appeared in the fastest-paced scenes.

Kaye also excelled in the movie verbally. Fast-paced, tongue-twisting dialogue worked so well in *Knock on Wood*, Panama and Frank expanded its use in *The Court Jester*. Mostly, Hawkins spouted the tongue-twisters to confound his adversaries, such as the King ("When the Doge did his duty and the Duke didn't, that's when the Duchess did the dirt to the Duke with the Doge"), and in a recurring exchange ("Get it?" "Got it." "Good."). But one routine, "The Vessel with the Pestle," would become the best-remembered bit of Kaye's film career.

The piece was based on an old Eddie Cantor routine that was conscripted by Bob Hope, who gave Panama and Frank their first jobs in radio and the movies. In *Roman Scandals* (1933), royal food-taster Cantor must remember that it's the entrée with the parsley that has been poisoned. In *Never Say*

Die (1939), co-authored by Don Hartman, Hope heads for a duel with confusing instructions on which weapon to choose ("There's a cross on the muzzle of the pistol with the bullet and a scratch on the barrel of the pistol with the blank."). Hope varied the bit before a gunfight in *The Paleface* (1948), as Hope jumbles the advice he's been given ("He draws from the left, so stand on your toes...").

For the facile-tongued Kaye, Panama and Frank knew they could up the ante. As Hawkins prepares to joust, the witch informs him that she's poisoned one of the goblets. The jester in shining armor must remember: "The pellet with the poison's in the vessel with the pestle; the chalice from the palace has the brew that is true." Our hero repeats every possible mispronunciation before finally getting it right—and then learns that the chalice from the palace was broken and has been replaced by a flagon with a dragon, which now contains the pellet with the poison. Now, the vessel with the pestle has the brew that is true.

Overall, the film's greatest asset was that, as Leonard Maltin pointed out in *The Great Movie Comedians*, "Panama and Frank were able to capture in a screenplay what Sylvia Fine had been able to encapsulate in her comedy songs for Danny over the years: his gifts for music, mimicry, pantomime, and fast-paced patter."

Indeed, the character, plot and setting allow Danny to blend into a film more seamlessly than ever. He cavorts *with* his co-stars, instead of in front of them, *inside* the story, rather than beyond it. His character is believable both as romantic lead and childish fool, alternating effortlessly between elegance and buffoonery.

Alas, artistic success did not guarantee financial success. The production was scheduled to take 70 days for rehearsals, primary filming, and second-unit work. It ended up taking 112. Its final cost—$4 million—made it the most expensive comedy ever produced. At the box office, it barely grossed $2 million.

Because the reviews were generally favorable, some onlookers blamed the film's losses on Danny's off-stage seriousness. A Paramount executive scoffed: "That's ridiculous Hollywood thinking. The picture didn't make money because it cost too much for today's market. It got out of hand."

Indeed, after making its way to television, *The Court Jester* found its audience. The film is now wildly popular and acknowledged by the American Film Institute as one of the greatest comedies ever made.

SEE IT NOW:
THE SECRET LIFE OF DANNY KAYE

(Filmed mid-April to June 3, 1956; aired Dec. 2, 1956, CBS 5 p.m.)
Producers: Edward R. Murrow & Fred W. Friendly
Associate Producer: Sylvia Fine
Cast: Danny Kaye (himself), Edward R. Murrow (host), Anthony Eden, David Ben-
Gurion, Josip Broz Tito, René Coty
Songs: "Thumbelina," "Ciu Ciu Bella," "Knock on Wood," "Minnie the Moocher," "Melody
in 4F: UNICEF Version," "Tritsch-Tratsch-Polka," "Stars & Stripes Forever,"
"Tschaikowsky," "I Never Knew"

Assignment: Children made Danny an instant figure of adulation. A
month after the film's release, he was presented an honorary Oscar, the Jean
Hersholt Humanitarian Award. Later in 1955, he appeared in a two-minute
film to promote UNICEF's Trick or Treat campaign, in which kids went
door-to-door on Halloween collecting donations.

Indeed, the trips had touched Kaye deeply, permanently. He knew the job
of promoting UNICEF wasn't finished. Sylvia, too, thought *Assignment:
Children* could have been much more effective. Because the film was shot
silent and Kaye added narration later, it failed to capture Danny and the
children at their most engaging. The film seemed too educational.

So, Kaye agreed to go on a third tour, one designed to disseminate the
message more widely and more accessibly. He would televise it. Danny
called on Edward R. Murrow of *See It Now*, and he didn't have to talk for
more than two minutes before the TV producer asked, "What do you need
and when can we get started?"

Kaye spent seven weeks, during the summer of 1956, cutting up for
32,000 miles across Italy, Greece, Yugoslavia, Switzerland, Turkey, Nigeria,
Spain, Morocco, France, England and Israel, all captured on film by two
CBS-TV camera crews. There were no rehearsals, no shooting schedules,
not even the tiniest hint of a plot—just Danny merrily pied-pipering through
the villages and the hearts of three continents. Kaye again paid all his own
expenses and carried only "a little bag of dried fruit, a little matchstick on
which to jot down little notes, and a pair of comfortable shoes."

The fruits of his labor were apparent everywhere. In a leper colony in
Nigeria, he got caught up in the music and jitterbugged with a youngster. In
Italy, a small child jumped out of a hospital bed and began singing a simple
Italian folk song, "Ciu Ciu Bella," which became the program's theme
song. In Yugoslavia, Kaye led the crowd through "I Never Knew," a song

THE SECRET LIFE OF DANNY KAYE

is an unforgettable experience marking a most unusual television debut in behalf of the United Nations International Children's Emergency Fund. Today you will follow the joyful trail of Danny Kaye at his best as he entertains' the children of Italy, Greece, Yugoslavia, Switzerland, Turkey, Nigeria, Spain, Morocco, France, England and Israel at the request of UNICEF. For an hour and a half through the cameras of **"SEE IT NOW,"** produced by **EDWARD R. MURROW** and **FRED W. FRIENDLY,** you will see the upturned faces of these children transfigured with delight as Danny clowns his way into their hearts on this unique program **TODAY AT 5** on **CBS TELEVISION ⬤ CHANNEL 2**

KID FRIENDLY: Kaye's first TV appearance, on Edward R. Murrow's *See It Now*, promoted the work of UNICEF.

they had never heard before. But the evidence was most obvious in the illuminated faces of every child he touched.

When Danny returned home, Sylvia took over. Because the show was to run 90 minutes, be watched by millions, and be her husband's television debut, she was insistent that it be not only informative, but entertaining. As part of the deal, she would act as associate producer and supervising editor. With Murrow and co-producer Fred Friendly, she trimmed the 32 hours, or 240,000 feet of film, down to 10,000 feet. Entitled "The Secret Life of Danny Kaye," the segment was broadcast on December 2, 1956, almost simultaneously in 24 countries. In fact, it was the first American program to air in the Soviet Union.

The episode won a prestigious Peabody Award and permanently distinguished Kaye as not just ambassador for UNICEF, but to children in general. He would spend the rest of his life touting and tirelessly traveling for the organization. His expeditions increased exponentially in 1960, when he bought his own private jet, enabling him to fly himself to UNICEF destinations. Each year, he would publicize its Trick or Treat campaign by flying across the country, collecting donations at airports in tens of cities in just a few days. His whirlwind tours earned him a spot in the 1977 Guinness Book of World Records by visiting 65 different U.S. and Canadian cities in less than a week—flying every mile of the journey himself and amassing $6 million for UNICEF along the way.

Kaye and UNICEF became inseparable. They continued to tie their activities together up until his dying days. When UNICEF received the Nobel Peace Prize in 1965, Danny flew to Oslo, Norway, to accept it for them. Likewise, in 1969, when Danny was asked to put his handprints in cement in the forecourt of Grauman's Chinese Theater, he requested the ceremony be just one part of a whole program devoted to UNICEF.

Kaye's innate wanderlust perfectly complemented UNICEF's constant need for funds and publicity. But the demands of worldwide travel did affect Danny's health, as Sylvia explained: "Coming back from these trips, you would expect him to be absolutely worn out and underweight, which he is anyhow; however, he comes back looking healthier than before he left. I ask him why and he says it's because he has such a wonderful time."

UNICEF WORK

1954 *Assignment: Children.*

1955 *Assignment: Children* promotional tour. Trick or Treat film.

1956 *See It Now.* Radio show for UNICEF's 10th anniversary.

1957 Preface for UNICEF book. Trick or Treat sequence added to rebroadcast of *See It Now.*

1960 Selects tales for *Danny Kaye's Around the World Story Book.*

1961 Two 30-minute films for 15th anniversary trip.

1964 Visits UNICEF-sponsored It's a Small World pavilion at New York World's Fair. Narrates *A New Fashioned Halloween.*

1965 Flies first Trick or Treat tour. Flies to Oslo to accept UNICEF's Nobel Peace Prize.

1966 Second Trick or Treat trip. Shoots two 20th anniversary films while touring Europe.

1967 Tours Israel. Third Trick or Treat trip. Promotes UNICEF at Montreal Expo.

1968 Fourth Trick or Treat trip. Promotes UNICEF at Paris gala.

1970 Leads UNICEF circus. Tours Japan.

1971 Tours internationally.

1973 Stars in German TV show. Tours Istanbul. Conducts UNICEF benefit concert. Appears in UNICEF radio show.

1974 *Pied Piper* film (with scenes from 1971 trip). Tours New Zealand.

1975 Trick or Treat tour. Stars in public service spot. Tours Japan.

1976 Tours Europe.

1977 Tours Denmark.

1978 Visits Geneva.

1979 Four trips to Europe. Stars in telethon. Tours Asia and Holland.

MERRY ANDREW

(Filmed July 1 to Oct. 17, 1957; released N.Y. March 20, 1958)
Producer: Sol C. Siegel, for Sol C. Siegel Productions, Metro-Goldwyn-Mayer
Director: Michael Kidd
Screenplay: Isobel Lennart, IAL Diamond (uncredited Casey Robinson, Arthur
Wimperis, Jean Holloway, Leon Gordon, Richard Schayer, Hugh Gray, Jan Lustig,
Paul Osborn, John Patrick)
Original Story: "The Romance of Henry Menafee" by Paul Gallico
Songs: Saul Chaplin & Johnny Mercer ("Pipes of Pan," "Salud"/"Buona Fortuna," "Chin
Up, Stout Fella," "Everything Is Tickety Boo," "You Can't Always Have What You
Want," "Square of the Hypotenuse," "Here's Cheers")
Cast: Danny Kaye (Andrew Larabee), Pier Angeli (Selena), Salvatore Baccaloni
(Antonio Gallini), Robert Coote (Dudley Larabee), Noel Purcell (Matthew Larabee),
Patricia Cutts (Letitia Fairchild), Rex Evans (Gregory Larabee)

Devoting so much time to UNICEF kept Kaye away from movie cameras
for more than two years. So by February of 1957, he had signed to star in
three films, back to back to back. He'd spend the summer filming a musical
comedy for MGM, the fall starring in a sequel to *Knock on Wood* for
Paramount, and the following spring doing a biographical musical, or
"biopic," for Paramount.

After the breakdown of *Huckleberry Finn* several years earlier, it took a
larger, $200,000 payday and the promise that the picture would be built
around him to convince Danny to give MGM another look. Certainly, the
studio had a vaunted reputation for crafting classy musicals. Comedies were
another matter. MGM was notorious for misusing such comedians as Red
Skelton, Buster Keaton, the Marx Brothers, Laurel and Hardy, and Our
Gang.

Kaye, though, trusted the studio had come up with an acceptable vehicle.
The project, ironically, had been in Hollywood just as long as Danny had.
MGM had bought the film rights to a short story, Paul Gallico's "The
Romance of Henry Menafee," just as it was to be serialized in the April and
May 1943 issues of *Good Housekeeping*. It centered on an uptight English
schoolmaster who is captivated during his first visit to the circus, particularly by two bareback riders—beautiful Serena and Peter, a small boy who
resembles a recently unearthed statuette of the Greek god Pan. A week later,
Peter is brought to the school Menafee's wife owns, but the boy runs away.
Menafee follows him to the circus, intending to bring him back, but instead
the schoolmaster ends up taking the place of an injured clown. He falls in
love with the job—and with Serena. He stays with the circus for three
months and becomes engaged to Serena. When Serena's father discovers

CHIMP CHEERIO: Danny, director Michael Kidd, and simian co-star Angelina enjoyed making *Merry Andrew*. [© 1958 MGM]

Menafee is married, the schoolteacher flees to South America. There, he becomes a world famous clown. After the war breaks out in Europe, he returns to England, to bring joy to frightened children and to reunite with Serena and Peter.

Gallico and a revolving door of eight other writers spent the next seven years trying to make the story work. The drama was actually budgeted and scheduled to start filming in 1947 with Spencer Tracy as the lead, but got shelved. Interest in the project renewed a few years later after *The Greatest Show on Earth* was a big hit and every studio in town began scrambling to develop its own circus picture. Storyman Maurice Zimm was handed a yellowing script for *The Romance of Henry Menafee* and asked for his thoughts. Zimm found the story charming and whimsical, yet poorly structured and vague in theme. "What, then, *is* our theme?" he asked. "That if a man stays away from home long enough, and returns looking ignominious enough, his wife will finally grant him a divorce? That a boy like Peter is better off in a circus than in a 'School for the Sons of Gentlemen'? That if a schoolmaster has the talent to become the world's greatest clown, true love will triumph in the end?"

Zimm passed on the assignment and offered the studio this advice: "Briefly then: This studio at this time would never buy this story. Why not put it back on the shelf?"

Yet producer Sol Siegel thought the story had potential, not as a drama but as a light musical. He hired screenwriter Isobel Lennart, who specialized in high-spirited musicals like *Anchors Aweigh*. Lennart turned Menafee into Andrew Larabee, who teaches under his domineering father and aspires to one day become headmaster and marry his joyless fiancée—until he discovers the circus and pretty aerialist Serena. Lennart renamed the picture after the British slang for a clown, *Merry Andrew*.

In the months before production began, Billy Wilder's writing partner, I.A.L. Diamond, was brought in to strengthen the story and build up the comic situations. Diamond modestly recalled, "My involvement with *Merry Andrew* was peripheral. I did a last minute doctoring job on a script by the late Isobel Lennart, and I was not around MGM during the shooting."

In actuality, Diamond spent fourteen weeks rewriting the script and introducing key elements to the storyline, such as having Andrew adopted by the circus after he persuades a developer not to evict the troupe and replacing the role of the boy with a chimpanzee, who would become one of the most marketable faces of the movie.

MGM did not allow Sylvia to participate, but gave Kaye's friend, *Knock on Wood* choreographer Michael Kidd, the opportunity to direct his first film, with a princely budget of nearly $2.8 million. Unfortunately, the popularity of Hollywood musicals was cyclical and, by the time production got underway, musicals were taking a dive. *Merry Andrew* was the only musical MGM had in production at the time and, a month into filming, the studio ordered Kidd to wrap up the film as quickly and inexpensively as possible.

By eliminating or cutting back eleven scenes, Kidd was able to complete the picture several weeks early and $250,000 under budget. Associate producer and composer Saul Chaplin insisted the cuts severely weakened the movie. After a decade of working on some of MGM's greatest masterpieces, Chaplin left the studio after *Merry Andrew*. Kidd would never direct another film.

Kaye, conversely, enjoyed the experience, even though he knew the end product was no work of art. Danny confessed, off the record to *Saturday*

Evening Post interviewer Pete Martin, "It's the kind of picture that if you don't see, you don't have to kill yourself. It is not the greatest picture in the world by a long shot. I think it's a very pleasant, entertaining musical, which is what we started out to make, and I think we succeeded in doing that. Mike (Kidd) and I worked very well together and all the people concerned with the picture were very creative and very easy to work with. It was a most pleasant experience, and I think it shows on the screen."

Indeed, *The New York Times* called the film "pleasant," "genial," and "blithesome"—not exactly ingredients for a Hollywood blockbuster. It grossed a paltry $1 million.

ME AND THE COLONEL

(Filmed Nov. 18, 1957 to Jan. 30, 1958; released N.Y. Aug. 26, 1958)
Producer: William Goetz, for Goetz Pictures, Court Enterprises, Columbia
Director: Peter Glenville
Screenplay: S.N. Behrman, George Froeschel (uncredited Gottfried Reinhart, IAL Diamond)
Original Story: 1944 play *Jacobowsky & the Colonel* by Franz Werfel, adapted by S.N. Behrman
Cast: Danny Kaye (Jacobowsky), Curt Jurgens (Col. Prokoszny), Nicole Maurey (Suzanne), Francoise Rosay (Madame Bouffier), Akim Tamiroff (Szabuniewicz), Martita Hunt (Mother Superior)

Next up was *Knock on Silk*, the *Knock on Wood* sequel that had Kaye running from spies in Japan. But, by the time production was supposed to begin, Danny wasn't happy with the script, now titled *The Bamboo Kid*. Having set aside his winter for moviemaking, he started searching for a quick project to fill the time. One of his closest friends, producer William Goetz, was an endless fountain of offers. The year before, he'd tried to interest Kaye in *Gulliver's Travels*. Now Goetz was casting a more serious picture, *Jacobowsky and the Colonel*.

The German play, adapted for Broadway by S.N. Behrman, followed a resourceful Jew desperate to escape France on the eve of the Nazi invasion. Jacobowsky convinces an anti-Semitic Polish colonel to drive them both out of the country, while falling in love with Suzanne, the officer's girlfriend.

Columbia paid $350,000 for the film rights to the play back in 1944, while it was still running on Broadway. But the property languished for nearly thirteen years, going through assorted producers and various stars

A TOUCH DARKER: A mustache, graying temples, and black-and-white photography gave Kaye a calmer, more serious presence in *Me and the Colonel*, here with Curt Jurgens and Akim Tamiroff. [© 1958 Columbia Pictures]

such as Peter Lorre and Leslie Caron.

The theme intrigued Danny. More often than not, he would have passed on such a radical departure. Not this time. Nevertheless, Kaye emphasized to the press that he was drawn by the message, not by a clown's secret desire to play Hamlet.

Behrman and successive screenwriters tried to stick closely to the original play, deviating primarily to add bits of action that would make the proceedings feel less like a filmed stageplay. But most of the added visuals didn't move the plot forward and were cut. Among the additions that were subtracted, the film was supposed to open with Jacobowsky feeding ducks, to illustrate his kindness. The colonel, before requisitioning Jacobowsky's car, was first to requisition a scooter, and then a street sweeper. When their car crosses paths with a German tank, instead of Jacobowsky bargaining for gasoline with the Nazis by trading the colonel's vodka, the tank was to fire at their car, creating a giant crater in the road and forcing their car to swerve out of the way and hide in a tunnel. Jacobowsky was then to steal the gasoline from a firetruck—that he lured by intentionally setting a fire outside Suzanne's cottage. The writers also wanted to play up the romantic tension between the three main characters by having Suzanne, during the journey, bathe in a stream and share a picnic with Jacobowsky. Finally, when the inebriated officer challenges Jacobowsky to a duel, instead of pistols, the colonel was to chase his pajama-clad rival all through a castle with a sword. The swordfight was retained in the final script, although Jacobowsky is fully dressed, instead of in his PJs.

During shooting, the film was renamed *Best of Enemies*, before ultimately changing to *Me and the Colonel*. Most of the interior scenes were shot on a Columbia Pictures soundstage in Los Angeles. For the exteriors, the crew journeyed to Lyons, France, where the filmmakers were assisted by local technicians. Kaye delighted in confusing the foreign film crew with his non-sensical French double-talk.

But the moment the cameras began to roll, Kaye put on a different face. The script gave him plenty of witty dialogue, but no broad comedy or zaniness. His was a completely controlled, believable performance. Yet there was something else different about *Me and the Colonel*. Kaye said, "It wasn't the touch of gray in my hair. I've had that before. It wasn't the mustache. I've had that, too, in other pictures. I finally discovered the answer: *Me and the Colonel* was the first black-and-white movie I'd appeared in. The black-and-white photography made my eyes smaller, and that was what changed my face."

As Danny's first non-musical, the film appeared to leave no room for Sylvia's involvement. That didn't stop her. In 1953, she had penned lyrics to the title song for *The Moon Is Blue*—and it garnered her an Academy Award nomination. A year later, she added words to the music from *Witness to Murder*, and in 1956 acquired the rights to Elmer Bernstein's soundtrack for *The Man with the Golden Arm*. She wrote lyrics for Bernstein's theme (she called the song "Delilah Jones") and "Molly-O," so Danny could record them for Decca. In the same way, she wrote lyrics for *Me and the Colonel's* main theme, called the song "Suzanne," and published it under her Dena Music label.

Reviews for the picture were wildly divergent. The National Board of Review voted it among the year's Ten Best American Films. Other critics were horrified that a film would mix anti-Semitism and humor. The Writers Guild of America honored it as the best-written American comedy of 1958. And, ironically, the comic's most restrained performance would be his most critically lauded. Kaye won a Golden Globe as Best Actor in a Comedy or Musical.

THE FIVE PENNIES

(Filmed Oct. 7 to Dec. 12, 1958; released N.Y. June 18, 1959; wide June 30, 1959)
Producer: Jack Rose, for Dena Productions, Paramount
Director: Melville Shavelson
Screenplay: Melville Shavelson & Jack Rose (uncredited Robert Parrish, Daniel Fuchs, David Shaw, Edward O. Berkman, Raphael D. Blau, John Michael Hayes)
Original Story: "Intermission" by Robert Smith
Songs: Sylvia Fine ("Five Pennies," "Five Pennies Saints," "Follow the Leader," "Good Night, Sleep Tight," "Lullaby in Ragtime," "Schnitzelbank")
Cast: Danny Kaye (Red Nichols), Barbara Bel Geddes (Bobbie Meredith), Harry Guardino (Tony Valani), Susan Gordon (Dorothy, 6), Tuesday Weld (Dorothy, 11), Louis Armstrong (himself)

Soon after signing his original two-picture deal with Paramount, Kaye inked an extension for Dena Pictures to produce two additional films that the studio would distribute. Don Hartman suggested a musical biography, like the highly successful *Glenn Miller Story*. He thought Danny would make a perfect Red Nichols, the carrot-topped bandleader who was in the midst of a comeback after leaving show business to care for his polio-stricken daughter. Hartman's own daughter had polio, and in 1954 he purchased the story rights to Nichols' life from director Robert Parrish. Robert Smith was commissioned to write a ten-page treatment, *Intermission*, that concentrated on Nichols' self-imposed exile from music, during which he settled down at his father's chicken ranch in Northern California, so he could fully devote himself to his daughter.

Hartman ran it through five more writers, but the script never seemed to jell. Sylvia recounted: "One script started in Ogden, Utah. Another started in the Catskill Mountains. Nichols and his wife had 'met cute,' 'met bitter,' or couldn't make ends meet. Red's father was in. Red's father was out. It was a drama. It was a comedy. It was a dramatic comedy. It was a comedic drama. From Danny's 'next picture,' it became a project, then a commitment. A commitment, of course, is any picture you're stuck with."

The various drafts made for interesting drama—they just didn't feel like a Danny Kaye picture. So, after completing *The Court Jester*, Panama and Frank briefly took over the project, to reshape the story for Danny's talents. By the summer of 1956, the story was turned over to Mel Shavelson and Jack Rose, who had just earned an Academy Award nomination for writing a similarly heavy musical biopic with Bob Hope, *The Seven Little Foys*. Having pored over the early drafts, Sylvia gave the writers firm but

friendly advice: "Don't read them." Shavelson and Rose agreed to start
from scratch. First, they interviewed Nichols and his wife to hear the story
firsthand. Next, Sylvia handed them a list of eight "musical notions"—ideas
for numbers tailored to Danny's talents she hoped they could work into the
narrative, such as Red, early in his courtship, performing a "tongued" rendition of "Carnival of Venice." And Red, at an informal party following a day
of auditioning singers, could do brief imitations of a scared and gulping
singer, a singer with a cold, and the over-exuberant, off-key "Begin the
Beguine." Red might also perk up the exhausted band with a rousing number on the bus, perform a novelty dialect number with the band in costumes,
and sing a lullaby to his young daughter.

Shavelson and Rose's first draft disappointed her. At a January 1957
story conference, Sylvia unloaded with both barrels. She thought that the
script was short on fun, excitement and, most critically, music. Worse, as
written, Nichols was not a sympathetic character. "He is just a SOB, and the
public is never shown what compels him to behave the way he does," she
complained, possibly revealing what she thought of her husband's real-life
moodiness. "Men of enormous talent are devoted to their work, not only
compulsively, but there is a good reason why they are only at ease with people in the same profession and cannot make more than passing contact with
'civilians.' Illustrating this, we must also show why (Nichols' wife) Willa
puts up with this kind of behavior."

With production set to begin within weeks, Paramount decided to shelf
the project for one year. The delay gave Shavelson and Rose more time to
add punch to the script, even if that meant straying from the facts. Sylvia
may have agreed that it was "vital that Danny faithfully portray Red," but
considered it "sheer insanity if we didn't try to use some of those potential
Kaye fireworks and the soft, warm charm of his singing style."

They compromised, at least musically. There would be two different
musical concepts of Nichols: one for Red the public figure, one for Red the
private figure. "All clowning and singing was to be done privately, informally, or when starving," she said. "Thus, standard songs for the 'public
Nichols' and original songs for the 'private Nichols.' That's when I started
to write some new songs for a picture rich with great old ones."

In place of Nichols' quiet nature, Danny became an at-times frantic,
extroverted scat-singer. He may have been cast, for the first time, as a real-
life person, but that didn't mean that real person couldn't be presented as a
lot more like Danny Kaye than Red Nichols. Shavelson and Rose changed

Nichols' wife from a dancer to a singer, so that she could perform with his band. Because so many better-known musicians (Jimmy Dorsey, Benny Goodman, Glenn Miller, Gene Krupa, Jack Teagarden) got their starts in Nichols' band, the writers tried to play up the roles of the jazz legends in their scenario. At odds with history, they even worked Louis Armstrong into a pivotal role. They also wanted Benny Goodman to play himself in the picture, but couldn't meet his salary demands.

That didn't stop the producers from filling the movie with cameos—Bob Hope (as himself, exiting the Brown Derby), eleven-year-old Dena (as a rehabilitation ward patient), Red Nichols (as a horn-blowing Clicquot Club Eskimo), and disk jockeys Peter Potter, Dick Whittinghill, and Ira Cook (as radio announcers). One scene was also filmed on location at the typically star-studded Hollywood Brown Derby—although the celebrity portraits on the restaurant's walls were fakes. To avoid having to obtain clearances from all the stars, the Paramount art department whipped up 150 caricatures of nobodies.

Just as filming was about to finally get underway in early 1958, the musicians' union went on strike. Other films were able to continue production by using canned background music. That was impossible on a musical that required not only new music, but on-screen musicians.

By the time the strike reached its third month, Paramount offered to release Danny from his contract, allowing him to make the film at United Artists, a smaller, independent studio with a greater chance of securing a separate, temporary agreement with the union. But no deal could be reached with United Artists. The project sat dormant at Paramount for six months, until the strike finally ended.

During the break, Kaye had plenty of time to learn to pretend-play the cornet. Nichols himself would record the cornet and trumpet tracks, but Danny still had to be able to convincingly duplicate Red's fingering.

"We would always pre-record (the musical numbers)," recalled director Shavelson, "and Danny was so good at lip-sync. He and Louis did a duet. First they did 'Battle Hymn of the Republic' and then they did 'When the Saints Go Marching In.' Well, Danny was doing it back to Red Nichols' track and had to get the fingering on the trumpet right—Danny doesn't play the trumpet and he doesn't read music. Louis had recorded his own track, and Danny bet Louis that he would get the fingering right and Louis would miss it. And he was right, because Louis would never do the same thing twice, and Danny—having done it once—could do it perfectly back every time."

Kaye and Armstrong worked wonderfully together, although Louis unintentionally was the cause of one ongoing frustration. Cinematographer Daniel Fapp said, "(Armstrong) perspired so much, and in those days they didn't want to see that perspiration under his sleeves. He'd do a number and have to change shirts. We'd lose so much time changing shirts that finally they let it go, which was the proper thing to do to begin with."

Still, Kaye was never fond of rehearsals or retakes, particularly for what to him seemed the triviality of precisely matching his motions in one shot to those in the previous shot. As a result, he constantly argued with the script girl, who kept correcting his varying improvisations.

"No, no, that's terrible, Danny," the girl would plead, "because people will notice in this scene you drank half the glass, and now they look at the glass and it's full again."

"You're crazy," Kaye would answer. "Nobody's going to notice that."

Shavelson recalled: "This funny fight was going on, so in part of one of the big numbers in the picture he played the trumpet with his left hand and part of the number he played it with his right hand. He told the script girl he would do things that she would not be able to detect, and he proved it."

"Danny liked to improvise," Shavelson continued. "On stage, that's fine because you're only doing it once and whatever the other actors do, you take off from that. But not in a movie, where you've shot it one way in one angle and you go to shoot it in another way and he won't repeat it. So Danny for a while said, 'I'll only shoot one take, so the first time I do it, that's it. And if I improvise something, that's set in the picture.' I fought with him, and finally Sylvia went to him and said, 'Danny, that's unfair to everybody else. You're only giving them one shot at the scene, too. And, besides, you're lousy in the first take.' We finally talked him out of it, but it took half the picture to do it."

Sylvia wrote all the original music for the picture, arranged the old Nichols standards, and acted as associate producer. But her role as the latter was limited to musical aspects of the film.

"What Sylvia was interested in was the quality of the music reproduction, and she could never get it through her head that whatever you put on a soundtrack, it was still being played on the lousiest sound systems in the world, which were the American motion picture theaters," Shavelson recalled. "A lot of us mixed six tracks and we had basically stereophonic sound and everything else, (but) it was only going to come out on those ter-

HORN BLOWER: Kaye learned to expertly finger a cornet for *The Five Pennies*, here with nine-year-old Susan Gordon. [© 1959 Paramount Pictures]

rible speakers. And she spent most of the time in post-production. I don't know, it might have taken her years after we finished before she was satisfied with the music tracks on the picture. That was her basic contribution."

Fine's score was as good as any she had ever written, and blended perfectly with the picture's story and era. Her "Five Pennies Saints"—a jazz rewrite of "When the Saints Go Marching In" climaxed by Kaye and Armstrong improvising for three scat choruses—would steal the picture.

For her song "Follow the Leader" (also a working title of the film), choreographer Earl Barton invented a "flapper's dance" he called the

"Flapistan," inspired by steps in the Charleston, Black Bottom, and Big Apple. "They asked me to make up a dance specifically for the film, which was indicative of a flapper's dance," Barton recalled. "It was kind of a cutesy thing; we did it with a gymnasium full of people, and Danny led it and sang it. It was a little complicated step."

First, though, Kaye wanted the choreographer to demonstrate. "It's easy," Barton explained. The choreographer went through all the steps, but as he came down from a big leap, he sprained his ankle. Barton had to wear a cast for two weeks.

Sylvia wrote three other songs—"Lullaby in Ragtime," "Good Night, Sleep Tight," and "The Five Pennies"—that, ingeniously, could each be sung as separate songs, interchangeably as duets, or all at once as a trio. Performing the three songs as a trio was no easy feat, particularly for young Susan Gordon. During rehearsals, she placed her fingers in her ears so she wouldn't be thrown off by Kaye and Armstrong. The filmmakers got so used to seeing her that way, they didn't notice that she plugged her ears in the final film, too.

The title song earned Fine an Academy Award nomination, although she lost to "High Hopes" by Sammy Cahn and James Van Heusen. "She was nominated," Shavelson added, "and also sued. It turned out to be an Italian song (called 'Anema E Core'), which she had heard some years earlier in Italy and then forgotten about, she thought. She said she thought it was brand new when she wrote it, and she had to pay off on it." Sylvia settled out of court for $10,000.

But as good as her numbers for Danny were, they indirectly added to one of the film's problems: people went home thinking that Red Nichols was like Danny Kaye, instead of believing that Kaye was Nichols. So, too, the storyline forced Kaye to spend much of the picture in a sour, dour mood—a poor match for a musical comedy. Yet *The Five Pennies* proved to be a genuinely touching picture. Although music-related expenses pushed costs a quarter-million dollars over budget, the film made back its $2.2 million investment. Critics were even more supportive. The film was nominated for five Oscars, a Golden Globe as best musical, and a Grammy for best soundtrack album.

The following summer, Kaye spent three weeks touring fifteen U.S. cities to promote *The Five Pennies*, before setting off for Australia. After two months of presenting his stage act in Sydney and Melbourne, Danny could tell the joy was slipping from his work. He was bored, distracted, exhausted. He sold the rights to *The Bamboo Kid* to Bob Hope, who had Panama and Frank rework it into *The Road to Hong Kong*.

Kaye vowed to take a year's break from show business. That didn't mean he wouldn't keep busy. In fact, the time off allowed him to jump head first into two new passions: flying and cooking.

His introduction to aeronautics began earlier in the year, when he took to the clouds with pal Michael Kidd, a new pilot. When they were at a steady altitude, Kidd passed Kaye the controls. Danny was hooked. Feverishly, he dove into learning everything about flying. It took months of study and difficult math exams, but on July 7, 1960, he received his pilot's license. Kaye returned to the books in order to earn successively higher ratings, until he was checked out on a DC-10 and purchased his own Lear jet.

It was flying that led to a second passion, Chinese cooking. Kaye had long been fascinated by cooking and had loved Chinese cuisine ever since his tour of the Orient 25 years earlier. The two intersected when Danny got a plane. Now, he could fly around the world in search of regional delicacies and ingredients.

One such mission brought him to San Francisco, where he visited famed Chinatown restaurateur Johnny Kan. Danny was entranced by what he saw. Over the next two years, he took every opportunity to fly to San Francisco to work in Kan's kitchen. Kan's head chef, Ming, took Kaye under his wing. Danny memorized Ming's technique and was soon chopping and frying at the master's side.

The cooking course was a long one because there was so much to learn, Kan's manager Guy Wong said, "because in Chinese cooking you don't do anything at the table except eat. There are no knives and forks so you can cut up the pieces. Everything has to be diced, sliced, and it has to be bite-sized because you have no utensil on the table other than chopsticks. So the preparation of it takes much longer than you would a hamburger or a steak."

Danny approached cooking as a serious art form. Wong said, "When it's something that he likes, he's very devoted to it. For instance, he liked cooking, and you cannot disturb him when he's standing there boning chicken. Anything he does, when he's concentrating, no one can disturb him. He will completely ignore you. That's a matter of understanding."

Rejuvenated by his newfound hobbies, Kaye was ready for new professional challenges.

VI.

TIPTOEING INTO TELEVISION

CONSIDERING THE WARMING EFFECT his stage act had over audiences, Kaye seemed ideal for television, precisely the type of performer families would happily invite into their living rooms. And through the 1950s, the TV networks would have liked nothing more than to facilitate that invitation. Danny chafed at the idea, convinced he would quickly exhaust his trove of elite-quality material. He averaged only one movie a year, and his stage act—while perpetually tweaked—always rested upon what he had done the night before. "I could do the stage show I've developed carefully over a period of years once or twice on TV, but after that I'd have to develop fresh, new material," Kaye explained. "Any medium which has to use as much talent as TV does is cannibalistic."

But as the decade wore on, Kaye realized television was inevitable. "I'm sure I'm going to go on TV eventually," he finally conceded. "It's silly to be mulish and close my eyes to it and say I'm never going to do it. I've never said that. What I've said was that I didn't want to go on at the moment I was asked."

Danny's agents at the William Morris Agency kept trying to catch him at that right moment. They had one deal, for instance, that would net Kaye $2 million for a certain number of guest shots during a five-year period. He refused.

Sylvia was interested in television only if she was given the time and money to produce something of quality. In April 1958, she unsuccessfully pitched NBC on a one-hour, color production of Gilbert & Sullivan's operetta *Trial by Jury*, to star Groucho Marx. NBC liked the idea and, two years later, starred Groucho in an hour-long *Mikado*—minus Sylvia.

She could never see herself, or Danny, doing television on a regular basis. "He'd never do a weekly show," Sylvia said while Kaye was touring Australia. "It sometimes takes me a week or even six weeks to write one big number." As well, she was nervous about the type of sponsor that might underwrite any program, since Danny had become so identifiable with children. For the same reason, they had declined big-money offers to take his one-man show to Las Vegas.

In April 1959, CBS suggested a 90- or 120-minute special promoting UNICEF. CBS marketing executive Victor Ratner explained, "Danny for a one-time must have every assurance that the material will be good enough so he can knock the ball out of the park and he must feel absolutely comfortable with it." But agent Abe Lastfogel advised Kaye to sign only "a big package," contending that a single TV appearance might "take the edge off it."

Lastfogel's team at William Morris had preached patience to Danny for 20 years, seeing him as a unique talent best rationed out to the public. Not long after returning from Australia, Kaye terminated his representation with William Morris and signed with the more aggressive MCA. Within weeks, in November of 1959, MCA had negotiated a television deal with sponsor General Motors. GM would pay Kaye's production company $1.5 million to develop three hour-long specials, one each fall for the next three years.

Soon after, MCA convinced Danny to take his one-man show to the Desert Inn in Las Vegas, marking his return to a nightclub stage after nearly two decades. Despite the adult-oriented environs of Sin City, Danny refused to alter his squeaky-clean stage act. Audiences loved it. With Sammy Prager at the piano and drummer Sidney Kaye leading the orchestra, Danny would play Vegas nightclubs throughout the 1960s.

AN HOUR WITH DANNY KAYE

(Taped Oct. 5, 1960; aired Oct. 30, 1960, CBS 8 p.m. EST)
Producer: Sylvia Fine
Director: Norman Jewison
Writers: Hal Kanter, Sylvia Fine
Songs: Sylvia Fine & Herbert Baker ("Stickfitz," "Cowboy;" Fine only "C'est la TV," "Drip Drop," "Contact Lens Bridge," "Flackeldack Store," "Five Pennies Saints," "The Crazy Harp," "Flamenco," "Minnie the Moocher," "GM Patter Commercial")
Guest: Louis Armstrong
Sketches: TV Commercial spoofs, International Chefs

As producer of Danny's first television special, Sylvia would be calling all the shots and, for the first time, have the title to prove it. She selected as director Norman Jewison and as writer Hal Kanter, from Kaye's old radio show. Musically, she would craft every note, from the background music down to the General Motors commercials ("Each chassis is classy...").

Sylvia spent months planning the show in minute detail. Kanter recalled, "There were constant discussions—a lot more talking than there was writing—because it was his first time on television. Obviously he wanted to make sure that everything was properly done and would present him in the best light and take advantage of as many facets of his many-faceted personality as possible."

As a result, Danny and Sylvia decided on a mix of proven numbers, peppered with a touch of fresh material. After fifteen minutes of spoofing TV programs and commercials, the rest of the program was pulled straight out of his stage act—"Minnie the Moocher," "Stickfitz," "Five Pennies Saints," his flamenco routine, a take-off on different types of laughs, spotlighting his dancing hands, and an often-told tale about five-year-old Dena's first trip to one of his shows. Kaye appeared on camera, non-stop, for the entire show, sharing the spotlight just once, with Louis Armstrong on "Five Pennies Saints."

Her idea, in fact, was to replicate the feeling of his one-man show. "You see, there is a sort of magical quality about Danny that you don't get in a movie," Sylvia related. "It comes across only on a stage. You can almost see the vibrations in the air between him and his audience. And I think it will happen on television."

To capture the spontaneous atmosphere of the stage, Sylvia insisted the show be videotaped straight through in front of a live audience. The entire program, except for a pre-recorded sketch with Kaye as four international chefs and one scene that had to be redone due to a technical problem, was recorded "live on tape," Danny said, "because I can get keyed up emotionally for a show just once. Also, when I work, I sweat. If the audience doesn't see me sweating after an hour, I feel they've been gypped."

For Satchmo, performing the scat-singing duet straight through for TV cameras proved even more difficult than in front of film cameras, where a director could better reign in Kaye and shoot multiple takes.

Sylvia, however, could not leave well enough alone. Unknown to the director, she went over every frame in the editing room. She substituted swatches in Danny's opening number with footage shot during the dress rehearsal, trimmed the closing number, and switched the order of others. But, because the show was shot straight through, the cuts weren't clean ones.

Days before the program was to air, director Jewison got wind of what Sylvia had done. He was livid. He immediately fired off an angry complaint to CBS, charging that once the program was taped, it should have been left alone.

He wrote to Sylvia more pointedly, complaining, "I was shocked to hear of the amount of experimentation and editing that was taking place... Indeed it was you who had the initial perspective and wanted a live, spontaneous and exciting performance, rather than a series of separate entities on tape. I was convinced then, as I am now, that to catch even some of Danny's greatness, it is necessary to have a live theatrical performance—that builds in intensity and communication and that the television show or, in this case, the videotape must be an experience—not a product of carefully interpreted editing and technical perfection."

He concluded, "The pre-taping of programs so far in advance invites too many second judgments—good or bad. A show is shot 'live on tape' to preserve the spontaneous and immediate experience of a live performance. Further editing and programming can only produce disastrous results."

The show aired exactly as Sylvia wanted. Aided by the prime 8:00 p.m. time slot on Sunday, pre-empting *The Ed Sullivan Show*, the special enjoyed solid ratings. Reviews, however, were modest. Curiously, critics were harshest on Danny's tried and true, "secure" bits, reasoning that much of the audience had already seen them.

ON THE DOUBLE

(Filmed Oct. 31 to Dec. 21, 1960; released May 20, 1961)
Producer: Jack Rose, for Dena-Capri Productions, Paramount
Director: Melville Shavelson
Screenplay: Melville Shavelson & Jack Rose
Songs: Sylvia Fine ("The Mackenzie Hielanders," "Darlin' Meggie," "On the Double Polka," "Cocktails for Zwei")
Cast: Danny Kaye (Pfc. Ernie Williams/Gen. Sir Lawrence Mackenzie-Smith), Dana Wynter (Lady Margaret), Wilfred Hyde White (Col. Somerset), Margaret Rutherford (Lady Vivian), Diana Dors (Sgt. Stanhope), Allan Cuthbertson (Captain Patterson), Jesse White (Cpl. Joe Praeger), Gregory Walcott (Col. Houston), Terence de Marney (Sgt. Twickenham), Rex Evans (Gen. "Puffy" Browne-Wiffingham)

The final movie comedy to be written expressly for Danny came about in an unlikely setting—a fake emergency room on the set of *The Five Pennies*. While shooting a somber hospital scene, with father Danny and mother Barbara Bel Geddes in tears and their polio-stricken daughter in an iron lung, Kaye looked past the camera, at producer Jack Rose and director Mel Shavelson, and asked, "How come you're not laughing? I'm a comedian."

The remark got the duo thinking. While Rose and Shavelson both started

FAMILIAR LOOK: *On the Double* was designed as a return to the kind of more carefree pictures Danny used to make. [© 1961 Paramount Pictures]

out as comedy writers, their most recent pictures had featured children contracting crippling diseases, husbands suffering heart attacks, and wives dying. They thought it high time for an out-and-out farce. Danny agreed to do the picture before seeing even a word of the script.

Rose and Shavelson got their idea from a recent British movie, *I Was Monty's Double*. The film was based on a true World War II incident in which an actor was forced to impersonate a British general, to shield the officer from assassination attempts. The writers saw Danny as perfect in both parts, especially considering his prior success with dual roles.

In their first screenplay, Shavelson and Rose envisioned Danny as Ernie, an Army private who's also a professional singer and comic. Officers call on him while he's performing in a USO show at the base. They allow him to finish his act, so long as he doesn't do his impression of General Sir Lawrence Trevelyan-Smith. "That's my best bit!" grouses Ernie. After he does his takes on Hitler, Jolson and Churchill, he begins imitating the general, and the military police suddenly drop the curtain. The officers inform Ernie that he's needed to impersonate the general, but must first fake his own death. Later, his stage helper, Corporal Joe Prager, takes over his stage act—and his girlfriend in the chorus. When Joe imitates Hitler, the audience roars. "He stole my whole act—and I died for his country!" Ernie complains. "And what's worse," the major adds, "he's getting laughs."

During his own memorial service and at a party, Ernie narrowly escapes assassination attempts. He must also contend with the general's sexy chauffeur/mistress, suspicious war buddy General Puffy, and wife, Lady Margaret, who quickly recognizes that he's not her cold, philandering husband. During an air raid, Ernie comforts Lady Margaret in the next bed by singing "Molly Malone."

The general's chauffeur, however, is actually a Nazi spy, who kidnaps the private. Ernie breaks away into the Berlin Opera House, disguises himself as the conductor, and leads the orchestra, as Hitler looks down from his private box. Fleeing, Ernie dresses as Hitler and, after entering a nightclub, as Marlene Dietrich singing "Lili Marlene." Drunk, amorous Nazis drag the singer to an airfield, where Ernie takes control of the plane. Amid gunfire, he parachutes to safety and escapes with the enemy war plans.

Although the script worked in two of Danny's greatest passions (flying and conducting), Shavelson and Rose figured they could heighten the suspense and the comedy by making Danny's character a weak-kneed hypochondriac and amateur mimic, rather than—as in *On the Riviera*—a professional impersonator and willing volunteer.

The film was completed in 37 days, on time, for pennies above the $1.5 million budget, despite the tricky dual photography. "This was a tough thing to do," Shavelson said. "You can do it much more simple now, but in those days, you blocked out one side of the screen in the camera and backed it up and re-shot it. If you made a mistake, you were in a lot of trouble. Danny had to have his timing perfect. And we had to feed his sound of himself as the one character to him while he was performing as the other character without the microphone picking it up."

Sylvia's contributions were kept to a minimum. She provided just two comedic songs—a tongue-twisting take-off on a Highland Fling and Danny's "ad-libbed" lyrics for "Cocktails for Zwei."

Sprightly and fun, *On the Double* returned Danny to the type of film that had given him a name. Yet, the audiences of old were nowhere to be found. It would be Kaye's final film with Shavelson, Rose, Paramount, and Sylvia.

THE DANNY KAYE SHOW

(Taped Oct. 1 to 2, 1961; aired Nov. 6, 1961, CBS 9 p.m. EST)

Director: Bud Yorkin
Producers: Bud Yorkin & Norman Lear
Writers: Norman Lear, Hal Kanter (uncredited Shirley Henry)
Songs: Mack David & Jerry Livingston ("I Am an Is," "Pipe and Slippers"), Sylvia Fine ("Airy Fairy Pipers," "German Concert Song"), "Begin the Beguine," "Turn Around," "Inchworm" (uncredited Billy Barnes, Bob Kaufman, Paul Smith)
Guests: Phyllis Avery, Alice Backes, Jesslyn Fax, Barry Livingston, James Millhollin, Bert Freed, Paul Mazursky, Barbara Morrison, Johnny Mann Singers
Sketches: Golf story, A Man Is Many Things pantomime, Hypnotic Party

For his second television special, Kaye had two directives: more of the material should be original and Sylvia should have no official role. Danny asked Hal Kanter to return. The writer agreed, provided he not have to work with Sylvia. Kanter wrote one sketch, then quit when director Bud Yorkin brought in his producing partner, Norman Lear, to assist with the writing.

Yorkin and Lear thought there was too much silliness in Kaye's first special. They wanted their show to have a deeper, psychological theme. Danny could sing a few established bits near the end, but the bulk of the show would be songs, pantomime and a dance number, all with a message.

Although Sylvia contributed no new material to the special, she was still the arbiter of what worked and what didn't for Danny. All numbers would have to meet her approval. Yorkin and Lear first asked revue specialist Billy Barnes to write two songs. "I was thrilled to be working with these people, so I wrote two numbers that I thought were wild, and they seemed to like them a lot," Barnes recalled. "The next thing I knew, they called up and said, 'We're terribly sorry, but we can't use your songs. Sylvia Fine will not have it.'"

The producers then enlisted Bob Kaufman to write a song, which was also rejected. They finally called in the big guns, Tin Pan Alley tunesmiths Mack David and Jerry Livingston, for nearly ten times the sum they offered to Kaufman. Sylvia gave the okay to David and Livingston's two songs, the cute "Pipe and Slippers" and the curious "I Am an Is."

Although several critics panned the latter song, a clunky paean to self-esteem, the show's main drawback was that it had to be taped in black-and-white. CBS—upset that NBC's color system had been accepted as the industry standard and aware that most color television sets were sold by NBC's parent company, RCA—had discontinued color programs on its schedule and deactivated its color transmission service with the telephone company. Sponsor General Motors was irked by the news. The company was even more upset to learn that NBC scheduled the first TV broadcast of *On the Riviera* one week before the Kaye special was to air.

GM, which advertised heavily on both networks, sent an emissary to encourage NBC to reschedule the movie. NBC agreed to push back the movie two months, in exchange for Danny taping the special at NBC's Burbank studios—for a rental fee, of course. The press was told that Kaye was producing his CBS show at NBC because NBC had better color facilities—a ridiculous excuse considering the show was taped in black-and-white.

THE MAN FROM THE DINERS' CLUB

(Filmed July 9 to late Sept. 1962; released April 17, 1963)
Producer: Bill Bloom, for Dena-Ampersand Productions, Columbia
Director: Frank Tashlin
Screenplay: Bill Blatty
Original Story: Bill Blatty, John Fenton Murray
Cast: Danny Kaye (Ernie Klenk), Cara Williams (Sugar Pye), Martha Hyer (Lucy), Telly Savalas (Foots Pulardos), Everett Sloane (Martindale), Kay Stevens (Bea Frampton), Howard Caine (Bassanio)

As Danny turned 50, he must have sensed that his days as a great movie clown were numbered. Certainly, few of the greats were crafting quality comedies by his age. The Marx Brothers, Stan Laurel, and Oliver Hardy were all in their late 40s when they made their last great films. Lou Costello and Harold Lloyd, perhaps wearing prematurely since they performed so many of their own stunts, slowed down in their early 40s. Charlie Chaplin and Bob Hope made their last great comedies at 50. Jerry Lewis, fifteen years younger than Kaye, had only a few more years of high-level pictures left in him.

With the exception of W.C. Fields, who played a cranky old curmudgeon, most of the great movie comedians played characters who were—like

SNAGGED: Bustling with outlandish sight gags, *The Man from the Diners' Club* would have been better suited for Jerry Lewis than Danny Kaye. [© 1963 Columbia Pictures]

Danny's—energetic and zany. But after two decades on screen, their bodies became less flexible and their faces began to show a wrinkled, world-weariness at odds with their youthful screen personas. And, as they—and their fan base—aged, they were no longer offered top quality scripts, directors or budgets.

After the lukewarm reception to *On the Double*, Kaye found himself in the same position. If he were to continue making comedies, he'd have to settle for something less, something like *The Man from the Diners' Club*.

It would be Danny's first comedy in black-and-white and first that wasn't written expressly for him. In fact, Columbia's casting director jotted down a list of 40 actors he thought could play the role, headed by Jack Lemmon,

Tony Randall, and Andy Griffith. Danny was choice number sixteen, between Bob Cummings and Alan Young.

The film was such a low-budget affair that Kaye's salary—$225,000, most of it deferred, plus a percentage of the profits—was nearly a third of the entire budget. The producers further defrayed costs by striking promotional deals with Diners Club International and Western Airlines.

The conventional script—about a meek Diners Club employee who must retrieve a credit card inadvertently issued to a gangster—was the first ever written by Bill Blatty, who a decade later would make a name for himself as author of *The Exorcist.*

Danny did what he could to energize what clearly would never be a classic. Co-star George Kennedy recalled, "I remember Danny Kaye quite fondly as being a very hard-worker, very concerned with making sure everything was as funny as we could make it—after all, for the most part it was a cartoon fashioned after the slapstick of Tom and Jerry."

Co-star Cara Williams, nonetheless, recalled Kaye's overreactions one afternoon when it came time to shoot her big drunk scene: "He had to wait a few minutes for me on the set, and he got a little angry in that scene and threw a tray down, because he was a little insecure that it wasn't his scene. He acted nice to me when I walked into the scene, but I could tell that he was annoyed. I think it's the only time I ever saw him show a poor disposition."

Interviewed one morning in his *Man from the Diners' Club* dressing room, Kaye remarked, "In all this talk about the dying movie industry there's only one thing that makes sense. A good picture today can make more money than ever. If you don't make a good picture, you don't deserve to make money."

Deservedly, then, *Man from the Diners' Club* died at the box office. In fairness, the picture wasn't dreadful. It had an intriguing premise and several amusing moments. It just wasn't a good fit for Kaye. It lacked what he usually had in his earlier colorful musical comedies—namely color, music and comedy suited to his unique gifts. There were two brief opportunities for dialect humor (pretending to be a Jersey tough guy and a German masseuse), but no fast-talking dialogue, no whimsy, no musical or specialty numbers, and, consequently, no Sylvia.

The mechanically simple slapstick and director Frank Tashlin's outlandish sight gags were better suited for Jerry Lewis, and the sequences involving beat poets only seemed to emphasize how un-hip Kaye was on the verge of becoming. Although reminiscent of his earlier roles as a sneezing, clumsy patsy, Kaye's Ernie Klenk could have been played equally well by anyone on that casting director's list of 40.

The Man from the Diners' Club would be Kaye's final comedy.

THE DANNY KAYE SHOW WITH LUCILLE BALL

(Taped Oct. 21, 1962; aired Nov. 11, 1962, NBC 9 p.m. EST)
Producer: Jess Oppenheimer
Director: Greg Garrison
Writers: Ernest Chambers, Herbert Baker (uncredited Jess Oppenheimer, Sylvia Fine, Roland Kibbee)
Songs: Sylvia Fine & Herbert Baker ("Hallelujah Twist"/"Nose to the Grindstone;" Fine only "Dry Bones," "Shortnin' Bread," "Cottonfields of Home," "Kent Cigarette Commercial"), celebrity medley, "Blue Nose Fly," "Ballin' the Jack," "Tschaikowsky"
Sketches: Restaurants
Guests: Lucille Ball, Johnny Mann Singers, Roger Til (French maitre 'd), Hollis Morrison (witch doctor)

For Kaye's third special, GM insisted on returning to color, even if it meant moving from CBS to NBC. So, too, the format needed to change. Danny admitted that he needed something extra, something sure to be a hit with television audiences. Sylvia suggested Lucille Ball, who was preparing to launch a new weekly series, *The Lucy Show*. Cleverly, Sylvia hired *I Love Lucy* producer Jess Oppenheimer to produce the special and then had Oppenheimer try to strike a deal with Lucy's executive producer—her ex-husband, Desi Arnaz.

Arnaz was reluctant. With her new series about to launch, Ball's schedule was packed. Desi finally agreed, with one caveat: Lucy would earn $100,000 for her guest appearance, convinced Kaye wouldn't pay the record sum. Arnaz was mistaken.

Oppenheimer had experience working with the temperamental stars of *I Love Lucy*, so he expected some issues with Danny and Sylvia. Oppenheimer remembered Kaye as having "an ego to match his talent. I had a couple of problems when I first got there. He had a way of answering very obliquely if you asked him anything. Almost right away, with everybody there in the room, I asked him what he wanted his opening song to be, and I got back a ten-minute discourse on psychology and philosophy and this and that and the other thing. And everybody's sitting there, nodding their heads. Then he goes to leave the room, and he hadn't answered the question that started the whole thing. So I stopped him, and I said, 'Danny, wait. You may not remember through all of this, but what started this was I wanted to know what song, a title.' I thought everybody in the room was going to die. Nobody talked to him like that. He would go on and on obliquely, and leave. Then they would get together and try to figure out what he really meant by that. They were scared to death of him. And it could have been the end of the job for me. He is capable of saying, 'I don't like that guy. Get him out of here.' But as it turned out, it was the start of a very nice relationship."

As preparations for the show began, Danny was appearing at Los Angeles' Greek Theatre. The conductor for his performances was Walter Scharf, who had directed the music on *Hans Christian Andersen* and was to conduct and arrange the music on Kaye's upcoming special. During one performance at the Greek, amid great fanfare, Scharf reached the point of Danny's entrance and, without thinking, threw out his hand to cue Kaye. After the show, Oppenheimer went backstage to see Danny, who was apoplectic. "Nobody cues me!" Kaye raved. "I don't need anybody to tell me when to come on! Get somebody else for the show." Scharf was fired from the special.

Sylvia would handle the songs herself and enlisted off-and-on partner Herbie Baker to assist. They decided to build half the show around Lucy's talents and cull half from Danny's stage repertoire. They considered "Deenah," "Otchi Tchorniya," "I am a Yogi from Goochbehard" (a spoof of an Indian yoga master), and the South African folk songs "Yon-u-ary" and "Yonny Mite Hoop Lebien'." Instead, Fine and Baker went with his spirited stage opener, "Hallelujah Twist," a medley of folk songs from the South, Kaye's comical dance-off with precision tap artists the Dunhills, and his impression of a French TV commercial for Kent cigarettes.

Lucy could contribute a comical dance and impersonations of Judy Garland, Carol Channing, and Marlene Dietrich (intercut with Danny as a progressively tipsier Dean Martin/Frank Sinatra). But music didn't play to Ball's strengths. She would be better utilized in skits. So Baker recruited Ernie Chambers, a young sketch writer who had approached him at a Writers Guild meeting.

Baker suggested Kaye and Ball perform the old vaudeville sketch "Goodbye Sam" (where a philanderer keeps ducking into the closet every time his lover's husband returns home), but in three or more versions—the original as well as how it would be done by other directors, such as Stanley Kramer ("Stella of Sunnybrook Closet"), Charlie Chaplin ("The Clothes Rush"), Tennessee Williams ("Sam in a Hot Tin Closet"), Walt Disney ("Sam in Closetland"), Alfred Hitchcock ("Psychloset"), or Billy Wilder ("Sam Like It Hot").

Then the writers learned that during the special Lucy wanted to plug her upcoming movie, *Critic's Choice*. Naturally, Danny would then have to promote *The Man from the Diners' Club*. And it's then that the writers decided dining out would make a perfect theme for the entire show.

Baker envisioned Danny and Lucy in a series of brief restaurant sketches (Kaye as a pizza chef or a waiter trying to uncork a champagne bottle, Ball as a diner struck by a pie, as a tyrant waitress, or as a server tossing a salad at Kaye, the couple getting drunk at a swanky restaurant or visiting an exotic, themed restaurant). Bridging the sketches would be a troupe performing short comic dances (waiting for a table, fighting for a seat at the counter, waiters carrying piles of dishes). In the end, the writers opted to keep Danny and Lucy a couple in all three sketches—as diners who get tipsy in a fancy French eatery, who make their first visit to a Japanese restaurant, and who battle the jungle décor of a Polynesian establishment.

The trickiest part to pull off was the drunk sketch, because Kaye and his producer had different ideas about how the scene should be played. "Whenever you're producing something with a big star like that," Oppenheimer said, "there has to be a little bit about who's going to ride the horse early on, otherwise you just get walked all over. People bypass you, and they go do whatever he says, and it's unbearable. But we had a restaurant scene, and it involved the fact that (Kaye) and Lucille Ball are getting progressively drunk. And in rehearsal, he started doing a typical Adirondacks comic thing of letting the food slop out of his mouth and so forth. Jerry Lewis and people like that, they think that's funny, and they do it all the time. I don't happen to think it's funny. So I said, 'Well, it's something I'd expect from Jerry Lewis, not Danny Kaye,' and he just froze over and turned on his heel, and I thought, 'Next I'll get a message from his manager that...' But, by golly, after he thought it over, he came back and took all of the gross stuff out. And maybe ten times after that, during the course of the show, any time there was a little discussion about something, he'd say, 'Do you think that's maybe what Jerry Lewis would do?' So it really touched him."

In large part thanks to Lucy, Danny's third special was by far his best.

But General Motors showed no interest in extending its sponsorship. Although each special generated nice ratings, Danny was delivering an older audience that already knew him. "The older people are already buying Cadillacs," GM explained. "We need somebody who delivers the younger people."

Choreographer Tony Charmoli recalled, "It was an excellent show, but unfortunately it was never shown again. Lucy got $100,000, which in those days was the highest paid anyone, and would have received 100 percent for reruns, so to have that rerun would cost a lot of money."

NBC promoted the special only half-heartedly, perhaps unhappy that it had to pre-empt its top-rated show, *Bonanza*. More likely, NBC didn't want to do any favors for CBS, which had just signed Kaye to a long-term deal. Danny, it seems, discovered that he enjoyed television, after all. It was certainly a more immediate medium than the movies, yet one that provided a massively larger audience than the stage. The downside with the specials was spending months crafting a single hour—and knowing that the critics expected perfection for having to wait so long. Kaye was ready to create an hour of entirely new material in a week, every week.

"Some say I've got nothing to prove anymore," Kaye said. "But it's like a guy playing a violin. He finds he knows how to play, but he practices every day so he can play better."

VII.

THE SERIES

TELEVISION'S FIRST BIG HITS had been variety shows, with some-times-motley collections of vaudeville-caliber sketches, monologues, musi-cal numbers, and novelty acts. The format—and the rag-tag rush of throw-ing together a new revue every week and performing it live—was exactly what Danny had been schooled in by Max Liebman at Camp Tamiment. In fact, Liebman himself used the Tamiment revues as the template for his seminal TV variety show, *Your Show of Shows*, featuring dialectician Sid Caesar and Tamiment alumnus Imogene Coca.

Certainly, a Tamiment-style revue would be the obvious choice of TV formats to show off Kaye's many talents. Yet in the 24 years since he left the Poconos, a Danny Kaye performance had become an event. It was a movie or a TV special, once a year. Or the stage act, carefully planned and perfected over decades, with mere tweaks from one night to the next.

Kaye hadn't had to come up with so much new material so often since his radio days. But he was ready for a challenge, and he figured, in at least one respect, doing a show once a week would be easier than doing one a year. "You have the luxury of doing a bad one occasionally and you needn't worry about being run out of town," he remarked.

More so, with his film prospects dwindling, hosting a weekly TV show would be the ultimate gauge of his acceptance by the public, to see if he still had it.

MCA alerted the three television networks simultaneously of Danny's availability. The first offer submitted—from CBS—was accepted. CBS agreed to let Kaye's production company run the show, with a budget of $160,000 per episode—making it the most expensive weekly hour on TV. As part of the deal, CBS would build Danny a mega-dressing room at the studio and his own Chinese kitchen at his home in Beverly Hills. Better yet, CBS at the time was the top network by a wide margin, airing all but four of the previous season's top 20 shows. Of the two open spots for variety shows in CBS's fall lineup, Danny's would receive the coveted 10:00 p.m. Wednesday slot, following *The Dick Van Dyke Show* and top-rated *Beverly Hillbillies*. The late hour would cost Kaye the adolescent audience he had been cultivating. But the alternative, pinned on *The Judy Garland Show*, was worse—9:00 p.m. Sundays, going head to head against NBC's powerhouse *Bonanza*.

CBS chairman William S. Paley was thrilled to sign Kaye. Embarrassed by the success of his "rural" sitcoms, Paley thought Danny would add a great deal of class to the network. The only drawback was that Paley demanded all CBS series be in black-and-white.

Another condition of the contract, after the difficulties of the annual specials, was that Sylvia be in no way involved with the series. In fact, she was not welcome on the set. Choreographer Tony Charmoli, a holdover from the Lucy special, perceived that "the series was a stepping stone for Danny because I felt perhaps he had to prove that he could make it on his own without Sylvia. Sylvia guided and wrote and had a lot to say about everything up until that point. This time Sylvia was in New York, and Danny was out here (in California)."

The rejection was doubly hard on Sylvia. She remained in Manhattan working on a Broadway musical, *The Scarlet Pimpernel*, and Danny's commitment to the weekly series spoiled her plans to cast him in the lead. It would take two longtime confidantes to replace her on the series as Danny's creative—and corporate—conscience. First would be his business manager, Herb Bonis, whom Kaye had met a decade earlier, when Bonis was managing the Palace Theatre in New York. As vice president and general manager of Dena Productions, Bonis would serve as executive producer on the TV series, writing the checks, helping to book guests, and making sure Danny got his way.

Then there would be someone who understood Kaye artistically, Herbie Baker. As Sylvia's frequent collaborator, helping to continually shape Danny's stage act, Baker was already under contract to Dena Productions. He ended up being the last writer to sign a contract for the series—holding out for lead billing among the writers and the largest salary of everyone on the crew.

Kaye insisted that everything on the show be thoroughly original, placing tremendous pressure on the program's creative staff. In assembling *The Danny Kaye Show* crew, Danny combined the Goldwyn philosophy (to get the best product, hire the best people) with his own: to do your best, work with people you respect.

Perry Lafferty recalled, "I was in New York doing some business, but I got the flu. I was flat on my back in my hotel room. I had a temperature of

103, and my agent called me up and said, 'You have an appointment tomorrow morning to meet Danny Kaye because he's trying to find a producer for his show.' Now I couldn't believe I would be a candidate because, although I had a fairly decent reputation, there were all these people who were much bigger than I was. So I said, 'Fine. Okay, I'll go.' I dragged myself out of my bed the next day and went up to the Sherry-Netherlands so sick I could hardly walk. I came through the door and there was the great man and his two agents, Ted Ashley and Ira Steiner. We sat down after the amenities were over. Ted Ashley said to me, 'Tell Danny how you think the show should go.' I was so sick that I could only respond with the truth, which was 'How the hell do I know how the show should go? The only way you can figure out how it should go is if you hire the best writers that you can find, get into a room, and bounce off the wall with it for two or three months 'til you come up with the format,' which apparently was the answer Danny was looking for. Apparently all the other guys that had come up had started to tell him how the show should go, and he thought it was better to do what I suggested."

The moment he recovered from the flu, Lafferty jumped into compiling a staff of writers and acquainting the group with Kaye. The producer screened every Kaye picture, attended his one-man show at Broadway's Ziegfeld Theatre, and watched him conduct a charity concert in Buffalo. He agreed that, with Danny's gifts for music, mimicry and dialects, Kaye would work best in a format like *Your Show of Shows*.

So Lafferty turned to former Sid Caesar writer Larry Gelbart, who had the hit *A Funny Thing Happened on the Way to the Forum* on Broadway. Gelbart also had begun renting out his services to help launch and set the tone for new TV series, as he would later do with *M*A*S*H*. Gelbart signed for two months—the first month developing ideas on his own, the second working with the rest of the staff to craft the first few episodes.

Filling out the writing staff were fellow Sid Caesar alums Mel Tolkin and Sheldon Keller, Herbie Baker's protégé Ernie Chambers, and Toronto writer Saul Ilson. The staff got together for the first time in Las Vegas, during the second weekend in June 1963, to watch Kaye's act at the Desert Inn and finalize the vision for the show. As Lafferty instructed the troops: "Danny Kaye is undoubtedly the most versatile entertainer in the English language. The challenge of writing a show for him isn't, for a change, fraught with compromises because the star is of limited abilities. No, sir! Our only problems now are how to best exploit his talents in a weekly situation."

One way to connect Danny with TV viewers was to end each broadcast with the "sit down spot" from his stage act. As Lafferty briefed his team: "In Danny's act, he sits down on a stool in the middle of the performance and talks informally with the audience. He kids, dances, sings and so forth. We all agreed that this type of a spot, possibly with Sammy Prager at the piano nearby, would be an ideal way to close each show, because it would allow certain vital parts of Danny's personality to come through. On television, he might tell the story of a song, then sing it. Or recount an anecdote about something that happened to him in his career. Or sing a song from some show that he was in. The song, however, would have originally been sung by somebody else in the production. Almost anything can happen here. Also this would be a good 'pad.' If we ran over during the hour, this spot could be compressed easily during airing."

The writers each brought to the conference their own stack of sketch suggestions, both one-offs and recurring segments, such as Kaye as an inept international spy, TV programs from foreign lands (such as a Japanese *Gunsmoke*), "Fairytale Courtroom Trials" (discovering that, say, Little Red Riding Hood and the Wolf were in cahoots or Humpty Dumpty was pushed off the wall), and "Press Conference," in which Danny would play various experts, such as a German missile specialist, being interviewed by reporters.

The idea for the show's first sketch was concocted during the Vegas trip, but not during the story conferences. During one of the meetings in the hotel suite, Gelbart mentioned he dreaded flying, and Kaye explained that people wouldn't be afraid of flying if they understood the process. So, Danny persuaded Gelbart and Mel Tolkin to join him on a brief flight. "Mel was sitting in the back seat, and I was sitting alongside Danny, (with) two sets of controls," Gelbart recalled. "And as we sped, flew, rolled, or whatever you do with a plane down the runway, he said, 'It's all yours,' and I was in control of the airplane. I took it up, and he had me fly it. It was exhilarating, and it was scary." Despite the terror, Gelbart and Tolkin had a great sketch idea—a nervous gentleman goes on his first plane ride. Kaye's jittery "victim" in the skit would become the show's first recurring character.

At least one celebrity guest would appear each week. Lafferty also wanted to assemble a regular supporting cast, like Caesar's, but was content to "discover" them as the season progressed. He'd already found the first addition— Lovelady Powell, a comedic actress and singer he saw perform in a revue in New York.

One major difference between Kaye's show and Caesar's was that Danny would not help construct the material. Kaye, said Lafferty, "was not a person like Sid Caesar was, when on *Your Show of Shows* he was actually in the room with the writers all the time while the material was being developed. That wasn't the case with Danny, because his wife Sylvia had written so much of his stuff before the television show, I think he'd gotten used to having the idea discussed with him, and then the finished product delivered to him, and then he would play with it. We would work out the ideas and then I would go down and discuss what we worked out with him. At that point, he would sometimes want to reject one or two. He spent more time with the musical people, but even then they would go and make the arrangements, after he'd approve what the idea was. And we would write the scripts after he'd approve the ideas. Then he'd come in and we'd go through the whole show with him, at which time he might like something, he might not like it, we might talk him into doing something if he was doubtful, or we might throw it out if he was absolutely adamant."

Among the writers, Herbie Baker always worked by himself. The others might break into pairs or work together as a large group, throwing ideas off the wall, with Mel Tolkin as de facto head writer, as he had been for Caesar, and Shelly Keller, the typist. According to director Bob Scheerer, "Shelly would never type a line the same way someone said it. Somebody would say a punchline, and he would write it in his own words, wielding his influence. He was saying, 'Sorry, pal, this is the way it's gonna be.' And people accepted it."

The ultimate success of the show would rest on how well it presented Danny as a weekly friend of the family. Lafferty said, "What we did have to build was Danny's person as Danny Kaye. In other words, not as a character he was playing, because in television they first must like you. Danny could do any act—sing, dance, comedy, do any accent—but what we had to bring forward was what he had when he would do his one-man show. In the theater, he'd be cute and silly and all that, but he also was very warm and very direct, and we addressed ourselves to developing that aspect, as well as utilizing all of his talents."

Kaye thought it best to downplay his frantic side and to limit the specialty material. "I don't want to overpower the audience," Danny said. "The television audience must yearn to know more about me. I feel communicating with people at home is different than in movies, theaters or clubs. The more they learn about you, the closer they feel. It's fine to entertain and do sketches, but at one point I want to sit down and communicate with the people rather than perform at them. If it doesn't work, we'll have to find something else."

According to Ron Friedman, who joined the writing staff in season three: "Danny was always reluctant to do special material. He, I guess, was always comparing it with his hits—'Tschaikowsky,' 'The Lobby Number' from *Up in Arms*, 'Anatole of Paris,' etcetera."

Director Scheerer confirmed, "He didn't want to do his 'dit-wat-diddle' on the show. He just didn't want to do it. And he would fight that. So anyone who would make any kind of a suggestion about that, he would be very leery about it."

That didn't always deter writers, like Ernie Chambers, who aspired to craft the next "Anatole of Paris." Kaye, said Chambers, "was excellent doing special numbers—that's what made him famous in the movies—but he couldn't do much on television because there wasn't time to perfect them. A number like 'The Lobby Number,' you couldn't learn that on a Monday and tape it on a Friday. The other reason is, on television, the public can't absorb them, they don't work. You look at what's done on television, and it's very rarely they are done."

Nonetheless, Kaye was adept at learning complicated material with minimal rehearsal. Bernie Rothman, a later addition to the staff, also continually pitched specialty material to Kaye, "the kind that Sylvia had written for years," he said. His first number for Danny had fun with CBS's prime-time schedule. "It was a real tongue-twister and real difficult," Rothman said. "I brought it to his penthouse, and he liked it. I could tell, because his only comment was 'It's too long.' So I shortened it a little bit and worked it over with him once or twice, and then I said, 'Okay, let's rehearse it.' 'No, no, no,' he said. 'It'll be fine. Go.' I didn't see it again until the run-through and it was lousy. I went up to Danny afterwards and said, 'Is there anything wrong with the number?' He said, 'No, it'll be fine.' I was petrified. I didn't see it again until he did it for the audience. He stood up and performed it like he'd been doing it for 20 years, the real Danny Kaye virtuoso-type number. I was amazed."

Writer Shelly Keller added, "I remember once we did a tour de force for (Danny). It was a musical. It was dynamite. The audience was screaming, and he said to me afterwards, 'If only I could take this out on the road for a month,' like he could do it better. He was a perfectionist. And every once in a while, if he didn't like what he did, he said so. He said to me once in the dressing room, 'I performed tonight like a tub of (manure).'"

Lafferty's plan was to tape five shows before the season started, to work out the bugs and to create a backlog of episodes that would allow for breathers throughout the year. For every five weeks of labor, the staff would get one week off, such as during the World Series and Christmas week, when one of the first five shows would be aired.

The crew would actually be working on four shows simultaneously — editing last week's show, fine-tuning and rehearsing this week's, writing next week's, and booking guests and submitting ideas for the following week. For the current show, Mondays began with planning meetings and assembling the week's script. On Tuesdays, the cast read through the script and music, and started rehearsing. On Thursdays came the first technical conference with the crew and a preliminary run-through of the show. Although there were no cameras, the entire cast and crew were present. Immediately afterwards, Kaye, Lafferty, Scheerer, Charmoli, Bonis, and the writers headed for the writers room to hash out what needed to be worked on. They considered the running time, the pace, the placement of sketches, songs and dance numbers, and then analyzed each individual component. When it came time to go over individual lines, the room was cleared except for the director, producer and three writers — Baker, Tolkin and Keller. Whether it took one hour or ten, they had to have a complete show written for Friday morning, when the cameras were brought in to block the show, the lights were set, and the cast and orchestra pre-recorded the music tracks, allowing the actors to bring home audiotapes to practice their lip-synching.

Saturday mornings saw the in-costume run-through, starting and stopping and starting again until every problem was corrected. The 4:00 p.m. dress rehearsal was taped with make-up, costumes, lighting, music and a live audience. A new audience was hurried in for the 8:00 taping, which usually ended on schedule 60 minutes later. The show was edited that night, although typically few cuts were needed, apart from some inter-cutting between the two taped shows. The final print was immediately shipped off to Canada, where it aired two days later. On Wednesday nights at 10:00 p.m., the four-day-old show hit American TV screens.

Danny carried the "live-on-tape" method of his specials over to his series, refusing to re-tape anything once the 8:00 show ended. "Television shouldn't have that antiseptic perfection you can get in a movie," Kaye said. "If you make a mistake on television, it only brings you closer to your audience."

Yet this desire for spontaneity was no excuse for smiling upon mistakes.

Danny jumped into the project with unbridled enthusiasm. He was intent on building Rome in a week, every week. Each show was to be a miniature masterpiece. He had to prove wrong the critics, who were convinced that the grind of a weekly series would dilute his genius.

THE DANNY KAYE SHOW
SEASON ONE
(32 shows)

Producer: Perry Lafferty • **Director**: Robert Scheerer
Writers: Larry Gelbart (shows 1-4), Herbert Baker, Mel Tolkin, Sheldon Keller, Saul Ilson, Ernest Chambers, Paul Mazursky (5-), Larry Tucker (5-), Gary Belkin (15-)
Cast: Harvey Korman (3, 5, 7-), Tony Charmoli Dancers, Johnny Mann Singers (1-8), Earl Brown Singers (9-), Clinger Sisters

Episode 1 (taped Aug. 10, 1963; aired Sept. 25, 1963)
Guests: Jackie Cooper, Lovelady Powell, Joe & Eddie, Jack Benny (cameo)
Songs: "Consider Yourself," "Cherry Pies Ought to Be You," "Love Me Lady Powell," Blues medley
Sketches: Cleopatra's Procession, Baseball Musicals (*The Baseball Man, My Fair Umpire, Horsehide Story*), Airline Passenger, Bandstand

Four days after tearing apart the premiere of Jerry Lewis' TV series, critics set their sights on *The Danny Kaye Show*. The program began with an extravagant fanfare and a never-ending procession of costumed Egyptians. At the end of the caravan, footmen carried in a royal "stretcher." Its curtains parted to reveal a robed prince kissing a beautiful maiden. The prince—Jack Benny—turned to the audience and remarked, "Wouldn't this have been a wonderful opening for Danny Kaye?" The final footman was a befuddled Kaye.

From there on, Danny effortlessly frolicked through story and song, joined by Jackie Cooper and Lovelady Powell, whose unusual name was turned into one of the musical numbers. The evening's highlights were variations on "Take Me Out to the Ball Game," in the styles of *My Fair Lady, West Side Story*, and *The Music Man*. In "My Fair Umpire," Danny's Professor Higgins explains that the aim of the game is mainly to complain, and that the runner who neglects to run with the hit has merely grown accustomed to his base. "The Horsehide Story" was a ballet that climaxed with players wielding switchblades after a cry to "Kill the umpire!" Finally, in "The Baseball Man," Kaye was joined by a band of marching Little Leaguers.

MAKE ROOM FOR DANNY: Kaye's weekly TV series, set to premiere September 25, 1963, was promoted as the crown jewel of CBS's fall season. [© 1963 CBS]

Danny ended the perfect evening by sitting back and fondly recalling his recent trip to Moscow. Flabbergasted, critics wondered how a show the quality of a Broadway revue ended up on their television sets. Even *New York Times* TV critic Jack Gould, who had ripped Kaye's three specials for lacking "the same magnetism felt in the theater," was gaga over the premiere. "How well Mr. Kaye survives the regular grind still hangs in the balance; a new show every seven days has shortened innumerable careers," Gould wrote. "But last night the omens hardly could have been more favorable. The true Kaye, both the performer and the personality, at long last found himself on the home screen."

Episode 2 (taped Aug. 17, 1963; aired Oct. 2, 1963)
Guests: Jose Ferrer, Red Norvo, Henry Beckman
Songs: "Brotherhood of Man," "Three Blind Mice," "To Be or Not to Be"

Sketches: *Hamlet* TV musical, Astronauts in Space, German Officer

Kaye did little improvising as far as the sketches went. During rehearsals he might experiment with his performance, but when the cameras rolled, he performed what was on paper. Pantomime routines provided the opportunity to add more, but Danny would "wing it" only in the final minutes of the show.

"Some of the best things on the show were on a spot at the end of the show we called the 'sit down spot,'" Perry Lafferty said. "It could be six minutes, four minutes, eight minutes, ten minutes, depending upon how things went—maybe we'd tape fifteen or 20 minutes, cut it down to five—where he'd just sit and talk about experiences he'd had or something that happened that week. That was all ad-lib. We only knew the area he was going to talk about."

In the final sketch on the second show, Kaye played a near-sighted British Army sergeant who kept messing up his superior's desk and getting his foot caught in the wastebasket. After the skit ended, there was a quick break for commercials. Yet when the cameras restarted, expecting Danny to amble out in a tuxedo for the sit down spot, there was no one. Suddenly, yelling erupted backstage. The audience began to laugh. Out came Danny in tux and tie, but also in the sergeant's pants. He sat down and spent the next few minutes talking about not being able to make the costume change. The audience loved it.

Episode 3 (taped Aug. 24, 1963; aired March 11, 1964)
Guests: Diahann Carroll
Songs: "Clock Song," "Old MacDonald," "Zip-A-Dee-Doo-Dah," "I'm Late," "Ugly Duckling," "Riverside"
Sketches: Interpreter, Son's First Haircut

Still searching for regular members of Danny's stock company, the producers auditioned a young actor named Harvey Korman in a barber sketch. They were so impressed by Korman, they invited him back for a future episode.

Episode 4 (taped Aug. 31, 1963; aired Oct. 9, 1963)
Guests: Carol Lawrence, Don Knotts, Joe & Eddie
Songs: "Together Wherever We Go," "Turn Around," "I Laid Around"
Sketches: Dancing Pagodas, Talent Playhouse's Diner, Toothache

Episode 5 (taped Sept. 7, 1963; new scenes taped Oct. 12, 1963; aired Oct. 23, 1963)
Guests: Gene Kelly, Michele Lee, Jackie Joseph, Henry Beckman, Myrna Ross

Songs: "Ballin' the Jack," "You Make Me Feel So Young," "You'll Never Get Away,"
"Side by Side," Kaye/Kelly medley, "Linguini Recipe"
Sketches: Business Lunch, Beauty Expert Miss Schmeckenvasser

One of Lafferty's dreams was to book Fred Astaire, which never came to pass. But he did get the next best thing—Gene Kelly. The star of *Singin' in the Rain* had just two requests. First, he wanted to sing "Ballin' the Jack." It was one of Danny's signature numbers, and Kaye was known to be fiercely protective of his material. Kaye, however, liked the idea—so long as he could present his own version immediately after Kelly did the number in his style.

Second, Kelly wanted to make sure the camera wouldn't dwell on close-ups of his feet. "Never in a million years, Gene, because I hate shots of dancers' feet. I hate 'em," assured director Scheerer, himself a former dancer. Scheerer and Kelly instantly became the best of friends.

Although Lovelady Powell proved acceptable in her first episode, her one-dimensional personality was proving a hindrance to the writers. Tall and sophisticated, she seemed to lack what Korman offered in spades—versatility. Yet her contract guaranteed she would appear in two of the first five shows, with options that could extend her all the way to season three. So, for the fifth episode, she taped a theater sketch and three songs. Three days later, Lafferty informed her the show would not be picking up her option. As he told her, "We have decided that it is better to pair Danny with different lady guests from time to time rather than with one specific person. We found good mileage with you on the first show, as we did with Diahann Carroll on the tape she did for us. The Gwen Verdon and Tuesday Weld scripts promise effective contrasting ways to present Danny and utilize different types of material."

Powell warned that the producers should be careful in how they scheduled her second episode, since her contract stipulated that it could not conflict with her appearance on other programs. Lafferty would make that possibility impossible. He cut Powell's appearances in the show and had Michelle Lee, who was rehearsing another episode, record three songs. He also had Korman tape a replacement sketch, thrown together by two improv artists from the Los Angeles chapter of Second City.

The contract Lafferty envisioned for Powell he instead offered to Korman. The more the producers saw of Harvey, the more they loved him. He was tremendously versatile and worked perfectly off of Danny. The producers kept picking up Korman's options, gave him several unsolicited raises, and insisted he be written into more and more episodes. Midway through the first season, Kaye made a special point of introducing Korman to the viewing audience and paying tribute to his work. Korman shared, "This prompted a letter from one viewer who said he was startled to learn who I was, since he always thought I was an actor named John Van Dreelen." Korman would appear in all but seven shows the first season, and never miss another.

So, too, those Second City improv artists—Paul Mazursky and Larry Tucker—were given short-term contracts to join the series' writing staff. Although they initially received little respect (a common request by new hires was that their billing at least be higher than Tucker and Mazursky's), they did turn out to be the longest-lasting writers—the only ones to survive from the first year to the series' final show—and go on to success in movies, creating cult hits like *I Love You, Alice B. Toklas*, *Bob and Carol and Ted and Alice*, and *Harry and Tonto*.

Episode 6 (taped Sept. 21, 1963; aired Oct. 16, 1963)
Guests: Mary Tyler Moore, Eddie Foy Jr., Dino Natali
Songs: "S'posin'," "Delightful Is the Word," "A Gypsy Cries," Area Code medley, "When the Song & Dance Man Came to Town"
Sketches: Talent Playhouse's gypsy musical, Sitcoms Around the World (*Father Knows Nothing* in U.S., *Father Knows Plenty* in France, *Osaka Hillbillies* in Japan)

Episode 7 (taped Sept. 28, 1963; aired Nov. 20, 1963)
Guests: Gwen Verdon, Don Penny, Zeme North, Clinger Sisters
Songs: "Alouette," "Two of a Kind," "What Is a Woman," "I Get So Lonely"
Sketches: Comedy Tonight, Anniversary at the Drive-in Restaurant

Episode 8 (taped Oct. 12, 1963; aired Feb. 12, 1964)
Guests: Peter Falk, Pete Fountain, Michele Lee
Songs: "Tea for Two," "Get Happy," "It's De-Lovely," "Gonna Build a Mountain"
Sketches: Victim in Hospital Room with Obnoxious Guy, Talent Playhouse's *Arabia*

Episode 9 (taped Oct. 19, 1963; aired Jan. 1, 1964)
Guests: Jack Weston, Nita Talbot, Clinger Sisters, Esquivel
Songs: "Top Hat, White Tie, & Tails," "Jalousie," "Everybody Out of the Pool," "Sugartime," "Record Store"
Sketches: Victim at Barbershop, Madame Schmeckenvasser's Kids' TV show, Phonograph Record vignettes
[This episode had originally being written for Tuesday Weld. But after the hard-living 20-year-old missed two days of rehearsal, Lafferty booked Nita Talbot to take her place. Nonetheless, a disoriented Weld showed up on the set Friday afternoon to record her musical tracks. The producer reminded her that she'd been written out of the show and suggested she go back to bed—and perhaps they could reschedule for a future show. "I made this very nebulous and did not promise anything," Lafferty informed CBS, which had no intention of welcoming Weld back.]

Episode 10 (taped Oct. 26, 1963; aired Oct. 30, 1963)
Guests: Juliet Prowse, Howard Morris, Jamie Farr, Levee Singers
Songs: "Breezin' Along with the Breeze," "Will Ye No Come Back Again?," "Everybody Clap Your Hands"
Sketches: Cowboys of the World parodies (*My Son the Gunslinger* in U.S., *Restless Kilts* in Scotland, *Frontier Cossack* in Russia), James Blonde vs. Dr. Yes

Episode 11 (taped Nov. 2, 1963; aired Nov. 6, 1963)
Guests: Art Carney, Joanie Sommers, Jamie Farr
Songs: "South Rampart Street Parade," "Romeo and Juliet," "The Story of Alice"
Sketches: Talent Playhouse's *Musketeers*, Victim in Hotel Room with Obnoxious Guy

Episode 12 (taped Nov. 9, 1963; aired Nov. 13, 1963)
Guests: Louis Jourdan, Eileen Farrell, Nita Talbot, Carl Ballantine
Songs: "Walk Right In," "Gypsy in My Soul," "Birth of the Blues"
Sketches: Opera parody of Football as a Dance, Jealousy movies (*Dial J for Jealousy* in U.S., *Jealousy, Italian Style* in Italy, *Quick Bernice, My Burnoose* in Turkey)

Episode 13 (taped Nov. 23, 1963; aired Nov. 27, 1963)
Guests: Nancy Walker, Mahalia Jackson, Sig Rumann, Marni Nixon, Dodo Denney
Songs: "When My Sugar Walks Down the Street," "Magnolia Blossoms of 1932," "Gypsy in My Soul"
Sketches: Three musicals (*Love: Then & Now*, *Magnolia Blossoms of 1932*, Talent Playhouse's *Svengalsky*)

As the weeks wore on, the demands of providing Broadway revue-quality material on a weekly basis intensified. Shelly Keller convinced his bosses to hire another Caesar show crony, Gary Belkin, whom they had courted months before. More importantly, they added a choral arranger and director, Earl Brown, who was adept at tailoring music and specialty pieces for Danny and guests.

For Kaye, the rigorous schedule and heightened pressure sharpened the edges of his already moody personality. Danny himself admitted, "I have moods. The span is great, but I don't think I'm abnormal in that respect. If a surgeon finds a procedure particularly difficult, he broods about how he could do it better. The process of learning requires enormous concentration. That's why on Friday and Saturday it is difficult to communicate with me."

Nevertheless, most of the crew adapted to his moodiness. "I remember once I was pissed off at him," Shelly Keller said. "Perry Lafferty, the producer, said to me, 'Suppose somebody said, 'Ladies and gentlemen, here's Sheldon Keller,' and 40 million people are watching you. You'd act pretty weird yourself.' But generally he was not a malevolent man, in pretty good spirits. We had a nice relationship. He was an actor, and actors are crazy. Actors are driven toward one thing: themselves. And to need that much approval is weird."

Lafferty conceded that Kaye was bound to rub some people the wrong way, "but that is not unusual when the whole reason for the show is one person. The whole reason for that show was Danny Kaye. If he wasn't there, there would be no show. Consequently, a tremendous amount of responsibility and pressure is placed upon the star of the show, because if it succeeds it will be to his credit, if it fails it will be to his detriment. They're not going to say it failed because Perry Lafferty did a bad job producing. They're going to say it failed because people didn't like Danny."

The crew discovered that Kaye was at his most engaging, his most heartfelt, when they themselves were at their lowest. Never was it more evident than when, as the crew was preparing for the next night's taping, news arrived that President Kennedy had been shot.

"We were all devastated," recalled writer Ernie Chambers. "Danny did for us what was his great gift. He, in a very warm and loving and amusing way, made us feel better. He was just as sad as we were, but I think people become comedians because somewhere in life they learn that this is something they can do that's good for people. I remember that day how he consoled us, made us all feel better and better able to handle the heartbreak. That week we were supposed to do a show with Mahalia Jackson, the black Gospel singer, and we were going to cancel it. But the show must go on; we were in a cycle. We decided we would go ahead and do it, and anybody who showed up at the taping was showing up to be entertained. Anybody who didn't feel they could handle it would not come. And during the rehearsal of her number, (Jackson) just broke down on stage, just cried, and he was comforting to her. He just rose to the occasion. When there was trouble, the gesture was there to help you laugh."

Episode 14 (taped Nov. 30, 1963; aired Dec. 4, 1963)
Guests: Glynis Johns, Jo Stafford, The Big Three, Jamie Farr, Laurie Ichino
Songs: "I'm in a Dancing Mood," "Timptation," "Be My Little Baby Bumble Bee"
Sketches: Train Caper, Office Party

Episode 15 (taped Dec. 7, 1963; aired Dec. 11, 1963)
Guests: Julie Newmar, Howard Morris, Ruffinos
Songs: "That Great Come & Get It Day," "Swingin' the News," "Truly Julie Newmar," "Anywhere I Wander"
Sketches: Talent Playhouse's *Robin Hood* spoof, Italian Kitchen

On screen, Danny continued to evolve. He was a work in progress. Yet his two stand-ins for Sylvia—Herb Bonis and Herbie Baker—had drastically different ideas about who Danny should be on TV. Bonis, the businessman, knew that there were basically two types of variety shows—ones in which an amiable host introduced the talent and ones in which the host *was* the talent. And he knew that the former type, with low-key emcees like Ed Sullivan, usually outlasted the latter type, with larger-than-life stars like Sid Caesar and Milton Berle. Proof positive was the disastrous performance of the fall's two other big variety programs, *The Judy Garland Show* and *The Jerry Lewis Show*.

So, Bonis argued that the material should not only be stronger, but should better emphasize Danny's masculinity, rather than his silliness. It wasn't enough to have great components; the show needed Danny warm, firm and confident, building a rapport with the audience rather than just performing for them.

Baker disagreed completely. He thought Danny bonded best with the audience through his performances. In a mid-season memo, Baker complained to Lafferty: "Bonis is 100 percent wrong when he says that entertainment alone cannot win a large audience, the connective talk and lead-ins are stilted, and that Danny must be made over in the image of Garry Moore and Art Linkletter. Danny has been true to himself, and mail and critics tell us he's the delight of the season." Instead, Baker argued that there was too much talking and not enough singing. The music, not the sketches, determined the pace of the show. And any time they led into the sit down spot with a sketch instead of a musical number, the sit down spot suffered. "Everyone seems to have a different reaction to a sketch—even a great sketch," Baker wrote. "But, for some reason, Danny doing a number seems to suspend the audience's critical opinion. We should take advantage of this."

With the addition of Earl Brown to the staff, Baker figured they now had the resources to develop a "Danny Kaye performance number" for every show—even if it wasn't from scratch. "Up to now," Baker wrote, "Danny has always insisted on original stuff rather than special versions of established things. Not on weekly television. Take 'em where you can find 'em."

Episode 16 (taped Dec. 14, 1963; aired Dec. 18, 1963)
Guests: Andy Williams, Dick Van Dyke, Mary Tyler Moore (cameo)
Songs: "Puttin' on the Ritz," "You Meet the Nicest People," "The Christmas Season"
Sketches: Courtroom, Nervous Groom
[Moore, who was set to guest-star the following week, received $500 for a cameo in a wedding sketch with her *Dick Van Dyke Show* co-star.]

Episode 17 (taped Dec. 21, 1963; aired Dec. 25, 1963)
Guests: Nat King Cole, Mary Tyler Moore, Clinger Sisters, Jamie Farr
Songs: "Comes Once in a Lifetime," "Jingle Journey," "In Vienna," "That's How I Feel,"
   "Baby, It's Cold Outside," "Let There Be Peace on Earth"
Sketches: Kinderspiel Light Opera Co.'s *Student Prince* spoof

Episode 18 (taped Jan. 4, 1964; aired Jan. 8, 1964)
Guests: Terry-Thomas, Marilyn Lovell, Laurie Ichino, Maori Dancers
Songs: "Up a Lazy River," "Tea for Two" parodies, "The New Baby," "I'm Five"
Sketches: Shipboard Waiter, *The Great Getaway* (*Great Escape* spoof)

The series gave Kaye the opportunity to showcase his dancing skills on a weekly basis, even though Danny didn't consider himself a dancer. Choreographer Tony Charmoli said, "Danny is a very physical person and I would say an excellent dancer—he might question that. He thinks he's an excellent *mover*. He moves very well, but he has the facility for movement that equals any good dancer. So he may call it movement. I call it dancing. And he liked to move and liked to dance, so naturally each morning on the series we'd start off with the dancing in the show."

The writers, however, always wanted to cut back on the dancing, particularly any numbers that didn't involve Kaye. "That was a constant fight because if it'd been up to (Charmoli, every night) it would have been an hour ballet," recalled Shelly Keller. "To have a seven-minute dance number in the middle of a show is death to comedy. So we used to scream and he wouldn't touch (the dance numbers) or cut them, so there were fights about getting those shorter."

Director Bob Scheerer was a former dancer and choreographer. Though he usually offered straightforward direction of sketches, his forte became clever dance numbers, such as having Danny perform "Breezin' Along with the Breeze" in front of an increasingly powerful wind machine. "We almost blew him off the stage," Scheerer remembered.

For one show, Charmoli thought it would be cute to have Danny dance with a pint-sized ballerina. "I auditioned many little girls from dance schools that I knew in the vicinity," Charmoli said. "They sent me different little students. And there were two girls. My assistant, Dick Beard, said, 'Look at that little girl!' But I said, "Look at *that* little girl at the end!" That little Asian girl was Laurie Ichino. We used her, and we received so much mail on her that she came back and did several more shows."

Ichino would soon find herself with Kaye on the cover of *TV Guide*. She made ten more appearances over the next two years, before moving on to the *Dean Martin Show* and ultimately a career as a professional dancer.

Episode 19 (taped Jan. 11, 1964; aired Jan. 15, 1964)
Guests: Dorothy Collins, Jackie Cooper, Marilyn Lovell, Clinger Sisters
Songs: "Hand Me Down My Walkin' Cane," "Ain't It Great to Be Crazy"
Sketches: Marriage Counselor Dr. Rheinmeddler, *Hit Parade* parody, Talent Playhouse movie

Wizard of Oz Hosting (taped Jan. 13, 1964; aired Jan. 26, 1964)
Director: Robert Scheerer
Writers: Sheldon Keller & Mel Tolkin
[As the new family-friendly face of CBS, Danny was hired to host the network's annual telecast of *The Wizard of Oz*. Kaye filmed four segments (airing before, during the two breaks of, and after the film), sitting on a giant toadstool in front of a painted backdrop of the Yellow Brick Road and Emerald City. CBS would rerun the segments each year, for as long as Kaye's series continued.]

Episode 20 (taped Jan. 18, 1964; aired Jan. 22, 1964)
Guests: Art Carney, Rod Serling, Joe & Eddie, Jamie Farr
Songs: "I Like the Likes of You," "Do You Ever Think of Me"
Sketches: Conducting Television City Philharmonic, *Safety Zone* (*Twilight Zone* spoof), Birthday Surprise

Episode 21 (taped Jan. 25, 1964; aired Jan. 29, 1964)
Guests: Diahann Caroll
Songs: "Put on a Happy Face," Nonsense Song medley
Sketches: *I'll Cry Tamale* (*Viva Zapata* spoof), New Father, It's Closing Time

Episode 22 (taped Feb. 1, 1964; aired Feb. 5, 1964)
Guests: Imogene Coca, Laurie Ichino, Joe & Eddie
Songs: "Crazy Barbara," "The Thank You Letter," "Shall We Dance?"
Sketches: Swiss Ambassadors, *Der Fledermountie*, Competitive Monopoly Players
[The show originally planned to reunite *Your Show of Shows* vets Coca and Howard Morris, but due to "writing problems," Morris' appearance was delayed two weeks.]

Episode 23 (taped Feb. 15, 1964; aired Feb. 19, 1964)
Guests: John Mills, Hayley Mills, Joe & Eddie, Maudie Prickett, Bernie Kopell
Songs: "Shine on Your Shoes," "When I Take My Sugar to Tea," "Just in Time"
Sketches: *The HMS Cruelty* (*Mutiny on the Bounty* spoof), Customs, Fraternity Pin

Episode 24 (taped Feb. 22, 1964; aired Feb. 26, 1964)
Guests: Buddy Ebsen, Howard Morris, Marilyn Lovell
Songs: "Let's Take a Walk Around the Block," "Hey, Look Me Over," "Mommy, I Wanna Drinka Water," "Marching Along Together"
Sketches: Folk Singing Hillbillies, Uninvited Dinner Guest
[Ebsen insisted he get to play Jed Clampett from his top-rated *Beverly Hillbillies*, but the writers thought that using the character would confine them to creating a standard sitcom sketch. Instead, they suggested casting him as Jed's twin brother.]

Episode 25 (taped Feb. 29, 1964; aired March 4, 1964)
Guests: Art Carney, Te Arohanui Maori Dancers Co.
Songs: "They All Laughed," "Now Is the Hour"
Sketches: Prospective Suitor, *Lawrence of Alcatraz*

Jamie Farr, who would later play cross-dressing Corporal Klinger on *M*A*S*H*, had played in sketches in nine *Kaye Show* episodes and appeared set to be offered a contract as a permanent addition to the series. His hopes, however, were dashed when the producers saw versatile comedienne Joyce Van Patten in action. "I got the job through Paul Mazursky and Larry Tucker, who recommended that they try me out," she recalled. "My first show was with Art Carney as my father and Danny as my boyfriend. Lucky for me, something went wrong and I covered, and that was it. I did about four shows to end that season and then was put under contract for the next three years."

Farr would never appear on the show again.

> **Episode 26** (taped March 7, 1964; aired March 25, 1964)
> **Guests**: Tony Bennett, Howard Morris
> **Songs**: "I Love a Piano," "Carnival of Venice," "Bunch o' Blues"
> **Sketches**: Giovanni Gets a Letter from His Son in America, James Blonde vs. Dr. Yes
>
> **Episode 27** (taped March 14, 1964; aired March 18, 1964)
> **Guests**: Nancy Walker, Jerry Stiller & Anne Meara, Joe & Eddie
> **Songs**: "I'm Old Fashioned," "Just Imagine," "Bathtub Admiral," "You're Under Arrest," "Heart of My Heart"
> **Sketches**: *Sheiks in Toyland*, Chronically Unemployed Rudy Loses His Job
>
> **Episode 28** (taped March 28, 1964; aired April 1, 1964)
> **Guests**: Dorothy Collins, Howard Morris, Laurie Ichino
> **Songs**: "Change Partners," "Cup of Coffee"
> **Sketches**: *Tequila Mockingbird*, Hit Parade parody, Jerome Goes to Friendship Club
>
> **Episode 29** (taped April 4, 1964; aired April 8, 1964)
> **Guests**: Jim Nabors, Bea Benaderet, Andy Griffith (cameo)
> **Songs**: "Whistle While You Work," "Gigi"
> **Sketches**: Look Out for Mama, *The Long, Hot Supper*
> [In a spoof of *The Long, Hot Summer*, Kaye played Fat Daddy, a comically ruthless Southern tyrant, who became a recurring character. More notably, the episode gave Jim "Gomer Pyle" Nabors his first opportunity to sing on television.]
>
> **Episode 30** (taped April 11, 1964; aired April 15, 1964)
> **Guests**: Mary Tyler Moore, The Youngfolk
> **Songs**: "Steppin' Out with My Baby," "It's That Time of Year"
> **Sketches**: Pronunciation, Irish Lovers

After taping show 29, Danny volunteered to prepare a late-night Italian dinner at the home of Tony Charmoli, who recalled, "He decided he was going to do the whole dinner himself, and he cooked the spaghetti. I said, 'Let someone else do that,' as he was taking the spaghetti off the stove to the sink to strain it. And as he carried it over to put it on the edge of the sink to pour the hot water off, the steam scalded his hand. So it slipped and the boiling hot water went into his boot. The pain was so terrific he didn't scream; there was nothing except an 'Uhhh…' Well, we got the boot off and got his foot into ice immediately. He seemed to be all right—little does one realize when one is in such terrific shock. He was able to complete his dinner, and he said, 'No, no. I'm all right.' Then about half-an-hour later, he said, 'I'm feeling a little chilly. I think maybe I better go home.' And his driver took him home, and he said halfway between my house and his house he just was on the ceiling of the car in such pain. It was just horrendous. But the doctor came over, took care of him, and knocked him out. Incidentally, the dinner was excellent."

Kaye was confined to bed for several days, his right foot and leg swollen and blistered. His doctor said he would be down for at least six weeks. CBS suggested they finish the season with reruns. But Danny was determined not to miss a beat. He rehearsed the upcoming show in a specially constructed wheelchair, with his burned leg in a cast, propped up and surrounded by a protective cage. Then, he hosted the show from a stool, with the action played around him. If a skit was about a floorwalker, it now concerned a cashier. The cameras taped him only in close-up—never below the waist and never moving around. One restaurant sketch couldn't be tweaked, so Howard Morris was called in to take Danny's place. The first show went so well, Kaye cracked, "maybe we should do them all sitting down."

Dance numbers were also modified. For one routine, Danny and Shari Lewis sang the first chorus, then Tony Charmoli sprang from the wings to dance with Lewis. For the rest of the number, she alternated between her singing partner and her dancing partner. For another song, Kaye and Lewis "danced" with puppets.

"We almost made a virtue out of the fact that he got hurt," producer Lafferty said. "I went to England and a few other places with him one week off when he was on crutches, and it was tough to get around, but he went. He said, 'I hurt myself, but here I am,' and he'd do his thing."

The injury made him perpetually irritable, but Kaye—and the rest of the crew—soldiered on. "The only time I ever saw him throw a tantrum was when he had that injury to his foot," recalled cue-card holder Tommy Grasso. "It was backstage when a cameraman or a cable puller dropped one of those big cable cords on his foot, and he let out a lot of profanities with an audience full of nuns."

Episode 31 (taped April 18, 1964; aired April 22, 1964)
Guests: Vincent Price, Shari Lewis & Lambchop, Howard Morris
Songs: "Ballin' the Jack," "My Ladies Love to Dance," "Around the World," "Tall Hope"
Sketches: Art Gallery, Autocratic Waiter

Episode 32 (taped April 25, 1964; aired April 29, 1964)
Guests: Pat Carroll, Ferrante & Teicher, Red Skelton (cameo)
Songs: "Mountain Greenery," "Mention My Name in Sheboygan"
Sketches: Sitcoms Around the World (*Donna Von Reedendorfer Show* in Vienna, *Danny Tomasetti Show* in Italy, *Pate fois Junction* in France), Vaudeville Act, Nurse Schmeckenvasser

Danny's first year ended in high style. The day the season's last new episode aired, *The Danny Kaye Show* was presented a prestigious Peabody Award. Less than a month later, the series took home Emmy Awards for Outstanding Variety Show of the Year, Outstanding Variety Show Performer (Kaye), and Outstanding Variety Show Director (Scheerer).

The show ended the season at number 30 in the ratings, averaging more than eleven million viewers a night. But despite winning its time slot handily, the series lost almost half the audience of its lead-ins, *The Dick Van Dyke Show* and *The Beverly Hillbillies* (which in 1963-1964 garnered the highest ratings for a sitcom in television history).

SEASON TWO
(32 shows)

Producer: Perry Lafferty • **Director**: Robert Scheerer
Writers: Mel Tolkin, Sheldon Keller, Ernest Chambers, Billy Barnes, Gary Belkin, Paul Mazursky, Larry Tucker, Ron Friedman
Cast: Harvey Korman, Joyce Van Patten, Tony Charmoli Dancers, Earl Brown Singers

For season two, CBS's programmers figured they could extend their good fortune by moving the two sitcoms up a half-hour and wedging in the new *Cara Williams Show* before Kaye. When Shelly Keller heard of the switch, he ran screaming to Danny.

"What can I do about that?" Kaye shrugged. "You can't tell a network…"

"Get in your airplane and don't come down 'til they make a change," Keller blurted, before realizing Danny's powerless position when it came to scheduling.

The only significant change Danny made was to the creative staff. Herbie Baker would not be back. Like Sylvia, he wrote slowly, laboring over every syllable, and was not as well suited to the weekly grind. In addition, since he always worked alone, he was frustrated that he was not as involved in the show as the others. For instance, when none of his submissions were used in the Don Knotts episode, Baker demanded his name be removed from the credits.

His spot was filled by another revue specialist, Billy Barnes. Barnes likewise wrote musical numbers off by himself and personally rehearsed Danny on the piano in Kaye's penthouse. With Baker gone, Barnes quickly joined Earl Brown as Danny's closest creative confidantes on the program.

Episode 33 (taped Aug. 8, 1964; aired Nov. 25, 1964)
Guests: Gwen Verdon
Songs: "Just in Time," "I've Got Your Number," "The Fair in a Day"
Sketches: Elopement parodies (silent movie, adult film *Fud*, musical *Great Elopement of 1935*), Anatomy of an Argument

Episode 34 (taped Aug. 15, 1964; aired Oct. 21, 1964)
Guests: Angela Lansbury, John Gary
Songs: "On the Street Where You Live," "A Buddy by the Name of You," "Lulu's Back in Town," "South Rampart Street Parade," "Ten Girls Ago"
Sketches: *Night with a Pirahna* (*Night of the Iguana* spoof), Late Snack

Episode 35 (taped Aug. 22, 1964; aired Sept. 23, 1964)
Guests: Gwen Verdon, Rhythm Masters
Songs: "Ain't She Sweet," "What Is Love," "Do You Ever Think of Me," "Tall Hope"
Sketches: Jerome's Blind Date

Episode 36 (taped Aug. 29, 1964; aired Feb. 10, 1965)
Guests: Gwen Verdon, Harve Presnell
Songs: "Runnin' Wild," "Little Boy Blue"
Sketches: Three-act musical *Top Hat, White Tie, & Green Socks*, Husband's Raise

Episode 37 (taped Sept. 5, 1964; aired Dec. 30, 1964)
Guests: Buddy Ebsen, Pat Carroll, Howard Morris, Bernie Kopell
Songs: "A Foggy Day," "Bidin' My Time," "Sentimental Journey"
Sketches: *Fort Aggravation*, New Supermarket Checker

Episode 38 (taped Sept. 19, 1964; aired Oct. 28, 1964)
Guests: Jose Ferrer, Dorothy Collins, Laurie Ichino
Songs: "Look Who's Dancing," "Folks Who Live on the Hill," "Rockin' Red Ridin' Hood"
Sketches: Red Riding Hood musical, Ruthless Job Seeker, English Courtroom

Episode 39 (taped Sept. 26, 1964; aired Sept. 30, 1964)
Guests: Phil Silvers, Barbara McNair
Songs: "Jamboree Jones," "You Make Me Feel So Young," "You're My Everything," "Don't Put a Tax on a Beautiful Girl"
Sketches: Family Burlesque, Neighbor's Late-Night Party

Episode 40 (taped Oct. 3, 1964; aired Oct. 7, 1964)
Guests: Imogene Coca, Joe & Eddie, Bernie Kopell, Dino Natali
Songs: "The Marching Adorables," "First Day on the Job," "No Strings"

Sketches: *Naughty Gypsy Yetta* operetta, Husband Picks Out a Gift for His Wife

Episode 41 (taped Oct. 10, 1964; aired Oct. 14, 1964)
Guests: Mary Tyler Moore, Danny Cox
Songs: "Old Piano Roll Blues," "I've Got a Lovely Bunch of Coconuts"
Sketches: Television Addiction, Fat Daddy in *Fat on a Hot Tin Roof*

Episode 42 (taped Oct. 24, 1964; aired Nov. 4, 1964)
Guests: Lucille Ball, John Gary
Songs: "Slap That Bass," "Way Back Home," "Pennies from Heaven"/"Nevertheless"
Sketches: Fire the Maid, The Show Must Go On

The biggest threat to Kaye's longevity on television wasn't the *Cara Williams Show*. For the first time, Kaye would be up against real competition. NBC began scheduling movies on Wednesday nights, starting an hour before the Kaye show—the first time a network ever scheduled weekly movies in prime time. Kaye's ratings suffered immediately. Within months, CBS and ABC began laying out plans for their own movie of the week, and NBC decided to broadcast films two nights a week.

As Danny's ratings inched lower, CBS pressured Lafferty to liven things up. Yet it was a gentle pressuring, since Lafferty was becoming a golden boy around CBS. He avoided cost overruns and kept the show running like clockwork. No detail escaped him, right down to sending the show's guests warm, personalized thank-you notes after every appearance. Danny, most of all, took an instant liking to the genial producer. Lafferty was constantly at his side, frequently dining among the celebrities in Kaye's Chinese kitchen.

In casting, Lafferty was adept at cross-promotion, regularly booking guests who had their own CBS shows, including *The Dick Van Dyke Show, Beverly Hillbillies, Petticoat Junction, Twilight Zone, Andy Griffith Show, Baileys of Balboa, The New Phil Silvers Show*, and *The Munsters*. But his biggest coup came in brokering a swap with Lucille Ball. She agreed to guest-star on Kaye's show, in return for him appearing a month later on *The Lucy Show*. Dena Productions paid top stars $7,500 per appearance—never more—but Lucy appeared for just $500, the same amount her company, Desilu, would pay Danny to appear on her show.

Although Danny and Lucy had worked together twice before—on Kaye's 1962 special and later co-hosting a local Emmy Awards presentation—this time around wouldn't go as smoothly. The two simply had diametrically opposed approaches to rehearsing. To retain an air of spontaneity, Danny would only rehearse a routine until he had the sense of it and adequately knew his lines. Lucy, on the other hand, preferred to practice scenes over and over again until everyone else could scream. Consequently, Ball kept complaining to Kaye that he should get up on his feet. After one argument on the day before the taping, the two didn't exchange goodbyes at the end of the day. Gossip columnists claimed a full-blown feud had erupted. Kaye and Ball said they were merely "kidding" each other.

Episode 43 (taped Oct. 31, 1964; aired March 17, 1965)
Guests: Imogene Coca, Enzo Stuarti
Songs: "Stairway to Paradise," "Do Re Mi," "Molly Malone"
Sketches: Irish Traveler, Amateur Doctor

Episode 44 (taped Nov. 7, 1964; aired Nov. 11, 1964)
Guests: Howard Morris, Shari Lewis & Lambchop
Songs: "You Are My Sunshine," "Cherry Pies Ought to Be You," "The Questions Children Ask"
Sketches: Italian Street Singers, James Blonde in *From Turkey with Stuffing*

Episode 45 (taped Nov. 14, 1964; aired Nov. 18, 1964)
Guests: Diahann Carroll, Don Knotts, Clinger Sisters
Songs: "Pick Yourself Up," "Up Above My Head," "Personality"
Sketches: Test Flight, Nervous Army Reservists, *The Spoiled Prince*

Episode 46 (taped Nov. 28, 1964; aired Dec. 2, 1964)
Guests: Art Carney, Pearl Bailey, Laurie Ichino, Ed Peck, Johnny Silver
Songs: "If This Isn't Love," "Who Wants to Be a Millionaire"
Sketches: Carpooling Neighbors, Three-act movie *Murder, Maestro, Murder*

Despite Kaye's many talents, he did have limitations. For one, the crew quickly learned to avoid having him display anger, like in the husband-and-wife sketches done so well by Sid Caesar and Imogene Coca. "Danny couldn't find a way to do it that worked," Scheerer said. "Anger is often a part of the sketches, and he did it too realistically. It wasn't comfortable when it is supposed to be comedy and it looks like the man is really going to get upset."

So, too, certain guests—like Gwen Verdon—clicked perfectly, and were asked back over and over again. Others not so much. Scheerer said, "If Danny liked a guest, it was wonderful. If he didn't like them, it was awful. *Awful*. And he sure let it be known, just by being cold." Most of the ones who had to suffer through a week of Kaye's moodiness weren't asked back, though Scheerer said, "I'm not sure any of them wanted to come back."

One who did was *The Honeymooners'* Art Carney, whose appearances were always hysterical. Kaye, though, was perturbed by the comic's ad-libbing, which he saw as scene stealing. "Art Carney could not read cue cards well because he loved to ad-lib," said cardholder Tommy Grasso. In one sketch, "Carney was supposed to catch Danny Kaye. Carney got busy trying to read the cards one time and missed him in rehearsal. Danny fell backwards off the stage, and they would not speak to each other for the whole thing."

In editing Carney's third appearance, Danny wanted to use a longer version of the sit down spot he'd recorded during the dress rehearsal, so—to make room—they cut out Carney's solo, "Down by the Winegar Woiks." Carney was asked back once in season two. His improvisations brought down the house, infuriating Kaye. After the taping, Danny stormed out of the studio without saying goodbye. It was one of the funniest shows of the year—but would be Carney's last.

Episode 47 (taped Dec. 6, 1964; aired Dec. 9, 1964)
Guests: Imogene Coca, Tony Bennett, Clinger Sisters
Songs: "Cute"
Sketches: Rudy Loses His Job as Santa, *Swan Lake* parody, *Fledermikado*

Episode 48 (taped Dec. 12, 1964; aired Dec. 16, 1964)
Guests: Howard Morris, Pat Carroll, Joe & Eddie
Songs: "Changing of the Guard," "Heavenly Music," "The Story of Alice"
Sketches: World War I Veterans Interview, French Goldilocks, Jerome Comes to Dinner
[The French Goldilocks was the first of what would become ten foreign language fairy
  tales. Later installments included a German "Three Little Pigs," a Mexican "Jose and
  the Beanstalk," and an Irish "Little Red Riding Hood," who was smuggling liquor in
  her basket for grandma.]

Episode 49 (taped Dec. 19, 1964; aired Dec. 23, 1964)
Guests: Gwen Verdon, Jo Stafford, Bernie Kopell, Victoria Paige Meyerink
Songs: "Waltz Around the Christmas Tree," "Jingle Journey," "Ugly Duckling," "It's
  Almost Like Being in Love"
Sketches: Christmas Fantasy, Giovanni's Phone Call, *The Spy Who Caught a Cold*

The annual holiday show featured a fantasy dance sequence in which Danny and Gwen Verdon portrayed rejected dolls in a little girl's bedroom. That little girl turned out to be the star of the episode. Adorable, precocious and a week shy of her fourth birthday, wee Victoria Paige Meyerink immediately hit it off with Danny. So she was asked to return for the next show, to chat on Danny's lap during the sit down spot. This time, she was even more engaging. The show was flooded with fan mail. Victoria was asked back again for the next show, and the next, and the next.

"She had the most extraordinary face and reactions to Danny," Lafferty recalled. "She was on for about four weeks and the ratings went up four or five share points. She was the talk of America, this little spot with Danny and this little tiny girl."

RATINGS BONANZA: Danny's series received a spike in viewership late in the second season, thanks to frequent "sit down spot" appearances by precocious four-year old Victoria Paige Meyerink. [© 1965 CBS]

After five consecutive appearances, she was offered a contract for the remainder of the season, with a series of options for the following year. She just had to stay off of other variety shows.

That didn't stop her mother—an ambitious actress who never made it big on her own—from quickly signing Victoria to appear in TV commercials and a television pilot with Shirley Temple. But as her success grew, Victoria's charm seemed less natural. She got temperamental. She feigned illness when she didn't want to perform. She looked confused or frightened.

She clammed up if she thought the audience was laughing at her.

"I don't know whether her mother was pushing the kid or what," Lafferty said, "but it started to where the kid wouldn't talk to Danny. We'd get her up on his lap in front of the audience, and he'd talk, and she wouldn't answer. All the magic was gone. We even tried putting her on the lap and taping 45 minutes with no audience present, just to see if that made a difference. But there was something that happened after a few weeks, chemically, that stopped that child from wanting to communicate."

No matter how much clowning Danny did, he couldn't get her to respond. Lafferty renegotiated Meyerink's deal, to pay her a lesser amount for any weeks that she wouldn't appear. A week later, the producer informed her mother that Victoria would not be used for any more shows.

During the final weeks of the season, the ratings continued to slide. But, for Danny, there was worse news. CBS offered Lafferty the job of vice president in charge of programming for the West Coast. Kaye felt betrayed. Soon after, Scheerer announced that he wanted to direct specials and would not be returning to the series. It was time for a fresh approach.

Episode 50 (taped Jan. 2, 1965; aired Jan. 6, 1965)
Guests: Peter Falk, Dorothy Collins, Laurie Ichino, Bernie Kopell, Victoria Meyerink
Songs: "Pretty Baby," "Mother Goose on the Loose"
Sketches: Problem Student, *Hit Parade* parody, *Please Don't Eat the Tacos* spoof

Episode 51 (taped Jan. 9, 1965; aired Jan. 13, 1965)
Guests: Vincent Price, Dyan Cannon, Victoria Meyerink
Songs: "Triplets"
Sketches: Jerome Visits the Dentist, *Days of Wine and Schnitzel*

Episode 52 (taped Jan. 16, 1965; aired Jan. 20, 1965)
Guests: Imogene Coca, Nancy Wilson, Victoria Meyerink
Songs: "Life Is Just a Bowl of Cherries," "Play a Simple Melody," "Do Re Mi"
Sketches: Acrobatricks, Love Scene (Hitchcock, Fellini, Disney), Russian Cinderella, New Wig

Episode 53 (taped Jan. 23, 1965; aired Jan. 27, 1965)
Guests: Irene Ryan, Bessie Griffin, Gospel Pearls, Victoria Meyerink
Songs: "We Belong Together," "Five Pennies," "Yankee Doodle," "Bigger & Better"
Sketches: Moms Learn Son's Engaged, *A Shot in the Mouth* (*Double Indemnity* spoof)

Episode 54 (taped Jan. 30, 1965; aired Feb. 3, 1965)
Guests: Fred Gwynne, John Gary, Maudie Prickett
Songs: "I'm Putting All My Eggs in One Basket," "Cool Water"
Sketches: Herman Munster, Jerome Stars in a Play, Night Court

Episode 55 (taped Feb. 13, 1965; aired Feb. 17, 1965)
Guests: Elke Sommers, Pat Carroll, Laurie Ichino

Songs: Folk Song duet, "Three Part Invention," "Won't You Dance with Me?"
Sketches: Jerome Backstage, Marriage Counselor Dr. Rheinmeddler, Sons-in-Law
  Evict Mothers-in-Law

Episode 56 (taped Feb. 20, 1965; aired Feb. 24, 1965)
Guests: Werner Klemperer, Shirley Bassey
Songs: "Pass Me By," "A Spoonful of Sugar," "Sometimes I'm Happy"
Sketches: *Ringfinger*, Jerome at Baby Class, French Little Red Riding Hood
[Klemperer, from *Hogan's Heroes*, filled in at the last moment as the villain in a James
  Blonde sketch written for Paul Ford.]

Episode 57 (taped Feb. 27, 1965; aired March 3, 1965)
Guests: Imogene Coca, Joe & Eddie, Victoria Meyerink
Songs: "It's a Lovely Day Today," "There Was a Little Girl"
Sketches: Commercials by Great Authors, Bavarian String Trio, Wife's Poker Game

Episode 58 (taped March 6, 1965; aired March 10, 1965)
Guests: Jim Nabors, Oscar Peterson Jazz Trio, Victoria Meyerink
Songs: "Jackie, Elaine & Nancy"
Sketches: Viennese Conductor, Fat Daddy in *Labanza*

Episode 59 (taped March 13, 1965; aired March 24, 1965)
Guests: Lauren Bacall, Jason Robards Jr., Danny Cox
Songs: "Like Yourself," "You're Under Arrest," "Iowa," "Irish Melody," "The Best Things
  in Life Are Cheap"
Sketches: Quiz Show, New Fathers Trio

Episode 60 (taped March 27, 1965; aired March 31, 1965)
Guests: Kit Smythe, Howard Morris, Laurie Ichino
Songs: "Mutual Admiration Society," "Pleasure," "Three Part Invention Second Time
  Around"
Sketches: Reformed Crooks, Giovanni's Daughter's Wedding

Episode 61 (taped April 3, 1965; aired April 7, 1965)
Guests: Nanette Fabray, Astrud Gilbreto, Gary Coster
Songs: "San Francisco Boy Oh Boy," "Sunny Side Up"
Sketches: Jerome Trapped in Elevator, Barbary Coast

Episode 62 (taped April 10, 1965; aired April 14, 1965)
Guests: Gwen Verdon
Songs: "Jump in the Line"
Sketches: Jerome Dance Lesson, Innermost Thoughts

Episode 63 (taped April 17, 1965; aired April 21, 1965)
Guests: Tony Randall, Shani Wallis, Sophia Mary Gruskin
Songs: "A Shine of Your Shoes," "Consider Yourself," My Home Town medley
Sketches: Japanese Musicians, Jerome & the Stewardesses, International Crooks

Episode 64 (taped April 24, 1965; aired April 28, 1965)
Guests: Charles Aznavour, Stan Worth
Songs: "Ridin' on the Moon," Aznavour medley
Sketches: Jose & the Beanstalk, French Film Fugitives

SEASON THREE
(30 shows)

Producer: Robert Scheerer • **Director**: Steve Binder (65-69), Robert Scheerer (70), Billy Foster (71-)
Writers: Ernest Chambers, Pat McCormick, Ron Friedman (65-77), Paul Mazursky, Larry Tucker, Billy Barnes, Norman Barasch, Carroll Moore, Bernard Rothman
Cast: Harvey Korman, Joyce Van Patten, Tony Charmoli Dancers, Earl Brown Singers

Starting with the 1965 season, CBS finally, begrudgingly decreed that the majority of its established series—including Kaye's—be broadcast in color. So, to keep costs in line, Kaye would now tape just 30 episodes per season, instead of 32.

More importantly, *The Danny Kaye Show* needed to get younger. As Lafferty recalled, "It's a rule with variety shows especially, the longer they're on, the older they get. The audience tends to get older, and the younger people start to go somewhere else. The older people stay, but the advertisers like to have a big hunk of young people."

Kaye and Bonis turned to the producer of the youthful *Patty Duke Show*, one of the highest rated programs on rival ABC. The Duke show was actually the first producing job for Stanley "Stash" Prager, who had cut his chops as a comic actor, before gaining notoriety as a director on Broadway and in TV sitcoms.

To direct, Kaye and Bonis selected 24-year-old Steve Binder—talked about as a hot young talent after directing *Hullabaloo, Jazz Scene USA*, and the concert film *The TAMI Show*. Binder wanted to bring a contemporary vibe to *The Danny Kaye Show*. He alerted record producers that he was after fresh, hip talent, like Herman's Hermits and the Righteous Brothers. He also vowed to invigorate the writing staff, which he found dispirited by Kaye's reluctance to try new material and new characters.

To be sure, Prager and Binder would expunge all traces of old-fashioned variety programs, like *Your Show of Shows*. Writers Tolkin, Keller and Belkin were not asked back. Performers Howard Morris, after a record ten appearances, and Imogene Coca, after six, would not be invited back, either. Upon hearing the news, Morris cracked, "You mean it's not gonna be the Sid Caesar show any more?"

On his way out, Keller could tell that Prager would not be a good fit for Danny. "For some reason," Keller recalled, Prager "kept agreeing with everything Danny said, which scared the hell out of Danny. You want a producer who knows as much or more than you, somebody who can say,

'You're wrong, Danny. This will work.'"

But Prager didn't seem to understand Kaye's unique talents. Billy Barnes was among those who thought the new producer and director "didn't know what they were doing." Barnes recalled that for one show Prager "wanted Danny to sing some sort of jazz number that had nothing to do with his salesmanship. I said, 'This isn't what *The Danny Kaye Show* is.' 'Well, we thought we'd bring new stuff to it, jazz it up.' We went to color; I thought that was enough jazz."

Worse, Prager lacked the expertise to keep the wheels moving on such a complicated show—and to pacify Danny. "Stanley was completely out of his element and Steve (Binder), at that time, was relatively new," said writer Ernie Chambers. "The two of them simply couldn't handle what they were doing. Danny made mincemeat out of Prager. Perry (Lafferty) had been his alter ego, constantly with Danny. Perry was like his roommate. When Perry took the new job at CBS, Danny was really lost, because he depended so totally on Perry. And he didn't get along with Stanley at all. Stanley really didn't know the form very well, television variety, so there was upheaval."

Lafferty agreed: "The problem was that Danny was so tuned in to me and to Bobby (Scheerer) and to our way of working that the first person they hired to produce, Stanley Prager, didn't really have any of the 'equipment,' other than his own creativity. He didn't have the discipline. Danny was used to that, and he couldn't give him that. And the director couldn't give him that, so it really became chaotic."

Finally, Lafferty asked former director Scheerer to stop by and peek in on how everything was running. "I went one day to see him in his office, and he was timing the one-minute commercials," Scheerer recalled. "It's nonsense. They're done, they're shot, and he's sitting there as if it had to be worked out as part of his job as producer. He didn't know what he was doing."

Production on the season premiere was set to begin in days. A train wreck looked inevitable. In desperation, Lafferty cornered Kaye, to encourage him to hire back Scheerer to produce, since he was familiar with how the show ran. Kaye had Bonis buy out Prager's contract for $85,000—his weekly $4,250 fee for 20 episodes, instead of 30.

Scheerer stepped in immediately to produce, for $4,500 per show. He figured Binder, who was guaranteed thirteen shows, wouldn't last much longer. Scheerer recalled that during their first run-through, Binder spent the whole time reading the newspaper. So as part of his deal, Scheerer agreed that, should Binder need to be replaced, he would serve double-duty as director, as well as producer.

Episode 65 (taped July 31, 1965; aired April 13, 1966)
Guests: Edie Adams, Fred Gwynne, Glenn Yarbrough, Richard Kiel
Songs: "CBS Schedule Song," "Looking at You," "Little Leaguers," "Turn Around"
Sketches: Munsters News Report, Boat Buyers

Episode 66 (taped Aug. 7, 1965; aired Dec. 1, 1965)
Guests: John Astin, Gwen Verdon, D'Aldo Romano
Songs: "Real Live Girl," "Popo the Puppet," "Look to the Rainbow"
Sketches: Russian Space Scientist, Pests, Jerome Goes to a Dude Ranch

Episode 67 (taped Aug. 14, 1965; aired Sept. 22, 1965)
Guests: Richard Crenna, Nana Mouskouri, Herman's Hermits
Songs: "I'm Henry VIII, I Am," "While We're Young," "Showmanship," "Lassie from Lancashire," "Old Man River"
Sketches: Olympic Runner Interview, *30 Seconds over Schnitzel*

Episode 68 (taped Aug. 21, 1965; aired Sept. 29, 1965)
Guests: Shirley Jones, Righteous Brothers
Songs: "Blame It on Love," "The Begat," "She," "Hello Young Lovers"
Sketches: Trial of Man vs. Woman, Adam & Eve's Long Engagement

As an omen, when the sponsors arrived at CBS headquarters for the taping of the season's first episode, their elevator broke down. The executives spent most of the show trapped in the stalled elevator.

The show's featured dance number contained dozens of quick camera cuts timed to the music. "I was calling the shots live, how many bars per shot," recalled Binder. "We started the number and no more than 30 seconds in, my shot direction was one count behind. I was calling it perfectly, but the technical director missed one of my sets. I called, 'Cut!' and the TD looked at me. Everyone in the booth froze. The edict was, you don't cut Danny Kaye. I thought this was ludicrous. We were not going to be able to use any of this. So I stopped everything. All the dancers stopped. Danny kept going. He was not used to being cut."

Kaye stormed off to the control booth, only to discover that—because the soundstage was being re-cabled for color—the booth was vacant. Binder said, "By the time he finally figured out where we were, his face was not red, it was crimson. In a controlled voice, he asked, 'Steve... what happened?' 'Danny, I'm really sorry. I screwed up. We were one shot behind, we can't use any of this, and I didn't want to burn out the dancers.' 'Well, don't let it happen again.' In two seconds I became the biggest hero at *The*

Danny Kaye Show. I protected my team."

Binder may have earned points with his crew, but he slipped even lower in Kaye's esteem. Bonis, however, did like the director's decision to film guest Glenn Yarbrough singing "Walk On Little Boy" on remote—playing with a young boy at the beach, on a rowboat, and at Griffith Park. "That's really inventive," Bonis told him. "Think of doing something with Danny out of the studio."

So, for an upcoming show with Shirley Jones, Binder suggested the writers devise a remote musical number inspired by the nursery rhymes about what little boys and little girls are made of. They would first shoot Jones, singing the girls' part, at a local park. Then Kaye would arrive and sing the boys' part, pantomiming to the various animals mentioned in the lyrics.

Danny arrived at the shoot on time and recorded the number. But reviewing the tape in the control booth, Binder realized that Kaye was singing about one animal while pantomiming another. The director hurried to the set, just in time to see Kaye and Bonis driving off. Binder was forced to patch the number together from what he had and hope no one noticed the mistakes.

"The chemistry was not working between Danny and me," Binder admitted. "When you're directing, you can feel the vibrations. I had a real insecure feeling that Danny was not listening to me or didn't care."

Episode 69 (taped Aug. 28, 1965; aired Oct. 6, 1965)
Guests: Buddy Ebsen, Clint Eastwood, Fess Parker, Charo, George Feyer
Songs: "Doodlin' Song," "The Good Guys," "Makin' Whoopee"
Sketches: Western Hero Lessons, Ballad of Pinky Dan

By the fifth show, Kaye was all but ignoring Binder. While taping a cowboy sketch with Clint Eastwood, according to Binder, Danny "was just out to lunch. (Tension) was building all week." The day after Binder finished directing his fifth episode, he was informed that Dena Productions "does not now intend to utilize your services in connection with the other eight programs." He was paid in full for the remainder of his thirteen-show contract.

Episode 70 (taped Sept. 10, 1965; aired Sept. 15, 1965)
Guests: Harry Belafonte, Nana Mouskouri
Songs: "Mama Look a Boo Boo," "Gonna Build a Mountain," "Hava Nagila," "Opa Neena Neena Naee," "Pavlova," "Who Will Buy?"
Sketches: Baseball Around the World

Scheerer stepped in direct show number six—and quickly realized that simultaneously producing and directing such a complicated program was beyond the capacity of a single person. To make matters worse, CBS was pressuring him to replace the week's guest, Greek singer Nana Mouskouri, because chairman Paley didn't like her. Paley also wanted her cut from a previously taped episode that had not yet aired. Unfortunately, week six's star attraction, Henry Belafonte, had agreed to appear on the condition that Mouskouri, whom he toured with, be given two guest spots. Running out of time, well past budget, and fearful of upsetting Belafonte, Scheerer pleaded for the shows to proceed, as planned.

The moment the show wrapped, Scheerer phoned another dancer-turned-choreographer-turned-director, Billy Foster, who had choreographed Kaye's first TV special and *On the Double*. Foster would direct all future episodes and, as Scheerer's handpicked successor, would help bring stability back to the show.

Episode 71 (taped Sept. 17, 1965; aired Oct. 13, 1965)
Guests: Benny Goodman, Caterina Valente
Songs: 1930s musicals medley, "I Hear Music," "Hi Ya, Sophia," "Mother Goose Bossa Nova," "We're Gonna Make It"
Sketches: Class of '22 through the Decades

Episode 72 (taped Sept. 24, 1965; aired Jan. 12, 1966)
Guests: Bill Dana, Caterina Valente, D'Aldo Romano
Songs: Foreign Language medley, "Like Yourself," "Straw Hat Song," "Do I Hear a Waltz?"
Sketches: Race Around the World

Episode 73 (taped Oct. 1, 1965; aired Dec. 29, 1965)
Guests: Eddie Albert, Wayne Newton
Songs: "Holiday Time," "Once a Year Day," "Time for Parting," "Cool Water," "Goodnight Irene"
Sketches: Father Time Interview, Morning After Office Party

Episode 74 (taped Oct. 9, 1965; aired Oct. 27, 1965)
Guests: Dinah Shore, Herb Alpert & the Tijuana Brass
Songs: "The Mood I'm In," "Happiness Is," Quick Change medley
Sketches: Tourists in Audience/Art Challenge, Workaholic Tycoon's Retirement

Episode 75 (taped Oct. 23, 1965; aired Nov. 3, 1965)
Guests: Pat Boone, Carolyn Jones
Songs: "Fascinatin' Rhythm," "Smiles," "Smilin' Through," "Those Ghoulish Things"
Sketches: Morticia, Christopher Columbus Interview, Samson Swinger & Delilah
[Bobby Darin had been originally slated to perform, but canceled due to illness. Darin rescheduled to appear a year later, but would pull out of that show as well.]

Episode 76 (taped Oct. 30, 1965; aired Nov. 10, 1965)
Guests: Marguerite Piazza, Freddie & the Dreamers
Songs: "I've Got No Strings," "Til Tomorrow," "Do the Freddie, the Danny, & the Marguerite"
Sketches: *Ben Paliagacci M.D.*, Jerome at Confidence Class, German Three Little Pigs

Episode 77 (taped Nov. 6, 1965; aired Nov. 24, 1965)
Guests: Tennessee Ernie Ford, Lainie Kazan, Kelton Garwood
Songs: "Bless This House," "Bunch o' Blues," "Like Love"
Sketches: Thanksgiving Turkey Interview, Exiled King

Episode 78 (taped Nov. 13, 1965; aired Nov. 17, 1965)
Guests: Ray Walston, Vikki Carr, Laurie Ichino
Songs: Bird medley, "Haven't We Met?"
Sketches: Nervous New Father's First Babysitting, *Goldbelly*, Props

Episode 79 (taped Nov. 20, 1965; aired Dec. 8, 1965)
Guests: Diahann Carroll, George Hamilton, Victoria Meyerink
Songs: "Anything Goes," "Could It Be," "Friendship"
Sketches: Lighthouse Keeper Interview, Christmas Toys, German movie

Episode 80 (taped Dec. 2, 1965; aired Jan. 1, 1966)
Guests: Tammy Grimes, Bob Crane
Songs: "That Face," "Elegance," "Friendly Star," "Love Birds"
Sketches: Beethoven Interview, Missing Movie Star, Hogan Tunnels Out opening

Episode 81 (taped Dec. 8, 1965; aired Dec. 15, 1965)
Guests: Vincent Price, Vikki Carr, John Gary
Songs: "Another Go Round," "All I Need Now"/"Little Girl," "A Fellow Needs a Girl"
Sketches: *Bikini Beach Frankenstein*, Window Washer on *Candid Camera*
[The taping was moved up one day to accommodate Kaye conducting the San Francisco Symphony.]

Although over the last year crooner John Gary had appeared on Kaye's show three times, it was this episode—centered around a lengthy Frankenstein spoof—that convinced the producers that the singer could perform equally well in sketches. They signed Gary to eight of the last thirteen shows, including the final four, as a run-up to Dena producing his own show, which would fill in for Danny's during the summer. And to make sure audiences got the connection, Kaye guest-starred on the first episode of *The John Gary Show*.

Episode 82 (taped Dec. 16, 1965; aired Dec. 22, 1965)
Guests: Jean Simmons, Laurence Harvey, John Gary
Songs: "Let There Be Peace on Earth," "Waltz Around the Christmas Tree," "We Won't Be in England for Christmas"
Sketches: *Fop at the Top* (*Room at the Top* spoof), Jerome Goes Skiing

Episode 83 (taped Dec. 23, 1965; aired Jan. 5, 1966)
Guests: Liza Minelli, Alan Young, John Gary
Songs: "A Fellow Needs a Girl," "Let's Talk It Over," "Pennies from Heaven"
Sketches: Grand Prix, Buckingham Guards, Laundromat

Episode 84 (taped Jan. 8, 1966; aired Jan. 26, 1966)
Guests: Robert Vaughn, Michel Le Grand, Joyce Cuoco
Songs: "Bonjour Michel," "Wonderful Child"
Sketches: Litterbug, Spy Goes Shopping, Prospectors

Episode 85 (taped Jan. 15, 1966; aired Feb. 2, 1966)
Guests: Eddie Albert, Morgana King
Songs: "Indiana," "New Ashmolean Marching Society & Students Conservatory Band," "Yellow Bird"
Sketches: Napoleon Interview, The Night Out

Episode 86 (taped Jan. 22, 1966; aired Feb. 9, 1966)
Guests: Cyril Ritchard, Eddy Arnold
Songs: "On a Clear Day You Can See Forever," "Petrov the Thinker," "Where I Come From," Broken Hearts medley, "You Gotta Love Everybody"
Sketches: Jerome Takes Diction Lessons, *Sahara Beach Party*

Episode 87 (taped Jan. 29, 1966; aired Feb. 23, 1966)
Guests: Inger Stevens, Woody Herman & His Band, Clinger Sisters, Maudie Prickett
Songs: "Let Me Entertain You," "Old MacDonald," "Station Break Blues," "Worry About Tomorrow Tomorrow"
Sketches: Giovanni's Visitor, George Washington Interview
[Stevens was originally booked for the Christmas show, but pulled out because she was a spokesperson for Clairol and among Kaye's advertisers was Alberto-Culver, which had among its products New Dawn hair-coloring shampoo. A month later, Stevens agreed to appear if Alberto-Culver advertised products other than New Dawn.]

In late January, CBS informed Kaye that it would proceed with a fourth season. The ratings had continued to slip, but the show tightened the gap behind NBC, which was airing a new show, *I Spy*. What really helped Kaye's show, though, was that his audience had gotten younger and had proven to be a valuable platform for guest recording artists.

Scheerer agreed to stay on one more year as producer, with a hefty raise. And, he had one more request. One of Scheerer's greater irritants was one of Prager's hires, a brash, young, motorcycle-riding Canadian writer named Bernie Rothman. Scheerer disliked how the new writer seemed to challenge him on every decision and contributed little. He asked Herb Bonis not to pick up Rothman's option.

Danny, however, liked Rothman and his work. So, Bonis went to Rothman with two demands. First, he had to let the producer do his job. And, second, he was to compile a list of all the numbers he'd written for the show so far. Bonis took the list to Scheerer, who was surprised to see that Rothman had written or contributed to fifteen numbers for the first 23 shows, including a few of the better-received pieces like "Petrov the Thinker" and, with Earl Barton, "Mother Goose Bossa Nova." At Danny's urging, Scheerer consented to let Rothman stay on.

As producer, Scheerer had worked hard to get the series back on track, production wise. He wasn't the politician Lafferty was, always at Kaye's side. He rarely dined at Kaye's home. Scheerer, in fact, didn't want to spend any more time with Danny than he had to. Consequently, the rest of the creative staff saw Kaye less frequently, as well. For Scheerer, it was all business. He concentrated on getting the show in a groove, a groove that in time became a rut.

Episode 88 (taped Feb. 5, 1966; aired Feb. 16, 1966)
Guests: Tim Conway, John Gary, Kimio Eto
Songs: "Lose That Long Face," "Plight of the Bumblebee," Japanese songs
Sketches: Pests, Nervous Skyscraper Workers, *Good Spy, Mr. Chips*

Episode 89 (taped Feb. 12, 1966; aired March 9, 1966)
Guests: Nancy Wilson, John Gary
Songs: "It's a Hoopety Hey Kind of Day," "Memphis Blues," "Hurry! It's Lovely Up Here"
Sketches: Chickenman, Library pantomime

Episode 90 (taped Feb. 26, 1966; aired March 2, 1966)
Guests: Joanne Woodward, Robert Goulet
Songs: "Company's Coming," "Foreign Movies," "Wee Hughie"
Sketches: Fat Daddy Forecloses on Plantation, Last Episodes (*Fugitive, Shenandoah, Run for Your Life*)

Episode 91 (taped March 5, 1966; aired March 30, 1966)
Guests: Vikki Carr, John Gary
Songs: "I'm Following You," "Let a Smile Be Your Umbrella," "Simple Melody," "Take Love," "William Tell & Son"
Sketches: Hand-Obsessed Violinist, Jerome Asks for a Raise

Episode 92 (taped March 12, 1966; aired April 6, 1966)
Guests: Vincent Price, John Gary, Stan Worth
Songs: "Ain't We Got Fun," Gilbert & Sullivan medley, "Make 'em Scream"
Sketches: Escaped Convict, Drunk Diner pantomime

Episode 93 (taped March 19, 1966; aired March 23, 1966)
Guests: Senta Berger, Chaim Topel, Herb Alpert & Tijuana Brass
Songs: "A Time for Singing," "Duty of a Sheik," "To Life," "Matchmaker, Matchmaker"
Sketches: German Hansel & Gretel, *The Sands of Hankie-Pankie*

Episode 94 (taped March 26, 1966; aired April 20, 1966)
Guests: John Gary, Judi Armstrong

Songs: "I Can't Sit Down," One of Those Songs," "Sometimes I'm Happy"
Sketches: Courtships, Returned Husband

SEASON FOUR
(30 shows)

Producer: Robert Scheerer • **Director**: Billy Foster
Writers: Pat McCormick, Paul Mazursky, Larry Tucker, Billy Barnes, Norman Barasch, Carroll Moore, Bernard Rothman, Ron Clark
Cast: Harvey Korman, Joyce Van Patten, Tony Charmoli Dancers, Earl Brown Singers

Episode 95 (taped July 30, 1966; aired Sept. 21, 1966)
Guests: Eddie Albert, Vikki Carr, Sergio Mendes & Brazil '66
Songs: "Let's Get Away from It All," "We're Gonna Stay at Home"
Sketches: Jerome Goes to Europe, Airplane, Around the World Tourists
[Bonis would book singer Carr as often as possible, since he was shopping a Dena-produced *Vikki Carr Show* to the networks.]

Episode 96 (taped Aug. 6, 1966; aired Sept. 14, 1966)
Guests: Andy Griffith, Ron Howard, Clint Howard, Susan Barrett, Donna Butterworth
Songs: "Live Life a Little," "Shiny Stockings"
Sketches: Ronny Howard Show, Store Dummy, Italian Snow White, Spy

To start the fourth season, Kaye insisted they shake up the format. He thought the program should be more cohesive by featuring a weekly theme, such as having every song, dance number, interview and sketch relate to vacations. "He said he wanted to try something different," Scheerer remembered. "So I said, 'Okay. I'm happy to try.' And we did (several) shows that had not the formula in any way that we had before. None of them worked. Not one. We did one show with Ron Howard and all young kids. It didn't work. Perry (Lafferty) called me after the show and said, 'What's going on? What's happening?' And I said, 'Listen, Danny wants to do something different, and I'm trying. I don't know what to tell you.'"

After the underwhelming reception to the season premiere—in which most of the songs and sketches were performed entirely by child actors and singers—Danny agreed to revert to the old revue format. He consigned himself to playing it safe, reworking timeworn material and relying on proven characters. In particular, he wanted to reuse his two favorite characters— Giovanni, an elderly Italian tailor created in season one, and Jerome (pronounced "Jevome"), a shy, stumbling, shoe clerk from Brooklyn—to the point that they were on almost every week.

By the fourth season, writer Norman Barasch admitted, "My feeling was that the show ran out of a lot of the characters that Danny had done the first two years. We found things that worked week after week, so we didn't have to vary it as much. The character of Jerome he liked a lot. He played that over and over again. He loved that. And we'd create different situations for Jerome to be in. He loved pantomime, so we did a pantomime thing that became almost a weekly feature."

By the end, Kaye wanted to do less dancing, since it required more rehearsing. Fewer non-musical guests were booked. And, according to Joyce Van Patten, as the final season wore on, Danny "requested to do sketches only with Harvey (Korman) and me, and let the guest stars sing or do interviews, but no sketches."

The writers who had left the show naturally felt the quality plummeted. Too much music, too much pathos, not enough comedy. Starting with year three, the show, according to Shelly Keller, "wasn't funny. I don't know if Danny got serious or what. It wasn't funny for two years. He had an Italian character he liked, an old man, that was kind of serioso. We had introduced it, but it had a funny payoff to it. But I thought the show—I couldn't believe it—there weren't any laughs in it."

Scheerer said they kept reusing characters and bits because "it worked," but admitted that in later shows, "I think the quality of the writing was not as good. I'm not sure that I contributed enough either. I think I probably could have done more. But I didn't, obviously."

By the end of year four, said Barasch, "I think it was running down a little bit. I think we were running out of ideas for Danny to do and, you know, everything the first two years was fresh and original, because he'd never done it on television before. After all, to get Danny Kaye to go on television at all was a major coup, and so everything that he had to offer was done in the first year or two. Everything he did then was new. The third and fourth years I think the audience had seen much of it. So we had to dig into new material and new ways of presenting Danny that he would like to do and that he thought an audience might like. For some reason, the audience liked the show opposite us (*I Spy*) better, and our show went way down in the ratings."

Two months into the season, *I Spy* had surged to thirteenth in the ratings. *The Danny Kaye Show* fell to 79. A month later, CBS—without informing Kaye—decided not to renew his contract. The network would give Danny the news when contract negotiations reopened the following month. In the meantime, they considered giving his timeslot to a new show being developed for Carol Burnett. At least Harvey Korman wouldn't be out of work for long.

STAND-BYS: In his series' final season, Danny kept returning to comfortable characters, such as shy Brooklyn shoestore clerk Jerome, who learned to sing with recurring player Joyce Jameson in episode 100. [© 1966 CBS]

Episode 97 (taped Aug. 13, 1966; aired Feb. 8, 1967)
Guests: Fred Gwynne, Vikki Carr
Songs: "I'm Forever Blowing Bubbles," Birds medley
Sketches: *Cyrano*, Guest Pests, Questions Children Ask

Episode 98 (taped Aug. 20, 1966; aired Sept. 28, 1966)
Guests: The Peanuts, Isa Watanabe, Frankie Randall
Songs: "Short, Short History of the USA," "Simple Melody"
Sketches: Jerome X-ray, Japanese mimicry, Anatomy of a Crime

Episode 99 (taped Aug. 27, 1966; aired Oct. 26, 1966)
Guests: Eddie Albert, Joe Williams, The Peanuts
Songs: "Last of the Big Time Gypsies," "Minstrel Days," "One Step Behind"
Sketches: Hunting Trip, Page Boy, Automation

Episode 100 (taped Sept. 10, 1966; aired Oct. 12, 1966)
Guests: Tim Conway, Barbara Minkus, The Peanuts
Songs: "Hey Babe Hey," "Old MacDonald," "Four Leaf Clover," "We Kiss in a Shadow"
Sketches: Santa Interview, Jerome Sings

Episode 101 (taped Sept. 17, 1966; aired Oct. 5, 1966)
Guests: Ella Fitzgerald, Buddy Greco, Sergio Mendes & Brazil '66
Songs: "It Don't Mean a Thing," "Mood Indigo," "We Like Each Other Fine," Ella medley
Sketches: Little Green Riding Hood, Beach Picnic pantomime, December-May
    Romance

Episode 102 (taped Sept. 24, 1966; aired Oct. 19, 1966)
Guests: Leslie Uggams, Steve Sanders, Victoria Meyerink
Songs: "Glow Worm, "Thou Swell," "I Wish You Love"
Sketches: Man's Man, German Hansel & Gretel, Giovanni Comes to America
[The episode had been written for Chuck Connors, but *The Rifleman* star had to pull out
    at the last minute due to the death of his father. His featured spot—a western dance
    hall sketch—was cut and replaced with a Giovanni sketch being prepared for the
    next week's show. To fill time, they also contacted season two's darling, Victoria
    Meyerink, now at age five-and-a-half a seasoned show biz veteran, to try to rekindle
    her magic with Danny. The results were pleasing enough to merit a contract for
    return appearances (usually to sing cute duets with Danny) for the rest of the sea-
    son—or as long as the magic lasted.]

Episode 103 (taped Oct. 1, 1966; aired Dec. 28, 1966)
Guests: Caterina Valente, Gilbert Becaud, Victoria Meyerink
Songs: "Chime In," "Conversation Bossa Nova"
Sketches: Father of the Year Interview, Instant Spy, *Battle of the Bilge*

Episode 104 (taped Oct. 8, 1966; aired Nov. 16, 1966)
Guests: Louis Armstrong, Caterina Valente
Songs: "It's Today," Salute to St. Louis medley
Sketches: Waiter pantomime, Paul Revere, Scottish Doctor

Episode 105 (taped Oct. 22, 1966; aired Nov. 2, 1966)
Guests: Tony Randall, Stan Worth, Vikki Carr, Victoria Meyerink
Songs: "I Must Know," "Sunny Disposish," "Frog in the Grog"
Sketches: Answering Service, Shirtboards, High School Reunion

Episode 106 (taped Oct. 28, 1966; aired Jan. 11, 1967)
Guests: Liberace, Vikki Carr, Victoria Meyerink
Songs: "It Takes Two," "Style," "Vickie"
Sketches: Rest Haven, James Blonde Meets Mr. 88, Giovanni Moves Out

Episode 107 (taped Nov. 5, 1966; aired Jan. 4, 1967)
Guests: Louis Armstrong, German Kessler Twins, Victoria Meyerink

Songs: "Top Hat, White Tie, & Tails," "Five Pennies Saints," "Aren't You Glad You're You"
Sketches: Cement Worker pantomime, Jose & the Beanstalk, Jerome's Surprise Party

Episode 108 (taped Nov. 12, 1966; aired Nov. 23, 1966)
Guests: Petula Clark, Stanley Holloway
Songs: "Today I Love Everybody," "You Do Something to Me," Music Hall medley
Sketches: Captain Ahab Interview, Bank, Giovanni Gives a Party, UNICEF Trick or Treat film

Episode 109 (taped Nov. 19, 1966; aired Nov. 30, 1966)
Guests: Peter Ustinov, Frank Gorshin, Nancy Wilson
Songs: "All of Me," "It All Started with the Wheel," Memphis Blues medley
Sketches: Old Tycoon, Conductor-First Violinist, *The Magnificent Two*

Episode 110 (taped Dec. 3, 1966; aired Dec. 7, 1966)
Guests: Shirley Jones, Sergio Mendes & Brazil '66, Victoria Meyerink
Songs: "Nothing Can Stop Me Now," "Walking Happy," "Bim-bom" "What's New at the Zoo"
Sketches: Revolving Door pantomime, Jerome Helps Arnold

Episode 111 (taped Dec. 9, 1966; aired Dec. 14, 1966)
Guests: Sergio Franchi, Sallie Blair, Maudie Prickett, Victoria Meyerink
Songs: "For Me & My Gal"
Sketches: Jerome at Home, Prop Dance, Mouse Patrol

Episode 112 (taped Dec. 16, 1966; aired Dec. 21, 1966)
Guests: Peggy Lee, Wayne Newton, International Children's Choir
Songs: "Waltz Around the Christmas Tree," "Jingle Journey," "Some Children See Him"
Sketches: French Goldilocks, Giovanni's Gift

Episode 113 (taped Dec. 23, 1966; aired March 1, 1967)
Guests: George Burns, Mirelle Mathieu
Songs: "Cabaret," "All of a Sudden My Heart Sings," Burns medley, "Lily of the Valley"
Sketches: Jerome Meets George Burns

Episode 114 (taped Jan. 7, 1967; aired Jan. 18, 1967)
Guests: John Gary, Godfrey Cambridge, Laurie Ichino, Harold Gould, Dabs Greer
Songs: "Come Dance with Me," "Down by the Station," "Change Your Name"
Sketches: Cinderolga, Barber Shop pantomime, Giovanni Finds a Friend

Episode 115 (taped Jan. 14, 1967; aired Jan. 25, 1967)
Guests: Peter Falk, Pat Carroll, The Lettermen
Songs: "Teamwork"
Sketches: Mama Visits Jerome, Jerome's Roommate

Episode 116 (taped Jan. 21, 1967; aired Feb. 15, 1967)
Guests: Eddy Arnold, Millicent Martin
Songs: "There's Always an Extra Potato," Western medley, "Who Can I Turn To?"
Sketches: Jerome's Soulmate, The Sounds of Words

Episode 117 (taped Jan. 28, 1967; aired Feb. 1, 1967)
Guests: Burl Ives, Barbara Rush
Songs: "Any Wednesday," "Plant a Radish," "Seven Ages"
Sketches: Cold Opening, Jerome Fixes Up His Sister, Fat Daddy
[Kaye so adored Billy Barnes' song "Seven Ages," based on Shakespeare's monologue from *As You Like It*, with Kaye aging from infant through old age, that he made it the only song written for his television show to be permanently added to his stage act.]

Episode 118 (taped Feb. 4, 1967; aired Feb. 22, 1967)
Guests: Tim Conway, Izumi
Songs: "Where Do You Worka John," Japanese medley, "A Fellow Needs a Girl"
Sketches: Little Green Riding Hood, Texas Tony, Working Man vignettes

Episode 119 (taped Feb. 11, 1967; aired March 8, 1967)
Guests: Harold Gould (landlord Marco), Amzie Strickland (fiancée Betty)
Songs: "What She Mean by That?," "I'm a No Jealous," "Too Old to Be Young"
[This week featured a five-act, hour-long musical, "Giovanni's Wedding." As soon as it aired, a record volume of fan mail arrived praising the episode—and also bemoaning the announcement that the series would not be returning in the fall.]

Episode 120 (taped Feb. 25, 1967; aired April 5, 1967)
Guests: Joanie Sommers, Brothers Four
Songs: "Love," "Let's Not Talk about Love," "Folks Who Live on the Hill"
Sketches: Jerome's Nightmare, Unrequited Love vignettes

Episode 121 (taped March 4, 1967; aired March 15, 1967)
Guests: Roddy McDowall, Blossom Dearie
Songs: "Big Beautiful Ball," "Flash, Bang, Wallop," "Wee Hughie"
Sketches: Roman Spectacle

Episode 122 (taped March 11, 1967; aired March 29, 1967)
Guests: Diahann Carroll (herself), Joyce Jamison (Denise), Herbie Faye & Buddy Lewis (detectives), Byron Morrow (Captain)
Songs: "Be Yourself," "Don't Look Now," "I Like You," "Jamaica Farewell"
[The hour-long Giovanni musical worked so well that the writers immediately began work on an hour-long Jerome show, in which Jerome falls in love during a Caribbean cruise, even as he's mistaken by detectives as a cunning jewel thief.]

Episode 123 (taped March 18, 1967; aired March 22, 1967)
Guests: Sergio Mendes, Brazil '66
Songs: "Color My World," "Lonesome Road," "One Note Flea"
Sketches: Italian Three Pigs, Jerome Takes Ballet

Episode 124 (taped March 25, 1967; aired April 12, 1967)
Guests: Robert Morley, Arbors Quartet
Songs: "Walking on New Grass," "Down by the Old Mill Stream," "Smile Awhile"
Sketches: Jerome Gets Speaking Lessons, Army pantomime

VIII.
SPECIALS & ONE-SHOTS

WORN OUT BY TELEVISION, Kaye looked forward to not being chained to a weekly series and to returning to more appreciative outlets: charity travels, nightclub performances, and—or so he thought—movies.

Certainly, he already had an inkling that the world of entertainment—like the world in general—had changed drastically since he submerged himself into his series. The hope and optimism that marked the beginning of the space race had suddenly transformed into an era of cynicism and protests. The difference was abundantly clear when, the previous spring, Kaye, Sammy Prager, and singer Vikki Carr spent two weeks on a USO tour in Vietnam. Danny returned from post-World War II and Korean War tours to throngs of adoring fans and glowing press coverage. His return from Vietnam was greeted by combative reporters. Kaye fielded their first questions with good humor, but grew defensive as the questions became more pointed. By the time he was asked if he approved of America's role in the war, Danny had run out of patience. "I was there fourteen days!" he snapped. "I don't think that's enough time to get well informed."

As production of his series was winding down in the spring of 1967, Kaye signed to start the summer at the Desert Inn in Las Vegas, immediately followed by an extra-special engagement. He would spend six weeks starting August 7, acting for $210 a week, in the English village of Chichester. While the town was small, its theater was one of the most professional in the western world. Its first director was Laurence Olivier. Flattered, Danny signed to star in *The Servant of Two Masters*, a classical Eighteenth Century Italian comedy that he had been urged to tackle fourteen years earlier by *Knock on Wood* co-star Leon Askin, who found the lead character delightful and seemingly "written for Danny Kaye."

Kaye had played no role on stage other than "Danny Kaye" for decades. He grew increasingly nervous as the date approached. Days before he was to report to the theater to start the five weeks of rehearsals, the Six-Day War broke out in the Middle East. Kaye cancelled the Chichester engagement and rushed to entertain the battling Israelis. Although the war lasted only a week, Danny remained in the region, checking in on UNICEF services.

He received no fan mail from Chichester. His co-star-to-be Fenella Fielding was "less heartbroken than outraged," and made it known she thought it was "deplorable letting a whole run be sold out on his name and then backing out." Not only was it too late to find a British replacement, but the show was being done in the first place especially for Kaye.

Danny promised to pay the theater back in full any losses it suffered and suggested he might jet in from Israel on weekends to put on his one-man show, all proceeds benefiting the theater. Kaye would make additional goodwill trips to Israel in the coming years, after two decades of downplaying his political beliefs.

Sylvia, meanwhile, had been busy hopping between Hollywood, New York, London and Paris, embroiled in a series of projects. Like Danny, she was determined to succeed on her own—and was also discovering that popular culture was beginning to pass her by. After years of work on *The Scarlet Pimpernel*, she shelved it temporarily after Kaye began his series and shelved it permanently near the end of the series, upon learning that the overseas rights-holder for the Pimpernel character renewed its license for another 20 years. In the interim, Sylvia drew up the first draft of a TV series, with Rex Harrison in mind for the lead. It, too, never came to pass.

Finally, she had a sure-fire idea for a Broadway musical, hatched during an evening she shared with Leonard Spigelgass in Greenwich Village. "I'd seen the Village in the Forties and the Fifties," Sylvia said. "It was exactly the same, just dirtier. We were sorry we'd bothered. It was a useless pilgrimage. When I got back to my hotel, I wasn't sleepy, so I found myself writing the finale involving three generations—the girl, her mother, and her grandmother. The next day Lennie called me. He had the same idea with two generations, and he had a title, *We're a Whole New Thing*. When I heard the title, I said, 'That's it.' Every generation thinks it's different, they all think it hasn't happened before. But it has."

Spigelgass started writing the book, based loosely on *Day of the Turtle*, an Italian musical that ran briefly in Paris. Sylvia began work on the score. She peppered her lyrics with double meanings—words that meant one thing to parents and another to kids. The duo latched on to Broadway producer Kermit Bloomgarden. Months later, they dropped the project, discouraged that a rock musical with a similar idea hit Broadway. As Spigelgass explained, "It was pretty obvious that *Hair* had taken advantage of (the idea), and we were too old, really."

THE MADWOMAN OF CHAILLOT

(Filmed Feb. 19 to late May 1968; released N.Y. Oct. 12, 1969)
Producer: Ely Landau, for Commonwealth United, Warner Bros.
Director: Bryan Forbes
Screenplay: Edward Anhalt
Original Story: 1943 play *La Folle de Chaillot* by Jean Giraudoux, adapted by Maurice Valency
Cast: Katherine Hepburn (Madwoman of Chaillot), Charles Boyer (Broker), Claude Dauphin (Dr. Jadin), Edith Evans (Josephine), John Gavin (Reverend), Paul Henried (General), Oscar Homolka (Commissar), Margaret Leighton (Constance), Giuleietta Masine (Gabrielle), Nanette Newman (Irma), Richard Chamberlain (Roderick), Yul Brynner (Chairman), Donald Pleasance (Prospector), Danny Kaye (Ragpicker)

Danny's offers, too, were growing fewer and increasingly offbeat. He finally agreed to one that afforded him the opportunity to play a somewhat whimsical character, but in a contemporary drama. *The Madwoman of Chaillot* was a morality fable against materialism, based on Jean Giraudoux's 1943 play in which an eccentric old woman foils the civic leaders' plans to rip up the streets of her Parisian suburb in search of oil. For the first time—notwithstanding the aborted *Huckleberry Finn*—Kaye accepted a supporting role, that of the scruffy philosophical Ragpicker. He signed for $70,000 plus half of one percent of the gross.

Producer Ely Landau had spent most of the five years since acquiring film rights to the play suing and being sued by the author's estate and producers of a Broadway adaptation of the property. He was finally ready to get to work, and no expense was to be spared on the $3-million production. Landau assembled an all-star, international cast headed by Katherine Hepburn, Charles Boyer, Edith Evans, Paul Henreid, Margaret Leighton, Richard Chamberlain, and Yul Brynner. He hired John Huston to direct. They would shoot on location in France, with extravagant, colorful sets and costumes, and with the cast and crew put up at the most lavish resort to be found.

Landau insisted on contemporizing the story—infuriating his director, who argued that the audience could draw their own parallels to the present without him literally resetting the story. Three weeks before shooting was to begin, Huston quit. Hepburn was also ready to walk, but Landau convinced her to return.

Troubles continued after shooting began. Kaye and company had to endure continual delays due, first, to striking French technicians, then because of student riots sparked by the Paris peace talks. "You know, you

WITH AN EDGE: Kaye's satiric Ragpicker made the most of his limited screen time in *The Madwoman of Chaillot*, with Edith Evans and Margaret Leighton. [© 1969 Warner Bros.]

forget how slow and boring making movies is," Danny said, wishing he could fly but "I've been grounded for the duration of the picture... insurance companies!"

Further hurting the film's prospects for mainstream acceptance, screenwriter Edward Anhalt added an extraneous character—an intolerant reverend—and spent interview after interview bragging that his script was "an all-out attack on religion." Worse, Anhalt made everything too literal—having characters repeat lines over and over again for emphasis, depicting gritty street riots that clashed with the story's fantasy setting, and adding constant references to current hot-button topics like nuclear missiles.

Not unexpectedly, the film bombed, both financially and critically. The only positive notices were reserved for Kaye. The headline in *The Hollywood Reporter* blared, "*Madwoman* Short on Style, while Danny Kaye Scores." He appeared in just four scenes, but his stirring performance "defending" the rich and powerful during a mock trial was the picture's high point. Immediately, columnists began whispering about a possible Oscar nomination. So, too, Kaye began receiving a flood of movie offers—all for similarly offbeat roles, such as the lead in a Frederico Fellini film and another chance at Don Quixote. "I don't think I'd like to go back to making the kind of movies I used to make," Danny sighed. "I don't even know if that could be done."

He was also invited to do a number of TV variety specials, but Danny passed. There wasn't much of a challenge in doing something that he'd already done every week for four years. He also tired of the grind of hopping around the country to do his one-man show. Sammy Prager retired in 1968 and, after fulfilling dates with replacement pianists through the end of 1969, Kaye had had enough. Reluctantly, he slipped into a rut of show biz inactivity. "I don't want to keep sitting on a pinnacle," Danny complained. "I don't want to spend the rest of my life protecting my success."

The forced relaxation didn't last. Several months in, Kaye received an intriguing offer: to return to Broadway, in a modern musical, with just eight characters and none of the usual trimmings. The score was being written by the legendary Richard Rodgers, and the book by Peter Stone, who had just won a Tony Award for *1776*. Accepting the invitation would mean no more flying and no more Chinese cooking. More significantly, it would mean—for the first time on stage in nearly 30 years—he would have to play a character other than Danny Kaye.

TWO BY TWO

Shubert Theatre, New Haven, Ct. (Sept. 14 to 26, 1970); Shubert Theatre, Boston (Sept. 29 to Oct. 25, 1970); Imperial Theatre, N.Y. (six previews start Oct. 28, 1970; performances Nov. 10, 1970 to Sept. 11, 1971)
Producer: Richard Rodgers • **Director**: Joe Layton
Book: Peter Stone, based on 1954 play *The Flowering Peach* by Clifford Odets
Songs: Richard Rodgers & Martin Charnin ("Why Me?," "You Have Got to Have a Rudder on the Ark," "Ninety Again!," "Two by Two," "Something, Somewhere," "When It Dries," "You," "Poppa Knows Best," "Hey, Girlie," "The Covenant")
Cast: Danny Kaye (Noah), Marilyn Cooper (Leah), Joan Copeland (Esther), Harry Goz (Shem), Madeline Kahn (Goldie), Michael Karm (Ham), Tricia O'Neil (Rachel), Walter Willison (Japheth)

Lyricist Martin Charnin hatched the idea for *Two by Two*, as a musical version of an old Clifford Odets play, *The Flowering Peach*. In Odets' Yiddish take on the Biblical flood story, Noah must contend with three difficult sons—the oldest who's looking to make a buck, the middle son who's estranged from his wife, and the unbelieving youngest, who's in love with his brother's wife. Charnin and playwright Peter Stone approached Richard Rodgers with the idea of writing the music. Rodgers had created hit after hit for 45 years, first with Lorenz Hart and then with Oscar Hammerstein II. But many thought Rodgers, now in his late 60s, had lost his touch. He hadn't had a smash since Hammerstein's death ten years earlier. *Two by Two* sounded so appealing to Rodgers that he purchased the rights to Odets' play—without telling Charnin or Stone.

Now, Rodgers was in charge. "Rodgers actually went and bought the material, (which) surprised us because he did it without our knowing it," Stone confirmed. "After that, suddenly it became a different ballgame. We were dealing with him as producer. We were hoping to do it only with him as songwriter."

Although an ensemble piece, with nagging wife and quarrelsome children, Noah was the central figure. The creators figured they needed someone "of a certain age to play a patriarch," but could go in three different directions—a comical actor like Jack Gilford, a singer like Richard Kiley, or an all-around performer like Kaye. With Kaye the most marketable name on their short list, they called his agent—and were delighted to hear he was interested.

Danny, now 59, hadn't acted on Broadway since *Let's Face It*. Over the years, the offers continued to trickle in, including originating the lead roles in *The Music Man* in the 1950s and *Fiddler on the Roof* in the 1960s, and filling in for Rex Harrison in *My Fair Lady* for three months. But Rodgers' new project sounded different. It would address modern themes—the generation gap, adultery, divorce. There would be no special material, but instead a role quite unlike his well-established stage persona. "I did not want to come back in a male version of *Hello, Dolly*," he insisted.

Kaye had one demand: the show *had* to be special. "Fellas," he informed his creative co-workers, "I either want this to be a huge success or the bomb of all time. If we are really going to make a contribution to musical theater, fine, and if not, well, too bad, we dived off the board and the pool was empty. I want it to be that quick and final. I don't want to have to say to myself, 'I got to go to the theater again tonight?' At my age, my time of life? I'm not doing this for money. Because for one concert, I could make... no, it's not money, or keeping busy. I've done that. I have done it all."

So, Kaye sold his airplane, returned full-time to his apartment at the

Sherry-Netherlands (meaning Sylvia returned to California), and jumped into the role of Noah. Before opening night, there would be five weeks of rehearsals in New York, two weeks of tryouts in New Haven, four weeks of tryouts in Boston, and finally a week of previews in New York.

The crew would need every day of those three months. At first, the show was too long and unfocused. In fact, by its first public performance in New Haven, the show clocked in at just shy of four hours—so long that one reviewer said it should be renamed *Three by Three*. Charnin and Rodgers naturally thought the culprit was the book. They suggested slashing the script, while adding three more songs to a score that already had sixteen numbers. Miraculously, by the time they reached Boston, the show was down to three hours.

Another challenge, as Odets first discovered, came in holding the audience's interest in the second act, while Noah and family were on the ark. Everyone knew the ark would land safely, so drama had to be created between the characters.

Danny became a tireless force in helping to shape the show, if only to protect his part. The show may have been intended as an ensemble piece, but Kaye wanted to ensure his character was never upstaged and never melted into the background. He insisted on casting a different actress as his wife, one he suspected would play the role less aggressively. He so admired one dance between the wife and son that he wanted to perform it. Kaye recognized that the youngest son's big number, "Something, Somewhere," would be the hit of the show, so he suggested that he reprise the song at the end of the first act. He also didn't want to follow the funniest song in the play, "Forty Nights," which was performed by his middle son, so the number was cut. Line by line, the supporting parts were all pared back.

Rodgers, the producer, kept giving Danny his way. Whenever he didn't, Danny would sulk and go through the motions. And Rodgers was painfully aware that the public was looking forward to a Danny Kaye show. In fact, the day that tickets went on sale in New York, the box office set a Broadway record for advance business.

The excitement over Kaye returning to the Broadway stage—in fact the same Imperial Theatre stage that he last stepped onto in *Let's Face It*—was palpable. Reviews, however, were mixed. Most critics panned the book and considered the score far from Rodgers' best. The vast majority of reviewers simultaneously considered Kaye sensational. The never-ending lines of patrons agreed.

Despite the personal plaudits, the show's tepid notices bothered Danny. There had to be a way to get a little more of himself into the show. He had always seen himself as "an instinctive performer" who let the audience "choreograph" for him. So, he would vary his performance slightly from night to night, feeding off the audience, while still being true to the character and the story. "This is not gonna turn into a concert," he promised, "with me flitting around the stage, and the audience saying, 'That's nice, but we've seen him do that for 100 years!'" Danny estimated that there were about 30 spots during the play in which he could work in a specialty number or a routine, but wouldn't because—even though the audience might enjoy it—it wouldn't serve the play.

So, too, as he repeated the same material and performance night after night, he began to grow bored with the show. But he kept his improvisations in check, until the evening of February 5, 1971. Late in the first act, during the number "Two by Two," Kaye landed poorly on his left foot. In tremendous pain, he slowly sat down at the edge of the stage, as the other performers finished the dance without him. As soon as the number ended, Danny whispered to his co-stars to have the curtain lowered. His understudy, Harry Goz, quickly changed into Noah's costume. Kaye was rushed to the hospital, where he was diagnosed with torn ligaments in his leg and a hairline fracture in his ankle. Beginning the next evening, Goz would take over Kaye's role indefinitely. Ticket sales evaporated. It appeared as if Danny's comeback and his comeback vehicle were finished.

Kaye's leg was placed in a knee-length plastic cast, and he spent four days in the hospital. The show's creative team could tell the show was doomed without a big-name star, and began brainstorming possible replacements. Fortunately, Danny agreed to return, albeit hobbled. Rodgers closed the show and had Stone rewrite the script to accommodate Noah wearing a cast. Playing the ark builder at age 600, Kaye would wheel around in a wheelchair. After being transformed into a spry 90-year-old, he'd hop about on crutches. Word spread quickly: "Danny Kaye is back—*in the cast.*"

The show reopened February 18. As Danny rolled out onto the stage for the first time in his wheelchair, the applause was deafening. The new gags got the biggest laughs, such as when Noah pointed to his cast—supposedly there to treat a bout of gout—and asked God, "Where were you when I needed you?" Or when Kaye prodded his fellow actors with his crutch or playfully threatened them with his wheelchair. Danny discovered that his new plastic prop had given him license to step slightly out of character—

and the audience loved it.

According to Stone, Kaye "was responsible to the script until certain situations happened which made it difficult and which I do not consider to be his fault. He broke his leg and the script had to be changed, and most of those ad-libs were written. Different things that called attention to the fact that the script was saying that he was doing one thing when he was, in fact, unable to do it. Like dance or like 'run over there' or such things as that. It was actually heroic of him to appear in that condition, and we were all very grateful and very admiring of his effort."

Yet this excuse to ad-lib like he did in his one-man shows, coupled with the audience's hysterical roars of approval, soon had Kaye off on tangents, pretending to forget his lines, mimicking his fellow actors, or unzipping his stage wife's dress. Every few minutes, he'd throw out a line like "Don't back up anymore or you'll be in *No, No, Nanette*," "Maybe I'd better call my orthopedist," "Shall I feed you the right line?" "Let's not cheat the audience," or "Where's my throat doctor?"

He also encouraged the other actors to break up at his antics and "ad-libs," as if they were seeing them for the first time, as his vaudeville co-stars had been expected to do during his old stage routines. Actors who refused to step out of character soon found themselves on Danny's bad side.

One angry patron accused Kaye of turning *Two by Two* into *One by One*. As he recounted in a letter to the *New York Times*: "Right off, in his opening soliloquy with God, he began with the jokes about his accident, and never really discontinued them until toward the end of the show. Not only that, he used his wheelchair, his crutches, and his encased leg to terrorize the cast into 'breaking up' at every available opportunity. With the single exception of the actor who played his youngest son (who absolutely refused to get out of character), the others at times could barely read their lines audibly, far less (portray) a decent role. They were too busy being chased down, prodded and kicked at by Kaye.

"Nor was that all. He regaled us by throwing lines at Dick Cavett (seated in the audience), goosing the actress who played his wife during what, I think, was intended to be a charming little love song, pretending to forget his lines, and yelling into the wings for cues. He didn't give up these shenanigans until the final fifteen minutes, from the time his wife died until his final chat with the Lord. During those brief minutes he gave some indication of what he might have been able to do with a role of sensitivity of depth had he given himself the chance."

Whenever Rodgers tried to rein in Danny, the star shut down. The producer backed off. After all, the audience seemed to enjoy the new show more than the original. So, even after doctors removed the original cast after seven weeks, Kaye continued wearing one, knowing the prop was indispensable to his new act. He'd keep it on for seven months and finish the run with it.

"There were problems with the show," admitted Stone. "The show was not as successful artistically as we had hoped it would be, but it certainly had a successful run. It made a great deal of money. I'm still collecting that money. I don't regret the show in any way. I wish all of us had been doing a little more of the same show than we ended up doing."

Danny's miserable co-stars likely were relieved when the star announced he would not be renewing his contract once his original term expired in mid-September. No matter that audiences, on the whole, loved the show, and that it probably could have run for years, if Danny were so inclined. A full year of nothing but Noah was enough for him. He had done what he had set out to do. Besides, the seven months of prancing about the stage on crutches wasn't good for him. "I really was left with a bad hip," Danny recalled. "It's funny how you're vaccinated as a kid about how the show should go on. What I should have done when I had the accident is I should have gone home and gotten better and that would have been that." Pain from the injury remained constant, and forced him to undergo hip replacement surgery in 1984.

After turning 60, Kaye saw his various ailments multiply. He reluctantly had to come to grips with the fact that he was no longer the elfin sprite, who could charm audiences by skipping around the stage.

There were things that still made him feel young: flying and children. So, as soon as Two by Two ended, Danny embarked on an extra-special UNICEF expedition. He toured seven Asian countries in five weeks, accompanied by cameramen. He hoped to edit the footage into a TV special called Reassignment: Children, commemorating UNICEF's twenty-fifth anniversary. The trip never made it to television, but the documentary, under the title of The Pied Piper, was used for decades to promote UNICEF.

Kaye also bought another plane, a necessity for making his whirlwind trips for UNICEF. In fact, most of the entertainment offers that yet awaited him would be targeted at children, his most marketable audience.

HERE COMES PETER COTTONTAIL

(Voice recorded June 8, Aug. 4, 1970; aired April 4, 1971, ABC)
Producers/Directors: Arthur Rankin Jr. & Jules Bass
Writer: Romeo Muller, based on book *The Easter Bunny that Overslept* by Priscilla &
Otto Friedrich
Songs: Steve Nelson & Jack Rollins ("Here Comes Peter Cottontail," "The Easter
Bunny Never Sleeps," "If I Could Only Get Back to Yesterday," "When You Can't Get
It All Together, Improvise," "The Puzzle of Life")
Cast: Danny Kaye (Seymour S. Sassafras/Antoine/Col. Wellington B. Bunny), Casey
Kasem (Peter), Vincent Price (Irontail)

Kaye foresaw that his career was headed toward kiddy-oriented TV specials years before it got there. Danny wasn't opposed to children's programming, so long as it was top quality. In April 1966, inspired by the popularity
of prime-time specials like *Rudolph the Red Nosed Reindeer* and *A Charlie
Brown Christmas*, his Dena production company began pitching a one-hour
special, *The Nonsensical World of Dr. Seuss*. Kaye, in live action, would
play the tongue-twisting Dr. Seuss who, with his animated companion the
Cat in the Hat, introduces and narrates five different Seuss tales.

One month later, CBS announced it was working on an animated version
of another Seuss story, *How the Grinch Stole Christmas*. Dena subsequently
tweaked its proposal, making Danny "a bold man of the world" who with
the Cat in the Hat is engaged by McGrew of Seuss's *If I Ran the Circus* and
McGurk of *If I Ran the Zoo* to head expeditions in search of rare creatures.

In 1968, Dena proposed another one-hour, combination live action-ani-
mated special, based on Hans Christian Andersen's *The Little Mermaid*.
When that fizzled, Dena teamed with animators DePatie-Freleng to widen
its scope—*Danny Kaye's World of Hans Christian Andersen*, a series of 30-
minute specials. Kaye would narrate and tape live-action beginnings and
endings for the cartoons at Andersen's home-turned-museum in Odense.

The networks, however, were more interested in holiday specials, which
could be re-run year after year. So while preparing for *Two by Two*, Kaye
was approached by Arthur Rankin and Jules Bass. The producers had
launched a cottage industry creating Christmas TV specials, typically using
stop-motion animation, that featured a likable entertainer as narrator—Burl
Ives for *Rudolph, the Red Nosed Reindeer*, Jimmy Durante for *Frosty the
Snowman*, Fred Astaire for *Santa Claus Is Comin' to Town*. Having seemingly saturated Christmas, Rankin and Bass were looking for new holidays
to exploit and asked Danny to narrate an Easter special.

Although *Here Comes Peter Cottontail* wasn't nearly as well received as

HOP/SING: By the 1970s, Danny had come to realize that his marketability was increasingly for kids, such as in TV's *Here Comes Peter Cottontail*. [© 1971 ABC]

their Christmas classics, Rankin and Bass thought Danny was a natural for their format. He injected the not-always-smooth claymation with wild energy, singing and playing multiple characters—the spirited narrator, a French caterpillar, and the blustery old Easter Bunny. The producers immediately tried to think of how they could reuse Kaye, who suggested his Hans Christian Andersen series.

THE ENCHANTED WORLD OF DANNY KAYE: EMPEROR'S NEW CLOTHES

(Voice recorded Aug. 1971; live action taped Sept. 27 to 30, 1971;
aired Feb. 21, 1972, ABC)
Producers/Directors: Arthur Rankin Jr. & Jules Bass
Writer: Romeo Muller

Songs: Maury Laws ("World of Enchantment," "Clothes Make the Man," "A Tailor's Tailor," "Creation," "All You Need Is Money to Be Rich")
Cast: Danny Kaye (Marmaduke), Cyril Ritchard (Emperor), Imogene Coca (Princess)

Programs based on not holidays but fairy tales intrigued Rankin and Bass. The source material was endless. The producers pitched ABC on a series of specials called *The Enchanted World of Danny Kaye*. They could produce a new installment once a year, five times a year, or even once a week. They suggested initially starting on eight tales—*Rip Van Winkle, Rumplestiltskin, Treasure Island, Raggedy Ann, Hans Christian Andersen Christmas, Jack Frost, Gilbert & Sullivan,* and *Marco Polo*. Others that could be added or substituted were *Punch and Judy, Puss 'n Boots, The Road to Oz, Little Juggler, Heidi's Christmas, The Prince and the Pauper, The Pied Piper, Johnny Appleseed,* and *World of Toys*.

ABC liked the idea, with reservations. First, the network wanted to gauge the reaction to a pilot before making a long-term commitment. Second, none of the story ideas were based on a recognizable Hans Christian Andersen fairy tale. ABC preferred to start with something distinctly Andersen.

The first became "The Emperor's New Clothes." Kaye traveled to Arhus, Andersen's Danish birthplace, to film live-action lead-ins, sharing the tale to a group of children. Alas, due to underwhelming ratings and Danny's erratic health, the series ended at one.

DANNY KAYE'S LOOK-IN
AT THE METROPOLITAN OPERA

(Taped April 10 to 11, 1975; aired April 27, 1975, CBS)
Producers: Bernard Rothman, Jack Wohl, Herbert Bonis
Executive Producer: Sylvia Fine
Director: Robert Scheerer
Writers: Herbert Baker, Sylvia Fine
Cast: Danny Kaye (host), James Levine (conductor), Robert Merrill, Beverly Sills

In 1971, Sylvia decided to make one final run at fulfilling her lifelong dream—writing the songs for a Broadway book musical. In late 1968, she had purchased the rights to produce a musical version of George Bernard Shaw's *Doctor's Dilemma*, hoping to update the 60-year-old play into a modern tale of medicine and sex. In the spring of 1971, she engaged an aspiring young playwright, Tommy Thompson, to write the book. Together, they created an outline and eighteen pages of dialogue. The project would go no further.

One evening, Sylvia was discussing musical comedy with friends. Impressed by her vast historical knowledge, one friend suggested she should be teaching the subject. Sylvia, referring to her short-lived mentoring sessions with Thompson, replied, "I am." Coincidentally, the next day the University of Southern California called, asking if she had interest in teaching. Sylvia, still shy, was at first apprehensive. Broadway musicals were at a low point, in terms of quantity, popularity, art and discipline. She felt she owed it to her craft. She figured she would take six months, assembling a library of recordings and films and analyzing them for young people. She spent fifteen-plus hours a day compiling her library, funded by a $50,000 grant from the National Endowment of the Arts.

Her husband, however, was not crazy about her spring 1972 semester of "History & Analysis of Musical Comedy." "You're a writer," Kaye told her. "You should be writing."

That didn't stop Danny from accepting a teaching gig of his own. Late that year, he received a call from Goeran Gentele, general manager of New York's Metropolitan Opera Company. He was looking for someone to host a special presentation that introduced children to opera. Ideally, it would make opera seem a little less daunting to kids and possibly get them interested in the field. "I like to poison their minds when they're young," Gentele smiled, having already instituted a similar program at the Royal Stockholm Opera.

Danny was unsure. "If you want an academic exercise, I don't think I'm your man," Kaye warned. So Gentele agreed to the actor's terms. The shows, on the fourth and fifth of January 1973, would not be overly serious. He could explain the rituals of opera attendance, such as when to applaud and when to shout "bravo" or "brava," give a lesson in standing ovations, and end by conducting the Met's orchestra. He'd also introduce the opera's principals, ballet, chorus, musicians, extras, technicians and even the accounting staff. At one point there would be 500 people on the stage.

The success of the two sessions convinced Danny to return the next year for three classes. But the following year, as the number of students requesting admission continued to increase, he realized he couldn't add enough performances to meet demand. Instead, the show would be televised. To make Kaye feel at home, producer Bernie Rothman (a former *Danny Kaye Show* writer) recruited a familiar crew—Bob Scheerer as director, Herb

Bonis as co-producer, Herbie Baker as writer, and Sylvia as executive producer. It would be the first time that Sylvia, who had encouraged Danny to
do the work for the Met in the first place, had officially worked with her
husband since his third TV special in 1962. And, true to form, with weeks
left until the taping, she stepped in and rewrote Baker's script.

The program won the producers an Emmy for Outstanding Children's
Special, although Sylvia admitted, "It wasn't designed for children. It was a
youth series. However, I don't despise any Emmy. I'm very happy to win.
It's the first thing I've won since I was in piano competitions when I was a
little girl."

PETER PAN

(Taped April 30 to June 9, 1975; aired March 27, 1976 ATV U.K.;
aired Dec. 12, 1976, NBC)
Executive Producers: Gary Smith, Dwight Hemion
Director: Dwight Hemion
Writers: Andrew Birkin, Jack Burns, based on 1904 play *Peter Pan* by J.M. Barrie
Songs: Leslie Bricusse & Anthony Newley ("By Hook or By Crook," "Rotters Hall of
Fame," "They Don't Make 'em Like Me Anymore")
Cast: Mia Farrow (Peter Pan), Danny Kaye (Captain Hook/Mr. Darling), Paula Kelly
(Tiger Lily), Briony McRoberts (Wendy)

As soon as he finished up his work on *Danny Kaye's Look-In at the
Metropolitan Opera*, Danny left for London to star in a musical version of
Peter Pan. This television special was the brainchild of producer Gary
Smith, who recognized that NBC's holiday chestnut, *Peter Pan* starring
Mary Martin, hadn't been updated since 1960. For years, Smith had been
calling Kaye up every few months with a new idea for a TV special. But
each time, Danny always had a new excuse—the role wasn't right for him,
it conflicted with another project or UNICEF tour, he didn't want to travel.
When Smith phoned to say he was remaking *Peter Pan* in London with Mia
Farrow and wanted Kaye to play Captain Hook, the entertainer immediately
agreed. Unfazed, the producer went right on with his sales pitch. "Gary,"
Danny finally interrupted, "I said yes ten minutes ago."

Kaye would be filled with surprises. During rehearsals, Smith asked
Danny if he would join him and two friends for dinner at the elegant
London restaurant San Lorenzo. Kaye begged off, saying that he was too
tired from traveling so far. Smith and friends went to dinner and were
enjoying a sumptuous meal when who should join their table but the chef

who had prepared it—Danny.

Kaye and Farrow would be the only Americans in the cast; the rest would be British. Laurence Olivier was cast as narrator, although John Gielgud replaced him at the last minute. Working for British TV mogul Lew Grade, Smith also assembled an A-list crew—Oscar winner Michael Kidd as choreographer, Tony winners Anthony Newley and Leslie Bricusse for the music, and J.M. Barrie scholar Andrew Birkin for the script.

Smith remembered Birkin as "a very intellectual writer. He really researched the life of Barrie. He discovered it was not a simple fairy tale. With the kidnapping and such, it has kind of a dark side. He played that up. Then we brought in Jack Burns, of the comedy team Burns and Schreiber, to add comedy dialogue, after Andrew did basic structure."

Because it was planned as a Christmas special, *Peter Pan* would not be televised in the U.S. until eighteen months after it was taped. Unfortunately, because it was darker, more melancholy, and more introspective than its carefree predecessor, the special did not become the annual classic that its producers had intended. "We liked it," Smith said. "I think people were just so in love with the Mary Martin version and its wonderful score, ours didn't quite measure up."

PINOCCHIO

(Taped Feb. 23 to March 3, 1976; aired March 27, 1976, CBS)
Producers: Bernard Rothman, Jack Wohl
Directors: Ron Field, Sid Smith
Writer: Herbert Baker, based on 1883 story "Pinocchio" by Carlo Collodi
Songs: Billy Barnes ("I'm Talking to Myself," "What's That," "I'm a No Worried," "More," "Look at Me Now," "I Wanna Go Home," "This Little Boy")
Cast: Sandy Duncan (Pinocchio), Danny Kaye (Geppetto/Collodi/Stroganoff), Clive Reville (Coachman), Gary Morgan (Candlewick), Liz Torres (Cat), Flip Wilson (Fox)

Eight months after taping *Peter Pan*, Kaye started work on another full-length fairy tale, *Pinocchio*. Producer Bernie Rothman said, "*Pinocchio* was my partner's and my idea, and actually it grew out of Sandy Duncan. We were producing *Sandy in Disneyland*, and we liked her a lot. She was a dancer and real kiddish, and we thought it would be real nice to have her play a boy. Not to our knowledge had Pinocchio ever been played by a woman. And as soon as we talked about the idea of Geppetto, I just couldn't imagine anybody else playing Geppetto (but Danny)."

As with the Met special, Rothman gathered a familiar crew—Herbie

Baker to write the script and Billy Barnes to write the music. Baker's idea was to present the tale as "a story within a story," with Kaye, as third-rate playwright Carlo Collodi, staging his new play *Pinocchio* for his restless daughter (Sandy Duncan). The narrative device helped explain why a woman played Pinocchio and allowed for the use of less expensive, two-dimensional stage backdrops. Kaye also appeared as the puppet-master Stroganoff and a wistful Geppetto, reminiscent of his old Italian character from his weekly series, Giovanni.

Unlike the more high-minded *Peter Pan, Pinocchio* employed a cast and crew with TV variety show backgrounds. Consequently, the program felt more like an extended variety show—and more closely hit its mark. Danny did have one qualm: "They do television these days like movies. We're taking three weeks to tape this show with the sort of stop-and-go, hurry-up-and-wait production you have in movies. I suppose technically it helps. But I had occasion the other day to look at one of my old variety shows and I was astonished at how well it played—it would be a special today. The point is that we taped those one-hour shows in one hour with an audience watching. They had something I think we've lost—a spirit, a sense of performance! This is a 90-minute show I wish we were doing in 90 minutes."

Soon after completing *Pinocchio*, Kaye took a years-long break from show business, to become part-owner of a new Major League baseball team, based in Seattle, where he owned several radio stations. Though neither a professional athlete nor businessman, Kaye participated in every imaginable aspect of running the Seattle Mariners.

"For me to be a part of a baseball team without having an active part in its operation," Danny said, "would be to have a plane and not fly it. People forget I've been around baseball almost all my life. I look at it differently than the average fan, just as I look on a movie or stage performance differently than the average person. I understand the intricacies. I understand what's involved in a good performance, what's gone on behind the scenes."

Unfortunately, as a young expansion team the Mariners were ill equipped to achieve Danny's expected results: success. After six losing seasons, Kaye sold his interest in the team.

KRAFT SALUTES
DISNEYLAND'S 25TH ANNIVERSARY

(Taped Jan. 26 to 27, Feb. 6 to 9, Feb. 28 to 29, 1980; aired March 6, 1980, CBS)
Producers: Buz Kohan, Phil May
Executive Producers: Dwight Hemion, Gary Smith
Director: Dwight Hemion
Writers: Marty Farrell, Buz Kohan
Songs: Larry Grossman ("Don't Be Anything Less than Everything You Can Be," "Once Upon a Time in Anaheim," Disney medley)
Cast: Danny Kaye, Michael Jackson, Adam Rich, Wally Boag

EPCOT CENTER:
THE OPENING CELEBRATION

(Taped late Sept. to early Oct., Oct. 23, 1982; aired Oct. 23, 1982, NBC)
Producer: Gary Smith, for *Walt Disney's Wonderful World of Color*
Director: Dwight Hemion
Songs: Earl Brown ("Gateway to Future World," "Hooray for the 21st Century," "Showcase of the World," "You Will Grow Up to Be a Kid")
Cast: Danny Kaye, Drew Barrymore, Eric Sevareid, Roy Clark, Alex Haley, Marie Osmond, Alan Shepard

Considering Kaye's long-standing association with children, it's surprising that he'd never before worked for the preeminent family-friendly studio, Disney. He finally did in 1980, at the behest of *Peter Pan* producer Gary Smith. In an hour-long special to celebrate the twenty-fifth anniversary of Disneyland, Kaye appeared as himself, as well as fourteen other characters, from another Giovanni-type Italian and a Jerome-like Brooklyner to Captain Hook, recalling his last role for Smith. And, as a finale, Danny conducted a choir and band performing "It's a Small World."

The special came off so well that two years later, Smith asked Kaye to host another Disney special, celebrating the opening of the company's new theme park in Florida. Unlike the kiddy-oriented focus of Disneyland, Disney targeted EPCOT Center at adults, hoping the park would educate visitors and better the world.

As a result, Danny wasn't to play characters. He had to ratchet down the silliness. But, to ensure there was material suitable to Kaye's talents, his TV series arranger, Earl Brown, was hired to write the musical numbers.

Danny arrived during the week before EPCOT opened to guests, so he figured his production crew would have the park to itself. Eleven years ear-

NO MORE DUCKING DISNEY: Kaye did not work with Disney, the premier family entertainment company, until he hosted a special promoting Disneyland's 25th anniversary at age 69. [© 1980 Walt Disney Co.]

lier, Disney had taped a similar special to mark the grand opening of Florida's Magic Kingdom. Production went smoothly, but Roy Disney hated one aspect about it. Because the special had been taped nearly two months before the park opened, the songs, dance numbers, and comedy bits took place in an otherwise empty park. Without any guests around, the Magic Kingdom just didn't look right.

The EPCOT special, too, would be taped in the days before the park opened, but whenever "guests" were needed, the crew would round up a gaggle of Disney cast members to play the part. As well, there was a continuous stream of private pre-opening tours walking around, much to the chagrin of Kaye. He preferred the solitude of taping his numbers for the Disneyland special at the Disney studio, against a green screen.

Producer Smith remembered, "The tour groups would stand off to the side while we were trying to film, and Danny would want us to get rid of those people. We explained that we couldn't, that we were on location, and they were on tours."

Kaye was already feeling grumpy about shooting in the middle of balmy Florida. "It was very, very hot," Smith said. "Danny doesn't like multiple takes. He was very proud his television show was done (straight through), with no retakes. So after each take, he'd call one of the Disney guides— *'Robert!'* — and Robert would run up with an umbrella, because Danny didn't like the sun. He was not easy to work with."

After the crew returned to Los Angeles to edit the show, Disney decided the unveiling of EPCOT was such an important event, that they wanted Danny on site for the opening ceremonies, to shoot a live introduction and, as a finale, to conduct an international orchestra.

Kaye was dead set against returning to the swamp, yet Smith persuaded him. His one caveat was that he be given a golf cart, with driver, to transport him from one end of the massive property to the other. The night before the ceremony, Danny rehearsed conducting the orchestra in front of the American Pavilion. As he finished, he climbed into his golf cart, only to see that his escape path was blocked by another golf cart with two ladies inside. "Move that (bleep)ing cart!" Kaye exploded. The ladies apologetically pulled their vehicle to the side. Danny later learned the two women were Walt's widow, Lillian, and daughter, Diane. Danny would serve penance. The next night, as he stepped into the park to begin his hosting duties, a rainstorm hit. So, too, after word of his behavior got around, Disney executives vowed that Kaye would never again work for the studio.

SKOKIE

(Taped mid-Nov. to Dec. 1980; aired Nov. 17, 1981, CBS)
Producer: Robert Berger, for Titus Productions
Director: Herbert Wise
Writer: Ernest Kinoy
Cast: Danny Kaye (Max Feldman), John Rubinstein (Herb Lewisohn), Carl Reiner (Abbot Rosen), Kim Hunter (Bertha Feldman), Eli Wallach (Bert Silverman), Brian Dennehy (Police Chief Buchanan)

In between the two Disney specials, Kaye agreed to appear in his first film in twelve years. The TV movie was to be shot in the Jewish enclave of Skokie, Illinois, where in the late '970s a group of neo-Nazis had sued for the right to march through tne streets. The producer, Robert Berger, and writer, Ernest Kinoy, didn't intend to create a "historical document." Since the problems involved were universal, they wanted to fictionalize the

HIGH MARKS: Kaye's most dramatic role, as a Holocaust survivor in *Skokie*, earned some of his highest honors. [© 1981 CBS]

events, capturing their dramatic essence and prodding the audience to think.

Danny's role, in fact, was a fictional, "composite" character. "The Kaye character and his family are archetypes," Kinoy explained. "I felt it was important to tell the audience about more than the experience of any one of the real Skokie families, so I created a family whose emotions are very true to what is known about Holocaust survivors and their children."

The original script described Danny's character as, Kaye recalled, "having a short fuse—an explosive man. It said he was stocky, the kind of guy who would walk through a wall. I went to New York to discuss it. There was no rewriting needed at all. I merely suggested that the man's attitude be modified, so that his involvement is gradual. The Holocaust was something he'd lived with but kept under the surface, and when it came out he was surprised at himself."

That first screenplay was titled *Defend to the Death*, based on Voltaire's quote about disagreeing with what opponents may say, but defending to the death their right to say it. CBS thought news headlines were more marketable than philosophical vagaries. The network demanded the show be renamed *Skokie* and that it use the characters' real names.

Suddenly, the filmmakers had to be a lot more careful. They sent drafts of the script to most of the personalities involved in the narrative. Anyone who wanted their real name left out—namely the ACLU lawyer who represented the Nazis—was obliged.

Kaye's biggest scene came when he, as one of the more outspoken concentration camp survivors, delivered an impassioned plea in a courtroom filled with his Jewish neighbors. He recalled, "I thought they were a group of typical Hollywood extras, but then I made my speech about 'If the Nazis march here...' and I turned around and saw tears running down the extras' cheeks. I thought that for extras they were inordinately moved... until I discovered that every one of those extras was a survivor of the Holocaust. Every one had a number tattooed on his arm."

Danny's reluctant rabble-rouser was the first wholly dramatic film role of his career, retaining none of the light comic touches of the *Madwoman of Chaillot* and *Me and the Colonel*. "He loves challenges," Bernie Rothman commented at the time. "When you think he played *Skokie*—just out of the blue, he went ahead with this major television movie, laid himself on the line, did a role that he hasn't ever in his whole life done. At his age, most performers are consolidating. They aren't breaking new ground. Danny loves breaking new ground. He uses the basic equipment that he's had for years, but he likes to apply it differently."

Critics considered his performance brilliant, leading Danny to believe he would be besieged by offers to play grumpy, old men. He was nominated for a Golden Globe as best actor. "I am not going to say, 'This is my last big hurrah,'" Danny noted. "Tomorrow I may do something completely different, also climactic. If you want to say this is the best thing I have done, fine—at this time. There may be something better a year from now."

MUSICAL COMEDY TONIGHT II

(Taped Nov. 6 to 7, 1980; aired Feb. 11, 1981, PBS)
Producer: Sylvia Fine
Executive Producer: Herb Bonis
Director: Tony Charmoli
Writers: Sylvia Fine, Herbert Baker
Songs: "Tschaikowsky"
Cast: Sylvia Fine, Danny Kaye, Richard Crenna, Irene Dunne, Jack Lemmon

Sylvia's musical comedy history class went over so well at USC that in 1975 Yale asked if she would bring her program to the East Coast for the coming fall semester. She agreed to teach one tiny class. For the fifteen seats, she received 217 applications.

Fine enjoyed sharing her insight into musical comedy, yet she realized her "solo act" was limited to a very small audience. So, she had audiotapes of her lessons transcribed, as the basis for a proposed book. Tellingly, one chapter, titled "Turkeys—and Why," was to profile four Broadway shows she didn't care for, among them *Two by Two*.

Soon after, director Tom Grasso sought Sylvia to do a little teaching on camera. Grasso recalled, "I was doing a thing for PBS. It was called *The Warner Brothers Musicals*, and we couldn't find anybody to host it for the wraparounds. And somehow I talked Sylvia Fine into doing it. She insisted that Roddy McDowall do it, and I said no. Finally, she said, 'You do all the research...'

"I took the movies that they were going to show, and then I'd write out different things about the director and about this and that. Sometimes she knew the people and sometimes she didn't, but she ad-libbed, and I don't think the woman's ever done that in her life, but she came off very, very well. It all went through the Midwest; it never aired (on the West Coast). A lot of people in the Midwest had no idea who she was, but she told a lot of anecdotes. She was just terrific."

Her appearances, really, were not much different from what she did at USC and Yale. She stopped work on the book. What if she brought her instruction to public television, as Danny had when he couldn't meet the demand for admission to his opera classes?

In 1976, Sylvia contacted PBS about producing thirteen one-hour shows patterned after her classes. She would share insights into and anecdotes about the history of the American musical theater, interview the creators of historic Broadway shows, and recreate memorable scenes using replica sets and, when possible, the original stars. Los Angeles affiliate KCET was interested, if she could secure the bulk of the funding—up to $500,000 per episode. Fine spent two years hacking her way through the bureaucratic jungle of public television, foundations, government agencies, and underwriters, until she finally received the backing of Prudential for a 90-minute pilot.

Sylvia persuaded Carol Burnett, Richard Chamberlain, John Davidson, Agnes DeMille, Sandy Duncan, Bernadette Peters, and Bobby Van to appear for a token $1,000 apiece, recreating scenes from four trend-setting musicals. She also wanted Ethel Merman to perform "You're the Top" with Danny, but he insisted on appearing in a later episode, performing one of his own numbers, not someone else's. Rock Hudson took his spot.

Still stage-shy, Sylvia was apprehensive about being too much the focus of the show. She had no superstar aspirations. She plotted the program so that she spent a third of the show lecturing at a piano off to the side of the stage. While she agreed to wear makeup, she also appeared in a 20-year-old dress from her closet.

Unfortunately, Sylvia's first production without Danny would not be a smooth one. Tom Grasso, who was directing other PBS programs at the studio at the same time, recalled, "She had all these big, beautiful sets built, and first of all they built the sets too high, so they had to cut them down. And then it rained. They were outside drying them out with hair dryers. It was a mess. And I know she had a lot of problems editing and re-editing the show. She's such a perfectionist and she wanted just—bang!—the right note, and I know she drove a lot of people nuts getting one note on a piano that she had missed put back in."

Sylvia also wanted the program to retain the sound of a live theater. When the sound engineers started removing audience noises and adding echo chambers to Ethel Merman's occasionally warbling singing, Fine stopped them. She redid the soundtrack four times, ignoring her budget.

Perfection—Sylvia Fine style—proved a slow, expensive process. Fortunately, when *Musical Comedy Tonight* finally aired on October 1, 1979, the response was tremendous. Critics unanimously loved it. *Time Magazine's* Frank Rich noted Sylvia's "enthusiastic narration packs in as many anecdotes as possible... *Musical Comedy Tonight* is billed as the pilot for a series. By rights, it ought to run as long as the great musicals it celebrates."

The program earned big ratings (a 4.4 share in Los Angeles and Chicago,

BACK ON THE HORSE: Capping his 40+ years with Sylvia, Danny repeated "Tschaikowsky" from *Lady in the Dark* in her PBS TV special *Musical Comedy Tonight II.* [© 1981 PBS]

a 6.7 in New York, and a 7.9 in San Francisco—heady numbers for any show on PBS). It also won a Peabody Award. Best of all, Sylvia had done it all by herself.

PBS ordered a follow-up, but—intimidated by the price tag—would proceed one show at a time. Danny had already agreed to appear. Yet, production this time around would be even more difficult. Sylvia learned that a lifetime of smoking had left her with lung cancer. Weakened by the disease and by the treatment, she nevertheless plowed through with work on the second special. According to her friend Leonard Spigelgass, "All the time she was doing the second show, it was touch-and-go whether she'd get through it." One year after the taping, she would have a lung surgically removed and would spend her final years with severe emphysema.

Her original plan had been to group together musicals chronologically. But since she had no idea how many—if any—additional installments she would get the chance to make, Sylvia decided instead to select musicals with a similar theme. Her "Musicals with a Message" would include *Finian's Rainbow, South Pacific, Sweet Charity*, and *Lady in the Dark*. Sylvia again insisted that all numbers be performed exactly as they had been on Broadway. But Danny would do "Tschaikowsky" twice. After performing the number in context, among his fellow actors, he joined Sylvia at the side of the stage, where he repeated his old nightclub stunt of trying to set a new record for how fast he could sing it.

This time, though, it wasn't just a stunt; Kaye actually did tie his record, 31 seconds. Director Tony Charmoli said, "We played the recording of 'Tschaikowsky' when he did it on Broadway in the theater and he does it much faster now. In the theater, he had to do it slower because it was difficult to understand. In the theater it takes longer for that sound to get around, but on television where we could do it with microphones up close, he could do it much faster."

After the song, husband and wife sat next to each other, to chat. "Appearing on stage with Danny, it was like being back at La Martinque, but not as informal," Sylvia said, "although we have never appeared on the stage together like this before—ever. I've played the piano for him in the past and worked on his motion pictures, but I never sat in front of an audience and talked with him. I was terrified. He's so unpredictable. I didn't know what he would say or do."

Sure enough, Kaye slipped several swear words into their conversation, "to shock her and see how good an editor she is." Asked if they would ever make another stage appearance together, Sylvia replied, "I'd love to, but he likes to work alone."

"Only if she sings and dances," Danny smiled.

Director Charmoli added, "There was no mention for writer, or producer, or director on the first episode of *Musical Comedy Tonight*, and I said, 'Well, we'll take care of that in the next one.' And I directed the second episode and she received an Emmy nomination for writing and I received a nomination for directing."

It would take nearly five years, but Sylvia would get the opportunity to create a third and final installment. And, as a capping tribute to her career, the show was named *Sylvia Fine Kaye's Musical Comedy Tonight III*.

LIVE FROM THE LINCOLN CENTER: AN EVENING WITH DANNY KAYE & THE NEW YORK PHILHARMONIC

(Taped and aired live Sept. 23, 1981, PBS)
Producer: John Goberman • **Executive Producer**: Herbert Bonis
Director: Robert Scheerer
Cast: Danny Kaye, Zubin Mehta, Patrick Watson (host)

In early 1981, Kaye finally consented to something he had long resisted—televising one of his conducting gigs in its entirety, preserving it for posterity. He and Zubin Mehta (acting "more or less as Danny's warm-up man") led the New York Philharmonic on PBS's *Live from the Lincoln Center*. Batons were destroyed; music and laughter ensued.

Although the format was tried and true, Kaye tweaked some elements. Director Bob Scheerer remembered, "He changed the format when he was in New York, and we came backstage after and (Sylvia) was furious with him. "What have you done? What have you done? What do you think you're doing?" Because he had changed the format slightly. He was trying it in a way that he hadn't done it. And obviously she'd been very involved in laying it out over the years so that it worked exactly right, and he just said, 'To hell with it,' and he just went ahead and did it his way, and it didn't work as well. She was right."

The taping went smoothly, considering it aired live, with director Scheerer having to make camera decisions on the fly. He kept the focus on Kaye early on and, as the show progressed, incorporated more shots of the orchestra and audience. "Afterwards," Scheerer said, "it got very difficult, because (Danny) was very irritated with me because I didn't use enough shots of him conducting. I was trying to make it into a show."

The show would be as close as Kaye would come to broadcasting a public farewell. Battling fast-declining health, he kept marginally active with occasional guest TV spots, charity conducting, and UNICEF appearances. In 1986, after Kaye played an impish Austrian dentist on an episode of *The Cosby Show*, Ernie Chambers wrote a pilot for a half-hour sitcom, *The Danny Kaye Show*, with Danny as Dr. Henry Becker, a baseball-loving, French-pastry-cooking medic at a children's hospital in Pittsburgh.

But the *Cosby* gig would be his last on American television. He passed on all major projects, particularly any that would have celebrated his career.

Herbie Baker, inspired by the success of *That's Entertainment*, unsuccessfully pitched two similar ideas for specials, both showcasing Danny's range
of talents alongside other celebrities, rather than retrospectives of his career.
In the first, *The Danny Kaye Variety Hour*, Kaye would conduct the Los
Angeles Symphony in one segment, perform a sophisticated Noel Coward
routine in tie-and-tails with Julie Andrews, cook for twelve in San
Francisco, join Elton John in a rock number, and pilot his plane.

Baker's second idea, *Inside Danny Kaye*, would begin by asking, "Who's
the real Danny Kaye?" Kaye would sing back, "I'm Anatole... Ludvig von
Stickfitz... Yogi from Cooch Behar... Stanislavsky..." Segments would
then feature him piloting a plane with Alan Alda, dancing "Ballin' the Jack"
with Gene Kelly, singing opera with Beverly Sills, performing a number
from *Gypsy* with Goldie Hawn, playing Jerome opposite Harry Belafonte,
acting as surgeon alongside Carol Burnett and pioneering heart specialist
Dr. Michael E. DeBakey, conducting with Leonard Bernstein, cooking with
master chef Soo Lon Chin, and performing ballet with Rudolf Nureyev and
Margot Fonteyn.

In the early 1980s, Bernie Rothman reached a handshake deal with HBO
to produce another Kaye special that never came off. "I don't think Danny
was ready to do it," Rothman explained. "It was almost like a blank check
in the sense that (HBO) wanted him so, so badly to do a special for them.
There were two schools of thought. There was one particular concept he
kind of liked, but it was something of the sort he'd been involved before,
and at this particular point in his life he wasn't about to repeat. And we
talked about a retrospective-type of special, (but) I think he thought better
of it. He thought, 'Well, no, not yet—maybe when I get old.' He was not
ready to create a monument for himself. The monument was already there,
with some of his old pictures and television shows. It's monumental, and
it's real good. People will be liking that a long time after Danny isn't here."

Decades have now passed since Kaye died—on March 3, 1987, after the
amateur surgeon contracted hepatitis from contaminated blood during
quadruple bypass surgery four years earlier. His legacy has dimmed with
the passing of time. His greatest works—his triumphs on stage—endure
today only as memories in the minds of aging members of his audiences.
When his recordings get play nowadays, it's usually because they're being
used as background music on a TV show or videogame. Most of his own
television work is unavailable for public viewing, due to the cost it would
take to pay rights-holders, as well as the fact that much of his TV work has

not aged particularly well. Whimsy was of another time.

That leaves us with his movies, a source of sporadically great entertainment, but one not typically looked back on as a collection, as one might view the body of work of Charlie Chaplin, or Fred Astaire, or Alfred Hitchcock. History has smiled on individual pictures—in particular the holiday staple *White Christmas* and *The Court Jester*. Once considered a *Cleopatra*-sized bomb, the medieval romp has steadily gained a reputation as one of the greatest comedies of all time, to the point that both specials Danny did for Disney worked in Hubert Hawkins' running gag "Get it?" "Got it?" "Good."

With so many talents, Kaye was an oft-times uncomfortable fit for the film frame. During Danny's last years, Everett Freeman, screenwriter of *The Secret Life of Walter Mitty,* said, "He's a great talent, and he's done many pictures, but being as talented as he is, I think the picture business might have hurt him more than helped him, because he completely went into every part he did. In short, in pictures there was no Danny Kaye. He was what he wanted to be, and unlike Gary Cooper, who's always Gary Cooper, or Cary Grant, who's always Cary Grant, Danny Kaye was the part he played."

Still, through his best moments as Walter Mitty, as Hubert Hawkins, as Hans Christian Andersen, we retain faint glimpses of the greatness that was Danny Kaye. His may not have been a perfect life, but on stage—conjoined with his audience—he was as good as it got.

Get it?

Good.

ON TELEVISION

Toast of the Town (CBS, Dec. 7, 1952) *Hans Christian Andersen* clip for Goldwyn tribute

Operation Entertainment (NBC, 1954) USO tour clip

Winter Olympics Opening Ceremonies (CBS, Feb. 18, 1960)

What's My Line (CBS, Oct. 16, 1960) • (Oct. 29, 1961) • (Nov. 5, 1961) • (March 24, 1963) • (Oct. 24, 1965) • (Oct. 2, 1966)

Academy Awards (NBC, March 30, 1955) Receives honorary Oscar • (ABC, April 17, 1961) Presents honorary award for Stan Laurel • (April 10, 1969) Presenter • (March 29, 1982) Receives Jean Hersholt Humanitarian Award

DuPont Show of the Week: USO– Wherever They Go (NBC, Oct. 8, 1961) USO tour clip

12 Star Salute (ABC, Dec. 9, 1961) Host

Merv Griffin Show (NBC, taped Nov. 8 to 9, 1962) • (Oct. 10, 1969) • (Nov. 7, 1969; taped Nov. 3, 1969)

Cultural Center (NBC, 1962)

Tonight Show (NBC, Nov. 8, 1962) • (May 22, 1970)

Andy Williams Show (NBC, Nov. 8, 1962)

Here's Hollywood (NBC, Nov. 9, 1962)

Jack Benny Program (CBS, Feb. 25, 1964)

Eamonn Andrews Show (BBC, Nov. 22, 1964)

Art Linkletter's House Party (CBS, 1965)

Lucy Show (CBS, Dec. 28, 1964) "All by Myself"

Salute to Stan Laurel (CBS, Nov. 23, 1965)

Evening with Carol Channing (CBS, Feb. 18, 1966)

John Gary Show (CBS, June 22, 1966)

Hollywood Talent Scouts (CBS, Sept. 5, 1966)

Password (Jan. 24 to 28, 1966) • (Sept. 26 to 30, 1966)

Tienerklanken (Belgium, Dec. 14, 1967)

David Frost Show (CBS, Oct. 29, 1969) • (March 3, 1971)

Dee Time (BBC, Nov. 1, 1969)

Mike Douglas Christmas Special (Syndicated, Dec. 7, 1969)

Rowan & Martin's Laugh In (NBC, March 2, 1970; taped Jan. 20 to Feb. 1, 1970)

Ed Sullivan Show (CBS, Nov. 22, 1970)

Fight of the Century (NBC, March 8, 1971) Audience member

Dick Cavett Show (ABC, May 28, 1971; taped Feb. 4, 16 to 17, 1971) • (taped Nov. 24, 1971)

VIP Schaukel (ZDF Germany, March 23, 1973)

AFI Life Achievement Award: A Tribute to John Ford (CBS, April 2, 1973)

Tribute to Jack Benny (CBS, Dec. 29, 1974)

Entertainment Hall of Fame Awards (NBC, Feb. 22, 1975)

An Evening with John Denver (ABC, March 10, 1975; taped Feb. 24, 1975) Denver medley, "Grandma's Feather Bed," "I Love to Laugh"

Emmy Awards (CBS, May 22, 1966) Co-host • (May 17, 1976) Presenter • (Sept. 9, 1979) Audience member • (NBC, Sept. 25, 1983) Presenter

Iltalintu (Finland, Nov. 27, 1976)

CBS Salutes Lucy—The First 25 Years (CBS, Nov. 28, 1976)

This Is Your Life (BBC, taped April 19, 1977)

CBS: On the Air (CBS, March 26, 1978) Co-host

Bing Crosby: His Life & Legend (ABC, May 25, 1978)

Bob Hope's All Star Comedy Salute to the 75th Anniversary of the World Series (NBC, Oct. 15, 1978) "Take Me Out to the Ballgame"

Muppet Show (Syndicated, Nov. 21, 1978) "Cheek to Cheek," "Inchworm"

Highlights of the Ringling Bros. and Barnum & Bailey Circus (NBC, Jan. 30, 1979; taped Jan. 7 to 8, 1979)

Billy Baxter Presents Diary of Cannes Film Festival with Rex Reed (July 16, 1980)

Kennedy Center Honors (CBS, Dec. 25, 1984; taped Dec. 2, 1984) Recipient

Night of 100 Stars II (ABC, March 10, 1985)

Twilight Zone (CBS, Nov. 8, 1985; taped Aug. 2 to 13, 1985) "Paladin of the Lost Hour"

Cosby Show (NBC, Feb. 2, 1986; taped Jan. 16, 1986) "The Dentist"

Auf Los Geht's Los (ARD Germany, March 1986)

NOTES & SOURCES

I – Interview by Author
Q – Quote
MS – Original Manuscript
PCA – Production Code Administration records (censor)
TS – Transcript

I. One Upon a Time in New York

Earliest years: Census & immigration records (Kaye's birthdate is listed as Jan. 28, 1911, on his birth certificate and, consequently, his passports, not Jan. 18, 1913. He was definitely born in 1911 and in his late 20s shaved two years off his publicized age. But why he would add back an extra 10 days is mysterious and suggests that perhaps the date written on the certificate is in error.)
Minstrel show *Q*: *Milwaukee Journal* 6/17/45
"Rowdies": Pete Martin *TS* 1958 (of interview for *Saturday Evening Post*)
Runaway: *Photoplay* 5/44, Martin *TS*
Lichtman: Locke *I*, Stein *I*, White Roe programs
White Roe, tummling: Weiner *I*, Goldfarb NYU oral history, White Roe brochures, programs 1930-35, *Colliers* 5/14/49
$5 under pillow: *Saturday Evening Post* 8/9/58
Eisen, Goldfarb: White Roe programs
Malamud in Cheder, *Q*: White Roe programs 8/33, Weiner *I*
Nat *Q*: Locke *I*
Terpsichoreans, Marcus: *Holiday* 8/59, La Vie Paree program 1934
Harvey, Young & Fine stay: Kaye letters to Holly Fine 1935
Return to White Roe: Weiner *I*, White Roe programs, *White Roe-Stir* newsletter
Song of the Miners: Program 7/4/35, Kaye letter to H. Fine 7/5/35, Weiner *I*

"Rusty & the Doctor" sketch: *MS* 1935
Labor Day show: Kaye letters to H. Fine 8/29, 9/5/35, White Roe program 9/1/35
Nick Long at coffee shop: Martin *TS*
President Hotel: Locke *I*, Stein *I*, program 7/4/37
Lichtman mentor, radio auditions: Stein *I*
Bestry, Educational contract: Kaye letter to H. Fine 11/21/37
Kaye *Q* on London reception: Martin *TS*
Jackson *Q*: *Life Story of Danny Kaye* (Dick Richards, Convoy, 1949)
Singer? Dancer?: *Washington Morning News* 4/8/41

II. Sylvia

Sylvia growing up, "Great American Tragedy": Paul Werth's "Evening with Sylvia Fine" undated
"Beat an Egg": Brooklyn College Class Nite program 5/13/33
Camp Geneva: Programs 8/7, 8/28/37
Tamiment, Liebman: *Every Week, A Broadway Revue* (Martha LoMonaco, Greenwood Press, 1992), Tamiment Playhouse programs 1938-1940
Sylvia's first show: Program 5/29/38 (In her first show at Tamiment, Fine titled the number "ILGWU School of the Theatre." In subsequent performances, it would go by "ILGWU Finishing School," "Commencement Day at the Garment Center," and finally just plain "ILGWU.")
"Spies": Fine *MS* ("Spies" was initially performed 7/23/38 as "Spritzinwasser, Belchikoff, Scaramouche & Madame Stinky," then repeated the next summer, 8/26/39, renamed "International Spies" with

Kaye filling Munshin's role.)
Cabaret TAC: *NY Times* 11/27/38, *Actors on Red Alert* (Anthony Slide, Scarecrow Press, 1999)

Sunday Night Varieties

Credits: (*Sunday Night Varieties* featured many more songs than are listed in these credits. However, this entry—like all others in this book—list only those songs that either Danny performed or Sylvia wrote.)
Creating show, Lichtman introduces Sylvia: Locke *I*
Garrett *Q*: Garrett letter to LoMonaco 1987
Political: Lloyd *I*
First show: Program 3/5/39
Review: *NY Daily Worker* 3/7/39
Last night at Club Miramar: *NY Times* 3/27/39
Barbizon-Plaza: Locke *I*, program 4/9/39, *Variety* 4/12/39 (Some sources remembered the show running through April, while others insist it closed after a single performance at the Barbizon-Plaza.)
Sylvia invites Liebman: Werth, *Holiday* 8/59
Lichtman: Locke *I* (Lichtman would follow Kaye somewhat, a year later, when Nat became entertainment director at the ILGWU-operated camp next to Tamiment, Unity House, and convinced the Shuberts to bring Unity's revue to Broadway in the fall, a la *Straw Hat Revue*. Nat's show, *Tis of Thee*, would play just one performance before being axed. Ever frail, Lichtman's health continued to deteriorate and he died of tuberculosis in 1944.)

Tamiment Playhouse

Danny's debut: Program 7/3/39
Sylvia labors over "Anatole": Werth
Week 4: Program 7/24/39, "Here He Comes Now" *MS*
"Anatole" simple: *LA Times* 6/30/67 (Under Liebman, Sylvia's political satire remained light, such as in one night's opening song, "Information Please," which made Tamiment's remote location the butt of the joke, rather than Hitler: "We know it pays to stay at Tamiment no matter what the bill, 'cause even if Hitler were in Bushkill, he wouldn't bother to come up that hill.")
Yiddish Mikado: LoMonaco (When repeated, "That There Mikado," written by Liebman

and Herman Shapiro, was renamed "Der Richtige Mikado," or "The Real Mikado." Although the number never made it to Broadway, in later years Kaye would occasionally dust it off to entertain at private parties, joined by guests like Judy Garland.)
Shubert scout: LoMonaco , *NY Times* 10/29/39

The Straw Hat Revue

Nine-week run: (Kaye appeared in 73 of the 75 performances, dropping out 11/23-24 due to a cold.)
"Soused": (Kaufman originally envisioned the Carmen Miranda spoof for British comedienne Beatrice Lillie, but Lillie decided against doing a show in the U.S.)
Content of show: LoMonaco, programs
The Great Chandeliers: (There were, in fact, dozens of different chandeliers used by the Shuberts over the years, although the fixture used in "The Great Chandelier" was the same one used in *Princess Flavia* and *The Great Waltz*.)
Liebman *Q*: Program
Non-union scenery: NYPL clipping 9/24/39
Review: *NY Herald-Tribune* 9/30/39, *Billboard* 9/39
Tamiment postcard: *NY Tribune* 10/15/39
Changes, critic *Q*: *NY World-Telegram* 10/4/39
Aborted tour: LoMonaco
Courtship: Locke *I*
Weddings: *Woman's Home Companion* 4/5/56
Pursuit of Happiness: Locke *I*, show records (Although records are sketchy, Kaye likely made his first appearance on the show during the *Straw Hat Revue* run and may actually have reprised his best-reviewed sketch from the show, "Two Cups of Coffee"—as was common for *Pursuit of Happiness*. Records show he played "a Russian immigrant" on his second appearance, although Sam Locke recalled Danny performed the just-finished "Stanislavsky.")
"Stanislavsky": Locke *I*, Fine *MS* with Locke's handwritten notations
Benny: *Jack Benny Show* (Milt Josefberg, Arlington House, 1977)
Kaye formally announcing songs: *Holiday* 8/59
Policing from the piano: *Woman's Home Companion* 4/5/56
Cockeyed hands, chunks of meat: *SE Post* 6/10/50

Tamiment 1940: Programs

Lady in the Dark

Hart at La Martinique: *SE Post* 6/10/50, Werth
Show background, "Tschaikowsky": *Lady in the Dark: Biography of a Musical* (Bruce D. McClung, Oxford University Press, 2007)
Nerves: Randolph *I*
Poor rehearsals: Werth
"Mendelssohn" cut: McClung (Ira Gershwin, as could be expected, was quite disappointed by the loss of one of his favorite songs, so Danny included the number among the six *Lady in the Dark* songs he recorded for Columbia.)
Premiere: Randolph *I*, McClung, *SE Post* 6/10/50
Mischief: (Kaye and Lawrence would work together once more. Several years later, they appeared together on the British radio show *Hi, Gang!* Gertie tackled "Tschaikowsky," while Danny sang a sultry "Jenny.")
Success: Green *I*
CBS exec at nightclub: Stein *I*

Let's Face It

MGM offer: *NY World Telegram* 1/11/41
Show background: *NY Times* 11/16/41, "Melody in 4F" genesis: *SE Post* 8/9/58
Liebman's influence: Baker *I*
Loused up "Melody": *Woman's Home Companion* 4/56
Catskills visit: Baker *I*
Shifting headlines: *NY Post* 3/14/42
Liebman on payroll: Fine ledgers 1942 & 1943 (Most weeks during the first half of 1942, Fine paid her collaborator about $155 a week, then $125 a week starting in the summer. Payments were typically lower and less frequent during 1943, with the last on 9/9/43.)
Bathroom: Locke *I*
Local Board Makes Good: *Theatre Arts* 9/42
LBJ songs: Fine *MS*s for "Round for Johnson," "Wish You Were Here," "How About You?"
Nervous exhaustion: *NY Times* 3/25/42
Kaye leaves: Baker *I*, *NY Times* 1/18/43 (Freedley originally had planned to move *Let's Face It* to a smaller theater a few weeks after Kaye left, but—due to Ferrer's unsuccess—scrapped the idea.)

III. Hello, Hollywood

Up in Arms

• *They Can't Get You Down* treatment (Hartman & Boretz, 10/26/42)
• *Up in Arms* screenplays (Hartman & Boretz, 1/16, 2/16/43; with Pirosh, 3/17, 4/15, 5/17/43; with Rapp, 6/18, 6/24, 6/30, 7/7/43)
Goldwyn contracts with Kaye, Fine & Liebman: Contracts 5/14/42
Spitz: Spitz telegram 5/20/41
Bidding on Kaye: Hyde memo 6/5/41
Goldwyn Qs: Shavelson *I*
Making fun of Goldwynisms: (Cole Porter also poked fun at Goldwyn in "Anything Goes," and Sylvia may have had in mind the Goldwynism "in two words: im-possible" when she penned "in two words: un-likely" in "Soliloquy for Three Heads.")
Goldwyn & Gilbert & Sullivan: *Goldwyn* (Arthur Marx, Ballantine Books, 1976)
Creating movie: Scripts, Pirosh *I*
Overexcited music listener bit: (In *Wonder Man*, Danny was supposed to perform the routine as he listened to songs on the radio.)
"Lobby Number": scripts, Pirosh *I*, Fine *MS*s ("Here He Comes Now," "Lobby Number," "Shubert Alley," "Opening Opening," "Cherry Blossom Time")
Screen test: Production records, *The Road to Hollywood* (Bob Hope & Bob Thomas, Bookthrift, 1979)
Nose job: Kaye contract
Unease Q: Pirosh *I*
Mayo: Mayo *I*, Goldwyn memo 2/20/43, *Focus on Film* 3/81
Bowing: *SE Post* 6/10/50
Green Sylvia: Locke *I*
Sylvia on the set: Humberstone *I*
Filming "Lobby Number": Production records, Baker *I*
Retakes: Production records, studio memo 8/17/43
Budget, costs: Production records
Animation: Production records, script, Disney letter to Avalon Productions 9/1/43
Publicity in Palm Springs: Marx

Wonder Man

• *The Wonder Man* story (Sheekman, 12/28/43)
• Treatments (Hartman & Shavelson, 1/27/44;

Jevne & Moran, 2/21, 3/10, 3/17/44)
• Outline (Hartman & Swerling, 3/25/44)
• Screenplays (Hartman & Shavelson, 5/9,
5/27, 6/6/44; Shavelson & Rapp, 7/6, 7/10,
9/20/44; Hartman & Shavelson, 1/12/45)
Story problems: Notes on story conference
5/29/44 (Goldwyn, Hartman, Humberstone,
Shavelson, Duggan)
"Opera Number": Fine outline 7/5/44
Christmas titles: George Glass memo 7/11/44,
Goldwyn memo 7/15/44
Humberstone's advice: Humberstone *I*
"Bali Boogie" accident, delay: Production
records, accident report, Humberstone *I*,
Humberstone memo 8/4/44 (Filming "Bali
Boogie," Vera-Ellen suffered a stone bruise
on her heel from jumping on the drum, and
blisters on her legs and chest from her
dancing costume. And, although the director implied that Rapp was first brought in
after the accident, Rapp actually started
working on the script in mid-June, and he
was helped in the rewrites by Shavelson
and, later, Hartman.)
Liebman out: (Although Fine and Liebman
would never work together again, he and
the Kayes remained friends and Goldwyn
still had to go through the formality of
releasing him from each of the next three
pictures, as well.)
Sylvia's role: Shavelson *I*, Mayo *I*,
Humberstone *I*
"Otchi Tchorniya": Script 9/20/44, Humberstone
I
Censors, retakes: *PCA*, production records

Radio
Forecast: Prospective sponsor brochure 1940
Rapp: *Billboard* 7-15-44
Content: *Danny Kaye Show* scripts 12/28/44 -
5/31/46
Goodman Ace: Alsberg *I*, Kanter *I*, *Billboard*
7/21/45, *Time* 3/11/46
Reusing old jokes, Benny: *The Laugh Crafters:
Comedy Writing in Radio & TV's Golden
Age* (Jordan Young, Past Times Publishing,
1999)
Hutton: *Danny Kaye Saga* (Kurt Singer,
Richard Clay & Co., 1957)
Lewis: Alsberg *I*
Exit: *Billboard* 3/23/46, *Zanesville Signal* 5/2/46
Warning Q: Humberstone *I*

The Kid from Brooklyn
• *The Kid from Brooklyn* screenplays (Hartman
& Shavelson, 3/15, 4/9, 6/1/45; Freeman &
Englund, 6/12/45; Moran, 8/30/45;
Shavelson, 12/8/45)
Mitty on backburner: Freeman *I*
Remake Q: Shavelson *I*
McLeod: Shavelson *I*, Freeman *I* (Freeman
didn't say when the incident took place, so
it may have occurred during the production
of *Mitty*, instead of *Kid from Brooklyn*.)
Loesser, Cahn: Cahn *I*, Miriam Howell letter to
Goldwyn 3/29/45
"Cavalcade Number": Seelen & Lee *MS*
7/21/45, production records
Boxing coach: (Indrisano appears in the film as
a referee.)
Berlin advises: *The Search for Sam Goldwyn*
(Carol Easton, Wm. Morrow, 1989)
Cahn & Styne: Pay records (Two of the eight
numbers they composed for the film—"Love
Didn't Stop to Think" and "It Is the Most
Unusual Weather"—were not used in the
film.)
Redo musical numbers: Thompson letter to
Goldwyn 8/20/45, production records
Sounding board: Mayo *I*
Head on shoulders Q: *Time* 3/11/46

The Secret Life of Walter Mitty
• *Secret Life of Walter Mitty* storyline (Freeman,
2/5/45)
• Treatment (Freeman & Englund, 3/27/45)
• Screenplays (11/14/45, 1/18/46; Rapp, 3/15,
3/29, 5/1, 5/13, 6/7, 6/12, 7/3/46; Englund &
Freeman, 7/26, 8/7/46)
Goldwyn acquires *Mitty*: Freeman *I*, Miriam
Howell letter to Goldwyn 1/2/45
Thurber, *New Yorker*, Englund visits Thurber,
Englund fired: *Point of View* 1963, *NY
Times* 8/10/47
Freeman fired: Freeman *I*
Cahn reads script: Cahn *I*
Rapp: *Point of View* 1963
Sylvia pregnant, wire: Fine telegram to
Goldwyn 4/6/46
Working on songs: Fine telegram to Goldwyn
5/19/46
Psychiatrist dream: Baker letter to Fine 3/10/46
"Symphony for Unstrung Tongue": *Milwaukee
Journal* 10/26/47 (Danny based the
Czechoslovakian accent for "Unstrung

Tongue" on a silly voice he'd heard done by pal Johnny Green.)

New titles: Goldwyn letter to Zanuck 9/30/46, Audience Research Inc. survey results, Jack Shawn memo undated

McLeod, skeletonized sets: Jenkins *I*

Stand-in gambler: *SE Post* 6/10/50

Sylvia on radio: *Life* 8/18/47

Retakes: Production records

Previews: Studio report 6/27/47

"Malone" cut: Production records, Mandell *I*, Goldwyn letter to Englund 1947, Fine telegram to Goldwyn 5/21/47, Goldwyn telegram to Fine 5/21/47 (The "Molly Malone" sequence was rumored to have been salvaged by Walter Winchell in hopes of including it in a short subject along with spots by Frank Sinatra, etc. It was to be sold commercially, with all proceeds bene-fiting the Damon Runyon Memorial Cancer Fund. Production of the short was kept a mystery—and while the short may not have survived, the mystery certainly has.)

Thurber disliked film: *Life* 8/18/47

Review: *NY Times* 8/15/47

A Song Is Born

• *That's Life* screenplays (Tugend, 3/6, 3/27, 4/22/47; Rapp, 5/20/47)

Arden: Green *I*

Mayo *Q*: Mayo *I* (Mayo, for her part, was ready for a change as well. As she wrote to her aunt 8/19/45, during filming of *Kid from Brooklyn*: "I'll be glad to get away from working with Danny—not because I don't like him personally, but because I think it will be good to get away from this type of picture.")

Book: Margaret Thompson letter to Kaye 3/18/36, ghostwriter Ethel Paige letter to Fine 10/23/46, Mandel letter to Fine 10/28/46

Hipplefinger: *Hip-Hip-Hipplefinger!* screenplay by Freeman, Englund & Shavelson 8/22/46, suggested by Robert Ardrey & Ellick Moll's 1944 script *The First Coed*

Goldwyn explodes at Tugend: *Wit & Wisdom of Hollywood* (Max Wilk, Scribner, 1971)

Sylvia vs. Goldwyn: Fine letter to Pat Duggan 4/5/47 (In defense of Sylvia's claims, Goldwyn, in a telegram to her a few weeks before she left for California, on 2/3/47, said

Tugend would be calling her "so that you can begin thinking about numbers" and mentioned that "we wish to God we were seeing you before the middle of March. Can't that be arranged?")

Hiring Hawks, basket case: *Howard Hawks: Interviews* (Howard Hawks, Scott Breivold, University Press of Mississippi, 2006)

Sylvia passes on Goldwyn's offer: Lastfogel telegram to Fine 4/10/47

Separation: Hedda Hopper 9/47, Louella Parsons 9/47, Green *I*

Title change: Publicity sheet, Audience Research Inc. report

No credits: Tugend letter to author, *NY Times* 10/31/48

IV. International Icon

Chicago *Q*: *Citizen News* 7/18/58

Opening night: *Woman's Home Companion* 4/56, *SE Post* 6/10/50

Swaffer: *SE Post* 6/10/50

Warmth *Q*: *Life* 6/13/49

Sit Down Spot *Q*: *SE Post* 8/9/58

Churchill, closing night: *SE Post* 6/10/50

Returns to Sylvia: Parsons 2/48

Sylvia criticizes: *SE Post* 6/10/50

Sullivan *Q*: *SE Post* 8/9/58

The Inspector General

• *Happy Times* screenplays (Hecht & Lederer, 12/8/47; with Kurnitz, 2/21/48; Kurnitz & Rapp, 7/23/48, 6/30/49)

Lastfogel's arguments: Lastfogel memo (At least one other studio was in the bidding. Dore Schary, head of RKO, proposed a three-picture, non-exclusive deal.)

Warners contracts: Kaye & Fine contracts 8/8/47

Sylvia's movie suggestions: Memo 4/47, Sylvia story ideas 10/24/47, Fine outline late 1947 (*Inspector General* was among the titles suggested to Sylvia in a 6/10/47 letter from her brother, Robert.)

Wald buys *Father Goose*: Warners acquistion sheet 9/2/47

Sylvia's ideas: Fine treatment 10/47

Problems with Hecht/Lederer script: Story con-ference notes 12/23/47

Kurnitz: Kurnitz memo 12/10/47

Second draft analysis: Memo 3/9/48, story con-ference notes by Fine, Wald, Millard

Lampell, Jack Rose 3/23/48; notes by Wald, Fine, Lampell, Rose 3/30/48
Integrate music into story: *Time* 3/11/46
Sylvia's song suggestions: Fine letter 5/48
Kurnitz unhappy: Kurnitz letter 8/19/48
Writers visit set: Memos 9/1, 9/8/48
Mayor: Casting notes 8/30-31/48, memo 8/19/48
Mayor's wife: Casting notes 8/31-9/17/48
Catlett: Baker *I*
Danny vs. Sylvia: Green *I*
First day of rehearsals: Al Alleborn memo to T.C. Wright 8/16/48
Sylvia resumes writing: Alleborn memos 8/16, 8/24/48
Editing with Sylvia: Fehr *I*, Fine memo to Trilling 5/3/49
Break for *Command Performance*: Alleborn memo to Wright 8/16/48
Filming schedule, Butler: Production records
Medicine show problems, previews: Production records, Fine memo 5/3/49
Censors: *PCA*
Title changes: Warners memos 6/15, 6/17/49
18 months Q: Fehr *I*
Stop, You're Killing Me: Production records, Bacall approval 1/9/50, postponement notice 1/10/50
Contract killed, may re-team: Termination of contract 2/9/50, *Hollywood Reporter* 2/10/50

On the Riviera

• *On the Riviera* screenplays (Davies, 1/6, 4/28, 6/6/50; Ephrons, 6/17, 8/9, 8/24, 9/5, 9/13/50)
Zanuck's home movies: *We Thought We Could Do Anything* (Henry Ephron, W.W. Norton, 1977)
Censors: *PCA*, memos 5/11, 9/21/50
Sylvia: Ephron
Deleted numbers: Fine *MS*s (Unused Sylvia songs included "Dreams Come Tumbling Down," a ballad of regret, and a "test number" that evolved into "Rhythm of a New Romance.")
Prager: Memel *I*
"Popo": Ephron, pressbook (The late addition of "Popo the Puppet" also prevented Kaye from accepting an invitation to play a non-singing role, Frosch the comic jailer, in special end-of-the-year performances of the

New York Metropolitan Opera's *Die Fledermaus*.)
Popo sues: *Billboard* 8/21/54 (Ironically, Danny's later work with UNICEF would inspire Popo to himself spend ten years traveling around the world, on his own dime, to perform for UNICEF.)
Ephron Q: Ephron, reprinted by permission of author
Crowther review: *NY Times* 5/24/51
Can Can: Fox letter to Kaye 9/11/56 (Kaye was offered from $200,000 to $250,000 in salary, plus 30% of the profits.)
Huck Finn: *A Hundred or More Hidden Things: The Life of Vincente Minnelli* (Mark Griffin, Da Capo Press, 2010)

Hans Christian Andersen

• *A Stranger at Home* treatments (Bercovici, 11/20/37, 4/6/38)
• Outlines (Gabriel, 5/26/38; Ardrey, 6/23/38)
• Treatments (Bercovici, 6/29/38; Lamb, 7/1/38; Connolly, 9/4/38)
• *Once Upon a Time* treatments (Connolly, 10/18/38; Scott, 1/3/39)
• Screenplays (Connolly, 2/8, 4/14, 5/1/39; Swerling, 7/3, 8/5/39)
• *Hans Christian Andersen* treatment (Bellous, 3/1/40)
• *Stagecoach to Odense* screenplay (Sears, 7/15/41)
• *Cobbler & the King* outline (Hartman & Shavelson, 1/6/45)
• *Hans Christian Andersen* screenplay (Swerling, 10/18/50)
• Story notes (Langley, 12/50)
• Treatment (Taylor, 2/16/51)
• Screenplays (Taylor & Langley, 3/10, 3/14, 3/30, 4/10, 5/1/50; Taylor & Partos, 1951)
• Treatments (Englund, 5/11, 5/19/51; with Taylor, 5/26, 6/11/51)
• Screenplays (Hart, 9/6, 9/21, 10/1, 10/29/51)
Best picture Q: Goldwyn letter to Kaye 6/5/51
Backstory: Production records, *American Cinematographer* 7/52
Problems with screenplays: Louise Heidelberg synopsis of biography by Signe Toksvig 4/16/34, Craig Livingston/A. Crue/E.J. Cantor synopsis of Rengert bio 8/26/37 and Bercovici treatment 4/2/38, Aileen Seilaz/Alfred C. Schiller synopsis of Bercovici 8/2/38

Kaye as Andersen Q: Hartman/Shavelson story
 memo undated
Stewart, Koster: Koster letters 11/16, 11/19/50;
 Langley letter to Goldwyn 11/28/50;
 Goldwyn letters to Sherwood 12/6, 12/8/50;
 Goldwyn letter to Kaye 6/5/51
Kaye's demands: Bert Allenberg (William
 Morris Agency) letter to Goldwyn 12/29/50
Heavyweights: Shavelson *I*, Goldwyn letter to
 Sherwood 12/6/50, Osborn letter 1/10/51,
 Gordon & Kanin letter 1/14/51
Hart unhappy with credit: *Variety* 7/2/52
Hart's approach: Hart letter to Goldwyn 1/22/51
Rodgers & Hammerstein: Goldwyn letter
 6/11/51
"Shoe Song": Production records
Vidor's changes: Vidor/Goldwyn memos undat-
 ed, Hart telegram to Goldwyn 11/24/51
Shearer: (Ironically, in the months leading up to
 rehearsals, before Goldwyn learned that
 Shearer was pregnant, the producer had
 repeatedly complained that he thought the
 dancer was too thin. Goldwyn wrote to
 Shearer that he thought she wasn't eating
 enough and would lack the stamina for
 such a demanding role. Shearer reminded
 him that she had a naturally slight build and
 was a professional ballerina, who was just
 completing an exhausting twelve-month
 engagement.)
Jeanmarie: *Variety* 10/22/52, *NY Times*
 6/29/52, Fine letter to Goldwyn 7/19/52
Kids Q: Qualen *I*
Troubles with Danes: *NY Times* 4/27/52
Kaye in Denmark: *NY Times* 7/22, 8/1, 11/25,
 12/6/52
Album: *A Most Remarkable Fella* (Susan
 Loesser, Hal Leonard, 1993)

V. Peaking at Paramount
Baker: Baker's notes c. 1951
Crook kid, crying baby: *SE Post* 8/9/58
Liebman Q: *NY Times Magazine* 1/18/53
Ormondy: *NY Times* 3/9/54
Boston Symphony: *SE Post* 8/9/58
Kerr: *Theatre Arts* 8/51

Knock on Wood
• *Knock on Wood* screenplays (Panama &
 Frank, 1/16, 2/27, 4/14, 4/19, 5/19,
 11/14/53)
Teams with Panama & Frank, no restrictions:

LA Times 3/28/54
Production company formed: *NY Times*
 11/16/52
Dialogue Q: Day *I*
Dummies: *Variety* undated
3-D: *Hollywood Reporter* 3/53
Budgets, costs, doubles, added scenes, over-
 seas plans: Production records
Cut fox hunt: Memo 2/9/53
Zetterling: *This Week Magazine* 12/53, Day *I*
Denise injured: *Hollywood Reporter* 7/23/53,
 production records
Ballet: Production records
Danny the dancer: Charmoli *I*
Guinea pig: Day *I*
Injuries: *PCA*
Retakes: Production records
Classic Q: *NY Times* 11/8/70

White Christmas
• *White Christmas* screenplays (Krasna, 9/29,
 11/11/52, 6/12/53; Rose & Shavelson, 7/1,
 7/7/53; Krasna, 8/17/53; with Panama &
 Frank, 9/14/53)
VistaVision: *NY Times* 10/24/54
Inspiration, deleted songs: *The Complete Lyrics
 of Irving Berlin* (Irving Berlin, Robert
 Kimball, & Linda Emmet, Applause Books,
 2005)
Story concerns: Curtiz and Dolan notes 5/4/53,
 memos 2/27, 5/16/53
Crosby, Astaire pull out: *Variety* 1/2/53
Crosby returns: *Variety* 1/22/53
O'Connor in: Cast wardrobe sheet 8/7/53
Crosby's concerns, GI mail: Story conference
 notes 2/27/53
O'Connor out: Paramount memo 8/19/53
Hartman asks Kaye: *Deseret News* 9/15/53
Berlin consents: Berlin letter 8/19/53
Lousiest story: Wilk
Cut miniature ending: Dolan memo undated
VistaVision Q: Bracht letter to author

Assignment: Children
Meets Pate: *Redbook* 11/60 (Many published
 reports erroneously claim Kaye met Pate
 during the flight that his plane's engines
 caught fire and had to revert course back to
 Europe. But that fateful flight was in 1949
 and returned to Shannon, Ireland, not
 London.)
Travel: *NY Times* 4/17, 7/16/54

Kaye Qs: Werth
Review: *Beverly Hills NewsLife* 2/10/55

The Court Jester
• *The Court Jester* screenplays (Panama &
  Frank, 10/12, 11/15/54)
Song ideas: Set estimate sheet 8/13/54
Songwriting: Cahn *I*
Deleted songs: *PCA*, *MSs*
Budgets, costs, crew changes: Production
  records
Music cost overruns: Roy Fjastad memo
  1/14/55
"Pass the Basket" cut: Hartman memo 3/2/55
Dena Music formed: *Billboard* 4/9/55 (Kaye
  served as vice president and Fred Raphael
  as secretary and general manager.)
Fencing instruction: *Cads & Cavaliers* (Tony
  Thomas, A.S. Barnes, 1973)
Maltin Q: *The Great Movie Comedians*
  (Leonard Maltin, Crown, 1979)
Final cost: Production records (The original
  schedule was to include 48 days of primary
  filming, twelve days to rehearse, and ten for
  second-unit work.)

See It Now: The Secret Life of Danny Kaye
Background, possessions: *LA Times* 12/2/56,
  Time 12/10/56
Fine edits: *Hollywood Reporter* 11/1/60

Merry Andrew
• *The Romance of Henry Menafee* story
  (Gallico, 2/18/43)
• Screenplays (Gallico, 3/15/43, 5/27/44)
• Outline (Gordon, Wimperis & Gray, 3/22/46)
• Screenplays (3/27/45; Wimperis, 4/13/46)
• *The Private Life of Henry Menafee* treatment
  (Gray, 4/22/46)
• *Mr. Menafee* screenplay (Holloway, 5/20/46)
• *Romance of Henry Menafee* screenplays
  (Holloway, 8/5/46; Wimperis, 8/14, 8/19/46;
  Lustig, 8/28/46; Schayer, 9/27, 9/30, 10/2,
  10/3/46; Wimperis & Holloway, 2/21/47;
  Lustig, 10/1, 11/1/47; Osborn, 3/2/49;
  Lustig, 3/16/49; Osborn & Lustig, 4/28/49;
  with Wimiperis, 5/25, 8/10/49; Lustig,
  8/11/49; Gordon, 10/11/49; Wimperis,
  10/25/49)
• *Merry Andrew* screenplays (Lennart, 5/7,
  5/31, 7/18, 8/13, 11/15, 11/21, 12/3,
  12/17/56; Diamond, 3/21, 6/3, 6/24, 7/1,
  8/1/57; Patrick, 5/16/57)

Upcoming movie commitments: Kaye note
  2/8/57 (At the time, Danny anticipated starting *Knock on Silk* in October 1957 as soon
  as he finished *Merry Andrew*, and then
  jumping straight into *The Red Nichols Story*
  from February to June 1958.)
Circus picture craze: *Billboard* 3/10/51
Story problems: Maurice Zimm memo to Milton
  Beecher 6/26/54, notes on 1949 script
Diamond Q: Diamond letter to author

Me and the Colonel
• *Jacobowsky & the Colonel* screenplay
  (Behrman, 8/15/56)
• *Best of Enemies* screenplay (12/21/56)
• *Me & the Colonel* screenplay (Diamond,
  10/7/57)
Columbia buys rights: *LA Examiner* 5/44
Radical departure: *SE Post* 8/9/58
Gulliver's Travels: Goetz letter to Kaye 6/21/56
  (Kaye was promised $200,000 against 50%
  of the profits, as well as approval of director
  and leading lady.)
Exteriors in France: Pre-production report
  11/57 (The first four weeks were spent in
  Paris, Lyons and Marseille, shooting all
  exteriors, as well as interiors at the airport,
  inside a barn, townhall, and castle halls and
  stairways. Filming in Hollywood and Europe
  contributed to the film's $2.5-million price
  tag.)

The Five Pennies
• *Intermission* outlines (Smith, 10/15, 12/10/54)
• Treatment (Shaw, 6/29/55)
• Screenplays (Smith, 12/14/54, 1/31/55; Shaw,
  8/23, 8/29/55; Berkman & Blau, 11/23/55;
  Shavelson & Rose, 12/11/56, 1/27, 8/15,
  10/3/58)
Background: Shavelson *I*
Fine Q: "How to Change a Nichols into Five
  Pennies" by Fine 1959
Musical notions: Fine letter to Shavelson &
  Rose 5/23/56
Sylvia's criticisms: Fine notes 1/5/57 in antici-
  pation of 1/8/57 story conference
Shelved: Paramount memo 1/23/57
Two music styles: "How to Change a Nichols"
Goodman: *Hollywood Reporter* 9/58, 10/58
Cameos: Publicity sheet
Strike, UA deal: *Hollywood Reporter* 5/58 (Don
  Hartman died in March 1958, before filming

began. But his influence continued on with the picture. Because of his daughter, Hartman had become such a supporter of County Hospital that when the producers needed 10 iron lungs for the picture, the hospital sent over ten respirators and a technical advisor.)

Pre-record: Shavelson *I*

Sweating: Fapp *I*

Retakes, Sylvia: Shavelson *I*

Flapistan, sprained ankle: Barton *I*, publicity sheet

Lawsuit: Shavelson *I*, settlement 8/60

Cooking: Wong *I*

VI. Tiptoeing into Television

Cannibal, mulish Qs: *SE Post* 8/9/58

Trial by Jury: Proposal 4/23/58

An Hour with Danny Kaye - TV Special #1

Constant discussions: Kanter *I*

Satchmo: *Louis Armstrong* (Scott Allen Nollen, McFarland & Co., 2004)

Sylvia's editing: Jewison letter to Fine 10/28/60

On the Double

• *On the Double* screenplay (Shavelson & Rose, 5/16/60)

Genesis: *NY Times* 5/14/61, Shavelson *I*

Trick photography: Shavelson *I*

The Danny Kaye Show - TV Special #2

Kanter exits: Kanter *I*

Barnes: Barnes *I*

CBS scheduling snafu: *LA Mirror* 8/23/61

The Man from the Diners' Club

• *The Man from the Diners Club* screenplay (Blatty, 11/20/61, 5/31, 6/12, 7/2/62)

Other actors: Casting list 12/11/61

Kaye's pay: Contract (The film was budgeted at $778,000 and cost $863,000.)

Kaye on set: Kennedy letter to author, Williams *I*

Kaye Q: *NY Times* 8/26/62

The Danny Kaye Show with Lucille Ball - TV Special #3

Lucy signed, Kaye's ego: Oppenheimer *I*

Scharf: Termination papers 9/27/62, Oppenheimer *I* (Kaye appeared at the Greek 7/23 - 8/4/62.)

Chambers recruited: Chambers *I*

Unused song ideas: Fine's notes

Unused sketch ideas: Baker's notes (The writers considered writing parts for the cast of *Bonanza*, whose show Kaye would be pre-empting, and Richard "Dr. Kildare" Chamberlain, but the former would have cost too much money and for the latter, MGM would have required script clearance.)

Drunk sketch: Oppenheimer *I*

No re-runs: Charmoli *I*

VII. The Series

No Sylvia: Lafferty *I*, Scheerer *I*

Wasn't ready earlier: *SE Post* 8/9/58

Networks bid: *TV Guide* 1/9/65

Stepping stone Q: Charmoli *I*

Baker: Employment contracts

Flu story: Lafferty *I*

Gelbart's role: Gelbart *I*, Lafferty *I*

Vegas trip, Lafferty Qs, segment ideas, supporting cast: Pre-trip report by Lafferty 5/27/63

Flying Q: Gelbart *I*

Kaye vs. Caesar: Lafferty *I*

Keller's method: Scheerer *I*

Danny as a person: Lafferty *I*

Specialty material: Friedman *I*, Scheerer *I*, Chambers *I*, Rothman *I*, Keller *I*, *Make 'em Laugh* (William Fry & Melanie Allen, Science & Behavior Books, 1975)

Lafferty's plan, schedule: Lafferty *I*, Vegas trip report, *NY Times* 1/19/64

Antiseptic Q: *Christian Science Monitor* 12/23/65

Premiere review: *NY Times* 9/26/63

Sit down spot Q, costume change: Lafferty *I*

Astaire: Vegas trip report

Gene Kelly: Scheerer *I*

Lovelady Powell: Powell contract 7/16/63, Lafferty letters to Powell 9/10, 10/3/63

Korman: Korman contract 9/19/63, raise and bonus notices, Korman letter to Bonis 11/9/64 (Q)

Kaye moods Q: *TV Guide* 1/9/65

Moodiness Qs: Keller *I*, Lafferty *I*

JFK: Chambers *I*

Bonis vs. Baker: Baker memo 12/63

Dancing: Charmoli *I*, Keller *I*, Scheerer *I*

Farr: Farr on Peter Anthony Holder radio show 5/24/95 (Other occasional supporting play-

ers included three-timers Dino Natali
[*Barney Miller*] and Dodo Denney [Mrs.
Teevee from *Willy Wonka & the Chocolate
Factory*], and six-timer Bernie Kopell [*The
Love Boat*].)
Van Patten: Van Patten *I*
Burned leg: Charmoli *I*, Lafferty *I*, Scheerer *I*,
Grasso *I*
Cara Williams Show, Baker gone: Keller *I*
Lucy appearance: Oppenheimer *I*, *TV Guide*
1/9/65
Anger: Scheerer *I*
Carney: Grasso *I*, Lafferty letter to Carney
12/2/64
Meyerink: Lafferty *I*, Meyerink contracts 1/26,
3/23/65; Lafferty letters 1/8, 1/27, 3/31/65;
TV Week Citizen-News 2/11/67
Youth: Lafferty *I*
Anti-Caesar: Tolkin letter to author, Keller *I* (By
not bringing back Tolkin & Keller, the show
was also able to dump the two largest
salaries from the writing staff.)
Prager: Keller *I*, Barnes *I*, Chambers *I*, Lafferty
I, Scheerer *I*, Prager contract 4/8/65, Bonis
memo 8/5/65
Binder reading newspaper: Scheerer *I*
Stalled elevator, cut Q, remote, chemistry Q,
tension Q: Binder *I*
Binder fired: Scheerer *I*, Binder contract
5/10/65, Scheerer contract 7/23/65, Bonis
memo 9/16/65
Mouskouri: Bonis memo 9/11/65
Rothman: Scheerer *I*, Rothman *I*, Rothman's
song list
Themes: Scheerer *I*
Rut: Barasch *I*, Van Patten letter to author,
Keller *I*, Scheerer *I* (Burnett's show would
actually debut Mondays at 10 p.m.)

VIII. Specials & One-Shots

The Madwoman of Chaillot
Vietnam Q: *NY Times* 5/1/66 (Although an
avowed liberal, Kaye began downplaying
his views in the late 1940s, after he was
accused of holding Communist sympathies
for joining celebrity protests against the
blacklist.)
Scarlet Pimpernel: *LA Times* 11/9/63 ("Margot"
first suggested Kaye do a musical *Scarlet
Pimpernel* in a 7/14/55 letter. Fine had Lew

Wasserman begin researching the rights to
the character in 1959, discovering that it
had fallen into public domain in the U.S.,
but London Film Productions held the international rights.)
We're a Whole New Thing, Sylvia Q: *LA Times*
6/30/67
Bloomgarden: Termination papers 12/67 (He
was hired to write the book 4/67.)
Spigelgass Q: Spigelgass *I*
Fellini: Clipping 5/10/68 (for film *The Voyage of
Frederico*)
Quixote: Fan letter to Kaye 10/24/69 citing
Hollywood Reporter item
Prager retires: (David Black played the piano
on many of Kaye's 1968 and 1969 show
dates, although the last recorded run for his
one-man show—11/10 - 12/7/69 at Las
Vegas' International Hotel—featured Doug
Talbert at piano.)
End of stage show: (One of the last specialty
numbers penned for Danny and his stage
act was written in the late 1960s by Herbie
Baker—"Coccaycoccayanakoos," a satire of
then-in-vogue sexy movies, in which Kaye
played famous film director Athinaxos
Aristotle Miklos Niklos
Coccaycoccayanakos, the "Grecian elf" ["So
tonight, as I accept the Homolka—that's the
Greek Oscar…"].)

Two by Two
Kaye pinnacle Q, genesis of show: *NY Times*
6/16/70, Stone *I*
Patriarch Q, Gilford or Kiley: Stone *I*
Kaye *Hello, Dolly*/fellas Qs: *NY Times* 11/8/70
Odets' problem: NYPL clipping 10/7/70
Reviews: (One of the few reviews to pan
Danny's performance appeared in *Women's
Wear Daily*. The reviewer, one Martin
Gottfried, would 20 years later write the
nasty, mistake-riddled Kaye bio *Nobody's
Fool*.)
Kaye not a concert Q: *NY Times* 11/8/70
Accident, Qs: *NY Times* 2/19/71, Stone *I*
Kaye's ad-libs: *After Dark Magazine*, *NY Times*
4/11/71
Problems Q: Stone *I*
Cast removed: Secretary Valerie Davidson let-
ter to lawyer Seymour Bricker 3/25/71,
which noted therapy was expected to last

another four weeks
Kaye bad hip Q: *NY Times* 8/16/81
Fizzled projects: *Nonsensical World of Dr.
Seuss* proposal 4/66, *Danny Kaye & Dr.
Seuss* proposal 1966, *Danny Kaye's World
of Hans Christian Andersen* proposal, *Little
Mermaid* proposal for 68-69 season

The Enchanted World of Danny Kaye
Genesis, follow-ups: Production records, proposal, Videocraft title suggestions 1/15/71

**Danny Kaye's Look-in at the Metropolitan
Opera**
• Teleplay (Baker & Fine, 3/12/75)
Doctor's Dilemma: Fine notes 1971
USC: Fine lecture notes 3/7, 3/24, 4/11/72
Gentele, Kaye Qs: *NY Times* 1/5/73

Peter Pan
Peter Pan teleplay (Burns & Birkin, 3/5,
4/18/75)
Idea, San Lorenzo: Smith *I*
Olivier: Script
Birkin, reaction: Smith *I*

Pinocchio
• *Pinocchio* teleplay (Baker, 4/18, 5/3/75,
2/18/76)
Idea: Rothman *I*
Kaye TV Q: *LA Times* 3/21/76
Baseball Q: *LA Times* 4/77

EPCOT Center: Opening Celebration
Idea for shows: Smith *I*
Roy Disney: *Realityland: True-Life Adventures
at Walt Disney World* (David Koenig,
Bonaventure Press, 2007)
Tour groups, heat, live, outburst: Smith *I*
Kaye banned: Ron Miziker presentation to
Disneyana Fan Club 7/14/11

Skokie
• *Defend to the Death* teleplay (Kinoy, 9/15/80)
• *Skokie* teleplay (10/16, 10/24/80)
Not a "historical document," Kinoy Q, Kaye Q:
Newsday 11/15/81
Challenges Q: Rothman *I*

Musical Comedy Tonight II
Proposed book: Fine *MS* notes, letters to tran-
scriber
Warner Bros. Musicals: Grasso *I*
Sponsors: Fine letters to PBS 12/13/78,
7/12/79; KCET's Chuck Allen letter to Fine

9/27/77
Modesty, old clothes: Spigelgass *I*
Production problems: Grasso *I*, *LA Times*
10/1/79, Allen letter to Fine 3/23/79
Review: *Time* 10/1/79
Cancer: Spigelgass *I*, *LA Times* 5/4/82
"Tschaikowsky" new record: Charmoli *I*
Kayes Q: *NY Times* 2/8/81
Credit for Sylvia: Charmoli *I* (*Musical Comedy
Tonight II* was also promoted as *Sylvia Fine
Kaye's*, but her name didn't officially
become part of the title until *III*.)

Live from the Lincoln Center
Reformatted, editing: Scheerer *I*
Baker specials: Baker's outlines
Sitcom: *The Danny Kaye Show* pilot script by
Ernie Chambers, Saul Turteltaub, & Bernie
Orenstein 8/26/86
HBO: Rothman *I*
Kaye dies: (Sylvia died 10/28/91, at age 78.)
No Kaye in pictures: Freeman *I*

INDEX

Books by David Koenig

Mouse Tales:
A Behind-the-Ears Look at Disneyland

Mouse Under Glass:
Secrets of Disney Animation & Theme Parks

More Mouse Tales:
A Closer Peek Backstage at Disneyland

Realityland:
True-Life Adventures at Walt Disney World

Danny Kaye:
King of Jesters

For more information on these books or to order your own copies,
contact Bonaventure Press, P.O. Box 51961, Irvine, CA 92619
or visit
www.bonaventurepress.com